CHASING
CHARIOTS

Sidestone Press

CHASING CHARIOTS

PROCEEDINGS OF THE FIRST INTERNATIONAL
CHARIOT CONFERENCE (CAIRO 2012)

EDITED BY
ANDRÉ J. VELDMEIJER & SALIMA IKRAM

© 2013 A.J. Veldmeijer & S. Ikram

Published by Sidestone Press, Leiden
   www.sidestone.com

ISBN 978-90-8890-209-3

Lay-out: A.J. Veldmeijer
Cover design: Sidestone Press
Photographs cover: front: Thebes, Egypt © Neilneil | Dreamstime.com;
   back: Tomb of Horemheb, Saqqara. Photography by André J. Veldmeijer.

In Memory of

Ros Eavis-Oliveira

19 December 1959 - 1 July 2012

TABLE OF CONTENTS

Abstracts	9
Preface	15
A Survey of the Diplomatic Role of the Charioteers in the Ramesside Period *Mohamed Raafat Abbas*	17
A Possible Chariot Canopy for Tutankhamun *Edwin C. Brock*	29
Vehicle of the Sun: The Royal Chariot in the New Kingdom *Amy M. Calvert*	45
Studying the Six Chariots from the Tomb of Tutankhamun – An Update *Joost Crouwel*	73
The Introduction of the Light, Horse-Drawn Chariot and the Role of Archery in the Near East at the Transition from the Middle to the Late Bronze Ages: Is there a Connection? *Hermann Genz*	95
On Urartian Chariots *Bilcan Gökce, Kenan Işık & Hatice Değirmencioğlu*	107
Chariots in the Daily Life of New Kingdom Egypt: A Survey of Production, Distribution and Use in Texts *Ole Herslund*	123
The Chariot as a Mode of Locomotion in Civil Contexts *Heidi Köpp-Junk*	131
The Chariot that Plunders Foreign Lands: 'The Hymn to the King in His Chariot' *Colleen Manassa*	143

A Glimpse into the Workshops of the Chariotry of Qantir-Piramesse – Stone and Metal Tools of Site Q I
    Silvia Prell   *157*

Wagons and Carts in the 3rd Millennium BC Syrian Jazirah: A Study through the Documentation
    Mattia Raccidi   *175*

Depictional Study of Chariot Use in New Kingdom Egypt
    Lisa Sabbahy   *191*

Art and Imperial Ideology: Remarks on the Depiction of Royal Chariots on Wall Reliefs in New-Kingdom Egypt and the Neo-Assyrian Empire
    Arianna Sacco   *203*

Chariots' Inner Dynamics: Springs and Rotational Inertias
    Bela I. Sandor   *217*

An Alternative Theory for 'Bit-Wear' Found on the Lower Second Premolar of the Buhen Horse
    Yukiko Sasada   *229*

Egyptian Chariots: Departing for War
    Anthony Spalinger   *237*

Charging Chariots: Progress Report on the Tano Chariot in the Egyptian Museum Cairo
    André J. Veldmeijer, Salima Ikram & Lucy Skinner   *257*

ABSTRACTS

A Survey of the Diplomatic Role of the Charioteers in the Ramesside Period

Mohamed Raafat Abbas

Charioteers were very significant in the Ramesside Period, evidenced for example by the frequent mention of them in texts dated to the reign of king Ramesses II. Charioteers also played an important role in diplomacy as many Ramesside charioteers held the title *wpwty nsw r ḫꜣswt nb* "the royal envoy to every foreign country". This paper will focus on the diplomatic role of the charioteers in the Ramesside Period and their status in Egyptian society.

A Possible Chariot Canopy for Tutankhamun

Edwin C. Brock

The tomb of Tutankhamun contained among the many objects a gilded wooden trapezoidal frame from which radiate a series of twenty-eight hinged ribs. This frame and rib assembly is supported by four poles, and is just over two meters in height. The assembly was strengthened laterally by two pairs of horizontal bars, each provided with cylindrical bronze sleeves at their ends which fit over the upper ends of the poles beneath the trapezoidal frame (Carter Archive, Burton photo p1663). Other ribs support the hinged rib pairs from below and these, in turn, are attached to the horizontal cross braces. It is supposed that the ribs served to support a canopy of cloth or leather or some combination of the two, which has not survived, or the remains of which yet wait to be identified. The present paper discusses the identification and use of this object as part of a chariot.

Vehicle of the Sun: The Royal Chariot in the New Kingdom

Amy M. Calvert

This paper will focus on the symbolic importance of the royal chariot later in the New Kingdom, using the chariot body discovered in the tomb of Thutmose IV as the basis for discussion. A detailed examination of the iconography of this vehicle, taken together with evidence from other royal chariots and the texts that refer to the pharaoh in his chariot in general, will suggest layers of significance for these vehicles. There is a strong use of solar imagery tied to the chariot, and it also appears to have connections to the $3ht$ and with the maintenance of cosmic order and regeneration. Relief evidence points to the use of the chariot as a mobile throne on the field of battle. Moreover, important elements of the iconography of chariot decoration are shared with thrones, Windows of Appearance, palanquins, and royal barques — all venues for royal appearance. Of particular interest are the aggressively apotropaic and potentially powerful terrestrial focus of the scenes on the chariot body of Thutmose IV, which suggests that the ritual significance of these vehicles was always balanced by their importance and functions in the real world. The iconography surrounding the king was particularly complex and a number of royal iconographic themes appear intertwined on this chariot. Beyond the aggressively protective elements designed to guard the king against his enemies (both terrestrial and celestial), these include a heavy emphasis on the king's solar connections, symbols relating to his place in the Egyptian cosmic view, and indications of the pharaoh embodying and merging with certain deities in particular contexts, with the chariot itself acting as a conduit for this interaction.

Studying the Six Chariots from the Tomb of Tutankhamun – An Update

Joost Crouwel

It was in 1985 that the late Mary Littauer and this author published the unique group of six actual chariots from a single, well-documented context – the tomb of pharaoh Tutankhamun in Thebes (KV62) (Littauer & Crouwel, 1985). In this paper the author returns to these vehicles and examine their discovery and subsequent history, as well as their construction and use, in the light of more recent work.

The Introduction of the Light, Horse-Drawn Chariot and the Role of Archery in the Near East at the Transition from the Middle to the Late Bronze Ages: Is there a Connection?

Hermann Genz

This contribution will review the role of archery in the Levant, Anatolia and Egypt throughout the Bronze Age. While bows played an important role in warfare throughout the 3rd and 2nd millennia in Egypt, decisive changes are noticeable at the beginning of the New Kingdom (second half of the 2nd millennium BC). Composite bows and new types of arrowheads were introduced, but more important is a noticeable change in iconography. While in the Old and Middle Kingdoms the pharaoh smiting his enemies is always depicted with a mace or a dagger, in the New Kingdom a new image emerges: the pharaoh in his chariot using a bow.

Equally in the iconographic record of Hittite Anatolia (second half of the 2nd millennium BC), the bow is frequently depicted as a royal weapon. The picture is most dramatic in the Levant. While for the Early (3rd millennium BC) and Middle Bronze Ages (first half of the 2nd millennium BC) almost no evidence for the use of bows and arrows is attested in the archaeological and iconographic records, in the Late Bronze Age (second half of the 2nd millennium BC) arrowheads are among the most frequently encountered weapons. Moreover, arrowheads are widely found in royal and elite tombs. It is suggested that the sudden rise in the social prestige of archery in warfare can be connected to the development of a new warrior ideology, linked to the introduction of the light, horse-drawn chariot.

Abstracts

On Urartian Chariots

Bilcan Gökce, Kenan Işık & Hatice Değirmencioğlu

The Urartian Kingdom had established sovereignty mainly in Eastern Anatolia and in Transcaucasia and North-West Iran between the 9th to the 7th centuries BC. In this study, the chariots in the Urartian State have been evaluated in the light of archaeological findings, written sources and visual arts. In addition, while this evaluation was undertaken, chariot accessories and their production, draft animals and intended uses of vehicles were examined and clarified by experiments carried out by the authors, in tandem with archaeological evidence. Two- and three-dimensional art and written sources show that this type of vehicle was used actively in martial, political, and civil life in Urartian culture. Additionally, archaeological evidence shows that the Urartian chariots were not the work of a single craftsman but a joint product of carpenters, leatherworkers and metal craftsmen. Although the vehicles have strong Neo-Assyrian and North-Syrian influences, characteristics unique to Urartu can be identified on them as well. As a result, it can be stated that the chariots had a significant role for the Urartians.

Chariots in the Daily Life of New Kingdom Egypt: A Survey of Production, Distribution and Use in Texts

Ole Herslund

This contribution surveys a range of socio-historic topics in New Kingdom texts and inscriptions, centred around the chariot as a constituent of everyday life. Although the written sources concerning chariots in civilian contexts are both rare and fragmentary, the consolidation of texts makes it possible to shed some light on a range of topics, such as production, distribution, civilian use, and certain meanings which the ancient Egyptians related to chariots.

The Chariot as a Mode of Locomotion in Civil Contexts

Heidi Köpp-Junk

Besides its use in war, hunting, and sports, the chariot was the supreme mode of locomotion for the elite – both men and women – for private and public purposes, and an important status symbol in New Kingdom Egypt. It was used for visits and inspections by kings, their families, or high officials on short and long distances, even in the desert.

The Chariot that Plunders Foreign Lands: 'The Hymn to the King in His Chariot'

Colleen Manassa

A new technical and literary analysis of the 'Hymn to the King in His Chariot' reveals important lexicographic identifications of elements of an ancient Egyptian chariot. The chief poetical device in the hymn, paronomasia, is employed with foreign loan words, turning the non-Egyptian origin of the chariot and its terminology into a literary vehicle for Egyptian imperialism. The literary context, including an important intertextuality with 'The Capture of Joppa', and possible performative settings are also addressed.

A Glimpse into the Workshops of the Chariotry of Qantir-Piramesse – Stone and Metal Tools of Site Q I

Silvia Prell

The excavation of site Q I, carried out by the Hildesheim Mission in Qantir-Piramesse from 1980 until 1987, allowed the intensive study of a highly specialized workshop area connected with the chariotry of the residence of Ramesses II. Stone and metal tools, as well as semi-finished and finished products unearthed here confirm that the armoury can be located in the excavated part of the originally much bigger workshop complex.

Wagons and Carts in the 3rd Millennium BC Syrian Jazirah: A Study through the Documentation

Mattia Raccidi

The first attestations of wheeled-vehicles in the ancient Near East come from Uruk. The proto-cuneiform signs of the end of the 4th millennium BC represent sledges sustained by four wheels or two rollers that could be considered as the archetype of the 3rd millennium BC wagons. The evolution of the wheeled-vehicles is confirmed by the discovery of wagons in tombs at Ur, Kish and Susa, dated back to the first half of the 3rd millennium BC, in addition to the so-called 'Standard of Ur' that represents a procession of the so-called 'battle car'. However, in Syria, during the second half of the 3rd millennium BC a rapid increase of the documentation relating to wheeled vehicles is attested. Terracotta models, seals or seal impressions and written sources from many Syrian sites (such as Ebla, Mari, Terqa, Tell Brak/Nagar, Tell Bi'a/Tuttul, Tell Beydar/Nabada, Tell Mozan/Urkesh, Tell Barri/Kahat, Tell Arbid, Tell Khuera, Tell Selenkahiye etc.) prove the use and diffusion of carts and wagons. Although no full-size vehicles have been found in Syria, a preliminary analysis on the morphology and functions of carts and wagons in the 3rd millennium BC Syrian Jazirah have been made, based on the documentation mentioned above.

Depictional Study of Chariot Use in New Kingdom Egypt

Lisa Sabbahy

This article surveys the use of chariots in the Egyptian New Kingdom, a period of approximately five hundred years. The study is based on depictions in temple relief scenes, private tomb paintings, stelae (both royal and non-royal) and ostraca. The depictions are divided by the context of use: procession, warfare, hunting, work, as well as who is using the chariot. Is there a driver as well as an occupant or occupants? Are they male, female, royal, non-royal or divine? Relevant textual evidence will be brought in as well.

Art and Imperial Ideology: Remarks on the Depiction of Royal Chariots on Wall Reliefs in New-Kingdom Egypt and the Neo-Assyrian Empire

Arianna Sacco

The present paper examines the use and significance of royal chariots as depicted in wall reliefs both in New Kingdom Egypt, especially during the 19th and 20th Dynasties (1298-1069 BC), and in the Neo-Assyrian

Empire (934-609 BC). Even though there are unquestionable differences between the two empires – apart from differences in time and space – in both cases we are dealing with Near Eastern empires that made propagandistic use of war scenes recalling recent military conquests. From Egypt, examples are discussed from the Great Temple of Abu Simbel, Ramesses II's temple and Seti I's temple at Abydos, the Beit el-Wali temple dedicated by Ramesses II, Karnak Temple, Luxor Temple, the temple at Medinet Habu and the Ramesseum. From Assyria, examples are examined from Nimrud, both from the Northwest and Central and the Southwest Palace, as well as from Nineveh's Southwest Palace. The study of the aforementioned scenes include comparing and contrasting the two empires, focussing on the way the king and his chariot are portrayed, and their relationship with the rest of the scene. Of great importance is the significance of the king and his chariot within the battle scenes and perceived role in warfare. Furthermore, the architectural context of the reliefs and the audiences for which the reliefs were intended are considered.

Chariots' Inner Dynamics: Springs and Rotational Inertias

Bela I. Sandor

The safety, comfort, and performance characteristics of a chariot depend on the vehicle's structural dynamics, which is a function of materials, geometry of components, and joint systems. Two areas are covered: spring systems and wheel structures. Every chariot has many springs, with a wide range of elastic properties. Leather is found as a tension spring in the yoke traces and in floor mats. The pole acts as a bending-and-torsion spring. The front floor bar acts as a bow spring, and also as an elastic warping element involved in the torsion of the pole. The subassembly comprising the axle, pole, yoke, pole-tail socket, and front floor bar is a shock-absorbing anti-roll mechanism, as long as the horses are running upright.

Wheel structures represent difficult design compromises in order to minimize the washboard effect, to provide spoke strength in compression, to resist bending in cornering manoeuvres, and to minimize both the linear and rotational inertias in order to achieve high acceleration. The concept of rotational inertia leads to a fresh view of the advantages and disadvantages of using iron tires and nave hoops in racing, as hinted in a crash scene in the Lyon circus mosaic; the conclusion is in favour of not using any iron in a high-performance racing chariot.

An Alternative Theory for 'Bit-Wear' Found on the Lower Second Premolar of the Buhen Horse

Yukiko Sasada

In 1958, the remains of a 19 year old male horse were found at Buhen by Walter B. Emery. The fact that it was found on top of the Middle Kingdom rampart caused excitement among academics since it signified the possibility that the Buhen horse dated back to 1675 BC, several decades earlier than previously found horse remains in Egypt. On closer examination of the skull, abnormal wear of the lower premolars was identified. There is controversy over whether this wear is evidence to suggest that the horse had been wearing a bit. This is an important concept since the use of a bit from this period would signify the first irrefutable evidence of use of domesticated horses in Egypt. This paper challenges this assumption as it is well-described in the veterinary literature that older horses may develop an abnormal pattern of wear on their molars that is commonly known as a 'wave mouth', which might be the cause for the Buhen horse's tooth wear, rather than a bit.

Egyptian Chariots: Departing for War

Anthony Spalinger

This study is the first of two that are concerned with the New Kingdom's army in formation. As befits the temporal development, we shall be concerned only with the departure of the king's troops and in particular concentrate upon the mustering of the soldiers. Furthermore, it is crucial to separate the advance across the Sinai from the later marches in Palestine and Syria.

Charging Chariots: Progress Report on the Tano Chariot in the Egyptian Museum Cairo

André J. Veldmeijer, Salima Ikram & Lucy Skinner

During the 2008 season of the Ancient Egyptian Leatherwork Project (AELP) in the Egyptian Museum, Cairo a cache of leather objects was traced in the magazine of the Museum. The cache consisted of several trays of red and green leather containing some 60 large and numerous small leather fragments, as well as objects made of thicker beige leather, decorated in green. This acquisition was recorded on Dossier du Service 32-2/101, as being purchased from Georges Tano, the well known Cairene antiquity dealer, in 1932. Upon investigating the contents of these trays, it seemed clear that they all came from a single chariot. The fragments included portions of the casing, the bow-case that was attached to the side of the chariot as well as parts of the harnessing. The current contribution presents the first results of the research as well as a report on the conservation.

PREFACE

André J. Veldmeijer & Salima Ikram

This First International Chariot Conference, jointly organised by the Netherlands-Flemish Institute in Cairo (NVIC) and the American University in Cairo (AUC) (30 November to 2 December 2012), was born out of the work of the Egyptian Museum Chariot Project's (EMCP) re-discovery of the chariot leather from a New Kingdom chariot housed in the Cairo Museum. Studying chariots – or indeed any object type – requires a great deal of interdisciplinary work. As the different strands of the EMCP started to be woven together, we became aware of the many people working on various aspects of chariots in the ancient Near East, and decided that an exchange of ideas would be most productive, hence the conference.

The intention of the conference was to make a broad assessment of the current state of knowledge about chariots in Egypt and the Near East, and to provide a forum for discussion. We accepted a wide variety of papers, varying from overviews to more detailed studies focusing on a specific topic, including philology, iconography, archaeology, engineering, history, and conservation. As the nature of the conference was exploratory, contributions show a varying state of the underlying research's completion.

As the contributions are from a wide range of scholarly specialties and for a diverse audience, the referencing system has been simplified so that it is accessible to scholars from different backgrounds, as well as anyone with an interest in ancient technology, transportation, or warfare.

We like to thank, first and foremost, our institutes (NVIC and AUC) for funding and offering a venue for the conference as well as their moral and practical support, particularly the staff of the NVIC for the latter. We are grateful to the AUC students (Ariel Singer, Nicholas Brown, Natalie Marquez, Amy Wilson, Kenaya Camacho, Laurel Darcy Hackley, Taylor Woodcock and Emily Layton) for their organisational help during the conference. The organisers would like to express their gratitude that the well known chariot specialist, Professor Emeritus Joost Crouwel (University of Amsterdam), was able and willing to come to Cairo for the key-note lecture. Professor Crouwel studied and published, together with the late Mary Littauer, the chariots that were found in the tomb of Tutankhamun (KV 62). We also like to thank the other participants for making the conference into such a success: speakers and audience all demanding a repeat of the event two years hence. The examination of chariots through many diverse lenses gave birth to new ideas and created a strong intellectual synergy, further stimulated by the lively discussion sessions, both during the conference and after hours.

We dedicate this volume to the memory of our friend Ros Eavis-Oliveira who died unexpectedly and tragically on 1 July 2012. She was an enthusiastic Egyptologist, keenly interested in diverse aspects of the discipline ranging from the evolving role of gods to royal hairstyles. She was always ready to participate in any and all experimental work and excavations, ready for stirring discussions over drinks, and always managed to maintain her keen sense of humour and appetite for life (and Egyptology) no matter the circumstances.

A SURVEY OF THE DIPLOMATIC ROLE OF THE CHARIOTEERS IN THE RAMESSIDE PERIOD

Mohamed Raafat Abbas

INTRODUCTION

During the Ramesside Period (1298-1069 BC), charioteers were very important in Egyptian society, judging from the crucial military role that they played in the battles of this period. The Ramesside Period is characterized by an increase in military positions, as a result of the great number of wars that were fought by the Egyptians during this period. We can observe the appraisal of the charioteers in the Ramesside Period from the famous texts of king Ramesses II (1279-1212 BC) regarding the Battle of Qadesh, where Ramesses II mentioned (Kitchen, 1979: 83-84): "It is whom which [...] I found them beside me in the fight, my charioteer and my shield-bearer Menna". Also Ramesses II is described in his texts as: "He is the savior of his army in the day of fighting, he is the great protector of his chariotry".

Charioteers also played an important role in diplomacy as many Ramesside charioteers held the title *wpwty nsw r ḫ3swt nb* "the Royal Envoy to Every Foreign Country". This paper will focus on the diplomatic role of the charioteers in the Ramesside Period and their status in Egyptian society.

THE IMPORTANCE OF THE ROYAL ENVOYS TO EVERY FOREIGN COUNTRIES (OR LANDS) DURING THE RAMESSIDE PERIOD AND THEIR RELATIONSHIP TO CHARIOTRY

The diplomatic title *wpwty nsw r ḫ3swt nb* "Royal Envoy to Every Foreign Country", or *wpwty nsw r t3 nb* "Royal Envoy to Every Land" was one of the most important administrative titles in the New Kingdom (1549-1069 BC; Al-Ayedi, 2006: 231-234; Taylor, 2001: 97). This title refers to the ambassadorial missions which were fulfilled on behalf of the king (El-Saady, 1999: 425).

The royal envoy was an important official, since he was a personal messenger to the king delegated to carry messages, both written and verbal, to the vassals of his kingdom, as well as to the kings of the neighboring countries (Abdul-Kader, 1959: 119-120). Such an envoy was usually of exceptional abilities and might have been charged with negotiations at the highest level. He presumably had to be an excellent writer, a convincing speaker, well-acquainted with the geography of the foreign countries in which he was going to serve, knowledgeable about the difficult paths, roads and the safe way, a wise guide, alert, a good horseman, an excellent bowman, well-acquainted with the different chiefs of the localities and their languages. For these reasons, some of these envoys were outstanding army officers, who had travelled to various places, and had the aforementioned requirements (Abdul-Kader, 1959: 120). Thus, during the Ramesside Period the majority of the royal envoys to foreign countries had a military background, particularly from the chariotry (El-Saady, 1999: 421). This was part of the social mobility in the 19th and 20th Dynasties in which the new military class became a more significant part of the aristocracy in Egyptian society. Being a member of the chariotry emphasized their expertise on the external routes as well as their administrative skills (*cf.* Kadry, 1982: 148-155; Kemp, 1978: 20).

The diplomatic duties of the royal envoy to foreign countries are, according to Abdul-Kader (1959: 121-122):

A) To inform his king about the neighboring countries, their people, chiefs and kings, their political interests, the internal situation and the power of the country;
B) To carry the diplomatic correspondence and to communicate oral messages;
C) To collect the tribute for the king from vassal-states;
D) Responsibility over all the gold, silver and the precious gifts exchange, including transferring the royal gifts to the vassals;
E) To convey the daughter of a foreign king to his own king for marriage. Usually an envoy of her own country accompanied her as well as the royal envoy of the king whom she was going to marry;
F) To conduct a prince of a subject country to the presence of the pharaoh at his own request;
G) To announce the accession of a new king to the throne;
H) To carry out political negotiations;
I) To investigate matters of unusual importance;
J) To reconcile differences between vassal chiefs and to interrogate them.

CHARIOTEERS AND DIPLOMACY IN THE RAMESSIDE TEXTS

During the time of Ramesses II, the charioteers played an important diplomatic role in the Egyptian-Hittite peace treaty in year 21 of Ramesses II' reign (figure 1). This role appears in a section at the

Figure 1. Egyptian-Hittite Peace Treaty. The Egyptian version on a great wall-stela. Temple of Karnak. From: http://www.memphis.edu/hypostyle/2004_season_report.php).

beginning of the treaty and clarifies the diplomatic role of the charioteers (as royal envoys) in this event as the following:

"[…] There came the Royal Envoy and Lieutenant-Commander of Chariotry [….], the Royal Envoy [….], and the Envoy of the Land of Hatti and of [….] Tili-Tesub, the Second Envoy of Hatti, Ramose, and the Envoy of Carcamish, Yapusili,[1] bearing the silver tablet, which the great ruler of Hatti, Hattusilis III, has caused to be brought to pharaoh, life, prosperity and health (l.p.h.), to request peace from the majesty of the king of Upper and Lower Egypt Wesermaatre-setepenre (Ramesses II) […]" (Kitchen, 1979: 226; 1996: 80).

The diplomatic role of the charioteers in the Egyptian Hittite peace treaty is noticeable in this text, which is considered as one of the most important historical texts in the Ramesside Period, throughout the military rank of chariotry *idnw n t-nt-ḥtr* "Lieutenant-Commander of Chariotry" (Gardiner, 1947: 28). The chariotry was divided into squadrons of 25 chariots, each commanded by a "Charioteer of the Residence", whose senior officer was the "Lieutenant-Commander of Chariotry" (Faulkner, 1953: 43).

From another important text of the Ramesside Period, Papyrus (P.) Anastasi III,[2] the diplomatic role of the charioteers can be deduced too. This papyrus dates to the reign of Merenptah, the fourth king of the 19th Dynasty (1298-1187 BC). The reference appears in a section at the beginning of the papyrus in epithets and titles of the first charioteer of his majesty,[3] Amenemopet, as the following:

"Fan-bearer on the Right of the King, First Charioteer of His Majesty, Lieutenant-Commander of Chariotry, King's Envoy to the Princess of the Foreign Lands of Khor Starting from Tharu to Iupa; [...] to the Princess of the Asiatics, Amenemopet" (Caminos, 1954: 69, 103; Gardiner, 1937: 21, 29).

From this text, which mentions the military and diplomatic titles of Amenemopet, we can conclude that Amenemopet was one of the most important charioteers in the second half of the 19th Dynasty, according to his two military titles and ranks of the chariotry: *ktn tpy n ḥm.f* "First Charioteer of His Majesty" and *idnw n t-nt-ḥtr* "Lieutenant-Commander of Chariotry". Amenemopet immediately mentions, after his two military titles of chariotry, his diplomatic career as King's envoy to the princes of the foreign lands of Khor, starting from Tharu to Iupa. That Amenemopet was a very important royal envoy is evidenced by the significance of the geographic places that he served. Khor or Kharo is the name of Palestine and its adjacent areas (Gardiner, 1947: 180-186; Gauthier, 1931: 151), Iupa is a city located near Damascus or between Damascus and Qadesh (Gardiner, 1947: 152, 181), and Tharu is the headquarters of the Egyptian army's defensive strategy on the eastern frontier, which has been identified by a number of scholars as Tell Abu-Seifa (Al-Ayedi, 2000: 53, 61, 95). This city lies 4 km to the east of the present city El-Qantarah, or Tell Haboua which lies in north-western Sinai, 9.5 km north-east of Tell Abu-Seifa.

THE CHARIOTEERS WHO HELD THE DIPLOMATIC TITLE "ROYAL ENVOY TO EVERY FOREIGN COUNTRY (OR LAND)"

We can recognize the charioteers with a diplomatic role by studying the inscriptions that were added by them to their statues, stelae and other objects. It reveals that the charioteers with such ambassadorial missions and who had a diplomatic role mentioned their title "Royal Envoy to Every Foreign Country (or Land)", next to their other military titles of chariotry.

It is not surprising that the largest number of the charioteers with this title date from the reign of Ramesses II, since foreign relations of the Ramessides, either military or diplomatic, reached their peak under this king (Kitchen, 1964: 47-70). Ramesses' long and eventful reign required many royal envoys of various ranks to fulfill the diplomatic affairs to the widest extent (Kitchen, 1982b: 43-95).

Therefore, reference to the charioteers who held the diplomatic title "Royal Envoy to Every Foreign Country (or Land)" during the Ramesside period is as follows:

1) Huy

Huy *ḥwy* was one of the viceroys of Kush during the reign of Ramesses II (Kitchen, 1980: 77). Information about his military and administrative careers mainly comes from his great stela (No. 17332) in the *Ägyptisches Museum und Papyrussammlung, Berlin*, which was discovered in Lower Nubia (figure 2). In the lower register of this stela there is an inscription consisting of five horizontal lines that

Figure 2. Stela of "Viceroy of Kush and Lieutenant-Commander of Chariotry", Huy, Ägyptisches Museum und Papyrussammlung, Berlin No. 17332. From: Habachi (1961: pl. 29).

reads (Habachi, 1961: 220, fig. 5, pl. 29; Kitchen, 1980: 79-80):

"An offering that the King gives to Amun-Re, Lord of the Thrones of the Two Lands, to Thoth, pleased with truth, to the Horuses pre-eminent in Wawat and to all the gods of Nubia, that they may give the receiving of offerings coming forth before (them) at the beginning of every season which happens in their temple, to the Ka of the Prince and the Mayor, the Viceroy, the Highest Authority in Nubia, the Fan-bearer on the Right of the King, the praised by the good god, Troop Commander, the Overseer of Horses, Lieutenant-Commander of His Majesty in the Chariotry, Troop Commander of Tharu, the Royal Envoy in Every Foreign Country, the one who comes from the (land) of Hatti, and who brought back its great one (princess); a person who can report where it (Hatti) is, has never existed, the royal scribe, Huy". The texts of Huy's stela refers to one of his important military titles and careers in the chariotry as *idnw ḥm.f m t-nt-ḥtr* "Lieutenant-Commander of His Majesty in the Chariotry". Huy played an important diplomatic role which is suggested by his diplomatic title *wpwty nsw ḥr ḫ3swt nb* "Royal Envoy in Every Foreign Country". It seems that this title was of particular importance for Huy because on the stela, this title is followed by: "the one who comes from Hatti, and who brought back its great one (princess)". Undoubtedly, by the great one of the land of Hatti, Maathorneferure, the daughter of the king of the Hittites, was meant and Huy would be, therefore, the man who accompanied the princess on her journey from her country to Egypt. Perhaps some time before the thirty-fourth year of the reign of Ramesses II, Huy was appointed as "Royal Messenger (Envoy) in Every Foreign Country", and thus he had the opportunity of bringing the Hittite princess to Egypt.[4] Having taken part in this great event, he was anxious to record his diplomatic participation on his stela (Habachi, 1961: 224).

2) Suti-em-hab

From his stela, which was discovered by Petrie in Abydos (figure 3), we know that Suti-em-hab *swti-m-ḥb* was one of the prominent charioteers in the reign of Ramesses II, judging his two military titles: *kḏn tpy n ḥm.f* "First Charioteer of His Majesty", and *idnw nt n ḥtr* "Lieutenant-Commander of Chariotry". Beside these two military titles, Suti-em-hab registered on his stela the diplomatic title *wpwty nsw r t3 nb* "Royal Envoy to Every Land" as one of his other positions (Kitchen, 1980: 246; Petrie, 1925: pl. 31).

3) Meryu

Meryu *mryw* was one of the charioteers and royal envoys during the reign of Ramesses II. He registered both of his military and diplo-

Figure 3. Stela of "First Charioteer of His Majesty" and "Lieutenant-Commander of Chariotry", Suti-em-hab. From: Petrie (1925: pl. 31).

matic titles on rock stela No. 20 at Abu Simbel. His military title of chariotry was *kdn n ḥm.f* "Charioteer of His Majesty", while his diplomatic title was *wpwty nsw r tȝ pn n Kš* "Royal Envoy to This Land of Kush" (Kitchen, 1980: 246-247). It is noticeable from this diplomatic title that Meryu was just a royal ambassador to the southern provinces of the Egyptian empire at Kush. Hence, Meryu probably erected this rock stela in Lower Nubia during one of his ambassadorial and diplomatic missions to the Egyptian administrative centers in Kush.[5]

4) Meryatum

Another charioteer and royal envoy from the time of Ramesses II, Meryatum *mry-Itm* registered both of his military and diplomatic titles on a door lintel, now in the *August Kestner Museum, Hannover*. He held the important military title *idnw n t-nt-ḥtr n nb tȝwy* "Lieutenant-Commander of Chariotry of the Lord of the Two Lands", and the usual diplomatic title of the royal envoys *wpwty nsw r ḫȝswt nb* "Royal Envoy to Every Foreign Country" (Kitchen, 1980: 242-243).

5) Amen-em-ent

The military commander Amen-em-ent *Imn-m-int* is considered to be one of the most significant military commanders during the reign of Ramesses II. He held various military ranks and titles, such as "Chief of Medjay-Militia"[6], 'Troop-Commander of the Army", "Officer of the Army" and "Charioteer of His Majesty". These military titles and ranks are registered on several of his monuments that were found in Thebes and are now housed in various international museums (Kitchen, 1980: 272-277). Amen-em-ent registered on the monument of his family in the Naples museum (No. 1069; Kitchen, 1980: 272) the military title of chariotry *kdn n ḥm.f* "Charioteer of His Majesty" (Kitchen, 1980: 273), and on his statue found at the Hathor temple in Deir el-Bahari (figure 4), now in the Luxor museum (No. 227), his diplomatic title *wpwty nsw r ḫȝswt nbw* "Royal Envoy to Every Foreign Country" (Kitchen, 1980: 274-275; Lipinska, 1966: 67, pl. 1).

6) Nui

Nui *Nwi* was an official and charioteer in the reign of Ramesses II. All of his military, administrative and diplomatic titles are listed on a stela, but unfortunately its present location is unknown. Nui held the important military title of chariotry *kdn tpy n ḥm.f* "First Charioteer of His Majesty", and the diplomatic title of the royal envoys *wpwty nsw r ḫȝswt nbw* "Royal Envoy to Every Foreign Country" (Kitchen, 1980: 239-240; Wente, 1963: 33-34). Moreover, he held a title, which indicates his political and diplomatic duties, *imy-r ḫȝswt ḥr ḫȝswt mḥt* "Governor of Northern Foreign Countries".[7] The main duty of the governor was to look after the interests of Egypt in the subject territories and to convey to the king full information about the activities of the vassals, hostile intrigues or the advance of any hostile army. Also, the governor had full authority over the local chiefs and could command them to defend the cities located in his area and to carry out fighting if necessary.

7) Penre

The military titles held by Penre. $pn\text{-}r^c$ shows that he was one of the more important military commanders in the reign of Ramesses II. He held the titles of "Troop-Commander", "Charioteer of His Majesty", "Chief of Medjay-Militia" and "Overseer of the Desert". These military titles are registered on many of his monuments found throughout Egypt and currently housed in several international museums. Additionally, Penre held the administrative title "Overseer of Works in the Ramesseum Temple"; but for the present work Penre's diplomatic and military titles are the main focus, as they give insight to his diplomatic role as charioteer. Penre registered on his stela from Koptos (figure 5), that is currently in the Ashmolean Museum, Oxford (No. 1894.106), his military title of chariotry $k\underline{d}n\ n\ \d{h}m.f$ "Charioteer of His Majesty", in addition to his diplomatic title $wpwty\ nsw\ r\ t\ni\ nb$ "Royal Envoy to Every Land" (Kitchen, 1980: 268-271). This diplomatic title is mentioned immediately after the military title (Gohary, 1987: fig. 1; Kitchen, 1980: 271), which may suggest that Penre had his military and diplo-

Figure 4. Statue of "Chief of Medjay-Militia", "Troop-Commander of the Army" and "Charioteer of His Majesty", Amen-em-ent. Luxor Museum, No. 227. From: Lipinska (1966: 67, pl. I).

Moreover, he was in charge of the infantry of the king and the chariots as well as the horses that were garrisoned in Palestine and Syria. He could deploy them during disturbances to the troubled area, without waiting for the command of the king (Abdul-Kader, 1959: 118-119). To the present author, this indicates that there is a clear relationship between the royal envoys, the charioteers, and the governors in their diplomatic, political and military missions. Nui held all of these titles and offices in the same time according to their common diplomatic, military and political duties.

Figure 5. Stela of "First Charioteer of His Majesty", Penre. Ashmolean Museum, Oxford No. 1894.106. From: Gohary (1987: fig. 1).

matic careers at the same time. It is remarkable, as can be seen on the aforementioned stela, that Penre also held the title of the Egyptian governor in Asia ⸗ *imy-r ḫ3swt ḥr ḫ3st mḥt* "Governor of Foreign Countries in the Northern Country" (Kitchen, 1980: 271) as well. This title is also registered, albeit in a different form, on a funerary cone of him as ⸗ *imy-r ḫ3swt ḥr ḫ3rw* "Governor of Foreign Countries of Khor", which is immediately followed by the military title ⸗ *kḏn tpy n ḥm.f* "First Charioteer of His Majesty" (Kitchen, 1980: 270). A comparable case has been shown for Nui (see above) who held the title ⸗ *imy-r ḫ3swt ḥr ḫ3swt mḥt* "Governor of Northern Foreign Countries" in the reign of Ramesses II. This again, suggests that there is a clear relationship between the royal envoys, charioteers and governors in their diplomatic, political and military missions. Therefore, it can be suggested that the Ramesside charioteer was able to hold the offices of the Egyptian governors in the north due to their great political and diplomatic experience which they gained from their diplomatic works as royal envoys to foreign countries.

8) Wennufer

Wennufer *Wn-nfr* was one of the prime charioteers during the reign of Merenptah, suggested by the military title ⸗ *kḏn tpy n ḥm.f* "First Charioteer of His Majesty". Wennufer also engraved his titles on his stela (No. 154) in the British Museum, London (figure 6). After this military title of chariotry, he registered his diplomatic title ⸗ *wpwty nsw r t3 nb* "Royal Envoy to Every Land" (James, 1970: 31-32, pl. 27; Kitchen, 1982a: 123).

9) Anhurnakht

Anhurnakht *'In-ḥr-nḫt* was one of the important charioteers during the reign of Siptah. He held two military titles related to chariotry: ⸗ *kḏn tpy n ḥm.f* "First Charioteer of His Majesty", and ⸗ *ḥry pḏt n t-nt-ḥtr* "Troop Commander of the Chariotry". These military titles are also regis-

Figure 6. Stela of First charioteer of his majesty, Wennufer, British museum, No. 154. From: James (1970: pl. 27).

tered on his block-statue in Linköping Museum (Smith Collection, No. 189), beside his diplomatic title ⸗ *wpwty nsw r ḫ3swt nb* "Royal Envoy to Every Foreign Country". This combination of titles suggests that Anhurnakht was one of the charioteers who played a diplomatic role during the later part of the 19th Dynasty (Kitchen, 1982a: 375).

10) Aipy

From a graffito in the South temple at Buhen (figure 7), we know that Aipy *3ipy* was one of the charioteers who played a diplomatic role in the reign of Siptah (1195-1189 BC), according to his listing of both of his military and diplomatic titles ⸗ *kḏn tpy n ḥm.f* "First Charioteer of His Majesty", and ⸗ *wpwty nsw* "Royal Envoy" (Caminos, 1974: 75, pls. 86, 87; Kitchen, 1982a: 374-375; Randall-MacCIver & Woolley, 1911: 26, 43).

Figure 7. Graffito of "First Charioteer of His Majesty", Aipy, South temple of Buhen. From: Caminos (1974: pl. 87).

11) Hori

Hori, Son of Kama ḥri s3 k3mꜥ, was viceroy of Kush under Siptah and is attested in year 6 of that king. He likely continued to serve under Setnakht (1187-1185 BC) and Ramesses III (1185-1153 BC), the first two kings of the 20th Dynasty (Reisner, 1920: 48-50). Before his appointment as viceroy, Hori registered both of his military and diplomatic titles in a graffito that was found at Buhen and dates to year 3 of the reign of Siptah (figure 8). He held the military title *kṯn tpy n ḥm.f* "First Charioteer of His Majesty", and the diplomatic title *wpwty nsw r ḫ3swt nb* "Royal Envoy to Every Foreign Country" (Caminos, 1974: 35-36, pls. 42-43; Kitchen, 1982a: 364-365; Randall-MacIver & Woolley, 1911: 38, pl. 15). Hence, Hori was one of the charioteers who played a diplomatic role in the Ramesside period. There is no doubt that he had an ambassadorial role at Kush, judging by the presence of his military and diplomatic titles at Buhen.

12) Webekhsenu

Webekhsen *wbḫsnw*, was the son of the viceroy, "First Charioteer of His Majesty" and "Royal Envoy to Every Foreign Country" Hori, Son of Kama. Exactly like his father, Webekhsenu listed his military and diplomatic titles in a graffito at Buhen dating to year 6 of the reign of Siptah (figure 9). He held the military title *kḏn tpy n ḥm.f* "First Charioteer of His Majesty", and the diplomatic title *wpwty nsw r ḫ3swt nb* "Royal Envoy to Every Foreign Country" (Caminos, 1974: 42, pl. 54; Kitchen, 1982a: 364-365; Randall-MacIver & Woolley, 1911: 36, pl. 12).

CONCLUSION

Several points become clear from the inventory, presented above, about the diplomatic role of the charioteers in the Ramesside Period. During this period, the majority of the royal envoys to foreign countries came from military backgrounds, particularly the chariotry, which was due to the social mobility in the 19th and 20th Dynasties where the

Figure 8. Graffito of "First Charioteer of His Majesty", Hori, Buhen. From: Caminos (1974: pl. 43).

Figure 9. Graffito of 'First Charioteer of His Majesty", Webekhsenu, Buhen. From: Caminos (1974: pl. 54).

new military class became part of the Egyptian aristocracy. Some of these envoys were outstanding army officers, who had travelled to foreign lands, became acquainted with their people, their rulers, their customs and habits, and the native language. Hence, the Ramesside charioteers often were chosen to be royal envoys. The various other diplomatic titles of charioteers during the Ramesside era is incontrovertible evidence for the importance of their diplomatic role during this time. This is notable in the Egyptian-Hittite peace treaty that dates to the reign of Ramesses II, and also in a section of P. Anastasi III that dates to the reign of Merenptah.

Charioteers who headed ambassadorial missions and who played diplomatic roles during the Ramesside period, used to stress the diplomatic title "Royal Envoy to Every Foreign Country (or Land)", in addition to their military titles of chariotry, on their monuments. No less than twelve charioteers from the Ramesside Period held this diplomatic title and inscribed it on their different monuments. Most of the Ramesside charioteers who held this title lived during the reign of Ramesses II. During the reign of this king, the international interaction of the Ramessides, being it militarily or diplomatic, reached its peak. Surely, Rammesses's long and eventful reign required many royal envoys of various ranks to fulfill the diplomatic affairs to the widest extent.

Ramesside charioteers succeeded in carrying out notable diplomatic missions during the Ramesside Period, such as carrying out the political negotiations in the Egyptian-Hittite peace treaty in year 21 of Ramesses II's reign, and accompanying the Hittite princess Maathorneferure on her journey to Egypt to marry king Ramesses II, in the 34th year of his reign.

Some Ramesside charioteers also held the office of the Egyptian governors in the north, due to the great political and diplomatic experience that they had gained from their diplomatic works as royal envoys to every foreign country. Clearly, in the Ramesside era, being a charioteer was but a step along the political and social ladder that led to greater glories.

NOTES

1 The treaty of king Ramesses II with Hatti (the Hittites) in his year 21 required the involvement of many envoys for its preliminary negotiations and consequences. It is conceivable that the period between the military conflict of the hostile powers and the agreement of peace, *i.e.* from year 11 to year 21, witnessed intense discussions for setting up an external peace along with its final codification. The royal envoys undoubtedly shuttled between Pi-Ramesses and Hattusas many times until a satisfactory treaty was agreed (Kitchen, 1982b: 75).

2 P. Anastasi III: This and the other British Museum papyri bearing the same name were purchased from Anastasi, the Swedish consul in Egypt, in 1839. Their provenance has not been recorded, but from what is known of the source of Anastasi's collections and from the internal evidence of the manuscripts themselves, Saqqara (Memphis) is the probable place of origin. P. Anastasi III (British Museum, London No. E10246) dates to the third year of Merenptah's reign (Gardiner, 1937: XIII-XIV).

3 Schulman (1963: 90) suggested that the first charioteer was leading a troop of ten chariots.

4 The diplomatic interactions between Egypt and Hatti reached their peak under Ramesses II with the first royal wedding, which is known as the first diplomatic marriage successfully practiced since the reigns of Amenhotep III and Akhenaten. This event, which took place thirteen years after the ratification of the peace treaty, was highlighted in the great temple of Abu Simbel (Kitchen, 1979: 233-257; Schmidt, 1993: 153-160; Schulman, 1979: 177-193).

5 Egypt's occupation of Nubia required administrative, religious and social centers, both for the Egyptian colonizers and the Nubian officials, as well as for the local people working for them. The Egyptian administration of Nubia was conducted from numerous outposts, but the residences of the high officials who helped administer the northern (Wawat) and southern (Kush) districts of Nubia were located at Aniba and Amara (Heidorn, 1999: 701-704).

6 The term 'Medjay' was held by some Nubian tribes who served in the Egyptian army in the times of the Old and Middle Kingdom. In the time of the New Kingdom, this term was held by the Egyptian military troops, which represented the police militia (Schulman, 1964: 25).

7 The pharaohs during the New Kingdom entrusted the administration of the cities in Syria and Palestine to local chiefs whom they appointed. In order to guarantee their loyalty, they installed Egyptian governors over them who were resident in their territories. The entire organization was sponsored by a department in the Egyptian capital. The pharaoh as head of the state and commander of the army was the supreme authority (Abdul-Kader, 1959: 106).

CITED LITERATURE

Abdul-Kader, M. 1959. The Administration of Syro-Palestine during the New Kingdom. – Annales du Service des Antiquités de l'Égypte 56: 105-137.

Al-Ayedi, A. 2000. Tharu: The Starting Point on the Ways of Horus. – Toronto, University of Toronto.

Al-Ayedi, A. 2006. Index of Egyptian Administrative, Religious and Military Titles of the New Kingdom. – Ismailia, Obelisk Publications.

Caminos, R.A. 1954. Late-Egyptian Miscellanies. – London, Geoffrey Cumberlege/Oxford, Oxford University Press.

Caminos, R.A. 1974. The New Kingdom Temples of Buhen. Volume I. – London, Egypt Exploration Society.

El-Saady, H. 1999. The External Royal Envoys of the Ramessides: A Study on the Egyptian Diplomats. – Mitteilungen des Deutschen Archäologischen Instituts Abteilung Kairo 55: 411-425.

Faulkner, R.O. 1953. Egyptian Military Organization. – The Journal of Egyptian Archaeology 39: 32-47.

Gardiner, A.H. 1937. Late-Egyptian Miscellanies. – Bruxelles, Fondation Égyptologique Reine Élisabeth.

Gardiner, A.H. 1947. Ancient Egyptian Onomastica. Volume I. – Oxford, Oxford University Press.

Gauthier, H. 1931. Dictionnaire des Noms Géographiques Contenus dans les Textes Hiéroglyphiques. IV. – Le Caire, Société Royale de Géographie d'Égypte.

Gohary, S. 1987. The Remarkable Career of a Police Officer. – Annales du Service des Antiquités de l'Égypte 71: 97-100.

Habachi, L. 1961. Four Objects Belonging to Viceroys of Kush and Officials Associated with Them. – Kush, Journal of the Sudan Antiquities Service 9: 210-225.

Heidorn, L.A. 1999. Nubian Towns and Temples. In: Bard, K.A. Ed. Encyclopedia of the Archaeology of Ancient Egypt. – London/New York, Routledge: 700-704.

James, T.G.H. 1970. Hieroglyphic Texts from Egyptian Stelae etc. Part 9. – London, The Trustees of the British Museum.

Kadry, A. 1982. Officers and Officials in the New Kingdom. – Budapest, Etudes publiées par les chaires d'histoire ancienne de l'Université L. Eötvös de Budapest.

Kemp, B.J. 1978. Imperialism and Empire in New Kingdom Egypt (c. 1575-1087 B.C.). In: Garnsey, P.D.A. & C.R. Whittaker. Ed. Imperialism in the Ancient World. – Cambridge, Cambridge University Press: 7-57, 284-297.

Kitchen, K.A. 1964. Some New Light on the Asiatic Wars of Ramesses II. – Journal of Egyptian Archaeology 50: 47-70.

Kitchen, K.A. 1979. Ramesside Inscriptions. Historical and Biographical. Volume II. – Oxford, Blackwell.

Kitchen, K.A. 1980. Ramesside Inscriptions. Historical and Biographical. Volume III. – Oxford, Blackwell.

Kitchen, K.A. 1982a. Ramesside Inscriptions. Historical and Biographical. Volume IV. – Oxford, Blackwell.

Kitchen, K.A. 1982b. Pharaoh Triumphant. The Life and Times of Ramesses II, King of Egypt. – Warminster, Aris & Phillips Ltd.

Kitchen, K.A. 1996. Ramesside Inscriptions. Translated and Annotated Translations: Ramesses II, Royal Inscriptions. Volume II. – Oxford, Blackwell Publishers Ltd.

Lipinska, J. 1966. List of the Objects Found at Deir El-Bahari Temple of Thutmosis III, Season

1961/1962. – Annales du Service des Antiquités de l'Égypte 59: 63-98.

Petrie, W.M.F. 1925. Tombs of the Courtiers and Oxyrhynkhos. – London, British School of Archaeology in Egypt.

Randall-MacIver, D. & C.L. Woolley. 1911. Buhen. – Philadelphia, University of Pennsylvania.

Reisner, G.A. 1920. The Viceroys of Ethiopia. – Journal of Egyptian Archaeology 6: 28-55.

Schmidt, H. 1993. Foreign Affairs under Egypt's "Dazzling Sun". – Revue d'Égyptologie 44: 153-160.

Schulman, A.R. 1963. The Egyptian Chariotry: A Reexamination. – Journal of the American Research Center in Egypt 2: 75-98.

Schulman, A.R. 1964. Military Rank, Title and Organization in the Egyptian New Kingdom. – Berlin, Verlag Bruno Hessling.

Schulman, A.R. 1979. Diplomatic Marriage in the Egyptian New Kingdom. – Journal of Near Eastern Studies 38: 177-193.

Taylor, J.A. 2001. An Index of Male Non-Royal Egyptian Titles, Epithets and Phrases of the 18th Dynasty. – London, Museum Bookshop Publications.

Wente, E.F. 1963. Two Ramesside Stelae Pertaining to the Cult of Amenophis I. – Journal of Near Eastern Studies 22: 30-36.

A POSSIBLE CHARIOT CANOPY FOR TUTANKHAMUN

Edwin C. Brock

INTRODUCTION

When Howard Carter opened Tutankhamun's tomb in November 1922, the world saw for the first time in over three thousand years the "wonderful things" forming the rich burial equipment of Egypt's kings, that had only been hinted at by the pillaged remains of the other plundered burials of the royal necropolis. Many of those surviving items pointed at what might be expected to be found in an intact royal burial. All the same, there were a number of unique objects found in KV 62 that even now remain poorly understood. In point of fact, the complete publication of this wealth of material was a daunting task for Carter and his team, especially when faced with numerous political and public relations concerns in addition to the work at hand. Thus, unfortunately, they were unable to publish the tomb and its contents fully (Carter & Mace, 1923; Carter, 1927; 1933). Until now, many of the objects still await detailed study and publication, some whose function remain uncertain. The notes of the excavation as well as the photographs can be seen on the website of the Griffith Institute: http://www.griffith.ox.ac.uk/tutankhamundiscovery.html, hereafter referred to as 'Carter Archive').

It is an object from this last category which is the focus of the present contribution: Carter Number 123, JE 60705, presently displayed in Gallery 7 on the upper floor in the northeast quadrant of the Egyptian Museum, Cairo (figure 1A & B). This object consists of a gilded wooden trapezoidal frame from which radiate a series of twenty-eight hinged ribs. This frame and rib assembly is supported by four poles which are just over two meters in height. The assembly was strengthened laterally by two pairs of horizontal bars, each provided with cylindrical bronze sleeves at their ends which fit over the upper ends of the poles beneath the trapezoidal frame (Carter Archive, Burton photo p1663). Other ribs support the hinged rib pairs from below and these, in turn, are attached to the horizontal cross braces. It is supposed that the ribs served to support a canopy of cloth or leather (Griffith Institute, Carter Archive, Index Card 123-4) or some combination of the two, which has not survived, or the remains of which yet wait to be identified.

DESCRIPTION OF COMPONENT PARTS

(Carter Archive, Index Cards 91a, 92a, 113, 123-01 through 123-12, 438, 465, 620 (118))

Canopy Frame

(Carter Archive, Index Cards 123-01, 123-02, 123-06, 123-09, 123-10 A; Burton photos p0011, p0012, p0013, p0035, p0036, p0042, p2004, p2005, p2008)

A wooden frame trapezoidal in plan (figure 2), takes the form in elevation of a cavetto cornice 9 cm

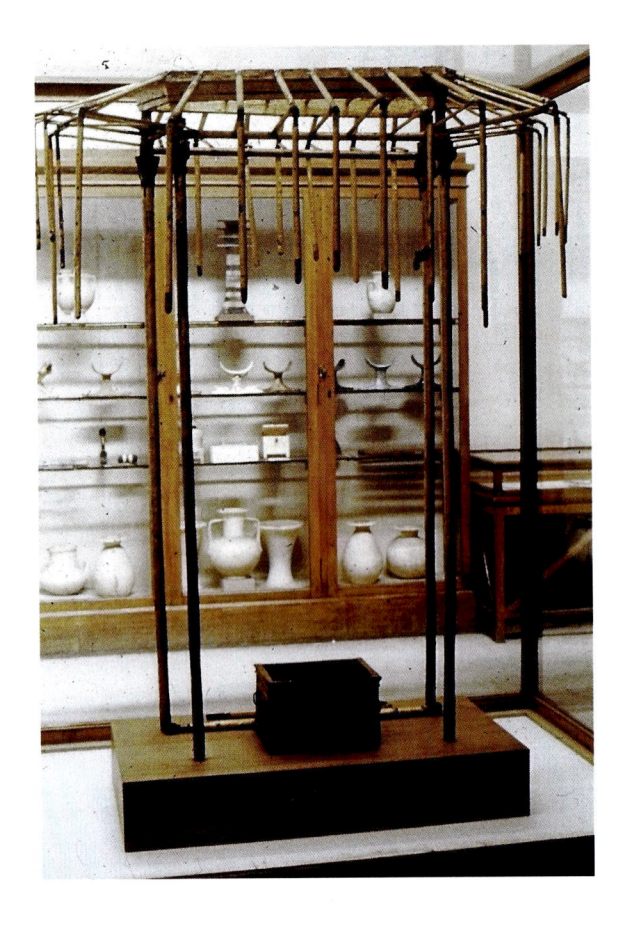

Figure 1A & B. Views of the front (A) and rear (B) of the assembled canopy as displayed in the Egyptian Museum, Cairo. Photographs by E.C. Brock. Courtesy of the Ministry of State for Antiquities/Egyptian Museum Authorities.

in height (see Index Card 123-06). The longer side has a length of 98 cm while the shorter side is 86 cm long. The ends are each 44 cm in length (not "43 cm" as stated on Index Card 123-06). The surface of the cornice itself is covered with gilded gesso and decorated with vertical lines above an ebony torus molding, with a band of running spirals incised on the horizontal surface beneath the torus molding. An upper vertical projection, inset above the top of the out-flaring of the cornice is gesso covered and cut at intervals by vertical notches, each flanked by an oblique hole passing from the top edge to the inside of the slot. In addition to a notch in each corner, there are seven notches on each of the sides and five on each end making a total of twenty-eight. The interior of the frame is divided into a grid formed by two bars parallel to the sides and six cross pieces perpendicular to these. A semi-circular sleeve of bronze covered with gilt gesso is placed vertically at each interior corner of the frame; two of these are now missing. The distance between the centers of these sockets is 86.5 cm at the long side and 76.8 cm at the short side.

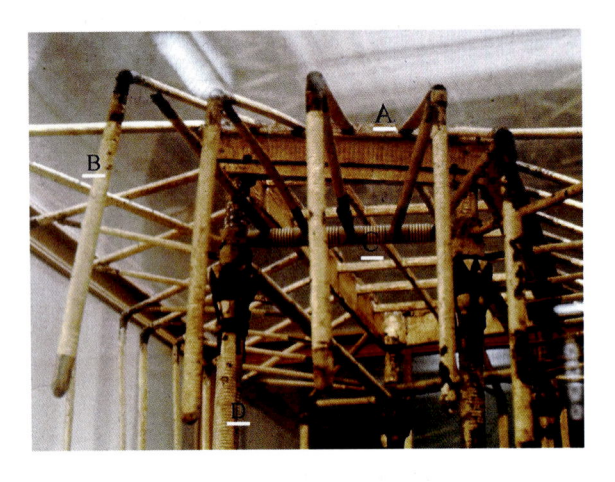

Figure 2. The left upper part of the canopy assembly showing frame (A), ribs (B), cross-bars (C), and poles (D). Photograph by E.C. Brock. Courtesy of the Ministry of State for Antiquities/Egyptian Museum Authorities.

Canopy Ribs or 'Slats'

(Carter Archive, Index Cards 091a, 092a, 113, 123-02 C, 123-03, 123-04, 123-05, 123-07, 123-09, 123-10 B-E, 367a, 620 (118); Burton photos p0032, p0033, p0035, p0036, p0043, p1231, p1671, p1673, p2004, p2005, p2008)

Sixty narrow wooden slats, flat on one side and convex curved on the other, are covered with gilt gesso and decorated with a series of incised parallel lines or ribs (see Index Card 123-07). Twenty-eight of these slats (referred to by Carter as 'Type a') are formed of two lengths joined together by bronze hinges (figure 3A & B). The outer end of the shorter element forms a narrow 2.5 cm projection, pierced horizontally near its tip, while the outer end of the longer element is beveled at each side and also horizontally pierced near the tip. Some of these hinged ribs are pieced vertically by two pairs of holes near the hinge on the short element while others have an additional pair of holes. Twenty-two additional ribs (Carter's 'Type b') are beveled from top to bottom at one end and vertically pierced at an oblique angle from outer end inwards. The excavators do not give details of the dimension of individual ribs other than indicating that there are variations in length as follows: Type a (28 pieces): 70 to 102 cm long, 1.85 cm wide; Type b (22 pieces): 32 to 33 cm long, 1.5 cm wide; Type c (2 pieces): 32.3 to 32.4 cm long, 1.5 cm wide; Type d (4 pieces): 38 to 40 cm long, 1.5 cm wide and Type e (4 pieces): 59 to 61 cm long. There is no indication of how Types c, d and e were employed. In the present display of the assembled canopy, the four longer Type e ribs (figure 4) and one of the cross bars (95b) are displayed on the floor of the display case together with Carter Number 511 the so-called 'traveling stool' (see below).

Figure 3A & B. Hinged ribs as presently displayed. Photograph by E.C. Brock. Courtesy of the Ministry of State for Antiquities/Egyptian Museum Authorities.

Cross-Bars or 'Pole Stays'

(Carter Archive, Index Cards 95b, 123-02 B, 123-08, 123-10B; Burton photos p0032, p0033, p0043)

Four rounded wooden bars, originally fitted with cylindrical bronze ends (see Index Card 123-08), were placed below the bottom of the canopy frame parallel to the sides and ends maintaining the same lengths as the inner corners of the frame. When found, only the two longer cross-bars appear to have survived and the longer of the two (Index Card 95b, Burton photos p0032, p0033) had lost its metal ends (figure 5). Each of the surviving pair of metal ends on the shorter side bar (Index Card 123-08, Burton photo p0043) is 4.6 cm in diameter and 2.5 cm in height. No indication of the two end bars is given in Carter's notes, and in the reconstruction both end bars and the longer of the side (rear) cross-bars are represented by modern wooden bars. The surface of each bar is coated with gesso alternating with gilt gesso into which a series of parallel grooves are incised and pairs of holes diagonally (but not in parallel) pierce these bars at un-gilded sections. These bars not only provided additional strength to the frame and pole assembly, but also, more importantly, served as attachment points for the lower ends of the supports for the hinged ribs.

Poles

(Cairo Museum JE 60704-60706, Carter Archive, Index Cards 438, 465, 123-08; Burton photos p1227, p1319, p1593, p1601, p1672, p1690)

Four wooden poles, 201 cm long, supported the canopy frame (see Index Card 123-08). They are covered with gesso and gilded for most of their length, with the upper and lower ends covered with red leather instead of being gilded. The thickness of the poles at the ends is less (2.9 cm) than the rest of the pole (3.3 cm), with a slight tapering at the bottoms and at the tops (2.75 cm). The entire gilded surface is decorated in a ridged pattern formed by parallel horizontal grooves incised in the surface of the gesso. A conical swelling (max. dia. 7.5 cm) near the upper end of each pole (ending 19 cm from the top) is decorated with pieces of ebony and colored ivory that form an open lotus blossom surrounded by lotus buds held in place by horizontal binding (figure 6). Another band of red leather 5 cm high is placed over the gilt surface just above the lotus

Figure 4. Unmounted Type e ribs on the floor of the display case. Photograph by E.C. Brock. Courtesy of the Ministry of State for Antiquities/Egyptian Museum Authorities.

Figure 5A & B. Ends of unmounted cross-bar 95b with modern replacement rings on the floor of the display case. Photographs by E.C. Brock. Courtesy of the Ministry of State for Antiquities/Egyptian Museum Authorities.

blossoms (and actually covers the top surface of each blossom), with a section between this and the leather covered end again decorated with the gilded grooves. Each pole is pierced by one hole above and one below the loti-form capital for an undetermined purpose (Index Card 123-08, Burton photo p1319). One possibility is discussed below as putative attachment points for inscribed gilt wooden strips. A second possibility might be considered: as attachment points for the ends of the Type e ribs to support the hinged corner ribs. As presently mounted, the inner ends of the support ribs at the corners are set into the interstices of the metal collars at the ends of the cross-bars.

PREVIOUS INTERPRETATIONS

The excavators (Carter & Mace, 1923: 120; Carter Archive, Index Cards 123-11) described the object as a 'traveling canopy' or 'portable pavilion', supposed to have been set up when the king was to have an alfresco audience or when he wished to sit in the shade. The frame is described as missing its base. The few others who have commented on this object follow this interpretation as well (James, 2000: 294; Reeves, 1990: 187).

At least two problems suggest themselves with regard to the reconstruction of this object and its presumed use. One of these is the lack of any base for the poles to be set into. The ends of the poles are blunt and covered in leather, appearing not to have been re-enforced with any stronger material such as metal ferules which might have aided in sticking them into the ground, whether the surface be alluvium or sand. The leather coverings of the lower ends were likely intended to protect the wood from abrasion. This certainly was the case on the upper ends and the areas above the loti-form capitals, where the metal corner sockets in the interior corners of the frame and the metal cylindrical ends of the cross-bars engaged the poles. It may be granted that if some sort of metal base or bases were originally present, they might have been stolen, as suggested by the excavators (Index Card 123-11).

Secondly, the trapezoidal plan of the canopy frame would necessitate a base comparable in plan to receive the bottoms of the poles. A square or rectangular base would be more likely for the function of the portable pavilion suggested by the excavators. An example of a pavilion frame with the expected rectangular plan was found in Tutankhamun's tomb, serving as a support for a linen pall or shroud between the first and second shrines surrounding the sarcophagus (Carter Number 208, Cairo JE 60665). This light wood frame was provided with its own set of feet (Carter, 1927: 43-44, pls. IV, LV, LVI; Carter Archive, Index Cards 208-1 through 208-8; Burton photos p1911, p1912, p1913). One of the earliest Egyptian pavilion frames to have survived is much older and quite different in design and possible function. This belonged to Queen Hetepheres I, wife of the early 4th Dynasty king Sneferu and mother of Khufu, the builder of the Great Pyramid at Giza. That artifact (Egyptian Museum, Cairo JE 57711) consists of a rectangular frame large enough to enclose a bed with room to spare. It could be broken down into units consisting of uprights, a roof frame and a base frame (Porter & Moss, 1974: 180; Reisner & Smith, 1955: 23-5, pl. 5-10). Any explanation for the unusual configuration of the portable pavilion should take into account the possibility that the form of the base imposed the plan of the frame and the arrangement of the poles. As will be seen, a suggestion can be offered to account for this, one that envisages a different method of utilization than offered by the excavators or the few scholars who have previously commented on this artifact.

Figure 6. Detail of loti-form capitals on support poles with attachments of top ends in interior corner sockets of trapezoidal frame. Photograph by E.C. Brock. Courtesy of the Ministry of State for Antiquities/ Egyptian Museum Authorities.

LOCATIONS OF PAVILION COMPONENTS

Before proposing an alternative use of the portable pavilion, however, it will be useful to review the locations in the tomb where the elements that comprised it were found. This small tomb was not likely to have been designed for a royal burial, differing completely in architectural components as well as size from kings' tombs immediately preceding and following it. However, it does fall into the pattern of tomb plans of the second half of the 18th Dynasty found in the Valley of the Kings, intended for members of the royal family or favored members of the court. In general these can be characterized as either a shaft opening at the bottom into a chamber, or a steep flight of stairs descending to a sloping corridor (or a pair of succeeding corridors) that leads to a rectangular room. Various subsidiary chambers may open off this room, depending on necessity, time and resources available. In the example of Tutankhamun's burial (for plan and sections of KV 62, see Weeks, 2003: 125), it appears that a large second chamber, namely the Burial Chamber, was cut into the north end of the first room which will be hereafter referred to as the Antechamber, following the excavators' designation. This burial chamber was provided with a floor that was sunk about 1 meter below the level of that of the Antechamber. A second smaller chamber called the Treasury was then added at the south end of this burial chamber, serving to house the canopic equipment, as well as numerous chests, shrines and two chariots. Near the south end of the Antechamber another small chamber, designated the Annexe, was cut into the west wall, again with its floor sunk below the level of that of the Antechamber. This Annexe was apparently intended for the storage of vessels of wine, oils and baskets of foodstuffs, along with various items of furniture such as beds and thrones, supplementing some of the material found in the Antechamber.

We are fortunate in possessing detailed photographs of the objects in situ in the tomb, as well as showing various stages of the removal of these objects (Griffith Institute, Carter Archive, Burton photos p0011, p0013, p0015, p0032, p0033, p0035, p0036, p0042, p0043, p2004, p2005, p2008). In addition, plans were made showing the location of many of the objects in the Antechamber and Burial Chamber, although none exist for the context of material in the Annexe or Treasury (Reeves, 1990: 80, 85). The trapezoidal frame, most of the ribs, and one of the cross-bars were all found grouped together at the south end of the Antechamber near the group of chariot bodies and wheels that filled the south east corner and comprising four of the total of six chariots from this tomb. One hinged rib and one support rib (Carter Number 113) were found to the west, between box 115 and the golden shrine 108 (Burton photos p0035, p2004). One of the cross-bars (Carter Number 95b) and two of the hinged ribs (Carter Numbers 91a, 92a), were found under throne 91, itself placed beneath the head end of the 'Ammut' ritual couch (Carter Number 137). One hinged rib (Carter Number 367a) was found on top of a box (Carter Number 367) in the Annexe (Burton photos p1231, p1671, p1673). In addition, more hinged ribs were found in the Annexe "scattered on the floor among other miscellanea" (Carter Index Card 620 (118)).

The other main elements of the canopy, the support poles, were located in the Annexe as can be seen from the photographs made during the clearance of this room (Griffith Institute, Carter Archive, Burton photos p1227, p1593, p1601, p1672, p1690). A more confused and jumbled situation of the objects was found here, and unlike the attempted restorations in the Antechamber, it seems that little was done here by the necropolis officials responsible for investigating and 'straightening up' after the two incidents of theft that occurred probably not long after the king's burial. One of the poles, designated as Carter Number 465, is said to have lain along the west wall more or less on top of the other objects, while the three other poles (Carter Number 438), lay on top of other material against the east wall, just to the south of the entrance to this chamber. It should be noted that while Carter's Index Cards for 438 and 465 give the find spots described above, the Burton photos seem to indicate the opposite situation. In photos p1227, p1593, p1601, and p1672, there appears to be at least one and perhaps two poles lying more or less horizontally behind the pole labeled 465. In photo p1790, it is possible to see one of these poles with its distinctive ridged surface at the middle right edge, behind the lower leg of the bed (Carter Number 377) and the end of one of the boats. Part of only one unlabeled pole is visible in the lower left of photo p1690, showing the view just inside the doorway to the Annexe, where the three poles collectively numbered 438 are said to have been found. The lack of detailed plans of location of the objects from this chamber frustrates attempts to suggest with certainty the original placement of the contents of the Annexe, although a general plan of the layout can be suggested by examining the photographs made during various phases of the room`s clearance. The separation of the poles from the rest of the pavilion elements in the Antechamber raises the question of whether or not they were always in the Annexe, although their occurrence on top of most of the other material and on the axis of the entry might allow for their having been re-deposited during one of the 'clean-ups' of the tomb after it had been violated in antiquity (Carter & Mace, 1923).

POSSIBLE CONTEXTUAL CHARIOT ASSOCIATION

The concentration of the four chariot bodies, with accompanying wheels and yoke poles at the same end of the Antechamber as many of the canopy elements might suggest some association by context, admittedly weakened by the disturbances associated with the robberies and restorations. Certainly such bulky objects as the chariot bodies would not likely have been moved far from their original position in any robbery attempt or subsequent re-ordering. In order to fit them through the doorways to the Antechamber as well as the Treasury it was necessary to remove the yoke poles from the bodies and to remove the wheels and cut off the ends of the axle trees. These various components, however, were all arranged together in proximity, while parts of the canopy frame, ribs and upper lateral supports were located under the chariot bodies.

Chariots had become items of prestige for several generations in Egypt's New Kingdom, having apparently been adopted from their contact with Syro-Palestinian peoples first encountered as the Hyksos usurpers of rule in Egypt (see summary in Littauer & Crouwel, 1985: 96-98; see also Crouwel in this volume) and following their expulsion in the mid-16th century BC, at the end of the Middle Bronze age, they quickly became key elements that helped bring about the rapidly expanding Egyptian empire of the 18th Dynasty. As conveyances of prestige they were particularly suited to the military elite that came to power under the pharaohs who extended Egypt's control into Syria-Palestine. These kings themselves were shown using chariots as mobile artillery platforms from which they and their accompanying chariot troops poured a deadly fire into the confused hosts of their enemies (see Spalinger, this volume). As vehicles denoting power, they also served as processional conveyances for the royal court as was often depicted in the reign of Akhenaten (see Sabbahy, this volume).

THE CHARIOT

Among the six chariots and associated equipment found in the tomb of Tutankhamun (Littauer & Crouwel, 1985), four were located in the southeast corner of the Antechamber (*Ibidem*: 1, 9-53), and two in the Treasury (*Ibidem*: 1, 53-63). Of the three most ostentatiously decorated chariots (Carter Numbers 120, 121, 122), two, which Carter referred to as 'State Chariots' (Carter, 1927: 54-63, pls. XVII-XXI), had solid gilt and inlaid front and side panels. One (Carter Number 120) was decorated with bands of running spirals, perhaps representing curls of fur (lion?), and Bes heads at the rear. The other 'State Chariot' (Carter Number 122) is decorated with alternating bands of feather patterns and bands combining running spirals and rosettes as well as two inlaid disks representing Horus eyes (falcon/sphinx or 'griffin'?). These hints of divine theriomorphic symbolism might reward further investigation. Carter's 'second State Chariot' (Carter Number 122, JE61990; A1 of Littauer & Crouwel, 1985: 9-17), may be singled out for our study with regard to the canopy. Close examination of the body reveals localized surface damage from material having been anciently torn away from the corners and near the rear of the sides (figures 7-8) The excavators had also noted this circumstance and assumed some metal elements had been wrenched off from these locations where lateral holes are also seen to have pierced the sides at these points. It bears significant traces at the outer (front) corners and rear ends of the body of possible semicircular sleeves

Figure 7A & B. Chariot 122 body, proper right exterior, front (A) and back (B) views, with indications by white lines of scars from lost elements. Photographs by E.C. Brock. Courtesy of the Ministry of State for Antiquities/Egyptian Museum Authorities.

Figure 8A & B. Chariot 122 body, proper left exterior, front (A) and back (B) views, with indications by white lines of scars from lost elements. Photographs by E.C. Brock. Courtesy of the Ministry of State for Antiquities/Egyptian Museum Authorities.

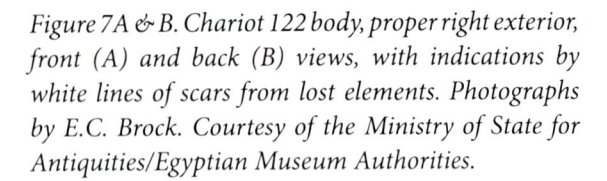

attached by pins having been anciently removed (*Ibidem*: 10; Carter Archive, Index Card 122-13). Providentially, the modern supports for the body of the reconstructed chariot as it is now displayed in Gallery 9 of the Egyptian Museum, Cairo (*Ibidem*: pl. VIII), suggested to this observer the same arrangement as that of the four support poles of the canopy frame. In plan, the position of these miss-ing parts approximates that of the bottoms of the poles as now displayed, with the two supports at the forward curved corners being closer together than the two at the rear edges of the body of the chariot. None of the other chariot bodies exhibit this evidence of attachments in such a location. It seems possible that some form of metal sleeve attached by pins against the exterior at these places may have served to receive the bottoms of the pavilion poles, in a manner similar to the leather-covered tops of the poles fitting into sleeves in the interior corners of the canopy frame. Unfortunately the chariot is presently inaccessible within its display case, so that exact comparative measurement with the spacing of the poles of the canopy cannot be made nor are any detailed measurements given in any publication other than a maximum rear width of 1.02 m (*Ibidem*: 9). While this rear width of the body exceeds that of the longer (rear) side of the frame, it may be possible that the poles tilted in slightly when mounted on the body, as do the sides of the body as well (*Ibidem*: pl. IX).

OBJECTS PERHAPS ASSOCIATED WITH PAVILION AND CHARIOT

Four Gilt Kneeling Captives

(Carter Archive, Index Card 122t, no Burton photos)

Described on Carter card 122t as "Four kneeling captive figures in gesso, gilt. Very much broken. The figures were hollow, and interior showed traces of glue. Meas. Inside at bottom 4 x 3.7 [cm]. They evidently served as sockets." It is tempting to see these objects as related to the missing elements from the exterior of the body of chariot 122 described above. They relate well to the 'imperialistic' subject matter of the decoration of both chariot 120 and 122. It is unfortunate that there are no drawings or photographs for these items.

Inlaid Wooden Strips

(Carter Number 150, JE 61998; Littauer & Crouwel, 1985: 51-52, pl. LXV (C)-LXVI; Carter Archive, Index Card 150; Burton photos p0037, p0041, p2006, p2007)

Five gilded and inlaid wooden strips bearing the names and titles of Tutankhamun were found in the south end of the Antechamber, some in chariot 122 and at least one on the floor beneath it, between chariot wheels 134 and 136 and calcite vessel 128. Four are identical in length (69 cm) and width (2.5 cm), while the fifth is shorter (56 cm) and slightly wider (3.3 cm). All five strips are slightly convex in cross section, and pierced at the top by a hole. The four longer strips (2-4) form two pairs as suggested by the composition of their texts, with two commencing with the Horus name and the other pair beginning with the epithet *nṯr nfr*, and all containing mention of Ankhesenamun as well. The shorter fifth strip also begins with the Horus name but omits the name and titles of Ankhesenamun. Mace tentatively suggested an association with chariot 121, without explanation (Carter Archive, Index Card 150). It is tempting to associate the two longer pairs with the four poles supporting the canopy frame, perhaps to be suspended by pins or pegs inserted into the holes piercing the poles below the lotiform 'capitals', mentioned above. The original placement of the shorter fifth strip is uncertain, although it is pierced at the top.

'Dagger-Shaped Objects'

(JE 61989G, 61990G, 61993E, 61994E; Carter Archive, cards 101n/122h, 120h; Burton photos p0534, p0534a, [note: Burton's photos show two of these objects from opposite sides, but the label of the upper figure changes from 101n to 122n. Carter Number 101n was an earlier designation for Carter Number 122h, based on the find spot of the piece in box Carter Number 101, placed on top of ritual couch Carter Number 137])

Four enigmatic blade-shaped objects, as yet inadequately explained, may also have formed a part of the chariot/canopy assemblage. These wooden objects have been described as some sort of ceremonial daggers or 'dagger-shaped objects'. They are flat and taper toward pointed ends with notches near the tips and at the wider opposite ends. An extension, angled between 45° and 55° from the horizontal plane, in two cases takes the form of a gilded bound figure of a Nubian enemy (Littauer & Crouwel, 1985: 49-50 [K1-K3], 63 [K4], 90, pl. L, LX; Griffith Institute, Carter Archive, cards 101n/122 h, 120 h), while the bent ends of the other two are plain cylinders topped with rounded knobs. To the rear of the enemies on the upper surface of each blade a slight circular depression can be observed, and each figure is pierced longitudinally by a hole. The floors of the chariot bodies were formed by a webbed network of interwoven leather strips; the well-preserved floor of the chariot from the tomb of Yuya and Thuiu best illustrates this feature (Littauer & Crouwel, 1985: pl. LXIX; Quibell, 1908: pl. 53). It may have been possible that the tips of these blades were inserted into the webbing at bottoms of the sides beneath the bottom edge of the chariot body below the missing putative metal sleeves and could have served to support the bottoms of the pavilion poles. The decorative program of both chariots 120 and 122 emphasize the subjugation of foreign enemies (the 'Nine Bows'), but on chariot 122 there is the added decorative detail at the lower back edges of the body showing pairs of kneeling bound Asiatic and Nubian prisoners flanking the narrow vertical column of the *smȝ* "union" symbol, bearing incised parallel bands, reminiscent of the poles supporting the canopy frame (Carter Archive, Burton photo p0541 [note similar image on gold foil fragment from KV 58, although the captives are standing, see refs in Littauer & Crouwel, 1985: 68.5, especially Daressy in Davis, 1912: 126, fig. 2]). Granted this interpretation is certainly speculative, particularly since there is no indication whether or not the missing sleeves lacked bottoms, and that one of the two undecorated pieces was found in the Treasury. Yet, given the uniqueness of these objects, as are the other components of the canopy, I present this as a hypothesis for their possible use for consideration. At the least Littauer & Crouwel (1987, *contra* Ritner, 1986) have convincingly demonstrated they could not have served as linch pins to hold the chariot wheels onto the axels.

Embossed Gold Harness Elements

(Cairo Temp. No. 30.3.34.52 (Littauer & Crouwel, 1985: 34-47, 87-88, pl. XLII-XLIX; Carter Archive, Index Cards 122 t-122qqqq; Burton photos p0531a, p1197a, p1774, p1775, p1776, p1777, p1779, p1781)

Although described as embossed gold elements with leather linen and gesso backing intended as appliqués to the harness, again it is tempting to see some of these as possible decorative elements attached to the covering of the canopy. It should be noted that a similar group comes from the Treasury, as well as from the robbers' cache from KV 58 (Littauer & Crouwel, 1985: 59-60, 68, 87). Given their relative fragility, it is difficult to imagine them holding up against the exertions of the chariot team, nor do all these sorts of items appear readily identifiable in contemporary depictions of chariot team harnessing. The shapes differ, as do the decoration although the themes of the latter are related by their bellicose and imperialistic subject matter. These items deserve further study particularly the possible inter-relationships of their shapes and decoration.

Traveling Stool

(Carter Number 511, JE 62044)

Reeves (1990: 187), following Carter, thought that the pavilion apparently was associated with object 511 from the Annex (Carter Archive, Index Cards 511-1, 2; Burton photos p1305, p1732, p1877), a rectangular box provided "with bronze staples, goose-feather filled cushion and leather carrying straps", identified by Carter as a 'traveling stool' and decorated with gilding and faience inlays depicting the *smȝ tȝwy* or union symbol and traditional bound foreigners. Eaton-Krauss (2008: 143-144, pl. LXXXII-LXXXIV) believes it may have been associated with a 'block throne', noting that one side is left undecorated as if abutting another surface. I do not feel there is any need to associate this item with the canopy, despite the fact that it is presently displayed in the same case as the pavilion in the Egyptian Museum, Cairo. As will be seen in the discussion below, a foot-stool was not likely to have been needed in the proposed means of use of the chariot with canopy. Other items from the tomb also were provided with metal staples on their exterior as a means of carrying, or securing the item, e.g. a semicircular box (Carter Number 79) with lid (Carter Number 574), apparently once containing unidentified objects carried in the funeral procession (Carter Archive, Index Cards 79, 574; Killen, 1994: 73, 77; Reeves, 1990: 188-193), and the bow-case (Carter Number 335; JE 61502; Carter Archive, Index Card 335; McLeod, 1982: 26-38, pl. VI-XVI).

REPRESENTATIONS OF CHARIOTS WITH CANOPIES

The only representations of Egyptian chariots with canopies known to this writer come from the reign of Ramesses II. Images from military scenes of the Battle of Qadesh, associated with depictions of his wars against the Hittites, Egypt's rival for the control of northern Syria, show a chariot provided with a canopy. This detail occurs in the Qadesh battle scenes on the north wall in the first hall of the main temple at Abu Simbel (Porter & Moss, 1962: 103-104), the south face of the west wing of the first pylon at Luxor Temple (*Ibidem*, 1972: 305 [14]) (figure 4) and on the exterior of the rear wall of the Abydos temple of Ramesses II (*Ibidem*, 1939: 39 [77 -78]). It does not occur in the preserved portions of the scene at the Ramesseum, although the main scene to which it belongs does survive. The representation of the battle at Karnak temple is very poorly preserved although it may once have been the most extensive of all, originally stretching along the exterior of the outer faces of the west walls between the 8th and 10th Pylons (*Ibidem*, 1972: 179 [535-537]). Unfortunately, little of the scene to which this detail belongs is preserved, and nothing remains showing the chariot with canopy. Where it is preserved, this detail occurs in a subscene beneath the representation of the enthroned king addressing his entourage, in association with the royal encampment being attacked. In this detail a chariot is shown with a richly caparisoned pair of horses held by either a groom or a soldier, apparently part of an honor guard of Egyptians and Shardana, guarding the entrance to the 'audience' venue. This item differs considerably from the Tutankhamun model in having only one pole and resembling in outline an umbrella. In the examples of the chariot with umbrella from the Qadesh battle scenes, only the one from Abu Simbel shows decoration on the umbrella, in the form of a vulture with outspread wings holding a fan in each of its feet, and flanked by pairs of cartouches of the king. A line of running spirals forms a border across the curved top, and a series of pendant flaps appear on the bottom edge of the canopy in alternating colors of red, black (blue?) and yellow, decorated with a feather pattern (Champollion, 1835: pl. XX-VII). These details were all apparently rendered in paint, since none survive in relief (see figures 9-11 for views of the examples from Abu Simbel, Luxor Temple and Ramesses II temple, Abydos).

Figure 9. Abu Simbel, Main Temple, First Hall, north side. Detail from Battle of Qadesh 'audience' scene with canopied chariot. Photograph by E.C. Brock.

Figure 10. Luxor temple, First Pylon, west wing, exterior. Detail from Battle of Qadesh 'audience' scene with canopied chariot. Photograph by E.C. Brock.

Figure 11. Abydos, Ramesses II temple, west wall, exterior. Detail from Battle of Qadesh 'audience' scene with canopied chariot. Photograph by E.C. Brock.

Another representation of a chariot sunshade from the time of Ramesses II is preserved at Karnak on a block now stored in a block yard outside the Bubastite Portal between the Ramesses III temple and the west wall of the Cour de la Cachette, near the south wall of the Hypostyle Hall (figure 12). It shows a prince driving a chariot with an umbrella-like canopy supported by a single central pole projecting from the top of the chariot body (La Saout, 1982: 232.4c; Van Siclen, 1990: 103-105). Like the unoccupied chariot described above in some examples as a sub-register of the audience scene from the Battle of Qadesh reliefs, a row of pendant 'flaps' are attached to the bottom of the umbrella beneath a horizontal strip. There is no other decoration on this umbrella.

In much later times and from another culture, we have examples from Assyrian reliefs of a king riding in a chariot provided with a sun-shade supported by a single pole. These come from Nimrud and Nineveh, dating to the reigns of Tiglath-Pileser III, Sennacherib and Ashurbanipal, from the latter half of the 8th to the third quarter of the 7th century BC and are now in the British Museum (WA/ME 118908, 124825, 124946; Barnett, 1975: pl. 65, 168; Van Siclen, 1990: 103).

CHARIOT AS VIEWING PLATFORM

There is an unrecognized possible use to which the combination of canopy and chariot may have been put. Some remains of Ramesside relief depict the king viewing the counting of battle trophies, that is body parts (mainly hands, but later penises, as well), severed from slain enemies, a tradition dating back at least to the beginning of the 18th Dynasty. In examples dating to the reign of Ramesses II at Abu Simbel (Porter &Moss, 1962: 103 [41-42], Upper Register), Abydos (*Ibidem*, 1939: 1 [3- 4],41 [87]), and Karnak (*Ibidem*, 1972: 179 [537], for example, the king is shown sitting in a chariot facing to the rear of the vehicle. Unfortunately, except for the Abu Simbel example, these scenes are poorly preserved, and show, at most, the king's feet and the lower part of the chariot (figures 13-14). From the 20th Dynasty comes a scene (figure 15) from the interior of the south wall of the second court of Ramesses III's temple at Medinet Habu of the same theme but much better preserved (*Ibidem*: 498 [93-95]). Given the recognized propensity of this king to copy scenes of his illustrious predecessor, it is not unreasonable to suppose that it presents an indication of what the scenes of Ramesses II may have looked like. Granted no form of shading device is shown, but it does suggest one use for a stationary chariot.

PROPOSED ASSOCIATION OF CANOPY AND CHARIOT

As presently reconstructed and displayed, the pavilion/canopy, if mounted on the chariot 122 as

Figure 12 . Karnak temple, south block yard, near exterior south wall of Hypostyle Hall. Ramesside prince in canopied chariot. Photograph by E.C. Brock.

Figure 13. Abydos, Seti I temple, second court, south at wall interior. Detail of remains of hand counting scene with Ramesses II (feet only) seated in chariot, viewing the count. Photograph by E.C. Brock.

Figure 14. Abydos, Ramesses II temple, north wall exterior. Detail of remains of hand counting scene with Ramesses II (feet only) seated in chariot, viewing the count. Photograph by E.C. Brock.

Figure 15. Medinet Habu, Ramesses III temple, second court, south wall interior. Detail of remains of hand counting scene with Ramesses III seated in chariot, viewing the count. Photograph by E.C. Brock.

described above and provided with a covering, would seem to have obscured forward vision (figure 16), and one wonders how stable it would have been under rapid movement. A partial solution to the first problem may lie with the incorrect arrangement of the hinged ribs, which as presently displayed seem to offer no useful function. If the hinged ribs are rotated axially 180°, however, so the flat sides are up and the flat inner ends of the hinge flanges are flush against each other, preventing any downward bending, the ribs would splay out at a much shallower angle, improving vision as well as extending the shaded area (figure 17). Compare this proposed re-arrangement, with the example of the configuration of the bronze hinges on the folding bed (Carter Number 586, Cairo JE 62018; Carter Archive, Index Card 586; Killen, 1980: 33-34).

This chariot, too elaborate and delicate for use in battle, was more likely utilized in state processions moving at a moderate pace (figure 18). The canopy, especially if decorated with equally ostentatious elements such as gilded pieces, would certainly have enhanced the display. In a stationary position it might also have served as an 'impromptu audience pavilion'. While this author believes that the association of the canopy with the chariot is a reasonable hypothesis, the means by which this configuration was utilized is problematic. Given its uniqueness, until now one can only hypothesize. Perhaps in the future, a replica to scale could be fashioned by which to test the hypothesis. One can only hope that when the objects from Tutankhamun's tomb are transferred to the Grand Egyptian Museum near the Giza pyramids, it may at least prove possible to make more detailed measurements of the body of the chariot in question, particularly the exterior scars from the loss of the putative sleeves.

Figure 16. Reconstruction of canopy mounted on chariot provided with covering in present display configuration. Computerized reconstruction by L. Pinch-Brock.

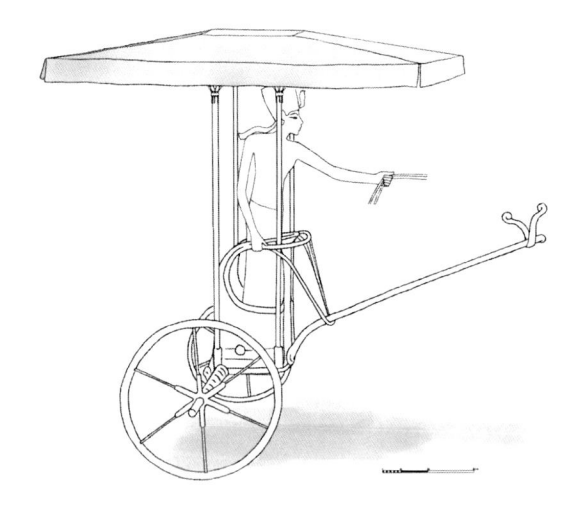

Figure 18. Reconstruction of chariot of Tutankhamen showing canopy with extended ribs in place in relation to figure of Tutankhamun. Computerized reconstruction by L. Pinch-Brock.

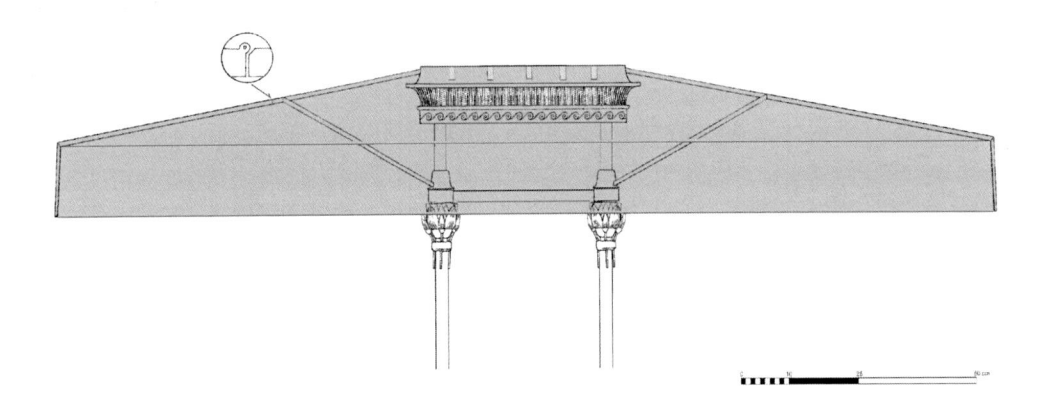

Figure 17. Side view of chariot canopy showing construction details of extended ribs. Computerized reconstruction by L. Pinch-Brock.

CITED LITERATURE

Barnett, R.D.1975. Assyrian Sculpture in the British Museum. – Toronto, McClellan and Stewart.

Carter, H. & A.C. Mace. 1923. The Tomb of Tut.ankh.amen I. – London, Cassel & Co.

Carter, H. 1927. The Tomb of Tut.ankh.amen II. – London, Cassel & Co.

Carter, H. 1933. The Tomb of Tut.ankh.amen III. – London, Cassel & Co.

Champollion, J.-F., 1835. Monuments de l'Égypte et de la Nubie. Planches, Tome I. – Paris, Firmin Didot Frères

Davis, T.M. 1912. The Tombs of Harmhabi and Toutânkhamanoun. – London, Constable.

Eaton-Krauss, M. 2008. The Thrones, Chairs, Stools, and Footstools from the Tomb of Tutankhamun. – Oxford, Griffith Institute.

James, T.G.H. 2000. Tutankhamun. The Eternal Splendor of the Boy Pharaoh. – Cairo, American University in Cairo Press.

Killen, G. 1980. Ancient Egyptian Furniture. Volume I: 4000-1300 BC. – Warminster, Aris and Phillips.

Littauer, M. & J.H. Crouwel. 1987. Unrecognized Linch Pins from the Tombs of Tutankhamun and Amenophis II: A Reply. – Göttinger Miszellen 100: 53-59.

Littauer, M.A. & J.H. Crouwel. 1985. Chariots and Related Equipment from the Tomb of Tutankhamun. – Oxford, Griffith Institute.

McLeod, W. 1982. Self Bows and Other Archery Tackle from the Tomb of Tutankhamun. – Oxford, Griffith Institute.

Porter, B. & R. Moss. 1939. Topographical Bibliography of Ancient Egyptian Hieroglyphic Texts, Reliefs and Paintings. VI. Upper Egypt: Chief Temples (Excluding Thebes). – Oxford, Griffith Institute.

Porter, B. & R. Moss. 1962. Topographical Bibliography of Ancient Egyptian Hieroglyphic Texts, Reliefs and Paintings. VII. Nubia, the Deserts, and Outside Egypt. – Oxford, Griffith Institute.

Porter, B. & R. Moss. 1972 [1929]. Topographical Bibliography of Ancient Egyptian Hieroglyphic Texts, Reliefs and Paintings. II. Theban Temples. – Oxford, Clarendon Press.

Porter, B. & R. Moss. 1973 (1964) [1927]. Topographical Bibliography of Ancient Egyptian Hieroglyphic Texts, Reliefs and Paintings. I. The Theban Necropolis. Part II. Royal Tombs and Smaller Cemeteries. – Oxford, Griffith Institute.

Porter, B. & R. Moss. 1974 [1931]. Topographical Bibliography of Ancient Egyptian Hieroglyphic Texts, Reliefs and Paintings. III. Memphis. Part 1. Abu Rawash to Abusir. – Oxford, Clarendon Press.

Quibell, J.E., 1908. The Tomb of Yuaa and Thuiu. Catalogue générale des antiquités Égyptiennes du Musée de Caire, Nos. 51001 -51191. – Cairo, Service des Antiquités de l'Égypte.

Reeves, C.N. 1990. The Complete Tutankhamun – New York, Thames & Hudson.

Reisner, G.A. & W.S. Smith. 1955. A History of the Giza necropolis. Volume 2. The Tomb of Hetep-her-es, the Mother of Cheops. A Study of Egyptian Civilization in the Old Kingdom. – Cambridge, Harvard University Press.

Ritner, R.K. 1986. Unrecognized Decorated Linch Pins from the Tombs of Tutankhamun and Amenhotep II. – Göttinger Miszellen 94: 53-56.

Van Siclen III, C. 1990. Editorial. – Varia Aegyptiaca 6.3: 1-5.

Weeks, K.R. 2003. Atlas of the Valley of the Kings. – Cairo, American University in Cairo Press. (See also the Theban Mapping Project website, Atlas of the Valley of the Kings: www.thebanmappingproject.com/atlas/index-kv).

VEHICLE OF THE SUN: THE ROYAL CHARIOT IN THE NEW KINGDOM

Amy M. Calvert

INTRODUCTION

The New Kingdom (1550-1070 BC) in ancient Egypt was a period of expansion and wealth, largely due to the military prowess of the pharaohs and the organization of their armies. Depictions of the pharaoh show him strong and athletic, able to defend Egypt from her enemies and subjugate her neighbors. The war chariot is central to many of these depictions. Introduced during the Hyksos period (*e.g.* Spalinger, 2005: 6), the two-wheeled horse drawn vehicle was an integral part of the imperial Egyptian army. Although the actual circumstances surrounding the introduction of this weapon to Egypt are much debated, the first textual reference to chariotry from Egypt occurs at the end of the Second Intermediate Period (1650-1549 BC), in the Kamose texts (Habachi, 1972: 36, note g). The present paper will focus on the symbolic importance of the royal chariot later in the New Kingdom, using the chariot body (Egyptian Museum, Cairo CG 46097) discovered in 1903 by Howard Carter in the tomb of Thutmose IV (1398-1388 BC) as the basis for discussion (Carter & Newberry, 1904: 24-33).[1]

A detailed examination of the iconography of this chariot body, taken together with evidence from other royal chariots and the texts that refer to the pharaoh in his chariot in general, will suggest layers of significance for these vehicles. There is strong use of solar imagery tied to the chariot, and it also appears to have connections to the *3ht* (akhet) and with the maintenance of cosmic order and regeneration. Relief evidence points to the use of the chariot as a mobile throne on the field of battle. Moreover, important elements of the iconography of chariot decoration are shared with thrones, Windows of Appearance, palanquins, and royal barques – all venues for royal appearance. Of particular interest are the aggressively apotropaic and potentially powerful terrestrial focus of the scenes on the chariot body of Thutmose IV, which suggests that the ritual significance of these vehicles was always balanced by their importance and functions in the real world.

NOTE ON THE CHARIOT IN WARFARE

It is important for the purposes of the current study to briefly examine the role of the chariot in Egyptian warfare. Earlier theories on the effectiveness of the chariot in battle have tended to exaggerate, comparing the weapons to modern tanks (Faulkner, 1953: 43), while others have considered them taxis for archers who would fire, mount the chariot, move to another spot, dismount and fire again (Schulman, 1979: 125). If that were the case, then there would be no need to have both a driver and an archer: the six chariots of Tutankhamun (1335-1325 BC), that of Yuya, and the chariot body found in the tomb of Thutmose IV were all designed to accommodate two people (Littauer & Crouwel, 1985: 70). Images of the pharaoh alone in his chariot withstanding, other depictions of Egyptian chariot teams regularly show two men in the vehicles. Textually, Pharaoh also mentions his driver, for example in the Qadesh inscriptions of Ramesses II (1279-1212 BC), he addresses "charioteer, Menena, my shield-bearer" (Lichtheim, 1976: 70). It has been noted that, with the proper sidelines and rigorously trained horses, Pharaoh could, in fact, steer his team by means of reins tied around his waist (Hansen, 1992: 177, note 19). However, the danger and difficulty of this manner of driving prevents seeing this as a common occurrence; it seems much safer and more practical to simply have a driver. The fact that this person is not usually depicted in the chariot should not be surprising – it is the king alone who is shown as sole victor and conqueror for the glory of Egypt and the gods.

With its high wooden sides covered with intricately detailed relief work, there may be a tendency to label the chariot of Thutmose IV as purely ceremonial and dismiss it as such. This is particularly true since the vehicle is relatively heavy. However, there is textual evidence for gilt and decorated chariots being used on the battlefield (see also e.g. Veldmeijer et al., this volume). A possible example, from Ramesses II's well-recorded Battle of Qadesh, suggests a gleaming vehicle in its description of the king in his chariot as being "like Re when he rises at dawn. My rays, they burned the rebels' bodies" (Lichtheim, 1976: 70). Although Ramesses might arguably have been forced to fight alone because of the surprise attack, other records of battle are explicit regarding the usual method of deployment.

In the Annals of Thutmose III (1479-1424 BC) at Karnak, it is reported that on the morning of the Battle of Megiddo the king appeared at dawn and "An order was given to the whole army…His majesty set out on a chariot of fine gold, decked in his shining armor like strong-armed Horus, Lord of Action, like Mont of Thebes, his father Amun strengthening his arm [...] his majesty was in their center, Amun protecting his person (in) the melee, and the strength of [Seth pervading] his limbs" (Lichtheim, 1976: 32). In light of such evidence, it seems implausible to dismiss the chariot of Thutmose IV, and the so-called 'state chariots' of Tutankhamun, simply as ceremonial vehicles. Indeed, while the king may have ridden to the battlefield in a light, rugged chariot, his high-sided war vehicle might have been brought along specifically for use in leading his army against the enemy (Littauer & Crouwel, 1985: 99). Even if he simply positioned himself in a prominent location above the field of battle, the substantial, gilt chariot would have made him far more visible to both his troops and the enemy, prompting greater bravery in one group while (hopefully) terrifying the other. There is no doubt that the pharaoh, covered in gleaming armor, would cut a much more awesome figure standing in a large, highly ornamented chariot embellished with shining metal than he would in a light, openwork vehicle – something that would have blended in with, and almost disappeared among, those of his own troops.

In his war vehicle, the king would have been extremely visible to both his troops and to the enemy forces. The physical appearance of Pharaoh in his chariot may have been intentionally constructed to lend courage to one group while striking fear into the hearts of the other. Due to this visibility, however, the pharaoh would have been an obvious target for his enemies, whether he was truly in the 'center' of the army or simply present on the field. Thus, chariots of the kings are often covered with protective iconography, enveloping the pharaoh on all sides. It was not only the body of the chariot that was endowed with protective imagery; literally almost every element that made up the chariot of the king, including horse trappings, was ornamented to serve an apotropaic function. The basic components that make up a chariot are the same whether it is an open-bodied, undecorated vehicle or the highly adorned chariot of the pharaoh. However, layers of decoration can be added to each element, and many were deliberately embellished in such a way that they actively protected the king. These individual protective elements seem to have been specifically selected to work together to encase the pharaoh in a divinely wrought and (theoretically) impervious shield.

THUTMOSE IV CHARIOT BODY

The Thutmose IV chariot body (figure 1) is constructed of wood covered with gesso and fine linen and decorated with minutely detailed low raised relief, which was originally silvered, both inside and out (Littauer & Crouwel, 1985: 72).² Although natural metallic silver was not found in Egypt, the Egyptians did have easy access to a material known as aurian silver (Gale & Gale, 1981: 113; Ogden, 2000: 170). This metal, which contains approximately 20% gold, was probably found in the same mines as the vast amounts of Nubian gold. It is a naturally silver-rich ore, similar to electrum, but with a larger proportion of silver. Most of the other surviving chariots from this period are overlaid with gold. Silver is not attested on any chariot body except for the one belonging to Thutmose IV, although silver does cover the ends of the axle and the pole on the chariot of Yuya (Littauer & Crouwel, 1985: 95). Textual evidence for other chariot bodies embellished with silver does exist, however. At the Battle of Megiddo, it is reported of the enemy that, "when they saw his majesty overwhelming them, they fled headlong [to] Megiddo with faces of fear, abandoning their horses, their chariots of gold and silver... then their horses were captured and their chariots of gold and silver became easy [prey]" (Lichtheim, 1976: 32). The description of the enemy chariots in both cases identifies them as of *nbw* and *ḥḏ nbw*, or gold and white gold (= silver). Although this kind of text could be propagandistic – an allusion to the importance of these vehicles as war booty – the examples of this type of statement are sufficiently numerous that they seem likely to be based on reality.

There are four panels of scenes on the chariot body (figure 2), two each on the interior and exterior, each set divided by what Carter & Newberry (1904: 26) described as "an exceedingly decorative and ornamental design." Hayes (1959: 150-151) elaborated on these unusual scenes thusly: "We see the pharaoh charging in his chariot into a confused mass of stricken foreign enemies [...] distributed helter-skelter over the field with no regard for ground lines or division into registers. This naturalistic and highly dramatic type of composition, thought to have been inspired by contemporary Helladic art, we shall find extensively employed in Egyptian relief, sculpture and painting from the end of the Eighteenth Dynasty onwards." Groenewegen-Frankfort (1951: 116) considered the scenes to be "simply an elaboration of the pictogram of the

Figure 1. General view of the chariot body, interior and exterior. From: Carter & Newberry (1904: pl. IX).

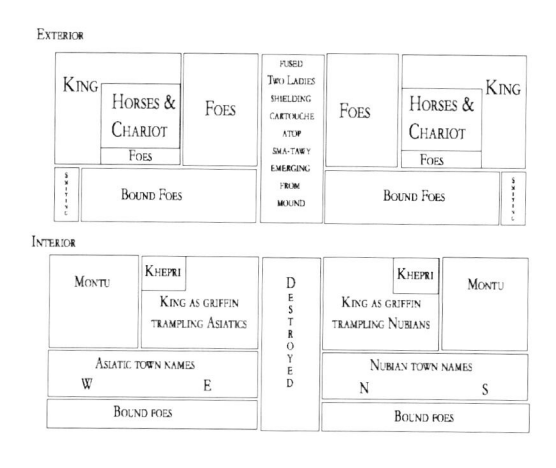

Figure 2. Schematic diagram of scenes on the chariot. Diagram by A. Calvert (with thanks to O'Conner).

victorious king." Extremely detailed and intricately incised, the scenes depict the enemies of Egypt not as an undifferentiated throng but as an army of individuals, with varying patterns of decoration on their weapons, clothing and jewelry. Petrie (1910: 144) noted that "it would be hard to find any point in which more details could be introduced."

On the exterior of the chariot body are two main scenes of Asiatic warfare. Both show the king riding in his chariot, horses rearing, his skill on the battlefield sending his Asiatic opponents into disarray. These are separated in the center and bordered on the bottom by a zone that includes a lion-headed bird, a large *smꜣ-tꜣwi* motif emerging from a mound, and bound foreign prisoners. On the inside of the chariot, two main scenes depict the pharaoh as a human-headed winged sphinx, trampling his northern (Asiatic) enemies on the interior left side (from the perspective of the king standing in the chariot) and those of the south (Nubians) on the interior right. Below these scenes are personifications of captured cities or regions, shown as human-headed name rings. There are six of these each for the north and the south, and the figures are rendered with the distinctive features of their region. At the bottom of the body interior are lines of bound prisoners, similar to those on the corresponding area on the chariot exterior. The central zone on the interior of the chariot is unfortunately very heavily damaged, but a *smꜣ-tꜣwi* was certainly part of the original design. In all of the scenes, Thutmose is shown fully surrounded by protective elements. Because these elements are layered one atop another, it is most efficient to examine each scene briefly before comparing and discussing the overall scheme and how they functioned together as a protective program. The description is always from the occupant's point of view.

Exterior Right Side

On the exterior right side (figures 3 & 4), Thutmose is shown in his chariot, firing his recurved bow as he charges furiously into the melee of his Asiatic opponents. At least five of the fourteen fallen enemies are missing one of their hands. This likely refers to the Egyptian practice of severing one hand of each of the enemy dead in order to get an accurate

Figure 3. View of the right exterior of the chariot. Photograph by A. Calvert. Courtesy of the Ministry of State for Antiquities/Egyptian Museum Authorities.

count of their numbers. The presence on the battlefield of handless enemy warriors could indicate a foreshadowing of this event. There was no doubt in the mind of the Egyptian artists who produced this scene that Thutmose would be victorious in his struggle against the Asiatics. By including in the battle scene images of enemy dead who have already been 'counted,' the imminent victory of the pharaoh is magically reinforced and becomes not only certain, but inevitable. And this is Pharaoh's victory. No other Egyptian force is visible; Pharaoh is alone except for the god Montu, who stands behind the king in his chariot, and the vulture goddess Nekhbet, flying above.

The fiercely rearing horses of the king visually separate the disorder of the enemy army, which is piled in hopeless disarray, from the neatly structured lines of text. Depicted in a stance better suited to predators than to benign equids,[3] this rampant pose seems to represent a transformation of their character while on the battlefield; like the king, they

Figure 4. Drawing of the right exterior of the chariot. From: Wreszinski (1935: pl. 1).

too may assume an aggressive nature through the assistance of a deity. The net-patterned housing shown here on the stallions of Thutmose might be indicative of this: the same pattern is often seen in the dress of goddesses (see JE 60794, the statue of Sekhmet from the tomb of Tutankhamun, for one example), a design that may allude to the horses being represented as a physical manifestation of a war-goddess on the battlefield, particularly since a war-goddess, Astarte, is specifically mentioned in the text directly above. The stallions of Pharaoh added to the emphasis on the virility and power of the king in these scenes and, when combined with the female aspects of a war-goddess, may represent the strength of both sexes, not just the male. After all, Sekhmet, perhaps the most vicious of all Egyptian deities, was female. There was an intense potency in androgynous forms (Troy, 1986: 15-20), and there is textual support for this concept being applied in this context. In the Qadesh inscriptions, for example, Ramesses' foes warn each other to steer clear of him because "She's (Sekhmet) with him on his horses, her hand is with him" (Lichheim, 1976: 70). Thutmose IV, together with his horses, form a sort of barrier between the chaos of the outside world and the ideal order of the Egyptian realm. Later texts, such as the Qadesh inscriptions, refer to the king in battle specifically as a wall, standing between his soldiers (and Egypt) and the chaos of the outside world (*Ibidem*: 62).

Egyptian order (*mꜣꜥt*) is personified by Thutmose, accompanied in his chariot by the war-god Montu, who stands behind the king steadying his aim. Most unusual about this scene is that the god is partially hidden by the king (Aldred, 1988: 130). The perception that the god is almost being absorbed by the body of the pharaoh is emphasized by the presence behind them of a personified ꜥnḫ holding a large, semi-circular fan of which only half is visible, with the remainder vanishing behind the head of the god. The flabellum was used as a signifier of a divine presence; the word šwit can be translated as 'spirit' or aspect of a god (Faulkner, 1996: 263). When it occurred behind the king it could indicate that he was in the 'shade' of the god, a position that would endow him with attributes of that deity. The reading is made particularly strong by the layering of the three (Schäfer, 1974: 180-181). This unusual merging of Thutmose, Montu and the flabellum may be seen as a rebus, the reading of which could be "<The shade of Montu is with Thutmose IV>" (Bell, 1985: 33-34). To take this a step further, the entire scene could be read "Then his Majesty appeared on the chariot like Montu in his might," a commonly encountered statement regarding the battling king (Lichtheim, 1976: 41).

Flying above the scene with her wings protectively spread to cover the king's vulnerable head and back, the vulture Nekhbet holds a šn-sign in her talons and offers him her eternal protection. Identified as the "Mistress of Heaven" in the text while always remaining the embodiment of Upper Egypt, Nekhbet's supports Thutmose's role as terrestrial king of that region just as Wadjet, the uraeus at his brow, implies the same dominion over Lower Egypt. Since she is also one of the deities who suckled and protected the divine child in the thickets of Chemmis, Nekhbet's presence also alludes to the king's role as the living Horus (Pinch, 2002: 212). Below the outstretched wing of the vulture is one of the many solar elements depicted on the chariot: a sun disc with two pendant uraei. Since the uraei are uncrowned, it is likely the "Eye of Re", embodying the violent heat of the sun and performing an apotropaic function, which is depicted here (*Ibidem*: 130).

Although Thutmose IV's vehicle in this scene is without figural representation, it has several important iconographic features (figures 5, 6 & 7). Its body sports a design of curved lines of dots, similar to that seen on the one remaining upright Asiatic chariot. This dotted pattern may indicate that

Figure 5. Detail of the king on the right exterior. Photograph by A. Calvert. Courtesy of the Ministry of State for Antiquities/Egyptian Museum Authorities.

these chariot bodies were covered in leather or hide – note the variety of patterned hides, apparently attached to a dark green-colored leather base, used on Tutankhamun's chariots depicted on the painted box (Egyptian Museum, Cairo JE 61467). The dotted pattern on Thutmose's chariot is mirrored in several of his quivers, including the stiff one worn slung across his back; this pattern is reminiscent of that depicted on a bow-case (attached to a green chariot) in the tomb of Rekmire (TT 100). The similarity of the pattern to that on the Asiatic chariots could additionally foreshadow victory and the claiming of booty (suggested by Katherine Eaton, Personal Communication, October 2010). The feathered design in the fenestration echoes Montu's costume as well as Nekhbet's body feather pattern, perhaps a visual device to symbolically project their protection around the king, completely enveloping him. This concept is more explicitly visualized in the left exterior scene discussed below.

Figure 6. Detail of the king on the right exterior. From: Wreszinski (1935: pl. 1).

Figure 7. Detail of patterns on the chariot in the right exterior scene. Photograph by A. Calvert. Courtesy of the Ministry of State for Antiquities/Egyptian Museum Authorities.

At the base of the king's chariot body in this scene, a small goose or duck head is visible above the horizontal median spoke (see also Sabbahy, this volume). Although there are several possibilities for its significance in this context, a rebus reading of *s3 Rˁ* (Son of Re), using the wheel itself as the solar disc, has been suggested (Stephen Harvey, Personal Communication, January 2000). Additionally, geese are closely related to the god Amun-Re and are notoriously aggressive birds, a characteristic that would have made it appropriate for battle (Houlihan, 1986: 62). The goose was also viewed as the "Great Cackler", a primeval bird that laid the world egg and initiated cosmos, adding a regenerative connotation to the depiction of this waterfowl (Pinch, 2002: 120).

Exterior Left Scene

In the left exterior scene (figures 8 & 9), Pharaoh has changed his weapon of choice. He holds his triangular compound bow and two of his enemies by the hair in his left hand. His right hand, raised high above his head, unusually wields a battle-ax in the traditional smiting pose (Hall, 1986: 20). The blade of the ax is turned away from the head of the king and overlaps the wing of the falcon hovering above him, while his hand covers the talons of the bird (figure 10). Unlike Nekhbet in the right scene the falcon is not specifically identified by text, but given the context, an identification with Montu seems most probable. Both Pharaoh's hand and the falcon are layered on top of a flabellum. This may allude to the pharaoh being seen here as embraced and sus-

Figure 8. Drawing of the left exterior of the chariot. From: Wreszinski (1935: pl. 2).

tained by the deity represented by the falcon. Also of note is the kilt that Thutmose is wearing here – it bears a feathered pattern intended to associate the king with a falcon and is very similar to the one represented on the purple quartzite statue of Amenhotep III (1388-1348 BC) as Re-Atum found in the Luxor Cachette (Kozloff & Bryan, 1992: 132-133). This regalia element and its connections will be further discussed below.

Since Pharaoh's hand and the talon of the falcon hovering above his head merge, the fist of the king that holds the battle-ax may in essence become the hand of the god, smiting the enemies of Egypt. The god could also be guiding the king's blow, or this could be viewed as the god granting the weapon to the king's hand as a divine commission to carry out battle. If the falcon can be seen as 'holding' the ax, this scene could also be related to much earlier images of personified falcons and other animals grasping weapons and prisoners, such as on the Libyan Palette (Egyptian Museum, Cairo; CG 14238). Regardless of the specific meaning, the fact that images of the smiting king often included the epithet "Strong-Armed Horus" seems potentially significant here.[4] This pose represents an incomplete action, one that is still in progress, rather than the completed one demonstrated by the handless soldiers in the exterior right scene.

The chariot body of the king in the left scene is decorated with a symbolic extension of the god's protection (figure 11). There is a representation of a falcon, holding a *šn*-sign in its talons, with his wings outstretched and wrapped around the side of the vehicle. The falcon relief is only seen in the fenestration

Figure 9. Detail of the king on the left exterior. Photograph by A. Calvert. Courtesy of the Ministry of State for Antiquities/Egyptian Museum Authorities.

Figure 10. Detail drawing of the king on the left exterior. From: Wreszinski (1935: pl. 2).

Figure 11. Detail of patterns on the chariot in the left exterior scene. Photograph by A. Calvert. Courtesy of the Ministry of State for Antiquities/Egyptian Museum Authorities.

area and not on the delineated zone of the front center/bottom sides of the chariot body. This suggests that a mirror image was evident on the opposite side of the body and that the fill of the fenestrations may have been a different material from the framework of the body. Many images show chariots with an open body and no fill, as for example seen on the painted box of Tutankhamun (Egyptian Museum, Cairo JE 61467). These lighter chariots were used for hunting by the king, but in battle, added protection was provided by filling in the sides with thin wood paneling or a leather or textile panel (Littauer & Crouwel, 1985: 72-73; see aslo Veldmeijer *et al.*, this volume). However, there are scenes, such as those of Seti I (1296-1279 BC) at Karnak (Epigraphic Survey, 1986: plate 28) where the king also uses an open-bodied chariot in battle, something that may expressly indicate contempt for his foes.

As in the right exterior scene, Pharaoh's enemies are in utter disarray; only two of the five enemy chariots are even shown upright. The enemy force is larger on this side of the chariot, both in terms of warriors and chariots. The clothing and hairstyles of the Asiatics are quite different for the majority of the men depicted, and there seems to be a higher proportion of elaborately dressed warriors than in the right scene. Six of the foes wear tight trousers, with several of the costumes being heavily embellished.

Central Zone

Separating the two scenes of battle is a complex apotropaic image, encompassing the front center of the vehicle as well as the bottom section of the sides (figure 12). This iconographically-dense image consists of a divine vulture shielding the king's cartouche, placed atop a symbol of unified Egypt to which rows of foreign prisoners are bound. Beginning at the top, surmounting the central area, is a lion-headed bird, presented frontally with wings outstretched and crowned with a solar disc. The rounded body and short tail of this bird identify it as a vulture, associated with the goddess Nekhbet. A number of goddesses were connected to leonine heads, including Wadjet, who was one of the four lion goddesses who guard Osiris (Pinch, 2002: 134). Thus, this image may represent a fusion of the Two Ladies into one form (*Ibidem*: 212). The leonine aspect of the image additionally links it with the "Eye of Re", which Pinch (*Ibidem*: 130) notes "represented royal power at its most brutal," and could perhaps also allude to the goddess Inana in her warrior aspect. The bird is crowned with a solar disc with two pendant uraei, appropriate headgear for the aggressive Eyes of Re. Like the similar image in this location on Tutankhamun's chariot A2 (Littauer & Crouwel, 1985: pl. XVII), these uraei hold *šn*-signs before them. However, instead of coming face-to-face with royal falcons as on Tutankhamun's chariot A2, they are turned out towards the depictions of the pharaoh's enemies. Here the uraei have an apotropaic function appropriate to the Eyes, spitting fire at the Asiatic armies and protecting the name of the king that appears below the talons of the bird.

In its claws the lion-bird holds two ꜥnḫs that it extends protectively around the top of the feathered crown capping the cartouche of the pharaoh. This headdress, which encompasses two ostrich plumes and a solar disc, is known as the *šwti* and was traditionally associated with the god Tatenen (Collier, 1996: 59). It also closely resembles the headdresses worn by Thutmose's chariot teams, as depicted on the sides of the vehicle. This cartouche in turn sits atop an unusual *smꜣ-tꜣwi*, apparently newly emerged from the mound below, to which are bound rows of foreign prisoners that wrap around the sides of the chariot. Both lines of prisoners are shown bound with the papyrus of Lower Egypt. This is presumably because they are all Asiatic like the enemies on both sides of the chariot, since enemies from Nubia in the south were generally depicted bound with the *wꜣḏ*-lily of Upper Egypt (see, for example, the alternating bound foreigners on Tutankhamun's A2 chariot linked by their respective hieraldic plants, Littauer & Crouwel, 1985: pl. XX).

The first two prisoners on either side of the *smꜣ-tꜣwi* face inwards towards the symbol of their subjugation, while the rest of the line is turned in the opposite direction and face the rear of the ve-

Figure 12. Front center view of the chariot. From: Carter & Newberry (1904: 25, fig. 1).

hicle. At the end of each of the lines of captives the cartouche of the king, Menkheperure, is shown endowed with human arms. In one hand he holds the end of the papyrus rope, which binds the captives, and the last of these kneeling figures by the hair, while the other arm is raised high and holds a mace in the traditional smiting pose. Although the arms of the figure are human, the rest of the personification is rendered as a falcon. On the head rests the double crown, and from the bottom of the cartouche sprouts the tail feathers and one of the talons of the bird, which grasps the head of an Asiatic prisoner. Depicted behind the cartouche are the words *nṯr nfr*. This term, 'good god', often precedes the names of pharaoh in texts, and, combined with the presence of the double crown, may indicate that this figure represents a fusion of the king and the god Montu. He is protected at the back by a uraeus, which faces in towards him.

Interior Scenes

The two interior scenes of the chariot are quite similar (figure 13). Montu is shown with wings outstretched to protect the vulnerable back of the king who is portrayed in the form of the powerful griffin, trampling three Asiatic foes underfoot in the left scene and three Nubians in the right. Similar to their use on temple walls, these ethnically differentiated depictions likely had cartographic connotations (McCarthy, 2007: 130-133). The king, here merged with the lion and with the wings of a falcon, wears an extremely elaborate version of the *3tf* crown situated atop a nemes headdress (Collier, 1996: 73-74). A thick, curving ram horn, which encircles the ear of the king, emerges from the band of the nemes. Since this type of horn is identified with the god Amun, the depiction of the king wearing it suggests an assimilation of him and the god (Bell, 1985: 33). The wings, evident on the back of the sphinx, also link him with the sun via an association to the solar falcon Re-Harakhte. Similarly, they may also refer to Montu and/or Horus; or perhaps to all falcon deities simultaneously. The open fan rising behind Pharaoh's back further indicates the divine nature of this representation of the king (Bell, 1985: 34). Above the fan is the god Khepri, who extends a *šn* towards the king and holds an-

Figure 13. Drawing of the left interior. From: Carter & Newberry (1904: pl. XII).

other sun disc in his front legs. Seen also in jewelry from the tomb of Tutankhamun, such as on his corselet (Egyptian Museum, Cairo JE 62627), the unusual lozenge wings of the scarab make one of their earliest appearances here.

Standing behind the king is the god Montu wearing his distinctive crown and protecting the king's back with his outstretched wings; this is the first preserved occurrence of Montu with wings (Werner, 1985: 125). Although wings are obviously appropriate for a falcon god, it is interesting that the configuration of Montu's outstretched wings echoes that of Nekhbet and the falcon in the exterior scenes. These images of Montu may suggest a merging of the protective forces of both male and female deities, similar to the combination of male and female aspects on the king's chariot horses mentioned previously. As discussed above, this type of male/female merging, combining the strengths of both sexes, can be extremely powerful.

Montu also extends several elements towards the king, including the ḫpš, or scimitar sword. The scimitar was another weapon introduced to Egypt during the Hyksos period; like the chariot, it makes its first textual appearance in the Kamose text (Smith & Smith, 1976: 65 note ff). During the New Kingdom, this weapon becomes a part of the standard royal military iconography. The king is shown in monumental temple reliefs receiving the sword from the gods as a symbol of their command to carry out military campaigns, conceptually identical to Montu's statement to the king in the interior right scene, translated by Bryan (1991: 194) as "I have given to you the ḫpš and valiance in order to trample the bowmen in their places." The connection between the chariot decoration and monumental battle reliefs indicated here will be further discussed below.

DISCUSSION OF THE ICONOGRAPHY

Thutmose's Chariot Body

From the above descriptions, it is clear that there is a dense, layered iconography in the scenes on the chariot of Thutmose IV. Many Egyptian concepts developed in the manner of accretion layers, where several meanings could exist simultaneously with no apparent conflict (Roth, 1998: 991). As might be expected, the iconography surrounding the king was particularly complex and a number of royal iconographic themes appear intertwined on this chariot. Beyond the aggressively protective elements designed to guard the king against his enemies (both terrestrial and celestial), these include a heavy emphasis on the king's solar connections, symbols relating to his place in the Egyptian cosmic view, and indications of the pharaoh embodying and merging with certain deities in particular contexts, with the chariot itself acting as a conduit for this interaction.

As an agent of cosmic order, the king was vulnerable to chaotic elements. The different levels of vulnerability inherent in royal public appearances may be evidenced by the density of protective iconography depicted on thrones, Windows of Appearance, palanquins, and royal ships. In other words, seated on his throne, in his palace, Pharaoh was surely surrounded by layers of human and divine protectors and in a completely controlled environment. There was a slight loss of this control when the king utilized his Window of Appearance, where he became more visible to his public, and where he interacted with them on a restricted level. When he travelled on land in his palanquin or by water in his 'falcon-ship', he would need to be protected symbolically more thoroughly than he did in his own throne room. This same train of thought may explain the extreme concentration of protective imagery seen on the chariot.

Out on the battlefield, Pharaoh is not in his palace, or a temple, or even on Egyptian soil; rather, he is in hostile territory, facing off against the 'wretched' enemy. Even if Pharaoh did not actually join in the battle, the same potential for damage to the body of the king was there. This danger would have made it most desirable for the king to wrap himself symbolically in the same protection he was afforded in his throne room. The basic theme of iconography and the images themselves do not change from throne to Window of Appearance to chariot, but it is the concentration of these emblems, which varies in each space. In his throne room, there are many surfaces that can be endowed with apotropaic treatment: floors, steps, footstools and walls, as well as the throne itself. The Window of Appearance, palanquins, and royal boats also provide a fair amount of surface area to work with. However, in the case of the chariot, only three surfaces are available: the horses, the chariot, and the king himself.

This might explain the existence of more thickly layered protective decorative elements on the chariot and its horse trappings. It is logical when under such constraints to embellish essential components with apotropaic devices, thus allowing them to serve double duty. Prime examples of this would be the Bes heads forming the ends of a pair of Tutankhamun's yoke saddles (Littauer & Crouwel, 1985: pl. XXXIV), which were designed specifically so that the end of the leather strap dangled from the god's mouth and created a long, lolling tongue, and linchpins from a relief of a chariot belonging to Ramesses II (1279-1212 BC) showing Asiatic heads being devoured by lions (Ritner, 1993: 122). This likely explains the density of the protective elements seen in the chariot as a totality, and might also offer another suggestion. The depiction of the chariot of the king *on* his actual chariot provided an additional canvas for protective iconography. In showing his 'double' symbolically so well-defended, this divine protection would surely have been seen to extend into the real world and surround his physical body as well. Embellishing an object with an image of itself in use may additionally suggest a level of perpetual activation.

Solar Iconography

The king in his chariot was increasingly associated with the sun over the course of the New Kingdom. In the Poetical Stela of Thutmose III, the first three verses of Amun-Re's speech include references to the king's likeness as brilliant and fiery light flanking a statement about Pharaoh in his chariot: "I let them see your majesty as lord of light, so that you shone before them in my likeness […] I let them see your majesty clad in your panoply, when you displayed your weapons on your chariot […] I let them see your majesty as a shooting star, that scatters fire as it sheds its flame" (Lichtheim, 1976: 37).

Texts from the reign of Amenhotep III (1388-1348 BC) specifically refer to the king as "speedy like the sun disc, an electrum star when he flashes by, chariot-mounted, strong-armed bowman, deadly shot," as well as "a runner like the disc when he moves, a star of electrum when he shines in a chariot," and "a dazzling sun disc appearing at the head of his army, a dazzling sun disc appearing in the war crown" (Redford, 1994: 169-170). The Qadesh inscriptions of Ramesses II include mention of the king appearing from his tent "like the rising of Re" and that in battle, when the king was fighting alone in his chariot, "All his ground was ablaze in fire; he burned all the countries with his blast" (Lichtheim, 1976: 60, 62). The speech of the king is even more explicit. Ramesses reports that "I arose against them in the likeness of Mont, equipped with my weapons of war […] I was like Re when he rises at dawn, my rays, they burned the rebels' bodies" (Lichtheim, 1976: 70). The very shape of the chariot body of Thutmose IV provides additional support for this concept of the king being portrayed in the chariot as the solar disk. Higher at both sides and sloping down in the front center, the outline is actually that of an *3ht*, wrapped around the king. The king taking the place of the solar disc being encircled by the *3ht* would have connotations of re-birth; indicative of his role as Khepri.

Akhenaten (1352-1335 BC), as an extreme example of this concept, by his daily procession in his chariot through Akhetaten provided a physical manifestation and imitation of the journey of his father as the sun disc traversed the sky and created the world anew each day (Redford, 1984: 178-179). In the text of the Earlier Proclamation of Akhenaten, the king "[appeared] on the great chariot of electrum – just like Aten, when he rises in his horizon and fills the land with the love and [the pleasantness (?) of] the Aten" (Murnane, 1995: 74). Akhenaten was identified directly as an earthly incarnation of his god in the created mini-cosmos of Akhetaten; they were seen as parallels, with the Aten in heaven and Akhenaten on earth. The daily procession of Akhenaten in his chariot paralleled the daily course of the Aten: "The fundamental point [being] the identification between king and disc as the two manifestations of a single divine power"(O'Connor, 1994: 289-290).

This link with the sun god is probably the reason chariots were placed in the tombs of the kings – one of the sections of the royal tomb is known as the "Chariot Hall" or the "Hall of Repelling Rebels" (Černý, 1973: 29). The role of the chariot in controlling chaos is emphasized by texts that parallel the king in battle in his chariot and the defeat of the enemies of the solar deity by Seth or Sekhmet. For example, Ramesses II in the Qadesh texts states that in the thick of battle he was "[…] before them like Seth in his moment" (Lichtheim, 1976: 66).[5] Not only useful in the physical realm, its connection to the sun might indicate that, in the afterlife, the chariot aided in the transformation of the king from the mortal plane to the divine. While he lived, the king became like the 'dazzling sun disc' in his chariot, showing his association with Re. Even more telling is that the chariot was considered to be the "earthly counterpart of the solar bark" (Kákosy, 1977: 57).

In the afterlife, the association between the king in his chariot and the sun god in his bark may have progressed to another level, where the king merges with the god and is no longer like the sun disc, but actually becomes the disc itself. This transition from the embodiment of the god to being seen as a god himself occurred over the 18th Dynasty (1549-1298 BC; Johnson, 1990: 26-46), and Thutmose IV certainly played a role in this trend towards solarization in his emphasis of solar deities and his tendency to have himself portrayed as an incarnation of the sun (Bryan, 1998: 51).

Thutmose IV expanded the importance of the cult of Horemakhetre ("Horus in the Horizon of Re"), the solar deity represented by the Giza sphinx. The Dream Stela identifies the god as "Horemaketre-Khepri-Ra-Atum" (all Dream Stela translations after Bryan, 1998: 43), although the sphinx is also referred to as "The Very Great Khepri". It is interesting to note in connection with the flabellum discussion above that the Great Sphinx is described as "powerful of respect, the shade of Re resting on him." Also, it may be telling that Thutmose "rested in the shadow of this great god." In the text of the stela, Thutmose is called "beloved of Horemaketre", and is told by the god, "Look at me, regard me, my son, Thutmose! I am your father, Horemaketre-Khepri-Re-Atum…my face belongs to you; my heart belongs to you, and you belong to me."

In addition to this textual identification of the king as the offspring of the falcon sun god, returning to the chariot body of Thutmose IV, there are a number of elements that support a solar connection. As Hartwig notes (2007: 122), in his chariot, Thutmose is "the manifestation of the sun god." Specific solar elements depicted include the disc with pendant uraei, which hovers directly above the king's head, the horse headdresses of feathers and sun-discs, and the curious occurrence of the *šbiw* collar around the neck of the king. Although it was rare for royal figures to be shown wearing this collar in a non-funerary context before the reign of Amenhotep III (Johnson, 1990: 37), Thutmose IV wears it on both sides of the chariot, on relief fragments found in the temple to Horemakhetre at Giza (Bryan, 1991: 154 No. 4.24), and also on an ivory gauntlet found at Amarna (*Ibidem*: 162-163). Given as the "Gold of Honor" to worthy subjects (Andrews, 1990: 181-183), the *šbiw* indicates the favor of the sun god when worn by the king (Bryan, 1998: 51). By wearing this collar he is considered to be fulfilling the role of the warrior sun god, ritually defeating the enemies of Egypt. However, recent research by Brand (Forthcoming) on the collar has suggested that this attribute was used "to depict the king as a hypostasis of any god including the royal ka – and not just Re – when the king acted in his official capacity as ruler."[6]

Another element of great interest is the large solar disc that appears behind the heads of the horses, just above the yoke saddle. From the time of Thutmose I (1503-1491 BC), this apotropaic panoply is consistently seen in representations of the royal chariot, and is always represented in two dimensions as facing sideways. However, examples recovered from the tomb of Tutankhamun clearly show that the solar disc actually faced forward (figure 14). Here it is the crown of a wooden falcon and stands on a base that would have been attached to the chariot pole. The solar disc in this example is carved with the anagram of the pharaoh's name, Nebkheprure, further solidifying the connection between the king and disc. This practice of embellishing even this solar element is not unique; reliefs at Medinet Habu of the chariot team of Ramesess III (1185-1153 BC) show traces of a scene carved onto their disc as well (Epigraphic Survey, 1932: pl. 24-25). These gilded elements would have been visible to any who saw the king in his chariot, gleaming in

Figure 14. Falcon attachment from the tomb of Tutankhamun. Photograph by H. Burton. Courtesy of the Griffith Institute, Oxford.

the sun even from a great distance. Framed by the heads of the horse team, which may have suggested the ꜣḫt, the 'dazzling' disc and the pharaoh would be seen as overlapping and, thus, merging.

As mentioned above, Thutmose IV's chariot preserves evidence of having originally been covered in silver. Silver was a divine material, considered to represent the bones of the gods, while gold was their skin (Aufrere, 1991: 412). Seen as the counterpart of gold and the sun, silver was closely connected to the moon and lunar deities, such as Thoth, Hathor and Khonsu. The metal's link with the moon as a counterpart of the sun is most interesting in this context. As a counterpart to the sun, the moon was also an "Eye of Horus" (Pinch, 2002:131). It is possible that the pharaoh had at least one chariot covered in gold and one covered in silver. This is a logical suggestion considering the emphasis the Egyptians placed on duality and the fact that texts refer to the king's "two great war chariots" (Aldred, 1969: 79). Other support for this hypothesis comes from the tomb of queen Ahhotep, where, along with the well-known gold boat model, a silver one was also found (Landstrom, 1970: 98). Additionally, pairs of objects – one gold and one silver – such as matched staffs in the Egyptian Museum, Cairo (CG 235a-b) topped with an image of the king, were found in the tomb of Tutankhamun.[7] The lack of a silver chariot in the tomb of Tutankhamun presents a difficulty, but with the supremacy of solar iconography during the period, it may not be surprising that Amarna-era chariots might be embellished primarily with gold. However, it should also be noted that his very name suggests the possibility that Thutmose had a particular affiliation with lunar deities.

Cosmic Order

As suggested above, the king in his chariot may have been portrayed intentionally as the sun disc just coming forth from the ꜣḫt, simultaneously repelling the demonic (= foreign) forces clustered at the horizon to prevent solar rebirth while bringing about the rejuvenation of the cosmos through its appearance. This concept would also have strong connections with the idea of the king as a living regenerative force. By subduing foreigners, the king symbolically transformed the anarchic life-potential of *isft* into the productive, actualized life of the cosmos in balance with *mꜣꜥt* (O'Connor, 2003: 178-179).

This chthonic, creative function of Pharaoh in his chariot finds additional support in the emblematic representation at the front of the chariot body of Thutmose IV. Although the use of the *smꜣ-tꜣwi* (representing the unification of the Two Lands of Egypt) dates back to the early Dynastic Period, the combining of this ancient symbol and bound prisoners did not appear, with one exception in the reign of Khasekhemwy (2690-2663 BC), until the New Kingdom (Baines, 1985: 245). At this time, the hieroglyph seems to take on a secondary meaning – making it not only symbolic of the unification of Egypt, but also the subjugation of foreign lands. The connection of the unification symbol and captive enemies seems to be a pictogram of the statement that "all lands and all foreign countries are gathered under your [i.e. the king's] sandals" (Baines,

1985: 245). Known from the Predynastic Period (5000-3000 BC) onwards, the bound prisoner motif becomes particularly prevalent during the New Kingdom (Ritner, 1993: 117-8). By placing depictions of trussed foreigners on objects such as footstools, cane handles and the soles of sandals, as well as on chariot elements such as the yoke and linch pins, the daily use of an otherwise benign object results in the ritual subjugation of the enemies of Egypt. Ritner (1993: 131) states: "Simply by making a state appearance, the king becomes a passive actor in the ritual destruction of the enemies of Egypt." However, it seems more appropriate to regard the king as an active participant, rather than a passive one. It is through his actions (*i.e.* stepping into the chariot) that the foreigners are ritually defeated and subjugated, and activation on his part is required to achieve this result.

However, the *sm3-t3wi* on the chariot of Thutmose IV is unusual. Depicted rising out of a mound, this image has the added connotation of creation and activation as well as being connected to the chthonic Sokar, the falcon-headed "[...] god of death as a transformative process" (Pinch, 2002: 202). The tumulus may be a representation of the primordial mound that emerged from *nnw* at the creation of the world. This mound was considered the center of the cosmos, a place of continuous creation (Pinch, 2002: 180). In one theology, from this mound came the first blue lotus from whence Nefertum, a manifestation of solar power at the time of creation, emerged. This deity's connection to the first, vitalizing ascent of the sun god, identifies this image as another solar reference. The king can even be depicted as Nefertum himself, as seen in a statue from the tomb of Tutankhamun in the Egyptian Museum, Cairo (JE 60723). The primeval mound was sometimes considered a manifestation of the creator god Atum, the primordeal "completed one" or "undifferentiated one" (Allen, 1988: 25), and was similarly connected to Tatenen, "the rising land" (Pinch, 2002: 60). This mound would then represent all potentials and all possibilities of creation, like the monad at the heart of a temple.

The *sm3-t3wi*, as monogram of the king and supporting his cartouche, rises out of the primeval mound, taking the place of the god and therefore identifying the king with the sun god who vitalizes the world and transferring the responsibility of activating the world from the creator god to the deified pharaoh. This concept of the king as a semi-divine intermediary would be supported by the visual hierarchy from earth to sky displayed here: the mound, the symbol of the combined Egypt, the king, the Two Ladies, and the sun. This hierarchy is made especially plain when the pharaoh was in his chariot with the real sun blazing above him. The entire pictogram at the front of the chariot represents the core of the Egyptian cosmos, the divine source of the king's strength, from which he emerged into the terrestrial realm to perform his role as "the excellent heir of Khepri," a phrase used to refer to Thutmose IV on the Dream Stela (Bryan, 1998: 42).

Chariot as Conduit

Pharaoh is often identified as the incarnation of various gods and becomes 'like' them in specific contexts. For instance, the war-like nature of the king and his knowledge of fighting and battle were considered to be attributes of Montu (Werner, 1985: 153). This is evident in a text from the reign of Amenhotep II (1424-1398 BC; Lichtheim, 1976: 41): "He was one who knew all the works of Montu; he had no equal on the field of battle". The Konosso text of Thutmose IV (Bryan, 1991: 333-334) identifies the king with other deities as well: "Then the Good God went forth like Montu in all his forms, equipped with his weapons of war, raging like Seth, Re having placed his fear in the lands like Sekhmet in a year of pestilence". Inscriptions such as these signify that each deity would endow the king with his or her own attributes. Comparing the king with Montu, Seth or Sekhmet would indicate specific aspects of raging prowess in war and strength in battle; aspects of the king which were customary in the New Kingdom. This aggression on the part of the pharaoh also played a ritual role in the cosmos (Baines, 1994: 14). Thus, Pharaoh's actions on the terrestrial plane paralleled the "divine processes which were occurring simultaneously in both the celestial realm and in the Duat" (O'Connor & Silverman, 1994: XIX). Like other venues which mirror the cosmos, such as temples and palaces, the chariot may almost be seen as a divine conduit through which the king channels these aspects, becoming the physical manifestation of these deities on earth while he is in action.

This concept of the conduit, where Pharaoh in his chariot can become 'like' a variety of deities depending upon the context ('like' Aten at Akhetaten or 'like' Montu on the battlefield), and the paralleling of terrestrial actions and celestial processes brings the focus back to the mound at the front of Thutmose IV's chariot. Its presence on the chariot body of the king may iconographically further demonstrate a relationship that certainly existed: that between Montu, Atum, and the king. Both Montu and Atum were, in addition to their primary functions, solar deities connected to the Theban region and Heliopolis respectively. From as early as the 12th Dynasty (1994-1781 BC), the pair is treated as representative of Upper and Lower Egypt, and they are often shown leading the king into the presence of Amun-Re (Werner, 1985: 236-251). In addition to being symbolic of the unified Egypt, these gods together represent the two sides of solar power, with Montu embodying the intensely aggressive solar heat burning the bodies of the sun-god's foes and Atum being related to solar benevolence, bringing cosmos to life by its appearance. By covering the body of the royal chariot with imagery linked to both of these deities, Thutmose IV was able to essentially 'become' Montu while in battle with human foes and 'become' Atum when he processed – whether he processed in triumphant return from military or hunting expeditions, both actions were symbolically related to the control of *isft* and the transformation of its potentialities into actualized ordered cosmos. Battle was paralleled in the celestial realm as the slaying of the foes of the sun bark in the *3ht*, while processing simultaneously set Pharaoh in the role of the primordial sun; the regenerative spark that sets off the creation of the cosmos.

The falcon wings on the royal sphinxes depicted in the interior scenes of the chariot body add another dimension to the imagery. It is well-known that Horus represented the living king, just as his father Osiris was identified with deceased pharaohs, and "the falcon becomes a principal symbol of kingship" (Lesko, 1991: 93). Thus, the king was the 'living falcon', and his titles and representations indicate this: for example, texts on the obelisk of Hatshepsut (1472-1457 BC) at Karnak identify her numerous times as "The Living Horus" (Lichtheim, 1976: 25-29). In his chariot, the king could also be identified as the "divine falcon, his horses (fairly) flying" (Bell, 1985: 46 note 45). From at least as early as the time of the Pyramid Texts, Pharaoh was believed to "fly to the horizon in the form of a falcon to unite with the sun disc" upon his death (Pinch, 2002: 120).

Besides the texts, there is also a vast amount of pictorial evidence of the pharaoh being viewed as a deified falcon. For instance, a statue of Thutmose IV depicting him as half-human and half-falcon was discovered in the Karnak Cachette (Bryan, 1991: 180). Another, similar statue is seen in a relief block from the peristyle court of Thutmose IV. The scene shows a group of statues Pharaoh is presenting to Amum; among these is one of Thutmose as a falcon, wearing a different headdress than the actual statue discovered in the Cachette (figure 15). This connection was also made literal on the living king through the use of royal falcon dress, most prominently by Thutmose III but seen on pharaohs throughout the New Kingdom (Giza-Podgorski, 1984: 103-121; Vogelsang-Eastwood, 1999: *e.g.* figs. 2:10 & 2:11).

As noted above, Thutmose IV wears a feathered kilt in the left exterior scene of his chariot body, tying him even more strongly to the falcon deity above him. Considering the context of these scenes, being on the body of a royal chariot, it is understandable that much of the falcon imagery on this vehicle refers to the virulent war-god Montu. However, the aforementioned feathered apron links the king with Re-Atum, the weary setting sun, and this imagery, combined with the mound at the front of the chariot and its connections to Tatenen and rebirth, makes the chariot iconography appropriate for use in both terrestrial battle and for the afterlife transformation into the primal creator whose regenerated daily appearance energized the cosmos.

Chariots, Thrones, and Other Venues for Royal Appearance

Since the chariot body of Thutmose IV and those of Tutankhamun's 'State Chariots' were so heavily embellished with relief work and metal, it may be assumed that their use was purely ceremonial.

Figure 15. Statue of Thutmose IV as a falcon. Karnak. Photograph by A. Calvert.

However, the extensive iconography on royal chariots indicates another function for these highly decorated examples. The main protective elements of the scenes on the chariot body occur on a variety of royal furniture and architecture, including thrones, Windows of Appearance, and royal ships. These were locations where the pharaoh was viewed by his public and where he could be vulnerable to the unknown. Especially on the battlefield, the king would require an extra level of protection to prevent anything negative from happening to him, a circumstance that would in turn affect the Egyptian cosmos. By incorporating into the body of the vehicle and harnessing all the protective elements seen on thrones, daises and canopies, he would have been properly protected and able to hold court, in a sense, even on the field of battle far from Egyptian soil (Schulman, 1979: 150).

Battle scenes of Seti I, Ramesses II, and Ramesses III (1185-1153 BC) show the pharaoh on the battlefield seated backwards in his chariot, receiving courtiers and being presented with the spoils of war. One relief from Medinet Habu shows Ramesses III dressed in full regalia and accompanied by fanbearers, being presented with captives and the severed hands and phalli of the enemy dead (figure 16; Epigraphic Survey, 1930: plate 23). He is sitting not on the floor of the chariot, but almost on the top rail – a seat of some kind having been inserted into the body of the vehicle. It is noteworthy that the chariot is harnessed, and the team of the pharaoh is also embellished with an elaborate housing, solar discs, and tall, plumed headdresses. Another example which lends credence to this concept is found on the north face of the pylon at Luxor temple built by Ramesses II. Depicting the Battle of Qadesh, the west side of the pylon shows the king seated on his throne as the central figure, while the east side presents the king, again central in the scene, in his chariot. These two scenes appear to suggest a parallel between the throne and the chariot (see also Sabbahy, this volume).

There may also be textual evidence for the use of the chariot as a throne. At the Battle of Megiddo, once the Egyptians had won, "the entire army jubilated and gave praise to Amun, [they lauded] his majesty and extolled his victory. Then they presented the plunder they had taken: hands, living prisoners, horses, chariots of gold, silver and of [painted work]" (Lichtheim, 1976: 33). Even the hieroglyphic words for chariot (*wrrt*) and throne (*st wrrt*) are similar and may indicate a connection (Kuhlmann, 1977: 28).

It was not only in his chariot that the king was identified as a god. The architecture of New Kingdom palaces clearly echoes that of temples. Sitting on his throne, Pharaoh could be identified with the cult image that was housed in the center of the

Figure 16. Ramesses III enthroned in his chariot at Medinet Habu. Photograph by A. Calvert.

temple (O'Connor, 1994: 291-292). On his throne, the king might have represented the solar, creator god – his appearance bringing the world to life. The decorative program evident in the remains of these palaces supports this concept. With tall, vegetal-form columns and depictions of wild animals and naturalistic flocks of birds, the palace decoration was teeming with life. The king on his throne was the incarnation of the creator, responsible for the activation of the land, represented in the human realm by the scenes that surrounded him in the palace (Kuhlmann, 2011).

More specifically, a useful comparison for the iconography on the chariot may be made with the golden throne from the tomb of Tutankhamun in the Egyptian Museum, Cairo (JE 62028). The chair displays lion feet, and the seat itself rests upon four openwork *smȝ-tȝwi* hieroglyphs, which are now unfortunately broken. At the front of the chair are two lion heads, molded in high relief and with inlaid eyes. These elements serve the same basic purpose as the leonine Bes head elements used on chariots (such as on the yoke saddles and at the rear of Tutankhamun's chariot A2) – to protect the king. However, unlike Bes, lions are inherently related to the ideals of kingship; the likely reason why their depiction was chosen rather than that of the dwarf god. Another reason that seems logical is that Bes, due to his ugliness, was more fearsomely apotropaic, and therefore better suited to protect the pharaoh in dangerous situations.

Forming the arms of the throne are the Two Ladies, both portrayed as winged uraei, wearing the double crown and seated atop *nb*-signs. Their wings envelope the pharaoh's physical body, effectively protecting his flanks, and encase him symbolically as well. At the back corners of the chair, and across the reverse of the chair back, are rearing cobras. While those that protect the back all wear solar discs, the two on the side corners each wear one of the crowns of Egypt, suggesting a geographic orientation.

While the back of the throne seat does not display the type of iconography discussed in the present work, it does show an interesting parallel with the chariot body of Thutmose IV. As on the chariot, the throne, as an object, is decorated with an image of itself in use. It may be possible that this type of depiction keeps the object 'activated' to a certain extent, even when the king is not present. Thus, Thutmose IV is constantly defeating the Asiatics on the exterior of his chariot, just as Ankhesenamun is forever anointing her young husband.

The chariot of the king may have reflected, in its particular design, the actual throne of the individual ruler to some degree. For example, two cedar throne panels were found in the tomb of Thutmose IV (Carter & Newberry, 1904: pls. VI & VII), one of which is now in the Metropolitan Museum of Art in New York (30.8.45a-c; figure 17), and the other is in the Museum of Fine Arts, Boston (03.1131). These show, on their interior, the king as a winged sphinx, trampling an Asiatic on the left side and a Nubian on the right. Above the king is a falcon with wings protectively outstretched and extending a *šn*. Below the falcon is a personified *ꜥnḫ* carrying a flabellum in its hands. These scenes are very similar to those found on the interior of the chariot body. A similar parallel may be drawn between the gold throne of Tutankhamun and his chariot (A2): both of these objects prominently display a running spi-

Figure 17. Throne panel from the tomb of Thutmose IV (MMA30.8.45a-c). Copyright: Metropolitan Museum of Art, New York.

ral motif. Parallel iconography being used on the king's chariot and his throne may emphasize their connection and support their function as venues for appearance.

Much of the same iconography that appears on thrones is also evident in Windows of Appearance, and thus the chariot can be linked to these venues as well.[8] In pictorial representations, as well as in actual remains, the Window of Appearance often shows *smȝ-tȝwi* scenes, bound prisoners, the Two Ladies, and the pharaoh as a sphinx trampling his enemies (Fjerstad, 2011: 37-49). Even the Window of Appearance at Amarna, where much traditional Egyptian iconography was not utilized, sometimes displayed a large *smȝ-tȝwi* scene with captive Libyans, Nubians and Asiatics, as shown in the tomb of Pernefer in Amarna (figure 18). At Medinet Habu, the main Window of Appearance in the first courtyard and several of the Windows in the East High Gate were embellished with three-dimensional carved heads of foreigners, serving as the ground line upon which the pharaoh stood (figure 19). These may be paralleled with depictions of chariots with living foreigners, or representations of them, tied beneath the chariot of the king, seated on the pole or even on the backs of pharaoh's horses; for instance in battle reliefs of Amenhotep II now in the Egyptian Museum, Cairo (JE 36360), scenes of triumph on a stela of Amenhotep III, also in the Egyptian Museum, Cairo (JE 31409), and in the battle reliefs of Seti I at Karnak (such as Epigraphic Survey, 1986: 31)

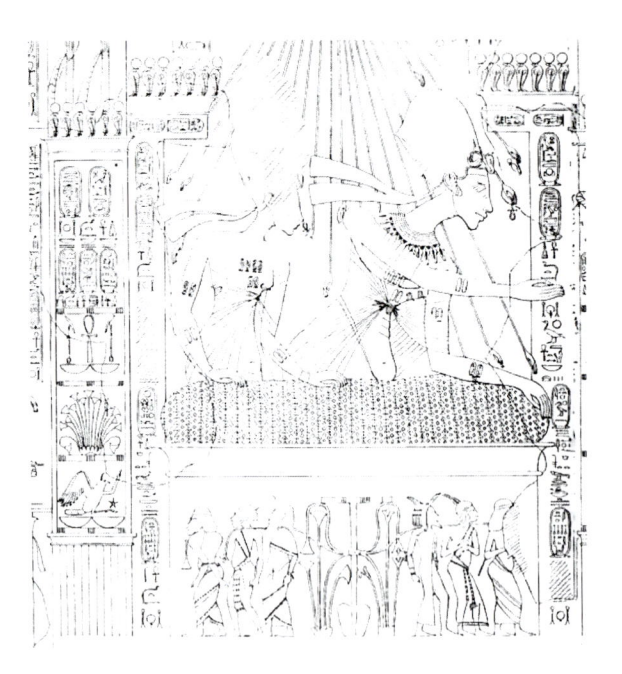

Figure 18. Window of Appearance at Amarna. Tomb of Pernefer. From: Davies (1905: pl. IV).

Royal palanquins and ships used to transport the pharaoh on land and by water also display protective images on them. Although it is from later in the New Kingdom and appears in the context of the Min Festival, the sedan of the king depicted in the northwest corner of the second courtyard at Medinet Habu can be seen as representative of the type (figure 20; Epigraphic Survey, 1932: pl. 197). The king is carried in a palanquin, the canopy of which is covered by an outer shrine consisting of tent poles (or *ȝms*-staffs), and the top of a *pr-wr*. This encircling layer strongly suggests an association of the living king with his cult image carried in its portable shrine. This framework is 'supported' by bound Nubian (front) and Asiatic (back) figures, atop whose heads the carrying pole appears to rest. The canopy is capped with a cornice and a frieze of solar-disc topped uraei.

Behind the king, and apparently standing on the carrying poles, are two winged goddesses wearing net dresses and ostrich feathers tucked into their headbands. The right arm/wing of the closest goddess is placed diagonally across the side of the king's throne, with the tip of the wing shown inside the armrest. The lion-legged throne has an elegant high back, covered with a thick rolled-topped cushion. At the fore of the side panel of the throne stands a uraeus wearing a *ḥdt* crown.

Representing Nekhbet and likely mirrored on the opposite panel by a *dšrt* crown-wearing Wadjet, this divine cobra stands directly in front of a falcon donned with a solar disc. Behind this falcon is the king himself, represented in solar form as a striding sphinx. The lower portion of the side panel depicts a *sm3-t3wi*. The king's footrest, a low rectangular form topped with a rounded cushion, is plain. Note that the long pointed toe of the king's sandal not only pierces the torso of the bound Nubian support figure but also crosses the figure's bent elbows at precisely the point where they are tied together.

The lion figures of the carrying poles (assuming there was a second mirrored on the opposite pole, which seems most likely) would also suggest a strong identification of the king with the sun. They likely represent the lions of *3kr* who guard the eastern and western horizons; an association which would relate the king between them to the sun itself. This would be particularly potent if the lions were gilded, as they probably were. It is interesting here to notice that the *sm3-t3wi* on the king's throne is almost completely hidden by the lion's body. This could be read as the 'unified Egypt between the horizons' and may relate to other cosmographical implications of the iconography, such as the possibility that the horizontal carrying pole delineates between the terrestrial and the celestial.

Similar to palanquins that transported the king on land, boats provided mobility on water. A boat model from the tomb of Amenhotep II in the Egyptian Museum, Cairo (JE 32217; figure 21) shows several elements that are similar to those on the chariot of Thutmose IV. A painted scene on the hull depicts the pharaoh as a sphinx, crowned with an elaborate *3tf*-crown and trampling a fallen enemy. From behind him rises the flabellum while a vulture hovers protectively above. Behind this image on the hull is another, more detailed scene which shows different incarnations of Montu, "Lord of Medamud", "He Who Dwells in Thebes", "Lord of Tod", and "Lord of Armant", in four vignettes, subduing representatives of different foreign lands (Werner, 1985: 129-136). In three of these, Montu is depicted as a falcon-headed man spearing the unfortunates who huddle before him, while in the fourth he is portrayed as a trampling hierakosphinx. Positioned behind this figure is the goddess Ma'at, kneeling with outspread wings to protect the rear of the scene. Rendered in relief, the cabin of the boat is decorated with anoth-

Figure 19. Window of Appearance at Medinet Habu. Photograph by A. Calvert.

Figure 20. Ramesses III in his sedan at Medinet Habu. Photograph by A. Calvert.

Figure 21. Amenhotep II's boat model. From: Daressy (1902: pl. XLIX).

er image of the pharaoh as a sphinx standing on the bodies of his enemies and protected by a goddess behind him. From the Ahmose reliefs at Abydos comes another protective element evident on a ship (Harvey, 1998: fig. 83 & 84). This fragment depicts a beautifully rendered vulture wrapped protectively around the aftercastle, very similar in position to the falcon wrapped around the chariot of the king in the exterior left scene of the Thutmose IV chariot body.

Battle Cycles

The scenes of the king enthroned in his chariot and being presented with spoil on the battlefield mentioned above appeared in monumental reliefs on temple walls. Battle cycle scenes (of which this presentation to the king is a part) seem to have developed through the 18th Dynasty, although they are best known from the reign of Ramesses II (see also Spalinger, this volume). However, discoveries of fragmentary reliefs at the Ahmose temple at Abydos provide evidence that this type of artistic program began as early as the outset of the 18th Dynasty (Harvey, 1994: 3-5). In addition, the reclassification of a relief block originally dated to the Ramesside period indicates that there were monumental battle scenes contemporary with the reign of Thutmose IV (Brand, 1995: 170-171). These monumental scenes of royal narrative (sometimes referred to as *Königsnovelle*) tend to follow the same basic sequence (Harvey, 1998: 308-314). This usually includes the commission of a god to the king, travel to the field of battle, the battle itself, the presentation to the king, the triumphal return to Egypt, and the king's offerings to the gods.

The imbalance of the scenes on the exterior of the chariot body of Thutmose IV, two Asiatic battles and no Nubian, is unusual and should be noted. There would be one of each type of battle expected according to traditional convention. The interior scenes of the winged sphinx-king trampling Asiatic and Nubian foes are more emblematic and should be distinguished from the 'real-world' battles of the exterior. There are several possible reasons for this imbalance. One is that it may indicate the relative threat of each to the Egyptian realm. Earlier pharaohs in the 18th Dynasty (for example Thutmose III and Amenhotep II) had subdued the southern lands with great success, and Nubia therefore required only occasional policing when a group of rebels harassed their Egyptian overlords. Asia, however, was a different story. Having been infiltrated by the Hyksos, Egypt was wary of her northern neighbors for centuries, and with good reason. Regions which had been defeated during the reign of Thutmose III had to be re-taken time and time again by his successors.

It may also be possible that this chariot was originally one of a pair, as mentioned before, with the lost vehicle's exterior being dedicated to Nubian battle scenes. A chariot symbolically related to the subduing of Nubian foes would be made all the more appropriate by gilding, perhaps providing a pair with the existing silver foiled Asiatic focused chariot body. The interior of this hypothetical second chariot would likely have been quite similar to the existing one. These emblematic trampling scenes represent total world rule, granted by the gods because of the king's regenerative actions as the "Sun of the Two Shores" while the exterior focused on terrestrial conquest over foreign foes that mirrored the defeat of the sun god's enemies, allowing him to rise and rejuvenate the cosmos.

Another possibility goes back to the idea that the scenes may be inspired by and/or copied from reliefs on the walls of a temple. As signaled long ago by Wreszinski (1935), it is possible that the vignettes on the chariot body of Thutmose IV were based upon one of these monumental cycles that has yet to be identified. Many of the elements associated with battle cycle scenes are present in the decorative program of the vehicle. As previously mentioned, the commission of Montu appears on the interior of the chariot, and the god extends the scimitar towards the king as a physical sign of this command. The scenes of actual battle are, of course, present as well. The detailed battle scenes incised onto the exterior of the vehicle act as a sort of billboard, advertising the symbolic prowess of the king and his inevitable victory. Whether Pharaoh actually led his troops into battle at the center of his army or he remained in relative safety to oversee and direct the action is moot. Since the army was an extension of the king, any victory by them would really be his. This may be why there is no army depicted in the scenes on the chariot body; they are symbolically absorbed into the body of the king. The entire scene on the chariot exterior may in essence represent the full battle sequence – past (fired arrows), present (smiting the leaders) and future (missing hands of defeated foes) – simultaneously by depicting a cycle in which Thutmose continuously fires his bow, smashes the skulls of the foreign leaders, and counts the enemy dead to triumph in his victory.[9]

There are some classic *Königsnovelle* vignettes missing from the chariot scenes – travel to and from battle, spoil being presented to the king, and Pharaoh presenting spoil to the gods. However, since travel to and from battle would have been enacted in the physical realm in the actual chariot, it may not have been necessary for these acts to be depicted on the chariot as well. The only major elements missing are the presentation scenes. As far as the king's presentation to the gods, one possible reason for their absence is that such depictions might be considered inappropriate on a war chariot. Perhaps that type of presentation scene was restricted to the temple venue, while the commission by the god and the depiction of battle held an apotropaic function as well as a narrative one. The presentation to the king, like travel, would be enacted in the chariot itself, so that could explain its exclusion. If the captured enemy were presented to the king as he sat in the chariot, this may have negating the need for this scene to be depicted on the vehicle itself. This suggestion seems likely, particularly since this future presentation is implied by the presence in the scenes of enemy dead with severed hands. Regardless, the chariot had to be 'activated' by the pharaoh in order to make the narrative sequence complete.

CONCLUSION

The chariot body found in the tomb of Thutmose IV is an exceptionally interesting object. Its extraordinary decorative program has provided a great deal of information regarding the myriad functions of the royal chariot in the New Kingdom. The solar aspect of the chariot is of particular interest. It seems that chariots played an important part in the general trend towards the solarization of the king's role, which occurred in the 18th Dynasty and reached its peak in the Amarna Period. This concept of the chariot as a solar vehicle is supported by its presence in tombs of the pharaohs of this period and the existence of a "Chariot Hall" specifically connected with repelling rebels aiming to halt the solar cycle. The king was seen as the sun disc in his chariot in life, and it is likely that this association was strengthened in the afterlife wherein the pharaoh truly becomes divine. Since he is compared in his chariot with Seth raging at the prow of the sun bark, its presence indicated an apotropaic as well as transformative function. Paired with these concepts, and emphasized in the iconographic program, is the chthonic, regenerative aspect of Pharaoh, with the chariot embodying the *ȝḫt*. While this idea is most clearly connected to the enthroned king in his royal palace, it is fundamentally related to the 'appearance' of the king, no matter where he was displayed.

The use of the chariot as a mobile throne is strongly indicated by its decorative program. On both the chariot and the throne, the *smȝ-tȝwi*, representing the physical realm of Egypt, is situated atop her defeated foes and protected from above by the gods. This is also clearly indicated in the decoration on the front of the Thutmose IV chariot where the cartouche of the king is placed atop the *smȝ-tȝwi* and below the divine lion-headed vulture. In its decoration, the chariot displays a visual hierarchy, representing the divine realm at the top, Egypt herself in the center, and the subjugated masses of the foreign lands in the bottom register of the scenes. In other words, the iconography visually describes the Egyptian ordering of the world. Besides these spatial references, there is also a strong implication of time sequence contained in the narrative relief on the chariot, in the sense that we see the commission of the god and the successful fulfillment of this charge in the form of the detailed scenes of battle. The foreshadowing evidenced by the severed hands of the dead implies the eventual presentation of these body parts to the king as he sits in his mobile throne. Pharaoh's 'activation' of the reliefs was essential; by stepping into his chariot, the king would have completed the cycle, bringing to life the potential victory the decoration represents.

NOTES

1 Sincere thanks to Stephen Harvey, David O'Connor, and Katherine Eaton for commenting on this research and providing their invaluable guidance.

2 The evidence for the silvering of the chariot is not explained by Littauer & Crouwel in their otherwise thorough discussion of the chariot (1985). Their assertion regarding the presence of silver leaf on the chariot body has been provisionally corroborated by Deborah Schorsch of the Metropolitan Museum of Art in New York (Personal Communication, March 2000). It is certainly possible that the metal in question is electrum, although it apparently has a high enough silver content to tarnish heavily.

3 The same stance is seen, to name but a few examples, in the lion at the king's side in a smiting scene from the palace of Merenptah (1212-1201 BC) at Memphis (University of Pennsylvania Museum, E17527), the hunting dogs on the painted box of Tutankhamun in the Egyptian Museum, Cairo (JE 61467), and the lion on the chariot body of Ramesses III in a relief from Medinet Habu (Epigraphic Survey, 1930: pl. 23). It is also present on several of the ceremonial slate palettes from the Predynastic Period, most notably the Louvre Palette (No. E 11052), the Small Palette from Hierakonpolis (Ashmolean Museum, Oxford No. E 3924), the Metropolitan Museum, New York fragment (No. 28.9.8) and the Hunter's Palette (British Museum, London No. EA 20790). Research into the iconographic programs of these palettes has suggested that they played a role in the repelling of chaos and maintaining cosmic order (O'Connor, 2002: 17-18; 2011: 33).

4 For example, Seti I at Karnak (Epigraphic Survey, 1986: pls. 15, 17, 28) and Ramesses III at Medinet Habu (Epigraphic Survey, 1932: pls 102, 111, 114).

5 Could this then suggest a parallel between non-royal fishing and fowling scenes (*i.e.* the nobleman's version of 'smiting' scenes – ritually controlling chaos) and the occurrence of private chariots in tombs, such as that of Yuya?

6 I am very grateful to Peter Brand for allowing me access to a draft of this forthcoming article.

7 Certain offerings were also presented in pairs, one of gold and the other of silver or faience (Katherine Eaton, Personal Communication, October 2010).

8 The similarity in the iconography of thrones and Windows of Appearance was initially pointed out to me by Tammy Hilburn (Personal Communication, December 1999).

9 Other possibilities (suggested by David O'Connor, Personal Communication, 2007) are that the exterior scenes should be viewed sequentially, with the right side leading to the left, or that the right side has more of a 'celestial' connotation, with the king defeating enemies of the sun god, and the left side being more 'terrestrial' (note the absence of the solar disc above the king's head and his personal engagement with the enemy).

CITED LITERATURE

Aldred, C. 1969. The 'New Year' Gifts to the Pharaoh. – Journal of Egyptian Archaeology 55: 73-81.

Aldred, C. 1988. Akhenaten. – London, Thames & Hudson.

Allen, J. 1995 [1988]. Genesis in Ancient Egypt. – Yale, Yale University Press.

Andrews, C. 1990. Ancient Egyptian Jewellery. – London, British Museum Press.

Aufrere, S. 1991. L'Univers mineral dans la pensée Egyptienne. – Cairo, Institut Français d'Archéologie Orientale.

Baines, J. 1985. Fecundity Figures. – Warminster, Aris & Phillips.

Baines, J. 1994. Kingship, Definition of Culture and Legitimization. In: O'Connor, D. & D. Silverman. Eds. Ancient Egyptian Kingship. – Leiden, Brill: 3-48.

Bell, L. 1985. Aspects of the Cult of the Deified Tutankhamun. In: Posener-Krieger, P. Ed. Mélanges Gamal Mokhtar I. – Cairo, Institut Français d'Archéologie Orientale: 31-59.

Brand, P. 1995. Tuthmoside Battle Relief. In: Thomas, N. Ed. The American Discovery of Ancient Egypt. – Los Angeles, Los Angeles County Museum of Art: 170-171.

Brand, P. 2006. The Shebyu-Collar in the New Kingdom. Part I. Studies in Memory of Nicholas B. Millet. – Journal of the Society for the Study of Egyptian Antiquities 33: 17-28.

Brand, P. Forthcoming. The Shebyu-Collar in the New Kingdom. Part 2.

Bryan, B. 1998. Antecedents to Amenhotep III. In: O'Connor, D. & E. Cline. Eds. Amenhotep III. Perspectives on his Reign. – Ann Arbor, University of Michigan Press: 27-62.

Bryan, B. 1991. The Reign of Thutmose IV. – Baltimore, Johns Hopkins University Press.

Carter, H. & P. Newberry. 1904. The Tomb of Thoutmosis IV. Catalogue général des antiquités égyptiennes du Musée du Caire v. 15, Nos. 46001-46529. – Cairo, Institut Français d'Archéologie Orientale.

Černý, J. 1973. Valley of the Kings. – Cairo, Institut Français d'Archéologie Orientale.

Collier, S. 1996. The Crowns of Pharaoh. Their Development and Significance in Ancient Egyptian Kingship. – Los Angeles, University of California Los Angeles (Unpublished PhD dissertation).

Daressy, M.G. 1902. Fouilles de la Vallee des Rois. Catalogue générale des antiquités Égyptiennes du Musée de Caire, Nos. 24001-24990. – Cairo, Institut Français d'Archéologie Orientale.

Davies, N. de G. 1905. The Rock Tombs of el Amarna. Volume VI. – London, Egypt Exploration Fund.

Drews, R. 1993. The End of the Bronze Age. – Princeton, Princeton University Press.

Eaton-Krauss, M. 2008. The Thrones, Chairs, Stools, and Footstools from the Tomb of Tutankhamun. – Oxford, Griffith Institute.

Epigraphic Survey. 1930. The Earlier Historical Records of Ramses III. Medinet Habu II. – Chicago, Oriental Institute of the University of Chicago Press.

Epigraphic Survey. 1932. The Later Historical Records of Ramses III. Medinet Habu I. – Chicago, Oriental Institute of the University of Chicago Press.

Epigraphic Survey. 1986. Reliefs and Inscriptions at Karnak. The Battle Reliefs of King Sety I. – Chicago, Oriental Institute of the University of Chicago Press.

Faulkner, R. 1996 [1962]. A Concise Dictionary of Middle Egyptian. – Oxford, Griffith Institute.

Faulkner, R.O. 1953. Egyptian Military Organization. – Journal of Egyptian Archaeology 39: 41-47.

Fjerstad, B. 2011. The Window of Appearance Re-Opened. New Perspectives on a New Kingdom Royal Venue. – Memphis, University of Memphis (Unpublished MA thesis).

Foster, J. 1996. Hymns, Prayers, and Songs. An Anthology of Ancient Egyptian Lyric Poetry. – Atlanta, Society for Biblical Literature.

Gale N. & Z. Stos Gale. 1981. Ancient Egyptian Silver. – Journal of Egyptian Archaeology 67: 103-115.

Giza-Podgorski, T. 1984. Royal Plume Dress of XVIII Dynasty. – Mitteilungen des Deutschen Archäologischen Instituts in Kairo 40: 103-121.

Groenewegen-Frankfort, H. 1951. Arrest and Movement. – London, Faber and Faber.

Habachi, L. 1972. The Second Stela of Kamose and His Struggle against the Hyksos Ruler and his Capital. – Glückstadt, J.J. Augustin.

Hall, E.S. 1986. The Pharaoh Smites his Enemies. – Munich, Deutscher Kunstverlag.

Hall, H.R. 1913. Catalog of the Egyptian Scarabs in the British Museum. – London, British Museum.

Hansen, K. 1992. Collection in Ancient Egyptian Chariot Horses. – Journal of the American Research Center in Egypt 29: 173-179.

Hardwick, T. & C. Riggs. 2010. The King as a Falcon. A 'Lost' Statue of Thutmose III Rediscoverd and Reuinited. – Mitteilungen des Deutschen Archäologischen Instituts in Kairo 66: 107-119.

Hartwig, M. 2007. A Vignette Concerning the Deification of Thutmose IV. In: D'Auria, S. Ed. Servant of Mut. Studies in Honor of Richard A. Fazzini. – Leiden, Brill: 120-124.

Harvey, S. 1994. Monuments of Ahmose at Abydos. – Egyptian Archaeology 4: 3-5.

Harvey, S. 1998. The Cults of King Ahmose at Abydos. – Philadelphia, University of Pennsylvania (Unpublished Ph.D dissertation).

Hayes, W. 1959. The Scepter of Egypt. Volume 2. – New York, Metropolitan Museum.

Heinz, S. 2001. Die Feldzugsdarstellungen des Neuen Reiches. – Wein, Verlag der Osterreichischen Akademie der Wissenschaften.

Houlihan, P. 1986. Birds of Ancient Egypt. – Warminster, Aris & Philips.

Johnson, W.R. 1996. Amenhotep III and Amarna. Some New Considerations. – Journal of Egyptian Archaeology 82: 65-82.

Johnson, W.R. 1990. Images of Amenhotep III at Thebes. Styles and Intentions. In: Berman, L. Ed. The Art of Amenhotep III. Art Historical Analysis. – Cleveland, Cleveland Museum of Art: 26-46.

Kákosy, L. 1977. Bark and Chariot. – Studia Aegyptiaca 3: 57-65.

Kozloff, A. & B. Bryan. Eds. 1992. Egypt's Dazzling Sun. Amenhotep III and His World. – Cleveland Cleveland Museum of Art.

Kuhlmann, K. 1977. Der Thron im Alten Agypten. – Glückstadt, J.J. Augustin.

Kuhlmann, K. 2011. Throne. In: Wendrich, W. Ed. UCLA Encyclopedia of Egyptology. – Los Angeles, UCLA (http://digital2.library.ucla.edu/viewItem.do?ark=21198/zz0026w9gt).

Landstrom, B. 1970. Ships of the Pharaohs. – New York, Doubleday.

Lichtheim, M. 1976. Ancient Egyptian Literature. Volume 2. – Berkeley, University of California Press.

Littauer, M. & J. Crouwel. 1985. Chariots and Related Equipment from the Tomb of Tutankhamun. – Oxford, Griffith Institute.

McCarthy, H. 2007. The Beit el-Wali Temple of Ramesses II. A Cosmological Interpretation. In: Hawass, Z. & J. Richards. Eds. The Archeology and Art of Ancient Egypt. Essays in Honor of David O'Connor. – Cairo, Supreme Council of Antiquities: 127-146.

Meilleur, A. 2000. A Re-Examination of the Chariot of Thutmosis IV. – Memphis, University of Memphis (Unpublished MA thesis).

Murnane, W. 1995. Texts from the Amarna Period in Egypt. – Atlanta, Scholars Press.

O'Connor, D. 1994. Beloved of Maat. The Horizon of Re. The Royal Palace in New Kingdom Egypt. In: O'Connor, D. & D. Silverman. Eds. Ancient Egyptian Kingship. – Leiden, Brill: 263-299.

O'Connor, D. 2002. Context, Function and Program. Understanding Ceremonial Slate Palettes. – Journal of the American Research Center in Egypt 39: 5-25

O'Connor, D. 2003. Egypt's View of 'Other'. In: Tait, J. Ed. Never had the Like Occurred. Egypt's View of Her Past. – London, University College London, Institute of Archaeology: 155-186.

O'Connor, D. 2011. The Narmer Palette. A New Interpretation. In: Teeter, E. Ed. Before the Pyramids. The Origins of Egyptian Civilization. – Chicago, University of Chicago: 145-152.

O'Connor, D. & D. Silverman. Eds.1994. Ancient Egyptian Kingship. – Leiden, Brill.

Ogden, J. 2000. Metals. In: Nicholson, P. & I. Shaw. Eds. Ancient Egyptian Materials and Industries. – Cambridge, Cambridge University Press: 148-176.

Petrie, F. 1910. Arts and Crafts of Ancient Egypt. – London, T.N. Foulis.

Pinch, G. 2002. Egyptian Mythology. – Oxford, Oxford University Press.

Redford, D. 1984. Akhenaten the Heretic King. – Princeton, Princeton University Press.

Redford, D. 1994. The Concept of Kingship during the Eighteenth Dynasty. In: O'Connor, D. & D. Silverman. Eds. Ancient Egyptian Kingship. – Leiden, Brill: 157-184.

Ritner, R. 1993. The Mechanics of Ancient Egyptian Magical Practice. – Chicago, University of Chicago.

Roth, A.M. 1998. Buried Pyramids and Layered Thoughts. The Organization of Multiple Approaches in Egyptian Religion. In: Eyre, C. Ed. Proceedings of the Seventh International Congress of Egyptologists. – Leuven, Peeters: 991-1003.

Schäfer, H. 1974. Principles of Egyptian Art. – Oxford, Griffith Institute.

Schulman, A. 1979. Chariots, Chariotry and the Hyksos. – Journal of the Society for the Study of Egyptian Antiquities 10, 2: 105-153.

Smith H.S. & A. Smith. 1976. A Reconsideration of the Kamose Texts. – Zeitschrift für Ägyptische Sprache und Altertumskunde 103: 48-76.

Spalinger, A. 2005. War in Ancient Egypt. – Oxford, Blackwell.

Troy, L. 1986. Patterns of Queenship in Ancient Egyptian Myth and History. – Uppsala, Uppsala Universitet.

Vogelsang-Eastwood, G. 1999. Tutankhamun's Wardrobe. Garments from the Tomb of Tutankhamun. – Rotterdam, Barjesteh van Waalwijk van Doorn & Co's.

Werner, E. 1985. The God Montu. From the Earliest Attestations to the End of the New Kingdom. – Yale University (Unpublished Ph.D Dissertation).

Werner, E. 1986. Montu and the 'Falcon Ships' of the Eighteenth Dynasty. – Journal of the American Research Center in Egypt 23: 107-123.

Wreszinski, W. 1935. Atlas zur altägyptischen kulturgeschichte. Volume 2. – Leipzig, Hinrichs.

Yadin, Y. 1963. The Art of Warfare in Biblical Lands. – Jerusalem, International Publishers.

STUDYING THE SIX CHARIOTS FROM THE TOMB OF TUTANKHAMUN - AN UPDATE

Joost Crouwel

In memory of Mary Littauer

INTRODUCTION

Egyptian and other ancient chariots were light, fast vehicles with a pair of (spoked) wheels, drawn by horses that were yoked on either side of a draught pole, and able to carry one or more standing persons (figures 1 & 2). Two other categories of wheeled vehicle are documented in Egypt and other parts of the ancient world: carts, that are also two-wheeled vehicles but designed to carry a stable load (goods or seated passengers), and four-wheeled wagons (these and other more technical terms are explained in the illustrated glossaries of Littauer & Crouwel, 1979a; 1985; 2002).

Three factors were of vital importance to the use of chariots. Firstly, spoked wheels (lightly and strongly made, thereby enabling fast transport); secondly, horse draught (strong and fast) and adaptation of the (originally ox) yoke to the horses' conformation; and thirdly, bridle bits allowing for directional as well as braking control over the animals. It should be noted that suitable timber was necessary, as well as craftsmen skilled in building and maintaining the vehicles, and professional horse trainers and drivers (see also Shaw 2001: 62-65).

Chariots were costly to make and maintain, and the draught teams had to be especially trained and matched in height. Under the right circumstances, they could be used for military as well as civil purposes. With their teams of horses (often stallions), the vehicles were at the same time an exciting

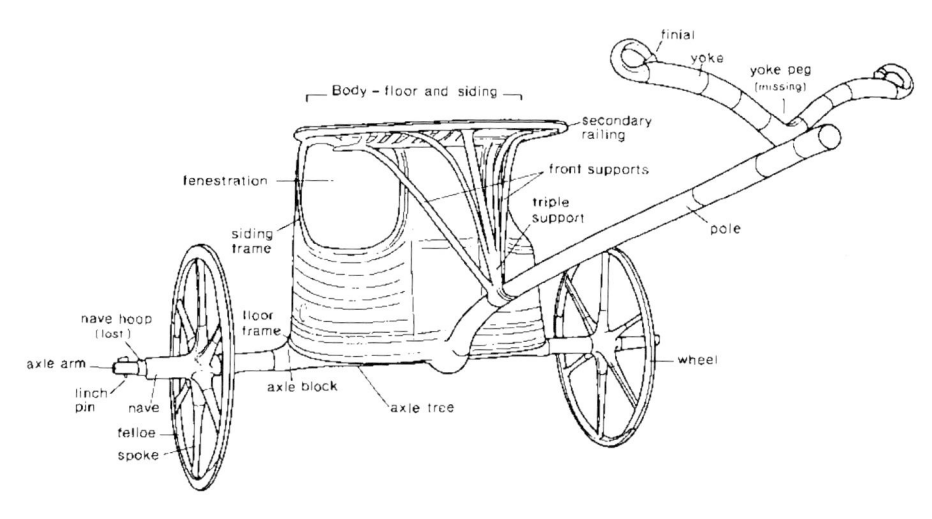

Figure 1. Terminology. Schematic drawing of chariot A1 from the tomb of Tutankhamun Drawing by P. Jacobs. After: Littauer & Crouwel (1985: fig. 1).

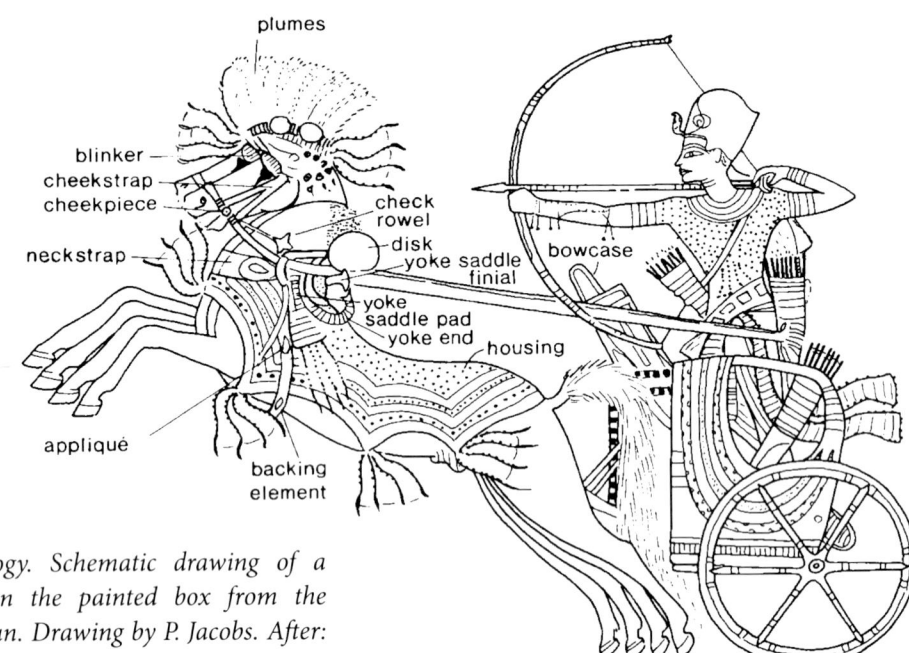

Figure 2. Terminology. Schematic drawing of a harnessed chariot on the painted box from the tomb of Tutankhamun. Drawing by P. Jacobs. After: Littauer & Crouwel (1985: fig. 2).

and impressive sight. Both the chariots and their draught animals were highly suitable for lavish decoration, thus catering for the love of ostentation of kings and an elite class. The equipages would have lent prestige to their owners, raising them literally and metaphorically above their fellows.

Chariots were not sudden inventions, but developed out of earlier vehicles that were mounted on disk or cross-bar wheels. This development can best be traced in the Near East, where spoke-wheeled and horse-drawn 'true' chariots are first attested in the earlier part of the second millennium BC (figure 3 [taken from a Syrian cylinder seal of the 18th-17th centuries BC]; for discussion, see Littauer & Crouwel, 1979a: 68-71;

Figure 3. Detail of Syrian cylinder seal. Drawing by J. Morel. After: Littauer & Crouwel (1979a: fig. 33).

1996a [= 2002]: 45-52; Crouwel, 2004: 78-82). It is generally agreed that the use of light, spoke-wheeled, horse-drawn chariots was introduced to Egypt from the Near East, as was the horse (Raulwing & Clutton-Brock, 2009: 59-78, with bibliography). The earliest osteological evidence for this animal in Egypt may be the skeleton of a ca. 19-years old stallion from Buhen in the south, its teeth possibly showing signs of wear from a bit (see Sasada, this volume). However, the proposed date of its find context (ca. 1675 BC) has not been universally accepted (Raulwing & Clutton-Brock, 2009). There are remains of horses and mules of the 15th Dynasty (1650-1535 BC) and the early New Kingdom from Avaris (present-day Tell el-Dab'a) in the eastern Nile delta (Boessneck, 1976: 25; Von den Driesch & Peters, 2001). To these can be added the recent find of the skeleton of a five-to-ten-year old mare from the same site, reportedly dating to the 15th Dynasty (Bietak & Forstner-Müller, 2009: 98-100).

In Egypt, chariots and/or their harness teams of horses are first attested in texts of the 16th century BC. These documents describe the struggle of the Theban pharaohs Kamose (1553-1549 BC) and Ahmose I (1549-1524 BC) to expel the Asiatic "rulers of foreign lands", better known as the Hyksos, from Egypt (Malek, 1989; Redford, 1997: 13-16, texts nos. 68-70). In one of the ancient texts, the chariot of Ahmose I, the first pharaoh of the New Kingdom and the 18th Dynasty (1549-1298 BC), is represented by a hieroglyph of an unharnessed four-spoked vehicle that was to be become standard in Egypt (Redford, 1997: 15, text no. 70 – the Autobiography of Ahmose, son of Abana, on a wall of his tomb at El Kab [Tomb 5; Porter & Moss, 1962: 182]). Recently found stone relief fragments from the pyramid temple of this pharaoh at Abydos in southern Egypt show horse-drawn chariots in scenes of battle between Egyptian and Asiatic forces (figure 4; Harvey, 1998: 314-372, figs. 76-78A, 97; Raulwing & Clutton-Brock, 2009: figs. 27-29). Spoked wheels also occur on the model-sized four-wheeled trolley carrying a gold boat that was found in the tomb of Ahmose I's mother Ahhotpe at Thebes (figure 5; Von Bissing, 1900: 20-21, pl. 10; Partridge, 1996: 139, fig. 121).[1]

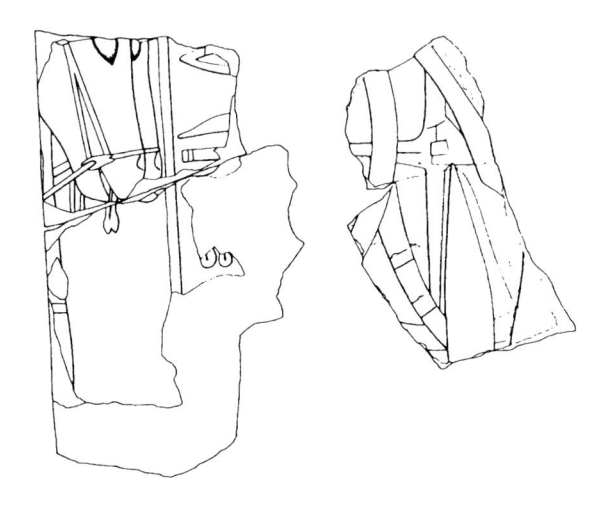

Figure 4A & B. Fragments of stone reliefs of Ahmose I from Abydos. From: Raulwing & Clutton-Brock (2009: figs. 27-28 left).

Figure 5. Trolley and model boat from the tomb of Ahhotpe, Thebes. From: Partridge (1996: fig. 121).

It should be noted that the craft of the wheelwright (who did not make spoked, but rather disk-type wheels), and the use of paired animals in draught (not horses but oxen), had not been entirely unknown in Egypt before the New Kingdom. There are two representations of siege ladders mounted on single-piece disk wheels, dating from the 5th(?) and 11th Dynasties respectively (figure 6; tomb of Kaiemheset at Saqqara: Quibell & Hayter, 1927: frontispiece; Senk, 1956/1957; tomb of Inyotef at Thebes: Arnold & Settgast, 1965: 50, fig. 2). Furthermore, among the many illustrations of sledges, there is one from the 13th Dynasty (1781-1650 BC) showing a sledge mounted on four such wheels. The vehicle is pulled by a team of oxen and carries a funerary boat (figure 7; tomb of Sebknakhte at El Kab: Tylor & Clarke, 1896: pl. 2; Stevenson-Smith, 1965, 23: fig. 34c; see also Dittmann, 1941). However, this ox-drawn conveyance does not really count as a local prototype for the light, horse-drawn chariot that became so common in Egypt in the New Kingdom.

Pictorial and textual evidence for the use of chariots in Egypt increases as the New Kingdom progresses, and by the 15th century BC they clearly played an important role in warfare and civil life (see especially Hofmann, 1989; 2004; Decker, 1986a; 1986b; 1994; Decker & Herb, 1994: 192-263; Rommelaere, 1991). Their military and sporting (hunting) use continued at least to the time of Ramesses III (1185-1153 BC). After his reign both representational and textual evidence for chariots in Egypt became quite scarce (Littauer & Crouwel, 1979b [= 2002]: 296-313).

Horse-drawn chariots were not suitable for the transport of goods or seated passengers. In Egypt, such transport was provided primarily by boats and donkeys (in later times, also by camels) (see a.o. Partridge, 1996: 3-75, 95-99). Sledges, pulled by oxen or groups of men, were used for moving building stone and sculptures to their destination, and litters for members of the elite, are also documented (see a.o. Partridge, 1996: 131-137, 88-94). As seen above, one relief of the Middle Kingdom (2066-1650 BC) shows an ox-drawn sledge mounted on disk wheels. The pictorial record of the New Kingdom includes a few representations of spoke-wheeled, ox-drawn carts, in one case in an agricultural setting (un-

Figure 6. Detail of stone relief from the tomb of Kaiemhesit, Saqqara. From: Quibell & Hayter (1927: frontispiece).

Figure 7. Detail of stone relief from the tomb of Sebeknekh, El Kab. From: Stevenson Smith (1965: fig. 34c).

known tomb: Hayes, 1959:164-165, fig. 90; tomb of Nebamun: Säve-Söderbergh, 1957: pl. 23, no. 17; Stevenson-Smith, 1965: 23, fig. 41. See also Hofmann, 1989: 290-293). Other spoke-wheeled carts are shown in the Egyptian army camp(s) on temple reliefs of Ramesses II (1279-1212 BC) depicting the Battle of Qadesh (1274 BC) (Wreszinski, 1935: pls. 22-23; Hofmann, 2004: 154, fig. 13).[2] They must have belonged to the army's baggage train. There are also actual remains of a single-piece disk wheel, which is now in the British Museum, London (E 29943), that must have belonged to a cart or wagon. Reportedly from Deir el-Bahari, the wheel has not yet been fully published (see Sandor, 2004a: 155-157, fig. 2; 2004b: 644, 646). This find recalls the similarly single-piece wheels belonging to the ox-drawn carts carrying families of the Sea Peoples on the move, depicted on temple reliefs of Ramesses III at Medinet Habu (Wreszinski, 1935: pls. 113-114; Yadin, 1963: 336-337). According to a passage in the Annals of Thutmose III, ox-drawn vehicles were used for the transport of boats for the army's crossing of the Euphrates river. The vehicles were built from local timber during a campaign in Syria (a.o. Decker, 1986b: 1132; Hofmann, 1989: 291).

DISCOVERY AND SUBSEQUENT HISTORY OF THE CHARIOTS OF TUTANKHAMUN

It was in November 1922 that the archaeologist and master draughtsman Howard Carter, then aged 49, first entered the tomb of Tutankhamun in the Valley of the Kings (Theban Tomb [TT] 62). This pharaoh of the New Kingdom's 18th Dynasty had ascended the throne as a boy and ruled for nine or ten years (1335-1325 BC). His tomb consists of a staircase followed by an entrance passage leading to four chambers. These have been known since their dis-

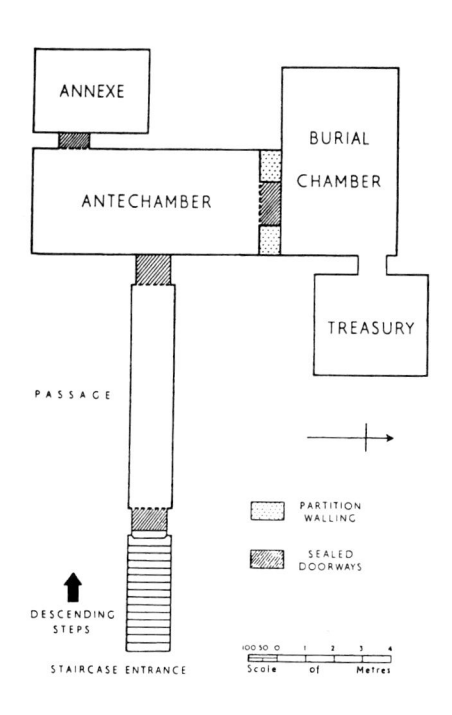

Figure 8. Plan of the tomb of Tutankhamun, Thebes. From: Littauer & Crouwel (1985: fig. 3).

Figure 9 (below). Isometric drawing of the tomb of Tutankhamun and its contents. Drawing by H. Parkinson. From: Littauer & Crouwel (1985: pl. I).

Figure 10. Chariots and other finds in the Antechamber of the tomb of Tutankhamun. Photograph by H. Burton. Courtesy of the Griffith Institute, Oxford.

Figure 11. Chariot material in the Antechamber of the tomb of Tutankhamun. Photograph by H. Burton. Courtesy of the Griffith Institute, Oxford.

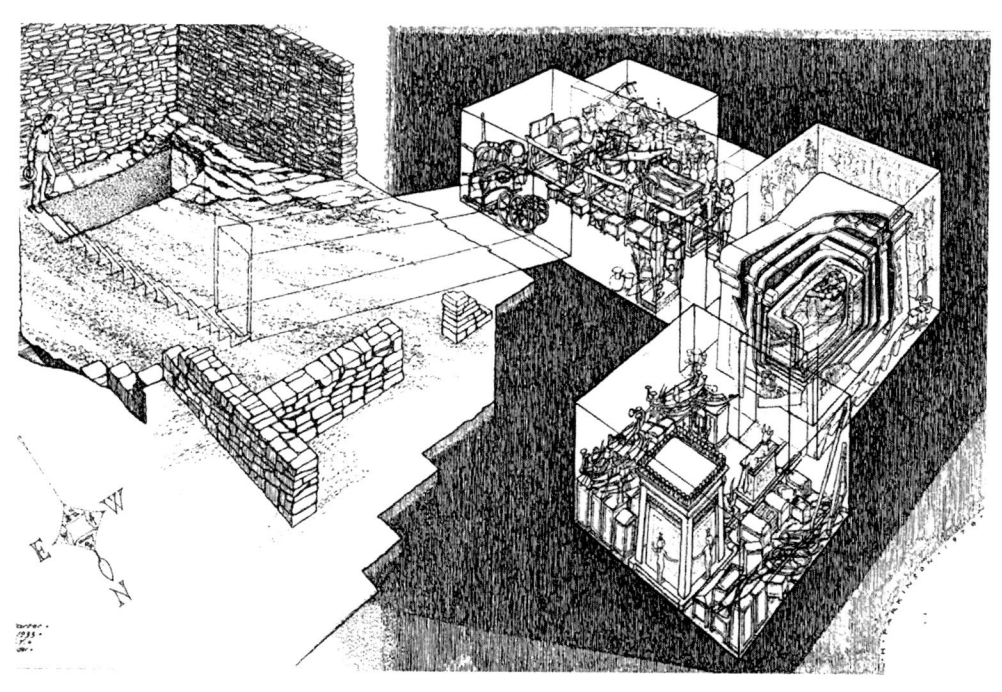

covery as the Antechamber, Burial Chamber, Treasury and Annexe (figures 8 & 9). The chambers, and the tomb as a whole, are very small in comparison with the other rock-cut royal sepulchres in the Valley of the Kings.

Among the wealth of finds from the tomb of Tutankhamun were no fewer than six chariots and fragments of harness and bridle elements. Four of the vehicles were found in the Antechamber and two in the Treasury. The former measures ca. 8 x 3.60 m, the latter ca. 4 x 3.50 m (for an idea of the find circumstances, see figures 10-12). The vehicles were found in different states of preservation, for a variety of reasons. The axles were too long (2.13 to 2.36 m) to be manoeuvred down the staircase and through the entrance passage to the Antechamber (ca. 1.60 and 1.70 m wide respectively) and two doorways (both ca. 1.40 m wide), so they had to be cut short and the wheels removed. It must have been particularly difficult to take two chariots still deeper into the tomb – from the Antechamber, through the Burial Chamber, to the Treasury, and this is probably why these vehicles were found completely dismantled (figure 12). Moreover, tomb robbers did considerable damage to the vehicles in antiquity by ripping off parts of their gold decoration, and carrying away, among other things, portable metal objects, elements such as nave hoops, linch pins and, possibly, horse bits. After the looting, the chambers were to some extent tidied up by the necropolis officials. This may explain the position in which the chariots and wheels in the Antechamber were found: stacked rather haphazardly upon one another against the south-east corner of the room (figures 10 & 11). Yet another source of damage was the intermittent humidity (particularly bad in the Treasury), which caused the glue and leather to 'melt' (see also Veldmeijer *et. al.*, this volume), and wood to expand and warp. It should be noted that one or two harness and bridle parts were found in the Annexe.

To his lasting credit, Carter did not rush to clear the tomb of its astonishing contents. On the contrary, he and his small team, which included the archaeologist Arthur Mace (if only during the first campaign), the photographer Harry Burton and the chemist Alfred Lucas, proceeded slowly and very carefully. For instance, it took them seven months – the first season (1922-1923) – to record and remove the objects from the Antechamber. The Treasury was only emptied in the fifth season (1926-1927). The work on the tomb ended in the spring of 1932, a little less than 10 years after it began.

Figure 12. Chariot material in the Treasury of the tomb of Tutankhamun. Photograph by H. Burton. Courtesy of the Griffith Institute, Oxford.

Figure 13. A.C. Mace and A. Lucas (seated) with the body of chariot A2 from the tomb of Tutankhamun. Photograph by H. Burton. Courtesy of the Griffith Institute Oxford.

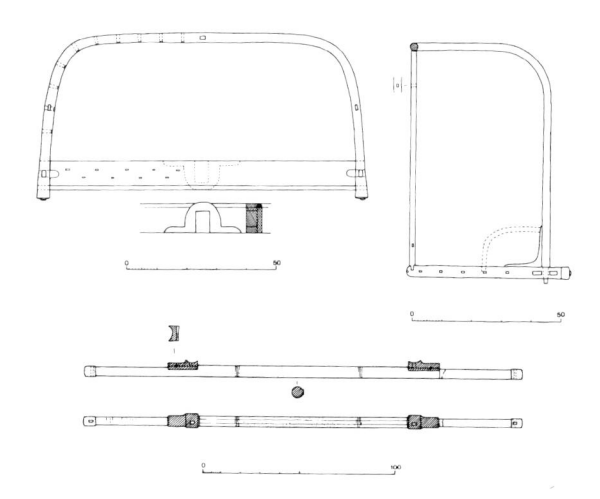

Figure 14. Details of chariot A5 from the tomb of Tutankhamun. Drawing by P. Jacobs. After: H. Carter index card.

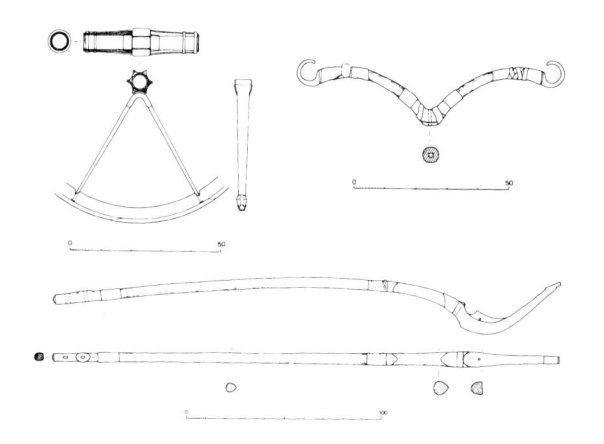

Figure 15. Details of chariot A5 from the tomb of Tutankhamun. Drawing by P. Jacobs. After: H. Carter index card.

Figure 16. Chariot A1 from the tomb of Tutankhamun, as reassembled. Photograph by R. Hurford. Courtesy of the Ministry of State for Antiquities/Egyptian Museum Authorities.

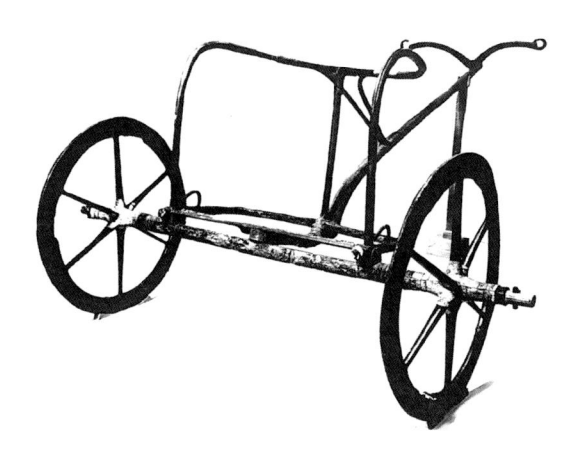

Figure 17. Chariot A4 from the tomb of Tutankhamun, as reassembled. Photograph by N. Scott. From: Littauer & Crouwel (1985: pl. XXX, top).

Figure 18. Chariot A6 from the tomb of Tutankhamun, as reassembled. Photograph by N. Scott. From: Littauer & Crouwel (1985: pl. LVI, top).

Carter arranged for measured plans of the tomb to be drawn, with and without finds shown on them (figures 8 & 9).[3] The objects were first numbered, then photographed *in situ*, and subsequently moved to the nearby empty tomb of Seti II (figures 11 & 13). There, descriptions and measurements of each object and copies of hieroglyphic texts were recorded on index cards, and sketches and scale-drawings made (figures 14 & 15). The necessary mending and conservation treatment were carried out and recorded. Next, the objects were taken outside for photography. At the end of each season, they were carefully packed and transported to the Egyptian Museum in Cairo, where they were en-

Figure 19. Mary Littauer and the author examining Tutankhamun's chariot A4 in the Egyptian Museum, Cairo. Photograph by N. Scott. Courtesy of the Ministry of State for Antiquities/Egyptian Museum Authorities.

tered and briefly described by Carter himself in the *Journal d'Entrée*. As for the chariots, five of them (A1-4 from the Antechamber and A6 from the Treasury) were reassembled, with the help of modern materials that conceal some of the details of the original appearance or construction. The vehicles were then put on display, each in its own large case, presumably under Carter's supervision (figures 16-19). Currently, four of the chariots from the Antechamber remain in their original display cases in the Egyptian Museum. The fifth (A3) has been moved to the Luxor Museum where it is on display. The sixth vehicle (A5), from the Treasury, was left in its dismantled state in a wooden box that was located in 1973 in the Tutankhamun storeroom of the Egyptian Museum at Cairo. Later, in the 1980s, this chariot was – most ably – reassembled by the Egyptian conservator Nadia Lokma.[4] It is presently exhibited in the Military Museum in the Citadel of Cairo.

Over the years Carter published a three-volume account of his work for the general public: The Tomb of Tut.ankh.amen I (1923, written jointly with Mace), II (1927), and III (1933). He also intended to present a full scholarly account, a daunting undertaking that did not come to fruition. Howard Carter died in London in 1939, aged 65, without having received any honours for his achievements from the British establishment, but with an honorary doctorate from Yale University.

The ample records made during the work on the tomb and its finds by Carter and other members of the team passed – through his niece Phyllis Walker – to the Griffith Institute of the University of Oxford.[5] In the 1960s, the Tutankhamun Tomb Series was set up at this Institute for the systematic publication of the various categories of finds. Several volumes appeared, the first in 1963 (Murray, 1963). Full publication of material from the tomb continues (see El-Khouli *et al.*, 1994: vii). For some time now, the whole documentation of the tomb has been digitalized and available on the website of the Griffith Institute (Tutankhamun: Anatomy of an Excavation: www.griffith.ox.ac.ak; see also Malek & Moffet, 2001).

Around 1970 Mary Littauer and the present author were invited by John Harris, editor of the Tutankhamun Tomb Series, to prepare the volume on these six vehicles and related equipment. Neither of us was an Egyptologist, but we were deeply involved in the study of chariots and other wheeled vehicles in the ancient world, including Egypt. After having consulted the records in Oxford and armed with many xerox copies and a set of photographs, in April 1973 we were able to examine all the chariots and most of the harness and other material in the Cairo Museum (figure 19). This was thanks to the permission and cooperation from the Egyptian authorities and to invaluable help from, in particular John Harris and Wim Stoetzer, then director of the Netherlands Institute for Archaeology and Arabic Studies at Cairo (currently known as the Netherlands-Flemish Institute in Cairo). In the museum we were given two hours to examine each of the five chariots on display inside their large cases, which had not been opened before. We were also allowed time in the storeroom to study the sixth chariot. Its entirely disassembled state permitted the verification of certain details of construction not accessible on the other vehicles. Furthermore, we travelled to Luxor to visit the tomb and see many of the temple reliefs and tomb paintings of the New Kingdom depicting chariots. It took until 1985 for the study to be published, as Volume 8 of the aforementioned series. The book, meticulously edited by John Harris, presented the fullest possible descriptions and discussion of the material. As comparative material, there were the extensive and detailed pictorial and textual records from Egypt and, in addition, the remains of five other actual chariots and of harness and bridle parts from Theban royal or elite tombs of the New Kingdom – of Amenhotep II, Thutmose IV (figures 20-22), Yuya and Tjuiu, Amenhotep III (figure 22) and probably Ay. There was also a chariot, now in Florence, from an unknown tomb at Thebes (figure 23). We were fortunate in being able to draw upon Jean Spruytte's examination of this chariot and upon David Pye's expertise in woodworking.

The six actual chariots from the tomb of Tutankhamun form a unique group of almost complete vehicles from a single, well-documented and well-dated context. They are of singular importance to the history of technology, and of the construction and use of this kind of wheeled vehicle in particular.

What follows is a brief review of the construction and use of these chariots, and of Egyptian and Near Eastern Late Bronze Age chariots in general, in the light of more recent work and discoveries. Special mention should be made here of the leather chariot trappings, newly found in the Egyptian Museum at Cairo (see Veldmeijer *et al.*, this volume), and the various chariot and bridle parts from Pi-Ramesse (present-day Qantir, see Prell, this volume), the 19th Dynasty's capital in the eastern Nile delta. At that site, stables and an exercise ground for horses were discovered (Herold, 1999; 2004: 131-132; 2006a).

Figure 20. Front and rear of chariot body from the tomb of Thutmose IV, Thebes. From: Littauer & Crouwel (1985: pl. LXVII).

Figure 21. Details of front and rear of chariot body from the tomb of Tuthmosis IV, Thebes. From: Carter & Newberry (1904: pls. X and XI).

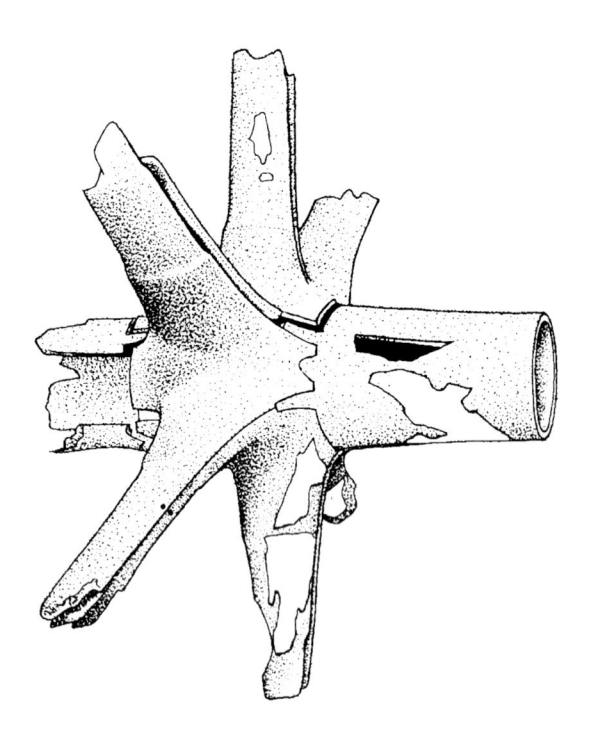

Figure 22. Part of wheel from the tomb of Amenhotep III, Thebes. Drawing by J. Morel. From: Littauer & Crouwel (1985: pl. LXXI).

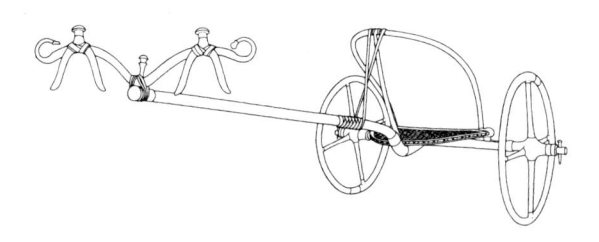

Figure 23. The so-called Florence chariot from an unknown tomb, Thebes. Drawing by J. Morel. From: Littauer & Crouwel (1979a: fig. 42).

CONSTRUCTION

The chariots from the tomb of Tutankhamun are characterized by a very wide wheel track (ca. 1.57-1.80 m), to ensure stability on fast turns, and by an approximately hip-high body, fully open at the rear for quick mounting and dismounting, and are wide enough to hold two persons standing abreast (figures 16-18). The floor has a shallow, D-shaped frame (0.92-1.11 m wide and 0.39-0.54 m deep) and is composed of interwoven rawhide thongs which not only help to keep the bent-wood frame in tension, but also provide some springiness (see Sandor, this volume). The light framework of the body has a vertical support at the centre front, and from two to five supports running diagonally out from the top rail to the draught pole, which also helps somewhat to reinforce the connection between the pole and floor frame. The siding is solid or fenestrated. The wheels are 0.90-0.97 m in diameter and revolve on a long axle that is fixed rigidly under the rear of the body. The six spokes are composite, as is the nave, which is elongated (0.34- 0.44 m) to reduce wobbling. The felloes or rims of the wheels consist of two sections of overlapping wood. These may have wooden and/or rawhide tyres. The single, long draught pole (2.43-2.60 m) runs all the way under the floor and helps support it. This pole, its rear end fitted into a socket under the rear floor bar and lashed to the front of the floor frame, rises in front of the chariot in a shallow, double curve before running forward to the yoke at an oblique angle.[6] The slender, two-horse yoke is fastened on top of the pole near its far end by means of lashings and a yoke peg. Two thongs run out from the pole to each arm of the yoke in order to keep the latter at right angles to the pole and to distribute tractive stress. The neck yoke was adapted to equine anatomy by means of two, padded yoke saddles of inverted Y-shape – one lashed to either yoke arm by its 'handle', its 'legs' lying along the horse's shoulders to take a large part of the pull (Littauer & Crouwel, 1985: 98-99). The two horses were harnessed by means of two leather straps: one crossing the front of their neck and the other passing beneath their belly (see Veldmeijer et al., this volume for an example of neckstrap). The animals were directed and controlled by a bridle, composed of a headstall and reins (figure 2). Remains of two neckstraps were found in the tomb, but no bits – possibly because these, being small and easily portable as well as valuable, had been stolen. Actual copper/bronze bits of two types are known from non-funerary contexts at Tell el-Amarna and Pi-Ramesse (Herold, 1999: 6-110).

The construction of the chariots from the tomb of Tutankhamun – and other extant chariots from Egypt – is based on the use of slender, bent wooden parts, held together by glue and rawhide, and sometimes further connected by mortise and tenon. This resulted in a light, resilient fabric, as has been confirmed by the full-scale reconstructions made by

Figures 24 & 25. Experiments with a reconstruction of an Egyptian chariot. From: Spruytte (1983: pl. 7, 2-3).

Figure 26. Partial reconstruction of an Egyptian chariot. Photograph by R. Hurford.

Jean Spruytte (figures 24 & 25; 1983: 23-51; 1999), by a team of the Roemer-Pelizaeus Museum at Hildesheim (Herold, 2006a: 375-386, pls. 14-23; 2006b) and, most recently, by Robert Hurford with the help of Egyptian craftsmen (see below; figure 26). Independently, mechanical engineers agree

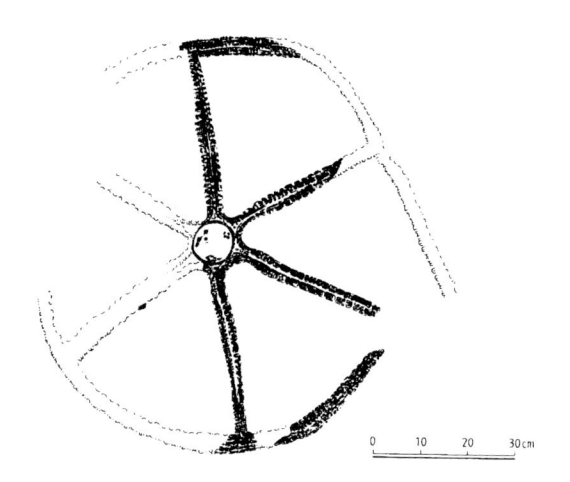

Figure 27. Part of wheel from Lidar Höyük. From: Littauer et al. (1991: fig. 3).

that, while it required great precision of workmanship, this technique of manufacture produced some of the finest examples of the wheelwright's and carriage maker's craft ever known (Rovetta, 2002; Rovetta *et al.*, 2000; Sandor, 2004a; 2004b; Svarth, 1986).

The experimental work is also relevant to the question of whether the wood for certain chariot parts was bent exclusively by steaming and heat-bending when already cut, or whether some parts were trained to approximately the shape desired during growth and then trimmed and heat-bent. It now seems likely that only the first method was used (see especially Herold, 2004: 132-133; 2006a: 376-379; 2006b: 8-9; also Robert Hurford – Personal Communication 2012; *cf.* Littauer & Crouwel, 1985: 93; Moorey, 2001: 8). It is known that the technique of heat-bending has a long history in Egypt, going back to the Old or, maybe Middle Kingdom (Killen, 2000: 356-357; Shaw, 2001: 63-64). The same is true of the use of rawhide, which was already known in Egypt in the Old Kingdom (Van Driel-Murray, 2000: 212). Rawhide, if applied wet to any wooden surface, will shrink as it dries to a yellow-white horny substance, producing a strong constricting effect.

As for the woods used in the construction of the chariots, only a few analyses have been made by botanists. The results show that elm was identified in various parts of the chariots of Tutankhamun (A4, 5 and 6). Elm and tamarisk were identified in the fragmentary six-spoked wheel from the tomb of

Amenhotep III (figure 22; Western, 1973). In addition, the bark of birch trees had been identified as a protective, waterproofing covering for the naves and felloe joins that were glued and bound with rawhide on chariots of Tutankhamun (A4 and 5). Birch bark, which retains its pliability for a considerable time, and even after drying, can be softened by moisture, and served the same purpose on composite bows from the tomb of Tutankhamun, as well as on other bows found in Egypt. Coloured birch bark, often in small patterns, was also used as decoration on some of the chariots (A1, 5 and 6) and related material, as well as on some of the bows from the tomb (for all this, see Littauer & Crouwel, 1995: 92-93; McLeod, 1970: 31-36).

The wood of the Florence chariot has been 'identified' several times, with somewhat different results each time (recently, Herold, 20002a: 379-380; but *cf.* Littauer & Crouwel, 1985: 92). Only the birch bark overlay on parts of the pole and wheels may be reasonably identified with the naked eye. It has often been observed that this chariot was only large enough to carry one occupant, and that parts of its body were incorrectly restored in the early 19th century (Littauer & Crouwel, 1985: 108 – based on observations by Jean Spruytte; see also Spruytte, 1989; Del Francia, 2002a; 2002b).

Tamarisk is native to Egypt, but elm and birch are not (Gale *et al.*, 2000: 345, 346, 336-337). There is little doubt that the latter two timbers were imported from the Near East, as elm and birch are indigenous in areas such as Anatolia and Armenia. Indeed, elm wood has been identified on an actual six-spoked wheel from a burnt building, dated to the early 12th century BC, at Lidar Höyük in southeastern Turkey (figure 27; Littauer *et al.*, 1991; reprinted in English in Littauer & Crouwel, 2002: 314-326). This wheel was made according to the same sophisticated technique of nave-and-spoke construction as the four- and six-spoked chariot wheels found in Egypt (for this construction, see especially Decker, 1984; Sandor, 2004a: 166-169; 2004b: 641-646; Spruytte, 1995).

While the obvious understanding of the waterproofing properties of birch bark and the use of elm in chariot making in Egypt clearly indicate northern influences, the combination of native tamarisk with imported elm in the six-spoked chariot wheel of Amenhotep III suggests manufacture of chariots in Egypt itself – as is vividly illustrated in workshop scenes in Theban New Kingdom tombs (figure 28; Drenkhahn, 1976:128-132; Hofmann, 1989: 182-202, 203-239; Shaw, 2001: 63). On the other hand, contemporary texts mention the import of timber from the Near East to Egypt, as well as the arrival of fully finished chariots as booty and as part of diplomatic exchange (a.o. Hofmann, 1989: 293-295). When such foreign chariots appear in the Egyptian pictorial record, they are usually similar to Egyptian ones (figure 29).

Taking all the evidence into account, it is clear that the type of chariot used in Egypt is of Near Eastern origin. The transfer of chariot technology

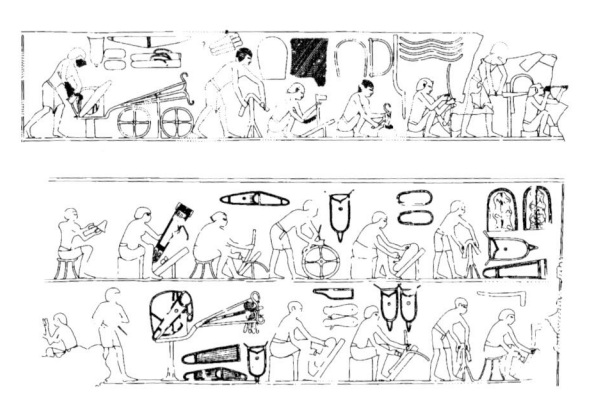

Figure 28. Details of wall paintings from the tombs of Puyemre and Hepu respectively. Thebes (TT 39 and 66). From: Littauer & Crouwel (1985: pl. LXXVI).

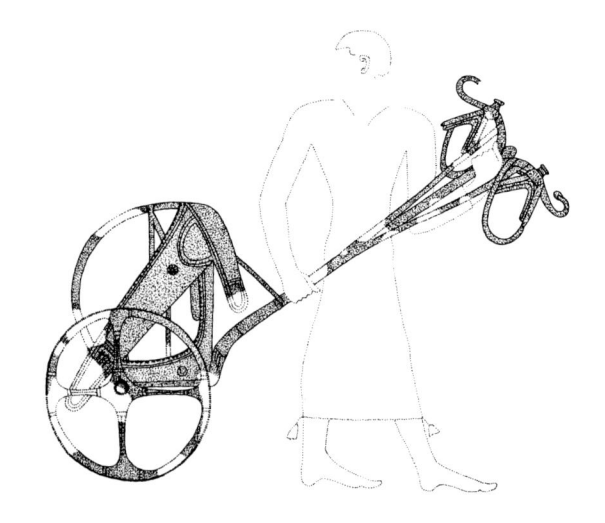

Figure 29. Detail of wall painting from the tomb of Rekhmire, Thebes. Drawing by J. Morel. From: Littauer & Crouwel (1979a: fig. 43).

– and the keeping of horses – from the Near East to Egypt not only included woods such as elm and birch (bark), but also skilled craftsmen, horses and their trainers, as well as the relevant technical vocabulary. Other cases of more or less contemporary, primarily military technology transfer from the Near East to Egypt are the composite bow and scale armour. Composite bows were used on the ground as well as from chariots, whereas scale armour was worn by chariot crews and draught teams of horses (Moorey, 1989; 2001; Shaw, 2001).[7]

USE

Despite their basic similarity, no two of the six chariots from the tomb of Tutankhamun are identical. In fact, hardly a single component part of one chariot actually duplicates that of another. The vehicles are clearly not the product of an 'assembly line', as each one is individually designed. It seems unlikely that any but the pharaoh's personal chariots would have been entombed with him, and the small differences in construction and proportions and the large differences in decoration between them must stem from the different purposes for which they were intended. There are traces of wear on parts of the rugged chariot A4, and segments of a wooden tyre of chariot A5, which is only simply decorated, appear to have been replaced. This indicates that at least these two chariots had not been specifically made as burial gifts, but had been well used before being deposited in the tomb.

Three chariots (A1, 2 and 3) from the Antechamber (called 'state chariots' by Carter) are conspicuous for their sumptuous decoration of gold and inlay, which would seem to restrict them to parade and ceremonial use (figures 1 & 16). Unlike A1 and A2, chariot A3 had a fenestrated siding of dressed leather rather than wood. This would give the vehicle less weight and more resilience. At the same time, the three chariots share a secondary rail at the top front of the body, and they have been reassembled with three other finds from the Antechamber: gilded figures of hawks with solar disks on their heads. These figures were fixed to bases that fitted over the draught poles. In the pictorial record, such disks are associated exclusively with the chariots of royalty (figure 1; see also Calvert, this volume).

In contrast, the fourth chariot from the Antechamber (A4) is undecorated and much more rugged (figures 17 & 19). It has no secondary railing. In its present state the body is entirely open, but it probably had a siding of dressed leather, like chariots A3, 5 and 6. Interestingly, there appears to be evidence that segments of a wooden tyre had been replaced. This chariot would have been the one suitable for hard wear and rough terrain, and might have been used by the pharaoh when on military campaigns or when hunting.

Of the two chariots from the Treasury, one (A5) was quite simply decorated (figures 14 & 15). Like

Figure 30. Scarab with cartouche of Thutmose I. From: Stevenson Smith (1965: fig. 34a).

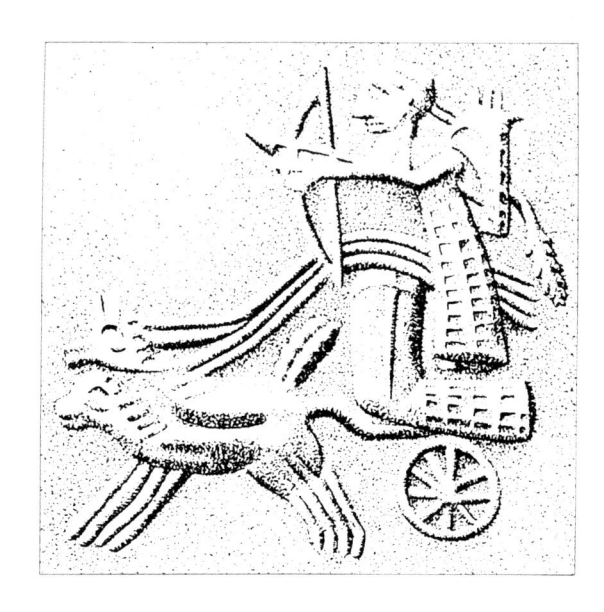

Figure 31. Detail of Syrian cylinder seal. Drawing by J. Morel. From: Littauer & Crouwel (1979a: fig. 36).

chariot A4, it had wooden as well as rawhide tyres, but it is of less sturdy construction. Carter considered chariot A5 and the other one from the Treasury (A6), with its considerable amount of gilt decoration (figure 18), to have been hunting chariots.

The fact that the six chariots of Tutankhamun – and the chariot body recovered from the tomb of Thutmose IV (figures 20-21) – all offered room for two people to stand abreast, but that, with rare exceptions, representations show the pharaoh alone in his chariot, raises the question of how frequently he drove himself. From the beginning there was a close connection between chariots and royalty in Egypt, as there was in the Near East. Textual sources make clear that driving was one of the accomplishments expected of a pharaoh.

There are many images of Tutankhamun and other pharaohs alone in a chariot. They are driving while holding the reins in their hands or, more often, with the reins tied around their hips to free their hands for the use of bow-and-arrow in a hunt or battle (figure 2).

Figure 32. Reliefs from the temple of Ramesses II. Abu Simbel. From: Raulwing (2000: fig. 15).

The theme of hunting or fighting with a bow from a chariot was very popular in Egyptian iconography, as a symbol of the pharaohs' prowess and exalted status. It is already represented on a scarab bearing the cartouche of Thutmose I (1494-1485 BC), showing him shooting down an enemy on foot (figure 30; Stevenson Smith, 1965: 22-23, 25). Probably, the theme derives from the Near East, where it is first seen on a Syrian cylinder seals of the 18th-17th centuries BC (figure 31). How realistic are these pictures? This ostentatious feat may have been performed with the hunting chariot in prepared hunts, in which the game was driven by beaters over selected terrain, and where comparatively little risk was involved. Much later, the same feat was performed by Etruscan and Roman racing drivers (see Crouwel, 2012: 64-69). It seems, however, extremely unlikely that a head of state would have attempted to control his team and use his weapons at the same time under battle conditions. More than likely, a separate driver, who could devote his entire attention to the draught team, would have been present if and when the pharaoh went into battle. Ramesses II, for example, is consistently shown alone in his chariot on the temple reliefs commemorating the Battle of Qadesh in Syria, although Egyptian textual accounts of this battle refer to his charioteer and shield-bearer Menna (Schulman, 1963: 88-89). The charioteer may actually be shown in some of the reliefs, standing behind the empty royal chariot (a parasol fixed inside it; see Brock, this volume, for a possible example) and holding the reins (Wreszinski, 1935: pls. 18, 81-82, 176). In fact, in Egypt artisans were not permitted to represent any mortal other than another member of the royal family or a deity in a chariot together with the pharaoh.

According to the textual and pictorial sources, the military forces of the Egyptian New Kingdom and contemporary smaller and larger kingdoms in the Near East comprised both infantry and chariotry (see Spalinger, this volume, for a detailed account on this topic related to the Battle of Qadesh). Mounted troops, playing an active role in battle, are first firmly documented in the 9th century BC (Drews, 2004, 65-69; Littauer & Crouwel, 1979a: 137-139; see also Sacco, this volume). The same sources also shed light on the often complex organisation of the armies, and their chariotry in Egypt (see especially Schulman, 1963; 1964; 1995; Gnirs, 1995; 1996; see also Spalinger, this volume) and the Near East (see especially Kendall, 1975; Beal, 1992; 1995; 2002). It is notable that cuneiform tablets from Nuzi in northeastern Iraq mention chariots of the left and right wings, suggesting that these operated on the army's flanks when in battle (Kendall, 1975: 32-33, 66-68, 130-131).

In warfare, chariots served primarily as an elevated firing platform for an archer, standing beside the driver. Bow-cases and quivers for arrows or javelins attached outside the chariot body provided reserve arms. Horse-drawn chariots combined speed with mobility and firing power, provided the terrain of operation was reasonably level and open (a.o. Archer, 2010; Littauer & Crouwel, 1979a: 90-94; 1996 [= 2002]: 66-74; Raulwing, 2000: 51-58; Schulman, 1979/1980). Small shields of varying shape, but always with a single handgrip, are seen carried both in the Egyptian and the Near Eastern chariots, to provide protection against enemy missiles (figures 20, 21, 32, 33 & 35). The Egyptian shields in the chariots at Qadesh and some other battles were held up in the hand of the inactive archer but, during the actual fighting, they were transferred to the hand of the charioteer (figures 32 & 33). The latter then, with his other hand, appears merely to have guided the reins, which were tied around the archer's hips, and against which the archer leaned (for charioteers/shieldbearers in Egyptian texts, see Schulman, 1963: 88-89; 1964: 67-68). This explains why Menna is called both driver and shield-bearer to Ramesses II at Qadesh (Schulman 1963: 88-9). Note that a tomb painting from Memphis (tomb 2733) shows such an archer, alone in his chariot, at target practice, with assistants picking up arrows lying on the ground (figure 34; Hofmann 2004: 152).

Practical experiments by Jean Spruytte with a full-scale reconstruction of an Egyptian chariot (based on those found in the tomb of Tutankhamun) demonstrated that this vehicle, with its rear axle and wide wheel track, was indeed eminently manoeuvrable and so stable that tight corners could be turned (Spruytte, 1983; 1999). This was subsequently confirmed by trials that were conducted in 2002 in south-eastern Turkey with reconstructions of Neo-Assyrian military chariots (made under the supervision of Robert Hurford, and based on Littauer & Crouwel, 1979: 101-134). These vehicles, depicted in detail on large-scale reliefs of the 9th century BC, were basically similar to the ones that were used earlier in the Near East and Egypt. The trials were filmed for a British television documentary called 'The Assyrian War Chariot' (2003), in which this author participated as a consultant. They also demonstrated that an archer standing beside the driver could quickly fire arrows in all directions, including to the rear, even when the chariot was moving at considerable speed (up to 28 km per hour) in stony but reasonably flat terrain (Crouwel, 2012: 53). Similar results were obtained in 2012, with reconstructions of Egyptian New Kingdom chariots (again made under the supervision of Robert Hurford, and based on Littauer & Crouwel, 1985). The trials took place (in flat and open terrain) near Cairo and were recorded

Figure 33. Detail of a stone relief from the temple of Ramesses III. Medinet Habu. Drawing by J. Morel. From: Littauer & Crouwel (1979a: fig. 44).

Figure 34. Detail of wall painting from tomb 2733. Memphis. From: Hofmann (2004: fig. 11).

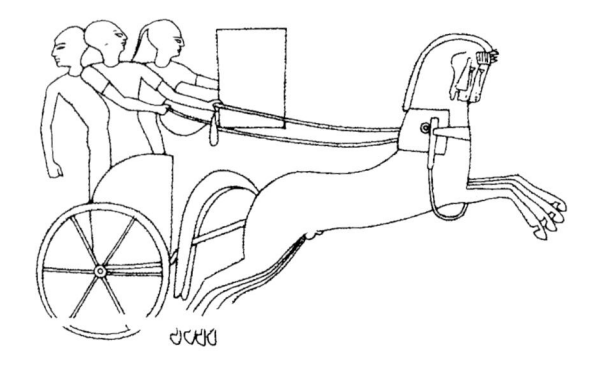

Figure 35. Detail of a stone relief of the temple of Ramesses II. Abydos. Drawing by J. Morel. From: Littauer & Crouwel (1979a: fig. 45).

for another TV documentary called 'Building Pharaoh's Chariot' (2013).[8]

These experiments suggested that Egyptian and Assyrian chariots probably did not, as had previously been thought, run along a well-prepared front line of enemy infantry to 'soften it up' with volleys of arrows (Littauer & Crouwel, 1979a: 91-94, 128-133; Spruytte, 1989). Rather, as was forcibly argued by Mike Loades who drove the chariots in both films, rows of chariots would have attacked the enemy line frontally, at full speed and at different places simultaneously, firing, before making a sharp turn and getting away quickly enough so as not to offer easy targets to enemy archers. This manoeuvre would be repeated again and again, until the enemy was sufficiently weakened for the infantry to come up and, together with chariots, finish him off.

There are, however, problems with such battle tactics. Would there not be chaos and loss of many precious chariots, draught teams and crews on the battlefield if both armies launched their chariotry at the same time, and at each other?

The often sizeable numbers of chariots of the armies in Egypt and the Near East mentioned in contemporary texts were not only limited in their field of operation to large stretches of level and open ground but, despite the use of protective scale armour for the crew and the harness team, they remained extremely vulnerable (for the limitations of chariotry, see also Crouwel 2011: 53-54; Littauer & Crouwel, 1996b [= 2002]: 66-74, in reply to Drews, 1988, 104-134, 1993: 10-14; Powell, 1963:165-167; Schulman, 1979:110-146). This stands in marked contrast to the modern armoured tank, to which ancient chariots have so often, fallaciously, been compared (a.o., recently, by De Backer, 2009).

Unfortunately, the Egyptian textual and pictorial documentation, which includes the scenes decorating the chariot body from the tomb of Thutmose IV (figures 20 & 21; see Calvert, this volume) and many large-scale reliefs on temple walls (see especially Harvey, 1988: 306-334; Heinz, 2001; Schulman, 1979/1980; Shaw 1996; Spalinger, 2005) shed only limited light on the exact handling of chariots in battle. Even in the case of the relatively well-documented Battle of Qadesh between the forces of Ramesses II and the Hittite king Muwatalli(s) II and his allies, it is often difficult to separate fact from fiction. Both the Egyptian pictorial and textual record are chiefly concerned with extolling the role played by the pharaoh (see especially the various contributions by Goedicke 1985; Mayer & Opificius, 1994; Spalinger, 2003; 2005: 209-234; more bibliography in Rauwling, 2000: 137. For images, see Wreszinski, 1935: pls. 16-25, 63-4, 81-9, 69-10, 92-106, 169-178). What is clear is that at Qadesh, chariots played a major part both in a surprise flank attack on an Egyptian division of infantry and chariotry on the march, and in a later counterattack by a freshly arrived force of the Egyptian army. Reliefs showing the battle seem to offer a rare glimpse of chariots attacking chariots (figure 32). The Egyptian ones carry the standard crew of archer and driver/shield-bearer. The chariots of the Hittites and their allies have an unusual three-man complement of driver, shield-bearer and, at the rear, spearman (quivers are absent), and must have therefore served essentially as a means of transport for military men who fought on the ground (figures 32 & 35). This would have given them a disadvantage in a confrontation with chariot-borne archers.[9]

To return to the six chariots from the tomb of Tutankhamun, it is uncertain whether any of them was actually used in battle by this pharaoh. Another use of these two-men vehicles – in racing – is very unlikely. There is no real evidence for this activity in ancient Egypt, or in the Near East (*cf.* Sandor 2004b: 646).

BIBLIOGRAPHICAL NOTE

Many of the books and papers that have been published since 1985 and are relevant to the subject of this paper, have been assembled by Peter Raulwing (1993; 2000: 132; In Littauer & Crouwel, 2002: xi-xii; also Raulwing & Clutton-Brock, 2009). Apart from those mentioned in my text, I have profited from reading the following publications: Feldman & Sauvage (2010); Hansen (1994); Hoffmeier (1995); Partridge (2002); Wilde (2003: 109-130).

ACKNOWLEDGEMENTS

I am most grateful to André J. Veldmeijer and Salima Ikram for their invitation to deliver the keynote lecture at the conference and for discussing chariot matters with me. Many thanks are also due to Robert Hurford for sharing his expertise in building Egyptian and other ancient chariots, to Oliver Graham and Willem van Haarlem for help with the bibliography, to Gillian Skyte-Bradshaw for correcting my English, and to Anneke Dekker, Jacob Eerbeek and Geralda Jurriaans-Helle for assistance with the preparation of text and illustrations.

NOTES

1. The model recalls the four bronze wheels, similarly four-spoked, belonging to a model of a trolley from the Burnt Palace at Açemhöyük in central Anatolia and usually dated to the first half of the 18th century BC (Littauer & Crouwel, 1986 [= 2002]: 289-295).
2. Wagons with spoked wheels, drawn by oxen and horses, are depicted in the Hittite army camp near Qadesh (Beal, 1992: 134; Hofmann, 1989: 291-292; Spalinger, 2003: fig. 13; Wreszinski, 1935: pl. 22).
3. Another plan, by Lindsey and Walter Hall, showing the position of the objects in the Antechamber, appears on a much reduced scale in Hoving (1978/1979: p. 17 of the plates).
4. Peter Raulwing (2000: 175) refers to N.I.A. Lokma, "Treatment and conservation of warped wood applied on one of the chariots of king Tutankhamun" (unpublished paper – in Arabic – for the fulfilment of the degree of Diploma (Master) in Conservation at the Faculty of Archaeology, Cairo University). Unfortunately, I have not seen this paper.
5. The Tutankhamun Archive also contains an unpublished seven-page manuscript on the chariots by Jane Waley.
6. According to Sandor (2004a: 161-163; 2004b: 639-641), the pole socket acted as a shock absorber. I am not convinced, nor is the carriage maker Robert Hurford (Personal Communication 2012).
7. Interestingly, another example of such a technology transfer took place at about the same time, involving Aegean fresco painters who became active in the Near East and at Tell el-Dab'a (Avaris) in the Nile delta (Brysbaert, 2008: 178, etc.).
8. I thank Martin O'Collins for sending me the film on DVD.
9. In contrast, in battle reliefs of Seti I Hittite chariots, like the Egyptian ones, carry a two-men complement, one of them armed with bow-and-arrow, the other with a shield (see Beal, 1992: 148-149; Epigraphic Survey, 1986: pls. 33-35).

CITED LITERATURE

Archer, R. 2010. Developments in Near Eastern Chariotry and Chariot Warfare in the Early First Millennium BCE and Their Contribution to the Rise of Cavalry. In: Fagan, G.G. & M. Trundle. Eds. New Perspectives on Ancient Warfare. - Leiden/Boston, Brill: 57-79.

Arnold, D. & J. Settgast. 1965. Erstere Vorbericht über die vom Deutschen Archäologischen Institut Kairo im Asasif unternommenen Arbeiten. - Mitteilungen des Deutschen Archäologischen Instituts Kairo 20: 47-61.

Beal, R.H. 1992. The Organization of the Hittite Army. Texte der Hethiter 20. - Heidelberg, Winter.

Beal, R.H. 1995. Hittite Military Organization. In: Sasson, J.M., J. Baines, G. Beckman & K.S. Rubinson. Eds. Civilizations of the Ancient Near East I. - New York, Simon & Schuster MacMillan: 545-54.

Beal, R.H. 2002. I reparti le armi dell'esrcito ittita. In: Guidotti, M.C. & F. Pecchioli. Eds. Ramesse II contro gli Ittiti per la conquista della Sira (catalogue exhibition, Florence 6 June-8 December 2002). - Livorno, Sillabe: 93-108.

Bietak, M. & I. Forstner-Müller. 2009. Der Hyksos-Palast bei Tell el-Dab'a. Zweite und dritte

Grabungskampagne (Frühling 2008 und Frühling 2009). – Ägypten und Levante 19: 91-119.

Boessneck, J. 1976. Tell ed-Dab'a III. Die Tierknochenfunde 1966-1969. – Wien, Verlag der Österreichischen Akademie der Wissenschaften.

Brisbaert, A. 2008. The Power of Technology in the Bronze Age Eastern Mediterranean. Monographs in Mediterranean Archaeology 12. – London & Oakville, Equinox Publishing Ltd.

Carter, H. & A.C. Mace. 1923. The Tomb of Tut.ankh.amen I. – London, Cassel & Co.

Carter, H. 1927. The Tomb of Tut.ankh.amen II. – London, Cassel & Co.

Carter, H. 1933. The Tomb of Tut.ankh.amen III. – London, Cassel & Co.

Carter, H. & P.E. Newberry. 1904. Tomb of Thoutmôsis IV. Catalogue général des antiquités égyptiennes du Musée du Caire v. 15, Nos. 46001-46529. – Cairo, Institut Français d'Archéologie Orientale.

Crouwel, J.H. 2004. Der Alte Orient und seine Rolle in der Entwicklung von Fahrzeugen. In: Fansa, M. & S. Burmeister. Eds. Rad und Wagen. Der Ursprung einer Innovation. Wagen im Vorderen Orient und Europa. – Mainz, Philipp von Zabern: 69-86.

Crouwel, J.H. 2012. Chariots and Other Wheeled Vehicles in Italy Before the Roman Empire. – Oxford, Oxbow Books.

De Backer, F. 2009. Evolution of War Chariot Tactics in the Ancient Near East. – Ugarit Forschungen 41: 29-41.

Decker, W. 1984. Bemerkungen zur Konstruktion des ägyptischen Rades in der 18. Dynastie. In: Altenmüller. H. & D. Wildung. Eds. Festschrift Wolfgang Helck zu seinen 70. Geburtstag. Studien zur altägyptischen Kultur 11. – Hamburg, Helmut Buske Verlag: 475-88.

Decker, W. 1986a [1965]. Der Wagen im alten Ägypten. In: Treue, W. Ed. Achse, Rad und Wagen. Fünftausend Jahre Kultur- und Technikgeschichte. – Göttingen, Vandenhoeck and Ruprecht: 35-59, 362-368.

Decker, W. 1986b. Wagen. In: Helck, W. & W. Westendorf. Eds. Lexikon der Ägyptologie. Band VI. – Wiesbaden, Harrasowitz: 1130-1135.

Decker, W. 1994. Pferd und Wagen im alten Ägypten. In: Hänsel, B. & S. Zimmer. Eds. Die Indo-Germanen und das Pferd. Bernard Schlerath zum 70. Geburtstag gewidmet. – Budapest, Archaeolingua Alvapítvány: 259-270.

Decker, W. & M. Herb. 1994. Bildatlas zum Sport im alten Ägypten. Corpus des bildlichen Quellen zu Leibes zu Leibesübungen, Spiel, Jagd, Tanz und verwandten Themen. – Leiden, Brill.

Del Francia, P.R. 2002a. La raccolta di armi del Museo Egizio di Firenze e la sua storia. In: Guidotti, M.C. Ed. Il carro e le armi del Museo Egizio di Firenze. MAAT- Materiali del Museo Egizio di Firenze 2. – Firenze, Soprintendenza per I Beni Archeologici della Toscana:16-37.

Del Francia, P.R. 2002b. Carro. In: Guidotti, M.C. & F. Pecchioli. Eds. Ramesse II contro gli Ittiti per la conquista della Siria (catalogue exhibition, Florence 6 June - 8 December 2002). – Livorno, Sillabe: 54-56.

Dittmann, K.H. 1941. Der Segelwagen von Medinet Madi. – Mitteilungen des Deutschen Archäologischen Institituts Cairo 10: 60-78.

Drenkhahn, R. 1976. Die Handwerker und ihre Tätigkeiten im alter Ägypten. – Wiesbaden, Harrasowitz.

Drews, R. 1988. The Coming of the Greeks. Indo-European Conquest in the Aegean and the Near East. – Princeton, University Press.

Drews, R. 1993. The End of the Bronze Age. Changes in Warfare and the Catastrophe ca. 1200 BC. – Princeton, Princeton Unversity Press.

Drews, R. 2004. Early Riders. The Beginnings of Mounted Warfare in Asia and Europe. – New York, Routledge.

El-Khouli, A.A.R.H. , R. Holthoer, C.A. Hope, O.E. Kaper & J. Baines. 1994. Stone Vessels, Pottery and Sealings from Tut'ankhamun's Tomb. – Oxford, Griffith Insitute.

Feldman, M.H. & C. Sauvage 2010. Objects of Prestige? Chariots in the Late Bronze Age Eastern Mediterranean and Near East. – Ägypten und Levante 20: 67-181.

Gale, R., P. Gasson & N. Heprer. 2000. Wood (Botany). In: Nicholson, P.T. & I. Shaw. Eds. Ancient Egyptian Materials and Technology. – Cambridge, Cambridge University Press: 334-352.

Goedicke, H. Ed. 1985. Perspectives on the Battle of Qadesh. – Baltimore, Halso.

Gnirs, A.M. 1996. Militär und Gesellschaft. Ein Beitrag zur Sozialgeschichte des Neuen Reiches. Studien zur Archäologie und Geschichte Altägyptens 17. – Heidelberg, Heidelberger Orientverlag.

Gnirs, A.M. 2001. Military: An Overview. In: Redford, D.B. Ed. The Oxford Encyclopedia of Ancient Egypt. – Oxford, Oxford University Press: 400-406.

Hansen, K. 1994. The Chariot in Egypt's Age of Chivalry. – KMT 5, 1: 50-61, 83.

Harvey, S. 1998. The Cults of King Ahmose at Abydos. – Philadelphia, University of Pennsylvania (Unpublished Ph.D dissertation).

Heinz, S.C. 2001. Die Feldzugdarstellungen des Neuen Reiches. Ein Bildanalyse. – Vienna, Verlag der Österreichischen Akademie der Wissenschaften.

Herold, A. 1999. Streitwagentechnologie in der Ramses-Stadt. Bronze an Pferd und Wagen. Wagen. Die Grabungen des Pelizaeus-Museums Hildesheim in Qantir-Piramesse. Band 2. – Mainz, Philipp von Zabern.

Herold, A. 2004. Funde und Funktionen. Streitwagentechnologie im alten Ägypten. In: Fansa, M. & S. Burmeister. Eds. Rad und Wagen. Der Ursprung einer Innovation. Wagen im Vorderen Asien und Europa. – Mainz, Philipp von Zabern: 123-142.

Herold, A. 2006a. Streitwagentechnologie in der Ramses-Stadt. Knäufe, Knöpfe und Scheiben aus Stein. Die Grabungen des Pelizaeus-Museums Hildesheim in Qantir-Piramesse Band 3. – Mainz, Philipp von Zabern.

Herold, A. 2006b. Auf Biegen und Brechen. Zum Nauchbau eines altägyptischen Streitwagens. Achse, Rad und Wagen. – Beiträge zur Geschichte der Landfahrzeuge 14: 4-19.

Hofmann, U. 1989. Fuhrwesen und Pferdehaltung im alten Ägypten. – Bon, University of Bonn (Unpublished Ph.D dissertation).

Hofmann, U. 2004. Kulturgeschichte des Fahrens im Ägypten des Neuen Reiches. In: Fansa, M. and S. Burmeister. Eds. Rad und Wagen. Der Ursprung einer Innovation. Wagen im Vorderen Asien und Europa. – Mainz, Philipp von Zabern: 143-156.

Hoffmeier, J. 2001. Military: Material. In: Redford, D.B. Ed. The Oxford Encyclopedia of Ancient Egypt. – Oxford, Oxford University Press: 406-412

Hoving, T. 1978/1979. Tutankhamun. The Untold Story. – New York, Simon and Schuster.

James, T.G.H. 2000. Tutankhamun. The Eternal Splendour of the Boy Pharaoh. – London/New York, Tauris Parke.

Kendall, T. 1978. Warfare and Military Matters in the Nuzi Tablets. – Ann Arbor, Brandeis University (Unpublished Ph.D dissertation).

Killen, G. 2000. Wood (Technology). In: Nicholson, P.T & I. Shaw. Eds. Ancient Egyptian Materials and Technology. – Cambridge, Cambridge University Press: 353-371.

Littauer, M.A. & J.H. Crouwel. 1979a. Wheeled Vehicles and Ridden Animals in the Ancient Near East. – Leiden/Köln, Brill.

Littauer, M.A. & J.H. Crouwel 1979b. An Egyptian Wheel in Brooklyn. – Journal of Egyptian Archaeology 65: 107-120.

Littauer, M.A. & J.H. Crouwel. 1983. Chariots in Late Bronze Age Greece. – Antiquity 57: 187-192.

Littauer, M.A. & J.H. Crouwel. 1985. Chariots and Related Equipment from the Tomb of Tutankhamun. – Oxford, Griffith Institute.

Littauer, M.A. & J.H. Crouwel. 1986. The Earliest Three-Dimensional Evidence for Spoked Wheels. – American Journal of Archaeology 90: 395-398.

Littauer, M.A. & J.H. Crouwel. 1996a. The Origin of the True Chariot. – Antiquity 70: 934-939.

Littauer, M.A. & J.H. Crouwel. 1996b. Robert Drews and the Role of Chariotry in Bronze Age Greece. – Oxford Journal of Archaeology 15: 297-305.

Littauer, M.A. & J.H. Crouwel (Edited by P. Raulwing). 2002. Selected Writings on Chariots and Other Early Vehicles, Riding and Harness. – Leiden, Brill.

Littauer, M.H., J.H. Crouwel & H. Hauptmann. 1991. Ein spätbronzezeitliches Speichenrad vom Lidar Höyük in der Südost-Türkei. – Archäologischer Anzeiger: 349-358.

Malek, J. 1989. An Early Eighteenth Dynasty Monument of Sipar from Saqqara. – Journal of Egyptian Archaeology 75: 61-78.

Malek, J. & J. Moffet. 2001. Tutankhamun On-Line. – Egyptian Archaeology 18: 11.

Mayer, M. & R. Opificus-Münster. 1994. Die Schlacht bei Qadeş. Der Versuch einer neuen Rekonstruktion. – Ugarit-Forschungen 26: 321-68.

McLeod, W. 1970. Composite Bows from the Tomb of Tut'ankhamun. – Oxford, Griffith Institute.

Moorey, P.R.S. 1986. The Emergence of the Light, Horse-Drawn Chariot in the Near East c. 2000-1500 BC. – World Archeology 18: 196-215.

Moorey, P.R.S. 1989. The Hurrians, the Mitanni and Technological Innovation. In: De Meyer, L. & E. Haerinck. Eds. Archaeologia Iranica et Orientalis. Miscellanea in Honorem Louis Vanden Berghe I. – Leuven, Peeters: 273-286.

Moorey, P.R.S. 2001. The Mobility of Artisans and Opportunities for Technology Transfer between Western Asia and Egypt in the Late Bronze Age. In: Shortland, A.J. Ed. The Social Context of Technological; Change. Egypt and the Near Easr, 1650-1550 BC. – Oxford, Oxbow Books: 1-14.

Murray, H. 1963. Handlist of Howard Carter's List of Objects from Tut'ankhamun's Tomb. – Oxford, Griffith Institute.

Partridge, R.B. 1996. Transport in Ancient Egypt. – London, Rubicon Press.

Partridge, R.B. 2002. Fighting Pharaohs. Weapons and Warfare in Ancient Egypt. – Manchester, Peartree.

Porter, B. & R. Moss. 1962. Topographical Bibliography of Ancient Egyptian Hieroglyphic Texts, Reliefs, and Paintings. Part V. – Oxford, Griffith Institute.

Powell, T.G.E. 1963. Some Implications of Chariotry. In: Foster, J.Ll. & L. Alcock. Eds. Culture and Environment. Essays in Honour of Sir Cyril Fox. – London, Routledge/Kegan Paul: 153-169.

Quibell, J.E. & A.G.K. Hayter. 1927. Teti Pyramid, North Side. Excavations at Saqqara. – Le Caire, Institut Français d'Archéologie Orientale.

Raulwing, P. 1993. Pferd und Wagen im alten Ägypten. Forschungsstand. Beziehungen zu Vorderasien, interdisziplinäre und methodenkritische Aspekte. – Göttinger Miszellen 136: 71-83.

Raulwing, P. 2000. Horses, Chariots and Indo-Europeans. Foundations and Methods of Chariotry Research from the Viewpoint of Comparative Indo-European Linguistics. – Budapest, Archaeolingua Alapítvány.

Raulwing, P. & J. Clutton-Brock. 2009. The Buhen Horse: Fifty Years after its Discovery (1958-2008). – Journal of Egyptian History 2: 1-106.

Redford, D.B. 1997. In: Oren, E.D. Ed. The Hyksos: New Historical and Archaeological Perspectives. – Philadelphia, The University Museum: 1-44.

Epigraphic Survey. 1986. Reliefs and Inscriptions at Karnak. Volume IV. The Battle Reliefs of King Seti I. – Chicago, Oriental Institute of the University of Chicago Press.

Rommelaere, C. 1991. Les chevaux du Nouvel Empire égyptien. Origines, races, harnachement. Connaissance de l'Égypte ancienne 3. – Bruxelles, Connaissance de l'Égypte ancienne.

Rovetta, A. 2002. Cocchi reali e cocchi virtuali. In: Guidotti, M.C. Ed. I carro e le armi del Museo Egizio di Firenze. MAAT - Materiali del Museo Egizio di Firenze 2. – Firenze, Soprintendenza per I Beni Archaeologici della Toscana: 10-15.

Rovetta, A., I. Nasry & A. Helmi. 2000. The Chariots of the Egyptian Pharaoh Tut Ankh Amun in 1337 BC: Kinematics and Dynamics. – Mechanism and Machine Theory 35: 1013-1031.

Sandor, B.I. 2004a. The Rise and Decline of the Tutankhamun-Class Chariot. – Oxford Journal of Archaeology 23: 153-175.

Sandor, B.I. 2004b. Tutankhamun' Chariots: Secret Treasures of Engineering Mechanics. – Fatigue and Friction of Engineering Materials and Structures 27: 637-646.

Schulman, A.R. 1963. The Egyptian Chariotry: A Re-Examination. – Journal of the American Research Center in Cairo 2: 75-98.

Schulman, A.R. 1964. Military Rank, Title and Organization in the Egyptian New Kingdom. – Berlin, Hessling.

Schulman, A.R.1979/1980. Chariots, Chariotry and the Hyksos. – Journal of the Society for the Study of Egyptian Antiquities 10: 105-153.

Schulman, A.R. 1995. Military Organization in Pharaonic Egypt. In: Redford, D.B. Ed. The Oxford Encyclopedia of Ancient Egypt. – Oxford, Oxford University Press: 289-301.

Senk, H. 1956/1957. Zur Darstellung der Sturmleiter in der Belagerungszene des Kaemhesit. –

Annales du Service des Antiquités de l'Égypte 54: 207-211.

Shaw, I. 2001. Egyptians, Hyksos and Military Technology: Causes, Effects or Catalysts? In: Shortland, A.J. Ed. The Social Context of Technological Change. Egypt and the Near East, 1650-1550 BC. – Oxford, Oxbow Books: 59-71.

Spalinger, A.J. 2003. The Battle of Qadesh: The Chariot Frieze at Abydos. – Ägypten und Levante 13: 163-199.

Spalinger, A.J. 2005. War in Ancient Egypt. The New Kingdom. – Oxford, Blackwell.

Spruytte, J. 1983. Early Harness Systems. – London, Allen.

Spruytte, J. 1989. Le char antique du Musée archéologique de Florence. – Travaux du LAPMO: 185-190.

Spruytte, J. 1993. Le trige de guerre assyrien au IXe siècle avant J.-C. – Travaux du LAPMO. Préhistoire anthropologie méditerranéenne 2: 192-200.

Spruytte, J. 1995. Technologie d'une roué du XVe siècle avant J.-C. (Char A 5 de Toetankhamon, no. 332 de l'inventaire de H. Carter). In: Chenorkian, R. Ed. L'homme méditerranéen. Mélanges offerts à Gabriel Camps. – Aix-en-Provence, Université de Provence: 239-247.

Spruytte, J. 1999. L'attelage égyptien sous la XVIIIe dynastie. Étude technique et technologique. – Kyphi 2: 77-87.

Stevenson Smith, W. 1965. Interconnections in the Ancient Near East. A Study of the Relationships between the Arts of Egypt, the Aegean, and Western Asia. – New Haven/London, Yale University Press.

Svarth, D. 1986. Aegyptiske stridvogne - konsturktion - materialer - metode. – Copenhagen, Idons Forlag.

Van Driel-Murray, C. 2000. Leatherwork and Skin Products. In: Nicholson, P.T. & I. Shaw Eds. Ancient Egyptian Materials and Technology. – Cambridge, Cambrige University Press: 299-319.

Von Bissing, F.W. 1900. Ein thebanischer Grabfund. – Berlin, Duncker.

Von den Driesch, A. & J. Peters. 2001. Frühe Pferde- und Maultierskelette aus Avaris (Tell el-Dab'a), östliches Nildelta. – Ägypten und Levante 11: 301-311.

Western, A.C. 1974. A Wheel Hub from the Tomb of Amenophis III. – Journal of Egyptian Archaeology 59: 91-94.

Wilde, H. 2003. Technologische Innovationen im Zweiten Jahrtausend v. Christus. Zur Verwendung und Verbreitung neuer Werkstoffe im ostmediterranen Bereich. – Wiesbaden, Harrassowitz.

Wreszinski, W. 1935. Atlas zur altägyptischen Kulturgeschichte II. – Leipzig, Hinrich.

Yadin, Y. 1963. The Art of Warfare in Biblical Lands in the Light of Archaeological Discoveries. – New York, McGraw-Hill.

THE INTRODUCTION OF THE LIGHT, HORSE-DRAWN CHARIOT AND THE ROLE OF ARCHERY IN THE NEAR EAST AT THE TRANSITION FROM THE MIDDLE TO THE LATE BRONZE AGES: IS THERE A CONNECTION?

Hermann Genz

INTRODUCTION

The origins of the bow can be traced back to the Epipalaeolithic (10th-9th millennia BC; Clark *et al.*, 1974: 324-326; Miller *et al.*, 1986: 180). Throughout the Neolithic (8th-5th millennia BC), the bow seems to have been one of the preferred weapons in the Levant (Gopher, 1994; Korfmann, 1972), Anatolia (Balkan-Atlı *et al.*, 2001) and Egypt (Debono & Mortensen, 1990: 44; Eiwanger, 1988: 35-36; 1992: 44-45), as attested by the discovery of numerous flint arrowheads. It seems that in the Near East during the Neolithic period the bow was mainly used for hunting. In contrast, from the Neolithic Period in Europe there is ample evidence for the use of bows and arrows in warfare, with arrowheads found embedded in bodies and concentrations of arrowheads around fortifications (Christensen, 2004). No such evidence has yet been found in the Neolithic of the Near East, and even the military nature of constructions such as the alleged fortifications of Neolithic Jericho have been questioned (Bar-Yosef, 1986). It is only after the Neolithic Period that evidence for the use of long-range weapons for warfare becomes available, and differences in the use of the bow become apparent in various regions of the ancient Near East (figure 1).

EGYPT

The use of the bow in Egypt from the Predynastic Period (5000-3000 BC) to the Middle Kingdom (2066-1650 BC) is amply attested in the iconographic record as well as by actual finds. Numerous arrowheads, mainly made of flint, but also of wood, ivory or fish bones, are known from the Predynastic Period onwards (Clark *et al.*, 1974: 326-356; Wolf, 1926: 16-18). Metal arrowheads only gradually appear from the 11th Dynasty (2160-1994 BC) onwards (Huret, 1990: 58; Petrie, 1917: 34). Bows from the Old (2663-2195 BC) and Middle Kingdom are attested, and are generally simple wooden self-bows.

When it comes to the use of bows, we mainly have to rely on picotrial evidence. The so-called Hunters' Palette attests to the use of the bow in hunting activities during the Predynastic Period (Mellink & Filip, 1974: Abb. 211). Further evidence for the use of the bow in hunting activities is provided by depictions from the Old Kingdom, for instance in the mortuary temple of Sahure (2464-2452 BC) in Abusir (Borchardt, 1913: Taf. 17). In the Old Kingdom the only person shown wielding a bow at the hunt was the king. This iconography was usurped by the elite at the end of the 6th Dynasty (2355-2195 BC). Evidence for the use of the bow in warfare is more limited. Possible indication for the use of archery in warfare is attested on a relief from Lisht, dating to the 4th (2597-2471 BC) or 5th Dynasty (2471-2355 BC) (Schulz, 2002: 24-25) and in the tomb of Inti in Deshasheh from the 6th Dynasty, which shows enemies pierced by arrows during the siege of a town (*Ibidem*: 29-31).

Evidence for the use of bows in warfare is more abundant during the Middle Kingdom. From the

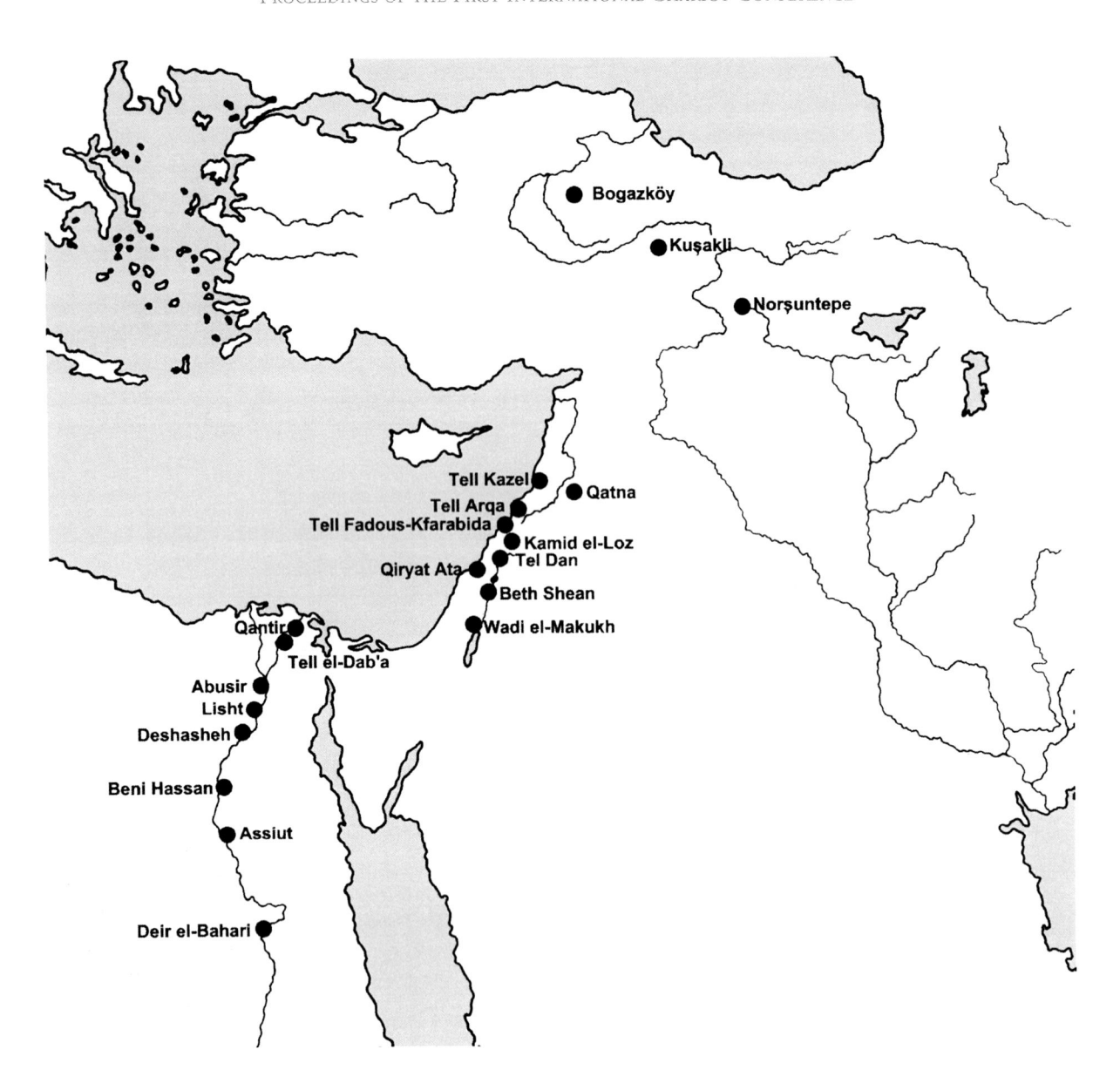

Figure 1. Sites mentioned in the text. Map by H. Genz.

Middle Kingdom we have a mass grave of soldiers from Deir el-Bahari (Winlock, 1945). Several of these soldiers were clearly killed by arrows, which were found embedded in the corpses. The exact date of this grave is rather controversial. While Winlock (1945) favored a date at the beginning of the 11th Dynasty in the time of Mentuhotep, a much later date during the 12th Dynasty (1994-1781 BC) cannot be ruled out (Vogel, 2003). Also in the iconographic record we have clear evidence for the use of archers in combat, for instance in the tombs of Beni Hassan (Shedid, 1994: Abb. 118) as well as in the tomb of Antef in Asasif (Schulz, 2002: 36-40 and Abb. 20). In addition to local archers, the use of Nubian mercenaries is attested by wooden models from Assyut (Wolf, 1926: Taf. 20), as well as by typical Nubian flint arrowheads from Tell el-Dab'a and other sites (Hein, 2001: 209). Generally bows are depicted as the typical weapons of common soldiers in the Middle Kingdom, whereas nobles and royalty only use bows for hunting activities, as for example shown in the tombs from Beni Hassan (Shedid, 1994: Abb. 27 & 96).

The use of the bow for both hunting and warfare continues during the New Kingdom. Several major new developments are noticeable, however. First, in addition to the local types of arrowheads, generally made out of flint (figures 2 & 3), bone, ivory or wood, all of which were produced from the Predynastic Period onward (Clark *et al.*, 1974: 358; McLeod, 1982:

Figure 2 (left). Silex arrowhead from Qantir-Piramesse. Inv. No. 0236.

Figure 3 Chalcedony (right). arrowhead from Qantir-Piramesse.

Photographs by A. Krause. Courtesy Grabung Ramses-Stadt, E.B. Pusch.

13-26; Tillmann, 2007: 64-69), bronze arrowheads of the leaf-shaped variety gained in popularity (Wolf, 1926: 85-86). This type clearly has its origins in the Levant (see below). Such arrowheads are attested in Ramesside levels in Qantir (figures 4 & 5) (Pusch, 2004: 253-258) and in the tomb of Tutankhamun (McLeod, 1982: 19-21). Second, in addition to the self-bow, composite bows now make their appearance (McLeod, 1970; Wolf, 1926: 81). This type of bow, most likely adopted from the Near East during the late Second Intermediate Period (1650-1549 BC; Moorey, 1986: 208; Shaw, 2001: 66-68), seems to have been exclusively used by higher-class warriors, and even the pharaohs, as attested by the presence of such bows in the tomb of Tutankhamun (McLeod, 1970).

Furthermore, there is a major change in the iconography of the pharaoh slaying enemies. Whereas from the Old and Middle Kingdom we have depictions of the pharaoh smiting his enemies with a mace, in the New Kingdom a new motif appears alongside the traditional one: the pharaoh charging into the enemies in his chariot, using a bow (figure 6). This clearly reflects a major social change, as the bow suddenly seems to become a proper weapon for the pharaohs (Shaw, 2001). The growing social prestige of the bow is also apparent in Amenhotep II (1424-1398 BC) boasting of his skills in archery (Schäfer, 1929; 1931).

THE LEVANT

The situation in the Levant is somewhat different. Already in the Late Neolithic there seems to be a marked decline in the use of the bow (Rosen, 1997: 43). In the Chalcolithic (4500-3500 BC) as well as the Early (3500-2000 BC) and Middle Bronze Ages (2000-1550 BC) arrowheads are rarely attested any more (Philip, 1989: 144-146; 2003: 186-187). It is only in the marginal areas in the south (Sinai, the Negev and Southern Jordan) that flint arrowheads, mainly of the transversal type, are still abundant (Rosen, 1997: 43).

That the bow did not totally disappear is attested by a few exceptional finds such as the so-called Tomb of the Warrior, a 4th millennium BC burial from Wadi el-Makukh in the vicinity of Jericho, where archaeologists discovered an actual bow as well as arrows (Schick *et al.*, 1998). Flint arrowheads are occasionally attested during the Early Bronze Age, for instance from Beth Shean (Bankirer, 1999) and Qiryat Ata (Bankirer, 2003). Flint arrowheads were also found in Early Bronze Age levels at Tell Fadous-Kfarabida (Personal Observation) and Tell Arqa (Thalmann, Personal Communication) in Lebanon. However, the preferred long-range weapon during these periods seems to have been the sling (Korfmann, 1972; Paz, 2011: 9-11; Rosenberg,

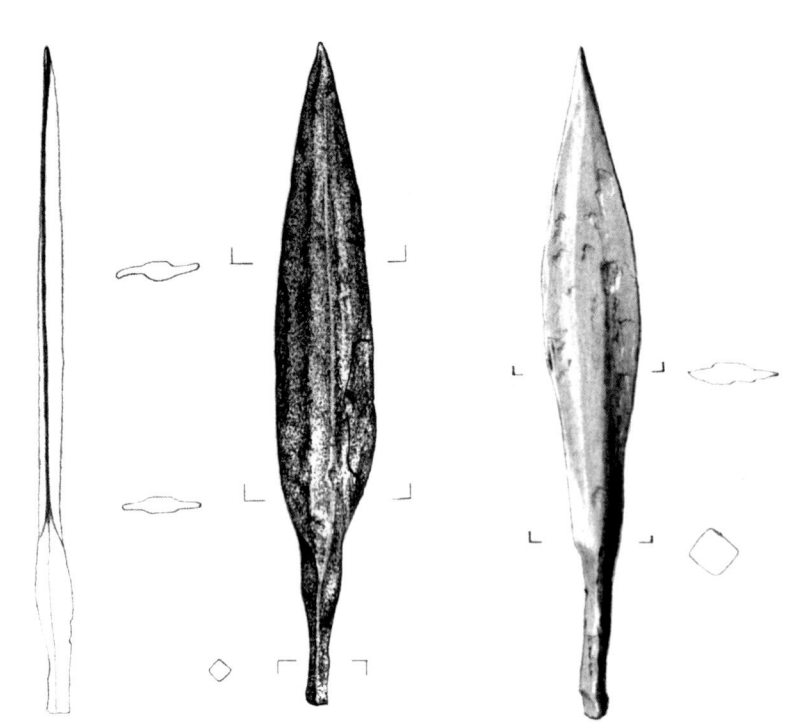

Figure 4 (left). Bronze arrowhead from Qantir-Piramesse. Inv. No. 0409, 01. Stratum B/2a. Drawing by K. Engel.

Figure 5 (right). Bronze arrowhead from Qantir-Piramesse. Inv. No. 2919. Stratum B/2a. Drawing by J. Klang.

Courtesy Grabung Ramses-Stadt, E.B. Pusch.

2009). Hardly any evidence for the use of bows and arrows is attested during the Middle Bronze Age.

One of the most pressing questions is the date of the introduction of the composite bow. The almost complete absence of actual bows and the paucity of the iconographic record preclude definite conclusions for the Levant. There are some representations of possible composite bows on seals from the late 4th millennium in southern Mesopotamia (Moorey, 1986: 209), but the often stylized depictions preclude a definite identification. The first secure attestation is found on a small stone slab from Early Dynastic Mari on the Euphrates (2600-2350 BC), which shows a siege scene involving an archer (Moorey, 1986: 209; Yadin, 1972). Further depictions of composite bows are found in the iconographic record of the Akkadian Period (2350-2150 BC; Moorey, 1986: 209). For the Middle Bronze Age the use of the composite bow as a regular combat weapon is attested in 18th century BC texts from Mari (*Ibidem*: 210).

A marked change is noticeable only at the beginning of the Late Bronze Age (around 1550 BC). At this time, metal arrowheads become extremely common (Genz, 2007: 50; Forthcoming; Philip, 1989: 146). They are usually made out of pure copper, but copper-based alloys are also attested (Philip *et al.*, 2003: 90). Flint arrowheads seem to have disappeared completely. Although no actual bows have survived, composite bows seem to have been widely used (Philip, 2003: 187), as attested in 14th century BC texts from Ugarit on the Syrian coast (Moorey, 1986: 208-209). With this type of bow it was possible to shoot heavier arrows for longer distances and with greater penetration force. This made the composite bow an ideal weapon for warfare, as well as hunting, as seen in two-dimensional images (Caubet, 2002: fig. 6: 4-5). Metal arrowheads become the most frequently attested weapon in the Levant during the Late Bronze Age. The majority of these belong to the leaf-shaped type with a square or rhomboid tang, of which several subtypes are attested (Cross & Milik, 1956: 16-19; figure 7: 1-2). Other types, such as barbed arrowheads, are rarely attested and presumably represent imports from Anatolia (Genz, Forthcoming; figure 7: 3).

The frequent occurrence of arrowheads in various contexts in the Late Bronze Age Levant – not only in tombs, but also in settlement contexts and in hoards – casts some doubts on Philip's (1989: 145) theory that we do not find arrowheads in the Middle Bronze Age because they were deemed to be unsuitable for inclusion in the warrior tombs. Even if this were the case, it clearly demonstrates a major change of attitude towards the bow in the Late Bronze Age. Arrowheads suddenly are the

Figure 6. Ramesses II in his chariot at the Ramesseum in Thebes. Photograph by H. Genz.

most frequently attested type of weapons in elite or even royal burials, such as the royal hypogeum at Qatna (Al-Rawi, 2011: 311-325; figures 8 & 9), the royal tomb at Kamid el-Loz (Miron, 1990: 62-65), tomb 387 at Tell Dan (Ben-Dov, 2002: 124-136) and many others. This fact clearly demonstrates the high social prestige of archery in the Late Bronze Age Levant.

ANATOLIA

The situation is again somewhat different in Anatolia. Despite the lack of actual bows, arrowheads are relatively well-represented in the Early Bronze Age (3rd millennium BC). Various types of flint (Baykal-Seeher, 1996: 57-65; Schmidt, 1996: 65-84) and bone (Obladen-Kauder, 1996: 300; Schmidt, 2002: 20-22) arrowheads are attested. Metal arrowheads occur with surprising frequency (Obladen-Kauder, 1996: 314; Schmidt, 2002: 51-54) and seem to become even more common in the Middle Bronze Age (first half of the 2nd millennium BC) (Boehmer, 1972: 104; Erkanal, 1977: 52), whereas other materials are less frequently attested. However, this may reflect the general lack of detailed studies of lithic inventories from second millennium contexts.

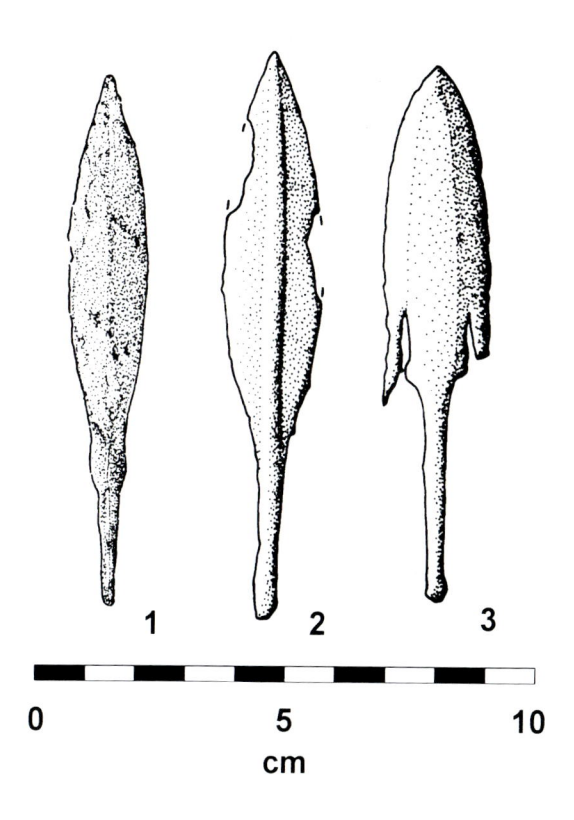

Figure 7. Late Bronze Age arrowheads from Tell Kazel, Syria. Drawings by H. Genz.

It is again during the Late Bronze Age (second half of the 2nd millennium BC) that metal arrowheads become the most frequently attested weapons in Central Anatolia (Siegelova & Tsumoto, 2011: 292). Most common are barbed arrowheads with a long tang (Boehmer, 1972: 104-109; 1979: 22-23; Erkanal, 1977: 53-54; Müller-Karpe, 2001: 227-228 and Abb. 4). This type is also attested in Southeastern Anatolia (Schmidt, 2002: 52-53). Leaf-shaped arrowheads of the Levantine type are also found in Anatolia, for instance at Boğazköy (Boehmer, 1972: Taf. XXVI: 816, 821; Taf. XXVII: 829; 1979: Taf. XIV: 3147A, 3149; Taf. XV: 3179-3180), Kuşaklı (Müller-Karpe, 1999: 65-66 and Abb. 10a-c) and Norşuntepe (Schmidt, 2002: 52 and Taf. 48: 609-617). In addition to the archaeological evidence, bows and arrows are frequently mentioned in Hittite texts, often in connection with chariots (Lorenz & Schrakamp, 2011: 137-139). This clearly shows that bows and arrows were widely used in Hittite Anatolia, both in hunting and warfare.

The high social status of the bow is again demonstrated by the fact that it is regularly depicted as the weapon of the Hittite king (Lorenz & Schrakamp, 2011: 137; figure 10).

DISCUSSION

It is clear that decisive changes in the technology as well as the social role of the bow are attested in all three regions at the beginning of the Late Bronze Age. While bows played an important role for warfare from at least the Old Kingdom in Egypt, decisive changes are noticeable at the beginning of the New Kingdom. On a technological level, these are the introduction of the composite bow and the now frequent use of metal arrowheads in Egypt. While in the iconographic record from the Old and Middle Kingdoms, the pharaoh smiting his enemies is always depicted with a mace, in the New Kingdom an additional image appears: the pharaoh in his chariot using a bow (Shaw, 2001: 60). This innova-

Figure 8. Arrowhead assemblage in the southern part of Chamber 1 in the Royal Tomb at Qatna. Photo Qatna-Project. Courtesy P. Pfälzner.

Figure 9. Arrowheads from the Royal Tomb in Qatna. Nationalmuseum Damaskus. Photo by P. Frankenstein & H. Zwietasch. Courtesy Landesmuseum Württemberg, Stuttgart.

Figure 10. Relief depicting Šuppiluliuma II carrying a bow over his shoulder in Chamber 2 in the Southern Fortress at Boğazköy-Hattuša. Photograph by H. Genz.

tion in royal iconography clearly emphasizes the growing role of the bow as a royal weapon.

The picture is most dramatic in the Levant. While for the Early and Middle Bronze Ages hardly any evidence for the use of bows and arrows is attested in the archaeological record, in the Late Bronze Age arrowheads are among the most frequently encountered weapons. Moreover, arrowheads are now commonly found in royal and elite tombs, for instance in Qatna, Kamid el-Loz and Dan, tomb 387 (Al-Rawi, 2011: 311-325; figure 8-9; Miron, 1990: 62-65; Ben-Dov, 2002: 124-136). This is in marked contrast to the situation in the Middle Bronze Age, where warrior burials only contain daggers, axes and spearheads (Garfinkel, 2001; Philip, 1995). Again this situation suggests a decisive change in the social and practical role of the bow and arrow.

Anatolia has a much longer tradition of metal arrowheads, as these are frequently attested already in the Early and Middle Bronze Ages. Yet again the number of arrowheads increases markedly at the beginning of the Late Bronze Age. Furthermore, just as in Egypt the iconographic record of Hittite Anatolia clearly shows that in the Late Bronze Age the bow became a royal weapon.

It has already been suggested that the sudden rise in the social prestige of archery in warfare can be connected to the development of a new warrior ideology. At the beginning of the Late Bronze Age profound changes in the political, social and economic systems of the Near East are noticeable (Akkermanns & Schwartz, 2003: 327-359; Bunimovitz, 1995). Many of the innovations noticeable in the Late Bronze Age Near East relate to military matters. Certainly one of the most profound changes was the introduction of the light, horse-drawn chariot (Littauer & Crouwel, 1979; Moorey, 1986; Philip, 2003: 188-189). Closely connected to the use of the chariot was the introduction of body armor (Deszö, 2003-2005: 319-323; Philip, 2003: 187; Ventzke, 1986) and the widespread use of the composite bow (Genz, 2007: 49; Philip, 2003: 187). The frequent use of metal arrowheads certainly is a reaction to the introduction of body armor. While the chronology certainly is not yet fine-tuned enough, it seems that these innovations were introduced at roughly the same time in Egypt, the Levant and Central Anatolia.

In popular accounts often the Hyksos are credited with introducing both the chariot and the composite bow to Egypt. However, neither in the Hyksos-controlled parts of Lower Egypt nor in the Southern and Central Levant is there any indication of a strong tradition of archery during the later Middle Bronze Age. Furthermore, in a study of the metalwork from Tell el-Dab'a, Philip (2006: 234-235; see also Shaw, 2001: 69) found clear evidence that the Egyptians deliberately seem to have rejected a number of technological innovations such as the socketed spearhead and the socketed ax, which where commonly used in the Levant, as well as by the Hyksos. The evidence currently at hand rather suggests that the Hyksos and the Egyptians simultaneously adopted the composite bow and the chariot from a third source, most likely from the Near

East (Littauer & Crouwel, 1996; Moorey, 1986: 208; Shaw, 2001: 66-69).

Another interesting point concerns the use of the Hittite chariots. Unfortunately our knowledge of Hittite chariots is extremely limited. Many scholars rely on Egyptian representations of Hittite chariots from the reliefs depicting the Battle of Qadesh. Here the Hittite chariot crews generally consist of three people, but are never depicted using bows (Shaw, 2001: 70). These depictions gave rise to the idea that the Hittites only armed their chariot crews with javelins or even lances, but not with bows. The impossibility of using lances from chariots was demonstrated by Littauer & Crouwel (1983). But even javelins are certainly inferior to composite bows when it comes to range and accuracy. The archaeological evidence clearly shows that bows and arrows were widely used in Hittite warfare. Furthermore, in Hittite texts arrows are frequently mentioned as part of the chariots equipment (Lorenz & Schrakamp, 2011: 139-140). Lastly, the adoption of the bow as a royal weapon by the Hittite kings demonstrates its high social value. It is therefore highly unlikely that the Hittites should put themselves at a disadvantage by rejecting the use of bows from their chariots.

While Hittite arrowheads show distinct typological differences from their Levantine and Egyptian counterparts, the basic technology was the same. Indeed, the study of the equipment of elite warriors shows that basically the same types of weapons and technological features were used in all regions of the Near East throughout the Late Bronze Age. This can be even shown in minor details such as the presence of stunning bolts (Genz, 2007). These blunt arrowheads served, in the opinion of the author, for training purposes of elite archers, and their presence in Egypt, the Levant and Anatolia suggests that in all regions the elite warriors received the same training and used the same weapons. Thus the Hittites seem to have been well aware of the potential of using bows and arrows for their chariot crews.

The changes affecting the equipment and training of elite warriors seem to appear almost simultaneously in all three regions discussed here, emphasizing once more the close connections between different regions of the Ancient Near East and Egypt during the Late Bronze Age.

ACKNOWLEDGEMENTS

I would like to thank all participants of the conference for very stimulating and fruitful discussions. Peter Pfälzner, Edgar Pusch and the Landesmuseum Württemberg (Stuttgart, Germany) provided me with illustrations. My participation in the conference was made possible through a short-term research grant from the Faculty of Arts and Sciences of the American University in Beirut.

CITED LITERATURE

Akkermans, P.M.M.G. & G.M. Schwartz. 2003. The Archaeology of Syria. From Complex Hunter-Gatherers to Early Urban Societies (ca. 16,000–300 BC). – Cambridge, Cambridge University Press.

Al-Rawi, A. 2011. Die Bronzewaffen aus der Königsgruft von Tall Mišrife/Qatna: Räumliche Verteilung und funktionales Spektrum. In: Pfälzner, P. Ed. Qatna Studien 1. Interdisziplinäre Studien zur Königsgruft von Qatna. – Wiesbaden, Harrassowitz: 311-327.

Balkan-Atlı, N., M. Kayacan, M. Özbaşaran & S. Yıldırım. 2001. Variability in the Neolithic Arrowheads of Central Anatolia. Typological, Technological and Chronological Aspects. In: Caneva, I., C. Lemorini, D. Zampetti & P. Biagi. Eds. Beyond Tools. Redefining the PPN Lithic Assemblages of the Levant. Proceedings of the 3rd Workshop on PPN Chipped Lithic Industries, Venice 1998. – Berlin, Ex Oriente Lux: 27-43.

Bankirer, R.Y. 1999. The 'Beth-Shean Point'. A New Type of Tool from the EB I-II at Tel Beth-Shean. – Mitekufat Haeven 29: 129-134.

Bankirer, R.Y. 2003. The Flint Assemblage. In: Golani, A. Ed. Salvage Excavations at the Early Bronze Age Site of Qiryat Ata. – Jerusalem, Israel Antiquities Authority: 171-182.

Bar-Yosef, O. 1986. The Walls of Jericho. An Alternative Interpretation. – Current Anthropology 27: 157-162.

Baykal-Seeher, A. 1996. Die lithischen Kleinfunde. In: Korfmann, M. Ed. Demircihüyük IV: Die Kleinfunde. – Mainz, Philipp von Zabern: 7-206.

Ben-Dov, R. 2002. The Late Bronze Age "Mycenaean" Tomb. In: Biran, A. & R. Ben-Dov. Eds. Dan II. A Chronicle of the Excavations and the Late

Bronze Age "Mycenaean" Tomb. – Jerusalem, Nelson Glueck School of Biblical Archaeology: 33-248.

Boehmer, R.M. 1972. Die Kleinfunde von Boğazköy. Boğazköy-Hattuša VII. – Berlin, Gebrüder Mann.

Boehmer, R.M. 1979. Die Kleinfunde aus der Unterstadt von Boğazköy. Boğazköy-Hattuša X. – Berlin, Gebrüder Mann.

Bunimovitz, S. 1995. On the Edge of Empires. Late Bronze Age (1500-1200 BCE). In: Levy, T.E. Ed. The Archaeology of Society in the Holy Land. – London, Leicester University Press: 320-331.

Caubet, A. 2002. Animals in Syro-Palestinian Art. In: Collins, B.J. Ed. A History of the Animal World in the Ancient Near East. – Leiden/Boston, Brill: 211-234.

Christensen, J. 2004. Warfare in the European Neolithic. – Acta Archaeologica 75: 129-156.

Clark, J.D., J.L. Phillips & P.S. Staley. 1974. Interpretations of Prehistoric Technology from Ancient Egyptian and Other Sources. Part 1. Ancient Egyptian Bows and Arrows and Their Relevance for African Prehistory. – Paléorient 2: 323-388.

Cross, F.M. & J.T. Milik. 1956. A Typological Study of the El Khadr Javelin- and Arrow-Heads. – Annual of the Department of Antiquities of Jordan 3: 15-23.

Debono, F. & B. Mortensen. 1990. El Omari. A Neolithic Settlement and Other Sites in the Vicinity of Wadi Hof, Helwan. – Mainz, Philipp von Zabern.

Deszö, T. 2003-2005. Panzer. In: Streck, M.P. Ed. Reallexikon der Assyriologie und vorderasiatischen Archäologie 10. – Berlin & New York, de Gruyter: 319-323.

Eiwanger, J. 1988. Merimde – Benisalame II. Die Funde der mittleren Merimdekultur. – Mainz, Philipp von Zabern.

Eiwanger, J. 1992. Merimde – Benisalame III. Die Funde der jüngeren Merimdekultur. – Mainz, Philipp von Zabern.

Erkanal, H. 1977. Die Äxte und Beile des 2. Jahrtausends in Zentralanatolien. Prähistorische Bronzefunde IX, 8. – München, C.H. Beck.

Garfinkel, Y. 2001. Warrior Burial Customs in the Levant During the Earlier Second Millennium B.C. In: Wolff, S.R. Ed. Studies in the Archaeology of Israel and Neighboring Lands in Memory of Douglas L. Esse. – Chicago, Oriental Institute: 143-161.

Genz, H. 2007. Stunning Bolts. Late Bronze Age Hunting Weapons in the Ancient Near East. – Levant 39: 47-69.

Genz, H. Forthcoming. Hittite Arrowheads in Tell Kazel? On the Use of Arrowheads as Ethno-Cultural Markers in the Late Bronze Age Levant. – Melanges Leila Badre.

Gopher, A. 1994. Arrowheads of the Neolithic Levant. – Winona Lake, Eisenbrauns.

Hein, I. 2001. Kerma in Auaris. In: Arnst, C.-B., I. Hafemann, & A. Lohwasser. Eds. Begegnungen. Festgabe für Erika Endesfelder, Karl-Heinz Priese, Walter F. Reineke und Steffen Wenig von Schülern und Mitarbeitern. – Leipzig, Verlag Helmar Wodtke und Katharina Stegbauer: 199-212.

Huret, T. 1990. Les pointes de flèches métalliques en Egypte ancienne. Essai de typologie. – Cahier de Recherches de l'Institut de Papyrologie et d'Egyptologie de Lille 12: 57-66.

Korfmann, M. 1972. Schleuder und Bogen in Südwestasien von den frühesten Belegen bis zum Beginn der historischen Stadtstaaten. – Bonn, Rudolf Habelt.

Littauer, M.A. & J.H. Crouwel. 1979. Wheeled Vehicles and Ridden Animals in the Ancient Near East. – Leiden, Brill.

Littauer, M.A. & J.H. Crouwel. 1983. Chariots in Late Bronze Age Greece. – Antiquity 57: 187-192.

Littauer, M.A. & J.H. Crouwel. 1996. The Origin of the True Chariot. – Antiquity 70: 934-939.

Lorenz, J. & I. Schrakamp. 2011. Hittite Military and Warfare. In: Genz, H. & D.P. Mielke. Eds. Insights into Hittite History and Archaeology. – Leuven, Peeters: 125-151.

McLeod, W. 1970. Composite Bows from the Tomb of Tutankhamun. – Oxford, Oxford University Press.

McLeod, W. 1982. Self Bows and Other Archery Tackle. – Oxford, Oxford University Press.

Mellink, M.J. & J. Filip. 1974. Propyläen Kunstgeschichte 13. Frühe Stufen der Kunst. – Berlin, Propyläen Verlag.

Miller, R., E. McEwan & C. Bergmann. 1986. Experimental Approaches to Ancient Near Eastern Archery. – World Archaeology 18: 178-195.

Miron, R. 1990. Kamid el-Loz 10: Das ‚Schatzhaus' im Palastbereich. Die Funde. – Bonn, Rudolf Habelt.

Moorey, P.R.S. 1986. The Emergence of the Light, Horse-Drawn Chariot in the Near East c. 2000-1500 B.C. – World Archaeology 18, 2: 196-215.

Müller-Karpe, A. 1999. Untersuchungen in Kuşaklı 1998. – Mitteilungen der Deutschen Orient-Gesellschaft 131: 57-113.

Müller-Karpe, A. 2001. Untersuchungen in Kuşaklı 2000. – Mitteilungen der Deutschen Orient-Gesellschaft 133: 225-250.

Obladen-Kauder, J. 1996. Die Kleinfunde aus Ton, Knochen und Metall. In: Korfmann, M. Ed. Demircihüyük IV. Die Kleinfunde. – Mainz, Philipp von Zabern: 207-384.

Paz. I. 2011. "Raiders on the Storm". The Violent Destruction of Leviah, an Early Bronze Age Urban Centre in the Southern Levant. – Journal of Conflict Archaeology 6: 3-21.

Petrie, W.M.F. 1917. Tools and Weapons. – London, British School of Archaeology in Egypt.

Philip, G. 1989. Metal Weapons of the Early and Middle Bronze Ages in Syria-Palestine. – Oxford, British Archaeological Reports.

Philip, G. 1995. Warrior Burials in the Ancient Near Eastern Bronze Age. The Evidence from Mesopotamia, Western Iran and Syria-Palestine. In: Green, A.R. & S. Campbell. Eds. The Archaeology of Death in the Ancient Near East. – Oxford, Oxbow Books: 140-154.

Philip, G. 2003. Weapons and Warfare in Ancient Syria-Palestine. In: Richard, S. Ed. Near Eastern Archaeology. A Reader. – Winona Lake, Eisenbrauns: 184-192.

Philip, G. 2006. Tell el-Dab´a XV. Metalwork and Metalworking Evidence of the Late Middle Kingdom and the Second Intermediate Period. – Vienna, Verlag der Österreichischen Akademie der Wissenschaften.

Philip, G., P.W. Clogg & D. Dungworth. 2003. Copper Metallurgy in the Jordan Valley from the Third to the First Millennia BC. Chemical, Metallographic and Lead Isotope Analysis of Artefacts from Pella. – Levant 35: 71-100.

Pusch, E.B. 2004. Piramesse-Qantir. Residenz, Waffenschmiede und Drehscheibe internationaler Beziehungen. In: Petschel, S. & M. Von Falck. Eds. Pharao siegt immer. Krieg und Frieden im Alten Ägypten. – Bönen, Kettler: 240-263.

Rosen, S.A. 1997. Lithics After the Stone Age. A Handbook of Stone Tools from the Levant. – Walnut Creek, Altamira Press.

Rosenberg, D. 2009. Flying Stones. The Slingstones of the Wadi Rabah Culture of the Southern Levant. – Paléorient 35: 99-112.

Schäfer, H. 1929. König Amenophis II als Meisterschütz. – Orientalistische Literaturzeitung 32: 233-244.

Schäfer, H. 1931. Weiteres zum Bogenschießen im alten Ägypten. – Orientalistische Literaturzeitung 34: 89-96.

Schick, T. 1998. The Cave of the Warrior. A Fourth Millennium Burial in the Judean Desert. – Jerusalem, Israel Antiquities Authority.

Schmidt, K. 1996. Norşuntepe. Kleinfunde I. Die lithische Industrie. – Mainz, Philipp von Zabern.

Schmidt, K. 2002. Norşuntepe. Kleinfunde II. Artefakte aus Felsgestein, Knochen und Geweih, Ton, Metall und Glas. – Mainz, Philipp von Zabern.

Schulz, R. 2002. Der Sturm auf die Festung. Gedanken zu einigen Aspekten des Kampfbildes im Alten Ägypten vor dem Neuen Reich. In: Bietak, M. & M. Schwarz. Eds. Krieg und Sieg. Narrative Wanddarstellungen von Altägypten bis ins Mittelalter. – Vienna, Verlag der Österreichischen Akademie der Wissenschaften: 19-42.

Shaw, I. 2001. Egyptians, Hyksos and Military Technology. Causes, Effects or Catalysts? In: Shortland, A.J. Ed. The Social Context of Technological Change. Egypt and the Near East, 1650-1550 BC. – Oxford, Oxbow Books: 59-71.

Shedid, A.G. 1994. Die Felsgräber von Beni Hassan in Mittelägypten. – Mainz, Philipp von Zabern.

Siegelová, J. & H. Tsumoto. 2011. Metals and Metallurgy in Hittite Anatolia. In: Genz, H. & D.P. Mielke. Eds. Insights into Hittite History and Archaeology. – Leuven/Paris/Walpole, Peeters: 275-300.

Tillmann, A. 2007. Neolithikum in der Späten Bronzezeit. Steingeräte des 2. Jahrtausends aus Auaris-Piramesse. Forschungen in der Ramses-Stadt 4. – Hildesheim, Gerstenberg.

Ventzke, W. 1986. Der Schuppenpanzer von Kamid el-Loz. In: Hachmann, R. Ed. Kamid el-Loz 1977-81. – Bonn, Rudolf Habelt: 161-182.

Vogel, C. 2003. Fallen Heroes? Winlock's 'Slain Soldiers' Reconsidered. – Journal of Egyptian Archaeology 89: 239-245.

Winlock, H.E. 1945. The Slain Soldiers of Neb-Hepet-Re Mentu-Hotpe. – New York, Metropolitan Museum of Art.

Wolf, W. 1926. Die Bewaffnung des altägyptischen Heeres. – Leipzig, Hinrichs'sche Buchhandlung.

Yadin, Y. 1972. The Earliest Representation of a Siege Scene and a 'Scythian Bow' from Mari. – Israel Exploration Journal 22: 89-94.

ON URARTIAN CHARIOTS

Bilcan Gökce, Kenan Işık & Hatice Değirmencioğlu

INTRODUCTION

As one of the great Near Eastern civilizations, the Urartians had established a strong state between the 9th and the 7th centuries BC, mainly in the basin of Lake Van, Eastern Anatolia Region (figure 1). Thus, as a result of expansionist policies of the Urartian kings, the boundaries of the state extended to Karasu-Euphrates River in the west, the Northern Armenia Mountains in the north, the Salavan Mountains in Iranian Azerbaijan in the east, and the Eastern Taurus Mountains which join the Zagros Mountains in the south (Salvini, 2006: 24-25).

The Urartians who dominated such a wide and rugged geography, became one of the important and greatest powers of the Near East in the 1st millennium BC. Undoubtedly, they owed this supremacy to their ability to use this mountainous country in the most efficient way, having a strong army and being the outstanding miners of their period (the Iron Age, 1200-400 BC), but the vehicles they had used in their social, religious and military life contributed to this dominance too.

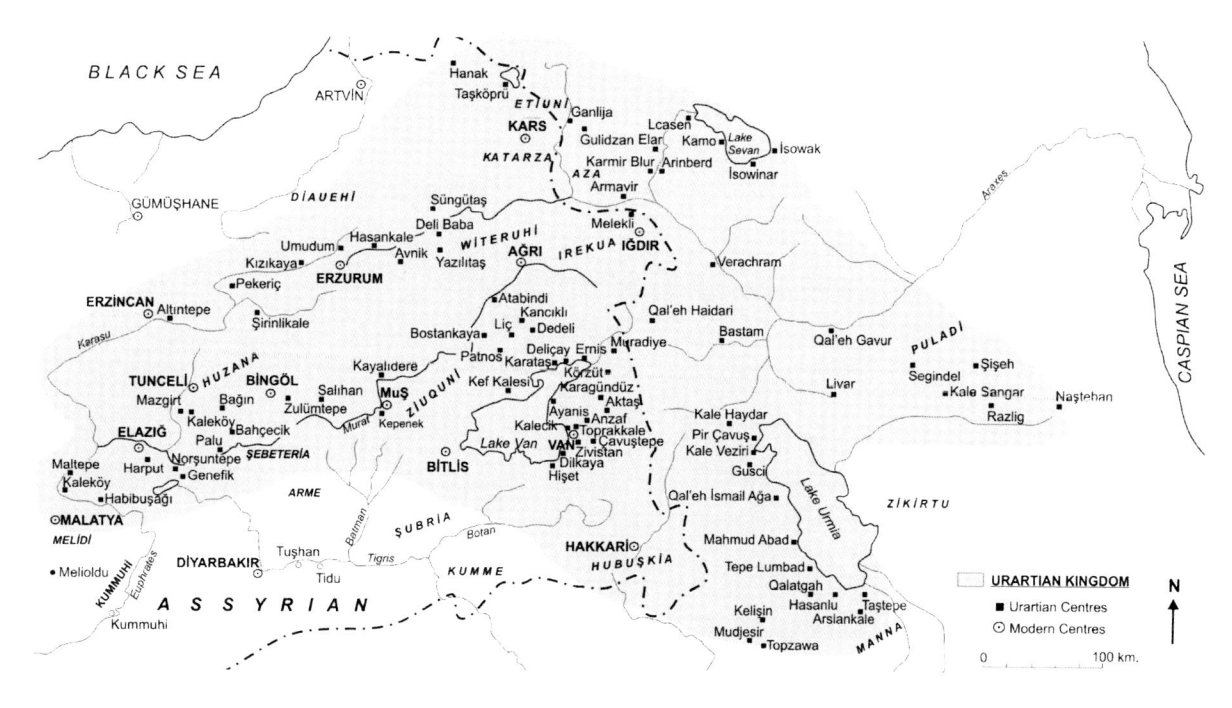

Figure 1. The Urartian Kingdom and its expansion. Map by B. Gökce.

The present study focuses on the importance of chariots in the social and military life of the Urartians, using archaeological finds, visual art and written sources. It also elaborates on the accessories of chariots, the materials out of which the accessories were produced, draft animals and their use. Additionally, comparisons were carried out with Neo-Assyrian and Persian parallels to clarify some subjects.

ARCHAEOLOGICAL FINDINGS

In archaeological excavations of the Urartian Period (859-638 BC), a chariot has been found in one of the chambers in the graves in Erzincan-Altıntepe. Unfortunately, the excavator has not given detailed information nor any drawings or pictures in the publications (Özgüç, 1969a: 6). Additionally, there are some chariot accessories that were found in legitimate as well as illegal excavations, which are being exhibited in various national and international museums as well as in private archaeological collections (Çavuşoğlu, 2011:115-130; Merhav, 1991: 53-78; Özgen, 1984: 91-152; Seidl, 2004: 93-103).

VISUAL DATA

Besides archaeological finds, chariots are depicted in a stone relief (Bilgiç & Öğün, 1964: 87, pl. XIX) and in wall paintings (*e.g.* Hovhannisjan, 1973: figs. 4 & 29) of the Urartian Period. Furthermore, chariots were also depicted together with miscellaneous figures such as animal, human, mythological creatures and motifs on metal works, such as helmets (Seidl, 2004: 68-72, figs. 29-32), chariot discs (Seidl, 2004: 102, fig. 74), quivers (Piotrovskii, 1970: fig. 49; Seidl, 2004: 90, fig. 56), plaques (Seidl, 2004: pl. 17/b; Sevin, 2007: 721-726, figs. 3 & 4), belts (Azarpay,1968: 47-49, fig. 11; Barnett, 1963: 197, fig. 46; Burney, 1966: 78, fig. 10; Çavuşoğlu, 2002: figs. 1-7; 2005: figs. 1-3; Kellner, 1991: pls. 1-9, 12-15, 34-35, 40-41 52-53, 87; Piotrovskii, 1967: 20, fig. 7; Seidl, 2004: pl. B.1) and breastplates (Çavuşoğlu, 2004: 67-77, figs. 1 & 2; Seidl, 2004: 113, fig. 85) (figure 2A-F).

WRITTEN SOURCES

Written sources of the period further provide important information about chariots. In Urartian

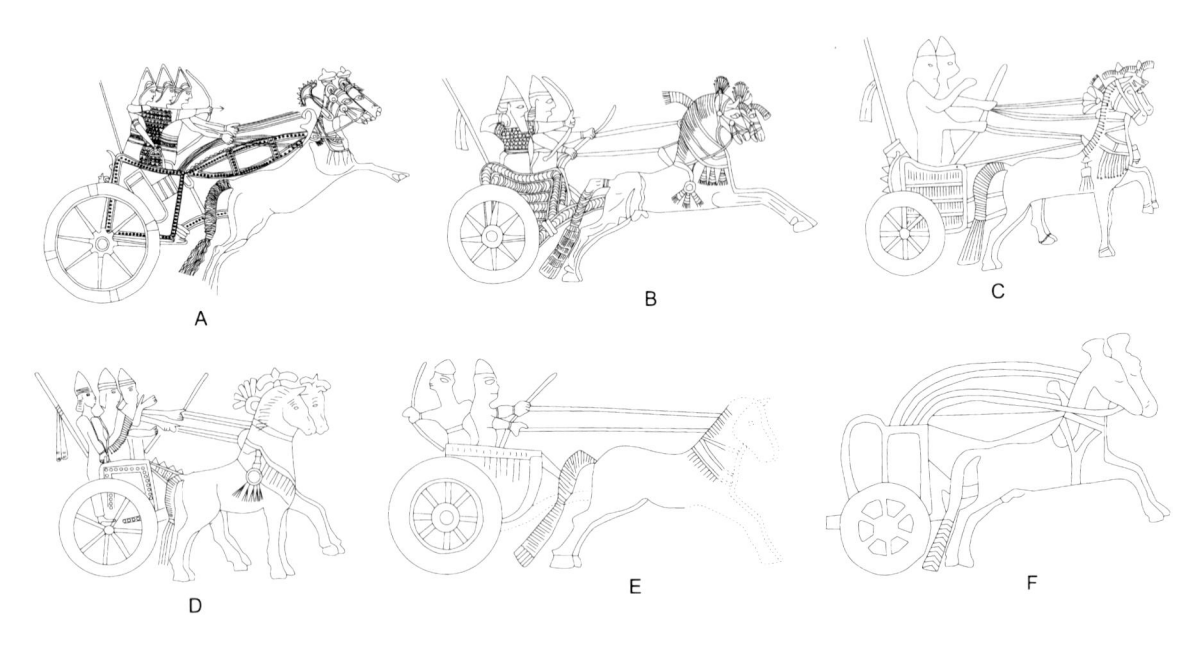

Figure 2. A) Chariot on bronze breastplate. Van Museum. Inv. No. 5.11.80. After: Çavuşoğlu (2004: figs. 1-2); B) Chariot on bronze belt. Van Museum. Inv. No.4.41.95. After: Çavuşoğlu (2005: fig. 2); C) Chariot on bronze helmet. Karlsruhe Badisches Landesmuseum. Inv. No. 89/1. After: Seidl (2004: detail from fig. 32); D) Chariot on bronze plaque. After: Sevin (2007: fig. 3-4); E) Chariot on bronze belt. After: Azarpay (1968: fig. 11); F) Chariot on stone relief. After: Bilgiç & Öğün (1964: pl. XIX). Drawings by B. Gökce.

texts, especially documents about military campaigns; ᴳᴵˢ**GIGIR**, a term understood as a Sumerogram generally used for chariots, appears (Salvini, 2008: 415).

One of the earliest of these inscriptions is dated to the co-regency period of the Urartian king İşpuini and his son Minua (820-810 BC). This inscription states that there were 106 chariots in the Urartian army that were used in a campaign around Lake Urmia (Salvini, 2008: Inscr. No. A3-9). Additionally, on another inscription of king Minua mentions that he deployed 66 chariots in the battle against the tribes who were living in the regions of present-day Erzurum and Kars (Salvini, 2008: Inscr. No. A3-5 Ro-Vo.).

In addition to these, an inscription dated to the period of the Urartian king Sarduri II (756-730 BC) mentions that during the king's campaigns against states such as Militia and Qalani in the west he eradicated 50 chariots (Salvini, 2008: Inscr. No. A9-1 Vo.). On another inscription from the period of Sarduri II, it is stated that the Urartian army contained 92 chariots when he ascended the throne (Salvini, 2008: Inscr. No. A9-3 VII).

It is understood from written sources that the highest number of the chariots in the Urartian army (106) was reached during co-regency period of Işpuini and Minua (Salvini, 2008: Inscr. No. A3-9). Considering this number, it is thought that except for the ones belonging to the king, chariots were used by provincial governors or noblemen who were close to the king. This indicates that Urartian chariots were only used by the elite. Thus, class of ᴸᵁ*ma-ri* ranked sixth in Urartian personnel list on a tablet uncovered in Toprakkale, Urartian settlement, has been interpreted as charioteers (Diakonoff, 1989: 99ff).

In addition to Urartian inscriptions, documents of the Neo-Assyrian Kingdom (1000-609 BC), contemporary with the Urartian Kingdom, provide additional information about Urartian chariots. In the inscriptions dated to the period of the Neo-Assyrian king Shalmaneser III (858-824 BC) it is recorded that the Urartian army consisted of a large number of cavalry and chariots during the conquest of Arzašku, the royal city of Urartian king Arame (Luckenbill, 1926-1927: Inscr. No. 605). Furthermore, Tiglath-Pileser III (744-727 BC) mentions that in the battle during which he defeated Urartian king Sarduri II (756-730 BC), he also captured numerous Urartian chariots including the chariot of the king (Luckenbill, 1926-1927: Inscr. No. 769). Furthermore, Sargon II (721-705 BC), one of the Neo-Assyrian kings, mentions in the narrative of his famous 8th campaign against the Urartian Kingdom that the Urartian king, Rusa I (730-714 BC), fought from his chariot (Luckenbill, 1968: Inscr. No. 154). Important pieces of physical evidence are the bronze sculptures of king Rusa I (730-714 BC), his two warriors and his charioteer, listed among the booty in the documents about the battle (Luckenbill, 1968: Inscr. No. 173).

CHARIOT ACCESSORIES

Our knowledge about chariot accessories is provided mostly by the archaeological record and two- and three-dimensional representations. The main chariot parts are the body, wheel, draught pole, body/draught pole supportive rod, yoke and upper supportive rod (figure 3). There are also additional related accessories to these (figure 4A-D). These accessories are discussed below.

Body

The bodies of chariots usually have a rectangular plan. An exception is the body of a chariot depicted on a belt fragment that was found in the grave of Nor-Areş II (Azarpay, 1968: 48, fig. 11), which has a form of a 'horizontal D' (figure 2E). In fact, the bodies with rectangular plan vary: some have the upper

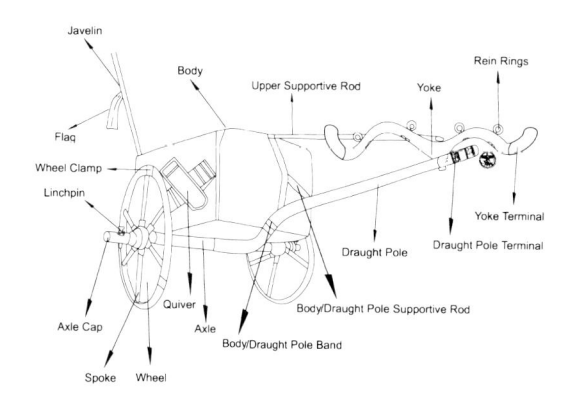

Figure 3. The chariot accessories and their positions. Drawing by B. Gökce.

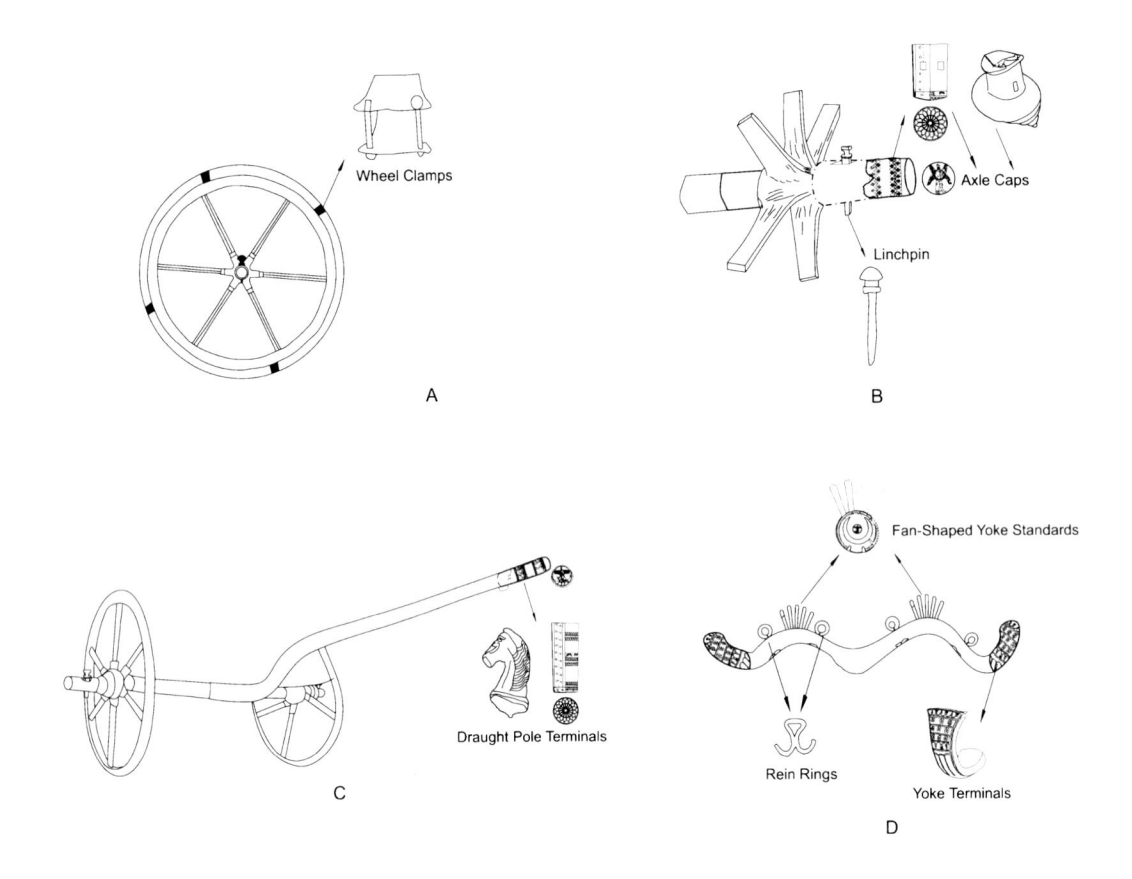

Figure 4. The chariot accessories related to each other. After: Çavuşoğlu (2011: fig. 4). Drawing by B. Gökce.

edge curving inward, others have the oval back upper edge getting lower towards the front, and still others have a flat upper edge. It is suggested that rectangular, small and light bodies were the influence of Northern Syria (Çilingiroğlu, 1984: 58-59). Additionally, it is suggested that one feature of having a camber in the front and back sides of bodies of Urartian chariots was also a common Neo-Assyrian characteristic (Çilingiroğlu, 1984: 59). Side-edge panels of the bodies are generally undecorated, but there are also some examples decorated with a series of spots, fish-bone motifs, horizontal stripes and checked patterns (figure 2A-E). These spots on the side panels of the bodies might indicate the presence of metal discs (Belli, 1983: 329, 335; Merhav, 1991: 76-77; on such decoration on Egyptian chariots see Calvert, this volume). Such metal discs have been found in illegal excavations at Urartian sites (Belli, 1983: figs. 1 & 2; Merhav, 1991: figs. 29 & 30/a-b; Seidl, 2004: fig. 74, pls. 24/a-c & 25/a-d). The diameters of these are between 24 and 32 cm. They usually have rivet holes on their outer surfaces

Figure 5. The accessories related to the body, the wheel, the axle, draught pole and the yoke. Drawing by B. Gökce.

(figure 5), and the dimensions suggest that the discs were hammered on wood and applied on textile or leather through these rivet holes. The surfaces were occasionally decorated with geometrical, floral motifs or various figures such as gods, humans and animals. Inscribed samples are dated to the periods of İşpuini (830-820 BC), Minua (810-785/780 BC) and Sarduri II (756-730) (Belli, 1983: 321-341; Merhav, 1991: 76-77). About the use of discs, Taşyürek (1975: 154) has stated that these could be used for decoration or protection.

Handles can be seen on the back and side upper panels of some depictions of bodies (figure 2 A & F). They are probably made of metal or wicker. Presumably, the people in the body must have protected themselves against jolts by holding these handles. A spear with a flag that is tied to its middle can be seen on the back inner side of some rectangular-shaped bodies (figure 2B-D). The flag was probably used as an indicator of power or to distinguish the chariot of senior commanders or the king in the battle area. Attached to the side-edge panels of some bodies there are also cross-placed quivers probably containing arrows (figure 2A).

It is quite difficult to determine exactly how the back part of these bodies was closed solely by using depictions of the Urartian vehicles in profile. However, from the depictions it is clear that the shields (saw-toothed or decorated in the center with lion-heads in relief) were used on the back panel of these bodies (figure 2A, C). Nevertheless, as a result of our trial restoration we think that the shields were not used to seal off the back part of the bodies, rather they were hung on the (possibly) wooden panel which closed the back part of the body (figure 6). This indicates that the shield was not only used as an indication of power, but also could be used for defence by the warrior when necessary. Additionally, in the chariot depiction on the Çavuştepe (Sardurihinili) plaque (Sevin, 2007: 721-726, figs. 3 & 4), the foot of the human figure in the back part of the body is on the axle (figure 2D). This depiction is important as it indicates that there are also chariot bodies with open backs.

Figure 6. Artist's impression. Drawing by O. Alpsar.

Usually two or three people were depicted standing in the bodies. Generally there is another warrior, hunter or elite individual near the charioteer, all of whom are in profile. This person wears a conical helmet and probably a two-piece garment. Sometimes they also wear bracelets.[1] The charioteer holds only a rein or sometimes a horsewhip combined with a rein. The warrior and hunter figures were depicted in the posture of shooting an arrow or a spear. The rulers were sometimes depicted in a greeting position (figure 2A-E).

Wheel

The depictions show six and eight spoked wheels. Generally the spokes run directly into the wheelhouse. However, in some samples it can be seen that the spokes had a small swelling in the part near the wheelhouse and the spokes ran through this cambered part before running into the wheelhouse (figure 2A-F). Çilingiroğlu (1984: 58-59) suggested that six spoke wheels were inspired by wheels of Northern Syria. In the depictions, wheel rims were often shown as double-circled parallel to each other. However, some samples of single-circled are also known from depictions (figure 2A-F).

Two or four 'U'-shaped elements are placed on the wheels (figure 2A). These are clamps used in connection with the wheels (figure 4A). Likewise, some metal wheel clamps were found in illegal excavations of the Urartian period (Merhav, 1991: 64-65, figs. 3a-b & 4). The clamps were made of bronze and have a length varying between 10 and 11 cm and a width between 8.6 and 9.3 cm. The connection between the ends of 'U'-shaped pieces is provided by a couple of iron or bronze rivets (figure 5). It is a common idea that these clamps were used to strengthen the wheels (Merhav, 1991: 59). Merhav (*Ibidem*) also concludes that outlines of the clamps provide information about the width and size of the wheel rim. Thus, the height of the Urartian wheel rims can be 13 to 15 cm, and the thickness can be 5 cm on the outer surface.

Axle

In Urartian art the chariots were mostly depicted in profile. Thus, the position of the axles cannot be understood precisely through images. However, considering the position of the wheels, it is possible to extrapolate the position: they are usually on the lower mid-center or lower back part of the body (figure 2A-F).

It is known from archaeological finds that some accessories were attached to the axle such as caps and linchpins (figure 4B). Among these, bronze axle caps can be separated into two types: mushroom-head shaped and cylindrical ones (figure 5).

The mushroom-head shaped axle caps have a length between 13 and 18 cm and rim diameter between 7.8 and 14 cm. On their cylindrical neck, there is a rectangular hole through which a linchpin can pass. Rivet holes can be placed in a specific order around the lower edges, suggesting that the object was hammered on wood. In all samples, the surface of the cylindrical base that lies beneath the cylindrical neck is decorated with embossed stripes (figure 5). The inscribed examples can be dated to the reign of Sarduri II (756-730 BC) (Özgen, 1984: fig. 43; Seidl, 2004: fig. 61; Taşyürek, 1975: pl. 32/d).

The axle caps of the cylindrical type have a length between 8.3 and 17.6 cm and a rim diameter between 5.2 and 7 cm. One end is open while the other is closed. The closed part is conical. In all examples, in the center of the cylindrical body two rectangular holes are situated facing one another, or sometimes a round hole for the linchpin to pass through. As well as undecorated examples, there are examples that are decorated with geometrical-floral motifs and figures of humans, gods and animals (figure 5). The inscribed examples can be dated to the periods of İşpuini (830-820 BC) and Minua (810-785/780 BC) (Çavuşoğlu, 2011: 115-117, fig. 1/A-D; Merhav, 1991: 66-67, fig. 9/a-b & 12/a-b; Seidl, 2004: 93, figs. 59-60).

Unfortunately, actual axles have not been found from legal excavations of Urartian sites. However, using the sizes of axle caps known from the illegal excavations, it can be said that thicknesses of the axles varied between 5 to 18.5 cm (Çavuşoğlu, 2011: 115-117).

Linchpins, another element connected to the axle, are made of bronze. Their length varies between 15 and 18 cm. These have a head in the shape of mushroom or a pinecone lying on a rectangular jut and a rectangular body (figure 5). Usually, there is a hole between the head and rectangular jut.

However, there are also some examples without any holes in this part. The inscribed examples can be dated to the periods of İşpuini (830-820 BC) and Sarduri II (756-730 BC) (Belli & Kavaklı, 1981: 15-20, pl. 1.2; Merhav, 1991: 66-67, figs. 5-8 & 13; Seidl, 2004: 94, fig. 62).

It is fair to assume that the wheel was fixed into its place and strengthened against jolts by the linchpin (Merhav, 1991: 54). Additionally, rectangular linchpins were uncovered in the excavations of Van-Toprakkale dated to the Urartian Period (Wartke, 1990: pl. XXIII/a-b). Likewise, these types of linchpins fit the rectangular holes on the of axle caps. However, in one example of the caps of the axle these holes are circular instead of rectangular (Merhav, 1991: 66, fig. 9/a-b). Even though no such examples have been found in excavated material, this data shows that the circular linchpins were also used in the Urartian kingdom.

Draught Pole

It can be seen by the depictions that 'Y'-shaped (figure 2F), double-centered (figure 2C) and single-centered (figure 2A-B, D-E) draught poles were used in chariots. The available data indicate that the Urartians usually used the single-centered draught poles. Draught poles could be undecorated or decorated with geometrical and floral motifs. In some depictions, the draught pole on the front side of the body was bound with a metal or leather draught pole band (figure 2A, B). The connection between the draught pole and the body would have been strengthened by this band.

From Urartian excavations in Erzincan-Altıntepe (Özgüç, 1969b: 263) and Karmir-Blur (Piotrovskii, 1967: 52, pls. 24 & 25) some draught pole caps in the form of a horse-head were found. Additionally, there are also some cylindrical draught pole caps dated to the Urartian Period (figure 5) (Çavuşoğlu, 2011: 118-120, figs. 3-5; Merhav, 1991: 72-73, figs. 24-26; Piotrovskii, 1970: fig. 59; Seidl, 2004: 95-99, figs. 63-71). These objects are separate accessories used in connection with the draught pole (figure 4C). The lengths of the pole terminals found in the excavations vary between 5 and 20.3 cm and their diameters are between 4.5 and 7 cm. As well as undecorated cylindrical draught pole terminals, there are also examples decorated with geometrical-floral motifs and figures of humans, gods and animals (figure 5). Inscribed cylindrical ones can be dated to the periods of İşpuini (830-820 BC), Minua (810-785/780 BC) and Sarduri II (756-730 BC) (Merhav, 1991: 72-73; Seidl, 2004: 95-99).

Yoke

Our knowledge about yokes of the Urartian chariots mostly depends on depictions (figure 2A-F). In the chariot depictions, the ending parts of the yokes are usually curved. This situation shows that the rest of the yoke can also be curved. Because some depictions are quite small, the form of the yoke cannot be discerned. In fact, even though we do not see the triangle and straight-stick formed yokes in Urartian art, we can find them in the art of Neo-Assyria, contemporary with the Urartian examples (Albenda, 1986: pls. 47 & 49; Littauer & Crouwel, 1979: figs. 52 & 61; Madhloom, 1970: pls. XIV/2, & XIV/ 7). Although there is no archaeological data from the Urartian Period for triangle and straight-stick formed yokes, they could be used in the Urartian as well as the Neo-Assyrian kingdom.

In addition to depicted examples, there are also some accessories found in excavations from Urartian sites that are thought to be used on the yokes (figure 4D). These include yoke-saddle terminals (Merhav, 1991: 69, fig. 14). These rectangular-shaped objects are 16 cm long and 7.5 cm wide. The narrow part of the pieces is closed while the wide part is open. The arms of each yoke saddle are provided with a finial equipped with a hole to accommodate the bridle (Merhav, 1991: 56) (figure 5).

Another accessory connected with the yoke is the yoke terminal. Some examples of these are known from illegal excavations (Çavuşoğlu, 2011: 120-121, fig. 6; Merhav, 1991: 68-70, fig. 17a). The length of these curved objects is 29 cm and their width is 9.5 cm. The yoke terminals were made of two different parts that were attached to each other. One end of the objects is closed while the other is open. On both ends of the open part are rivet or loop holes. There are undecorated examples, while others were decorated with floral motifs (figure 5).

Another accessory used on the yoke are fan-shaped standards. Some examples of these are also known from illegal excavations (Merhav, 1991: 74-75, figs. 27-28; Rehm, 1997: 214, 216-217, 387, 389, 391 U23-25). The diameter of the disc-shaped part of the standards varies between 25 to 27 cm, the length of the finger-shaped extensions is 35 cm, and their total length is up to 65 cm. There are rivet or loop-holes placed closely along the width of disc-shaped part. Besides, the surfaces of these parts were surrounded with two embossed stripes or bands and on the upper part of these pieces there are finger-like extensions. These extensions were secured by three rivets set around discs. Both undecorated and decorated examples are known, showing floral motifs and figures of gods and animals (figure 5). The inscribed ones are dated to the period of İşpuini (830-820 BC) (Merhav, 1991: 74-75).

Although the standards are shown, in depcitions, as part of the yoke (figure 2A, C, D), Merhav (1991: 57) suggested that they can be related both to the yoke and the draught pole, but added that it was quite hard to understand whether these parts were related to either of the two. However, considering the Salamis vehicle model Merhav concludes that they could be used on the yoke only. This seems to be supported by the fact that these objects were found in pairs in the excavations. Merhav (*Ibidem*: 58) also states that standartds could be used on the double-centered draught poles. However, the terminals used on the draught poles have a diameter not much more than 7 cm, which provides some information about the draught poles of the Urartians. In our opinion, it is not possible that the fan-shaped decorations with the diameter of 30 to 35 cm could be used on the smaller sized draught poles. We think that the fan-shaped objects were used in the yoke in the Urartian chariots as well as the Persian ones. Notably, this type of objects seems to appear on the yokes in Persian reliefs (Littauer & Crouwel, 1979: fig. 80) and as actual findings (*Ibidem*, 1979: fig. 82).

Another accessory connected with the yoke is rein-rings, mostly made of bronze and rarely of iron (Çavuşoğlu, 2011: 120-121, fig. 7; Merhav, 1991: 68, fig. 15). The lengths of these types of oval rings vary between 5.5 to 9 cm and they have a diameter varying between 2.5 to 5 cm (Çavuşoğlu, 2011: 120-121). In some examples, the ends of the pieces were attached to each other with three rivets. The ends of some rings were bent in the shape of a hook (figure 5). There are some rein-rings uncovered from illegal excavations (Çavuşoğlu, 2011: 120-121). However, rein rings are not found in two-dimensional art of the Urartians. This might be so as drawings/engravings of chariots are often stylized, small, and without detail.

Rein-rings are shown on a stone relief in Persepolis (Littauer & Crouwel, 1979: fig. 80), a vehicle model found in Oxus Treasure (*Ibidem*: fig. 82) and in Neo-Assyrian reliefs (*Ibidem*: fig. 61). In Persian and Neo-Assyrian art, these rings were placed on the yoke and the rein passed through them. The rings were placed in such a way that there would be two rings for each draft animal; the reins coming from the bits passing through them. Based on its use in Assyria and Persia, Çavuşoğlu (2011: 212) concludes that in the Urartian kingdom the large sized rings were fixed onto the yoke and the rein straps passed through them; he (*Ibidem*: 121) has suggested that the small-sized rings were probably used for fixing an object between chariot accessories or parts of horse trappings onto the ring or hanging an object.

Upper Supportive Rod

The upper supportive rod is a unit that at one end leads to the front upper side of the body and at the other end leads to the yoke. This part is generally in the form of stick and elliptical. While stick-shaped ones are undecorated, elliptical-shaped ones are decorated with geometrical motifs. The upper supportive rods probably provided power balance by connecting the body to the draught pole in chariots needed to move fast (figure 2A-F). Çilingiroğlu (1984: 58-59) has stated that the elliptical rod was an influence of Northern Syria.

Body/Draught Pole Supportive Rod

One end of the body/draught pole supportive rod is connected to the front part of the body and the other is diagonally attached to the draught pole. This part is usually a flat rod. However, in some depictions of chariots the end connected to the body is forked or curved (figure 2A, B, E).

By the evidence presented above, it is obvious that Urartian chariot accessories were both undecorated as well as decorated, consisting of various figures, motifs and inscriptions. Due to the lack of written sources, it is quite hard to say what these decorations on certain pieces mean. However, based on the depicted scenes it can be said that as well as the function of decoration they also had symbolic value, used for protection against evils and to giving power.

The diversity of chariot accessories such as decorated, inscribed or plain ones seems to verify the class distinctions in Urartian socio-organization: the pieces with elaborate decoration and inscriptions were meant for royalty, whereas the simpler ones were meant for the elite.

MATERIALS OF CHARIOT ACCESSORIES

Despite the lack of archaeologically attested chariot wood, textile and leather, these materials must have been an important part in the production of chariot accessories. Metal was involved too. Numerous metal chariot accessories have been found at Urartian Period sites (Çavuşoğlu, 2011: 115-122; Merhav, 1991; 56-77; Rehm, 1997: 214, 216-217; Seidl, 2004: 95-99).

Metal

The Urartians made important progress in metallurgy as in many other areas and thus produced a large part of their chariot accessories from metal. Bronze alloy had an extensive usage in Urartu. It should be noted that bronze is mentioned in the Urartian inscriptions as "URUDU" which is a Sumerogram (Salvini, 2008: Inscr. No. 491). Despite the numerous iron objects found in necropolises and settlements belonging to the Urartian Period, the Urartian inscriptions rarely mention iron pieces or weapons. Iron is referred to as "AN.BAR" which is a Sumerogram in the Urartian inscriptions (Salvini, 2008: Inscr. No. 397).

Bronze and iron were also used for other parts such as wheel clamps, axle caps, linchpins, yoke-saddle terminals, yoke terminals, yoke standards, pole terminals and rein-rings.

Wood

Even though modern geography of Urartu shows very few trees, we know especially from Neo-Assyrian written sources that trade in timber was active in ancient times.[2] In addition to textual sources, actual wooden pieces have been found in the excavations of the settlements belonging to the Urartians, verifying the usage of this material in so many aspects in the kingdom. Chairs, tables and a throne found in Erzincan-Altıntepe graves (Özgüç, 1969a: 24) and small trestle found in Adilcevaz H reef (Seidl, 1993: 185; fig. 4) are good examples of wooden objects. The Urartians also used timber in architecture (Forbes, 1983: 5ff).

Based on the data mentioned above and observation of ancient or modern horse-drawn vehicles the authors think, despite the lack of archaeological evidence, that wood is likely to have been used in the production of units of chariot accessories such as the body, wheels, yokes, draught poles, upper supportive rods and body/draught pole supportive rods. The absence of Urartian wooden chariot accessories undoubtedly can be explained by the absence of chariots in graves. Because most royal and noble graves were robbed, we do not know whether they ever contained chariots. However, a single example of a chariot is known, claimed to have been found in the grave of a nobleman at Erzincan-Altıntepe.

The climate and humid soil structure of Urartian geography must also have affected the survival of wooden objects. Interestingly, one finds charred and decomposed wooden material among metal objects in many graves.

Textile and Leather

The archaeological record as well as written sources and two-dimensional art shows that woven cloth was a major part of the life of the Urartians, as attested by words for and images of looms, female weavers, spindle whorls, needles, and other tools of the craft (Belli & Ceylan, 2003: 34, fig. 6; Burney, 1966: pl. XXV: g; Çavuşoğlu & Biber, 2008: 192, fig. 16; Erzen, 1978: 42, fig. 23, pl. XXXV/a-I; Kellner, 1991: pl. 70: 282, 71: 282; Martirosjan, 1974: pl. 107, fig. 82/1, 4, 8, 9; Öğün, 1978: 674; Seidl, 2004: pl. A-3; Yıldırım, 1989: 78).

Notably, numerous tools made of bone in area No. XI and pieces of weaving looms in pillared hall No. X have been found during the excavations in Çavuştepe (Erzen, 1978: 39). Based on these data, it has been suggested that these areas were workshops for weaving, wool working or leatherworks (Erzen, 1978: 39).

Besides these archaeological data, we know that leather referred to as "KUŠ" Sumerogram in the Urartian texts were traded between Urartian cities. On a tablet related to this found in Karmir-Blur (*Teišebai URU*) it is mentioned that leathers of 126 cows, 172 sheep and 16 goats were sent to the city of god A? in Aza Country (Diakonoff, 1963: Inscr. No. 10; Melikishvili, 1971: Inscr. No. 463; Harutjunjan, 2001: Inscr. No. 521).

It is seen from some chariot depictions in two and three-dimensional art of the Urartian period that especially the body, draught poles and upper supportive rods were ornamented. Many of these were possibly covered or decorated with textile or leather, especially plausible in light of the Urartian facility with textile and leather.

DRAFT ANIMALS

Depictions shows that horses were harnessed to the chariots. Likewise, Urartian written sources, archaeological findings and visual arts provide further information about horses and their role in Urartu.

In Urartian inscriptions, the horse is referred to as ANŠE.KUR.RA (Salvini, 2008: 395ff), which is a Sumerogram. Apart from that, it has been noted that the word *hušaa* inscribed on the clay bullae uncovered in Ayanis Fortress is the phonetic spelling of the horse in Urartian language (Salvini, 2001: 285, note 21).

Horses were a major part of the booty seized in the military expeditions to surrounding regions by the Urartian kings. Additionally, the Urartians supplied themselves with horses by breeding them; stables were found in Urartian sites such as Upper Anzaf Fortress and Bastam Fortress (Belli, 1998: 510; Kleiss, 1980: 300; 1988: 16-17; Kroll, 1989: 329-333). Neo-Assyrian written sources state that the Urartians and their contemporary Neo-Assyrians provided horses especially from countries such as Manna, Zikurtu and Parsua localized around Lake Urmia and obtained these both through taxation and purchase (Lanfranchi-Parpola, 1990: Inscr. No. 169; Luckenbill, 1968: Inscr. No. 786;).

Urartian two- and three-dimensional arts provide important information about horses. They were depicted on different metal objects (discs, quivers, belts, horse trappings, chariot accessories, helmets, etc.), wall paintings and stone reliefs, together with various other motifs and figures.

The horses shown in these scenes were used both for riding and for harnessing to the chariots. Depictions show that usually two (and more rarely one) horses were harnessed to the chariots. Additionally, based on the number of reins, it can also be argued that three or four horses were harnessed to chariots.

INTENDED USE

Two- and three-dimensional art and written sources show that chariots were used during the battles in military life (figure 7), in processions or parades (figure 8) and during hunting in civil life (figure 9) in the Urartian State.

Depictions show that chariots in the Urartian army played an active role in battle area, chasing the enemy, and during sieges. Images show that there were offensive and defensive weapons such as spear, shield and quiver in the bodies of the chariots that were used in battles (Çavuşoğlu, 2004: 75, figs. 1-2; Kellner, 1991: pl. 1, 26 & 35/117; Seidl, 2004: 71-72, figs. 31-32, 56, 74, 90 & 102). In Urartian art, injured enemy soldiers are shown in different ways lying under the chariots in the battlefield (Çavuşoğlu, 2005: 366, figure 1/a; Seidl, 2004: 102, figs. 74, 85 & 113) (figure 10).

The images also show that chariots played an important role in processions for state and military triumphs (Kellner, 1991: pl. 1/1; Seidl, 2004: 69-72, figs. 29-32, pl. 17/b; Sevin, 2007: 721-726, figs. 3 & 4).

Chariots were also used during hunting of bulls and lions in civil life. In depictions one can see the bodies of animals, attached to the front or back of the chariots, were impaled by the hunter's arrows and spears (Kellner, 1991: pls. 2-3, 6-7, 9, 26-27 & 41; Seidl, 2004: pl. B1; figs. 11 & 12).

Besides, bull figures were displayed under the feet of draft animals harnessed to chariots while

Figure 7. The chariot in a battle scene on bronze disc. Karlsruhe Badisches Landesmuseum. Inv. No. 89/18. From: Seidl (2004: fig. 74).

lion figures were in the position of biting the wheel or touching the wheel with one of their paws in hunting scenes (figure 11 & 12).[3]

CONCLUSION

Archaeological data and texts show that chariots had an important place in Urartu, despite its difficult and rough terrain. They were useful to control and expand the state, as well as being symbols of power. The maximum number of the chariots in the Urartian army is seen during the co-regency period of Işpuini and his son Minua: 106. The number of chariots in the Urartian army was less in comparison to the increasing number of military campaigns carried out at this time. According to the Urartian texts, some of these requirements for chariots were augmented by chariots seized as war booty. Besides the military function of chariots, chariots were used for state and military ceremony processions as well as for hunting by the Urartians. Chariots seen in both military and hunting scenes share some stylistic features. Regardless for which purpose they were used, the available data shows that horses were harnessed to Urartian chariots.

Archaeological finds show that metal, wood and probably leather, were used in the production of chariot accessories, indicating that the chariots were not produced by a single craftsman but were joint products of different craftsmen, including carpenters, blacksmiths, weavers and leatherworkers (for Egyptian chariot production see Herslund, this volume).

It is suggested that body, six-spoke wheel and elliptical upper supportive rods of Urartian chariot accessories were inspired by Northern Syrian and Neo-Assyrian cultures (Çilingiroğlu, 1984: 58-59). However, some chariot accessories were produced

Figure 8. The chariots procession scene on bronze belt. From: Seidl (2004: fig. 105).

Figure 9. The chariot in a hunting scene on a bronze belt. From: Kellner (1991: pl. 7/19).

Figure 10. The figures of injured enemy soldiers lying under the chariots. From: Çavuşoğlu (2005: fig. 1/a).

Figure 12. The chariot on bronze belt and scene of bull hunting. From: Kellner (1991: pl. 87/446).

Figure 11. A scene of a lion hunt by chariot on a bronze belt. From: Seidl (2004: detail from pl. B).

exclusively by Urartu. Especially, ornaments and inscriptions depicted on chariot accessories used in connection with the draught pole, axle and yoke display characteristics peculiar to Urartu. The accessories which are ornamental or plain and inscribed or uninscribed can be thought of as a reflection of class differences in Urartian society. The chariot accessories with rather ornate decorations, royal symbols and inscriptions must have been used for royal chariots, while those with simple decorations or undecorated and uninscribed ones were peculiar to chariots of lower classes in hierarchy.

Consequently, regarding the written, archaeological and visual data about the Urartian chariots it can be concluded that the chariots had an important place in Urartian social and military life.

ACKNOWLEDGEMENTS

We would like to thank Orhan Alpsa for proof reading the manuscript. Also our sincere thanks go to Rafet Çavuşoğlu from the University of Yüzüncü Yıl-Van for valuable advice and encouragement.

NOTES

1 On a military relief dated to the Neo-Assyrian Period, an Assyrian ruler is depicted as rewarding the soldier standing in front of him with a bracelet because of his victory (Parpola, 1987: fig. 11). Although there is no such information in Urartian visual arts, this Assyrian depiction might have a similar meaning as for the Urartians.
2 According to the information of Assur spies, the Urartian king Argişti II (714-685 BC) has bought timber with the rulers of the city of Harda from the district called Eziat (Preiffer, 1967: Inscr. No. 6). In an Assyrian letter, it is mentioned that 470 trees have been taken to the city of Ura by river by 160 men in total, coming from different cities (Preiffer, 1967: Inscr. No. 109). In a letter of another Assyrian spy 500 large timbers cut by the Urartians are mentioned (Harper, 1892-1914: Inscr. No. 705).
3 For lion hunting see Burney, 1966: 78, figure 10; Seidl, 2004: pl. B/1; for bull hunting see Kellner, 1991: pl. 87/446.

CITED LITERATURE

Albenda, P. 1986. The Palace of Sargon, King of Assyria. – Paris, Recherche sur les civilisations.

Azarpay, G. 1968. Urartian Art and Artifacts. A Chronological Study. – Berkeley/Los Angeles, University of California Press.

Barnett, R.D. 1963. The Urartian Cemetery at Igdyr. – Anatolian Studies 13: 153-198.

Belli, O. 1983. Urartu Kralı Išpuini'ye Ait Çivi Yazılı ve Resimli Tunç Eserler. – Anadolu Araştırmaları IX: 325-356.

Belli, O. 1998. 1997 Yılı Aşağı ve Yukarı Anzaf Kaleleri Kazısı. – 20. Kazı Sonuçları Toplantısı 1: 507-527.

Belli, O. & A. Ceylan. 2003. 2002 Yılı Aşağı ve Yukarı Anzaf Urartu Kaleleri Kazısı. – 25. Kazı Sonuçları Toplantısı 2: 29-41.

Belli, O. & E. Kavaklı. 1981. Çivi Yazılı İki Urartu Kral Asası. – Anadolu Araştırmaları 7: 15-25.

Bilgiç, E. & B. Öğün. 1964. 1964 Adilcevaz/Kef Kalesi Kazıları/Excavations at Kef Kalesi of Adilcevaz 1964. – Anatolia (Anadolu) 8: 65-124.

Burney, C.A. 1966. A First Season of Excavations at the Urartian Citadel of Kayalıdere. – Anatolin Studies 16: 55-111.

Çavuşoğlu, R. 2002. Urartu Kemerleri. – Erzurum, Atatürk University (Unpublished Ph.D dissertation).

Çavuşoğlu, R. 2004. Van Müzesi'nden Savaş Sahneli At Göğüslük Parçası. – Anadolu Araştırmaları 17, 2: 67-77.

Çavuşoğlu, R. 2005. A Unique Urartian Belt in the Van Museum. – Archäologische Mitteilungen aus Iran 37: 365-370.

Çavuşoğlu, R. 2011. Van Müzesi'nden Urartu Taşıt Aksamları. – 28. Araştırma Sonuçları Toplantısı 2: 115-130.

Çavuşoğlu, R. & H. Biber. 2008. Van-Kalecik Urartu Nekropolü Üzerine Bir Değerlendirme. In: E. Genç & D. Çelik. Ed. Aykut Çınaroğlu'na Armağan. Studies in Honour of Aykut Çınaroğlu. – Ankara, Ekici Form Ofset: 189-212.

Çilingiroğlu, A. 1984. Urartu ve Kuzey Suriye Siyasal ve Kültürel İlişkiler. – Ankara, Türk Tarih Kurumu Basımevi.

Diakonoff, I.M. 1963. Urartskiye Pisma i Dokumenti. – Moscow-Leningrad, İzdatel'stvo Akademii Nauk CCCP.

Diakanoff, I. M. 1989. On Some New Trends in Urartian Philology and Some New Urartian Texts. – Archäologische Mitteilungen aus Iran 22: 77-102.

Erzen, A. 1978. Çavuştepe I. Urartian Architectural Monuments of the 7th and 6th Centuries BC and A Necropolis of the Middle Age. – Ankara, Türk Tarih Kurumu Basımevi.

Forbes, T.B. 1983. Urartian Architecture. – Oxford, British Archaeological Reports.

Harper, R.F. 1892-1914. Assyrian and Babylonian Letters Belonging to the Kouyunjik Collection of the British Museum I-XIV. – Chicago, The University of Chicago Press.

Harutjunjan, N.V. 2001. Korpus Urartskich Klinoobraznych Nadpisei. – Erevan, Nacional'aja Akademija Nauk Respubliki Armenii, İzdatel'stvo 'Gitityun' NAN RA, Natsionalija Akademija Nauk Armenija Institut Vostokovedenija.

Hovhannisjan, C. 1973. The Wall-Paintings of Erebooni. – Yerevan, Armenian SSR Academy of Sciences Publishing House Press.

Kellner, H.J. 1991. Gürtelbleche aus Urartu. Prähistorische Bronzefunde Abteilung XII. Band 3. – Stuttgart, Steiner.

Kleiss, W. 1980. Bastam. An Urartian Citadel Complex of the Seventh Century BC. – American Journal of Archaeology 84, 3: 299-304.

Kleiss, W. 1988. Bastam II. Ausgrabungen in den Urartäischen Anlagen 1977-1978. – Berlin, Gebr. Mann Verlag.

Kroll, S. 1989. Chemische Analysen. Neue Evidenz für Pferdestalle in Urartu und Palastina. – Istanbuler Mitteilungen 39: 329-333.

Lanfranchi, B.G. & S. Parpola. 1990. The Correspondence of Sargon II. Letters from the Northern and Northeastern Provinces, State Archieves of Assyria V. – Helsinki, Helsinki University Press.

Littauer, M.A. & J.H. Crouwel. 1979. Wheeled Vehicles and Ridden Animals in the Ancient Near East. – Leiden, Brill.

Luckenbill, D.D. 1926-1927. Ancient Records of Assyria and Babylonia I. – Chicago, Histories & Mysteries of Man Limited.

Luckenbill, D.D. 1968. Ancient Records of Assyria and Babylonia I. – New York, Histories & Mysteries of Man Limited.

Madhloom, T.A. 1970. The Chronology of Neo-Assyrian Art. – London, The Athlone Press.

Martirosjan, A.A. 1974. Argištichinili. – Yerevan: Izdatel'stvo Armyanskoj SSR.

Melikishvili, G. A. 1971. Urartaskie Klioobrazny Nadpisi II. – Moskova, Otkritiya i Publicatsiyi, Vestnik Drevnej Istorrii.

Merhav, R. 1991. Chariot and Horse Fittings. In: Merhav, R. Ed. Urartu. A Metalworking Center in the First Millenium BCE. – Jerusalem, The Israel Museum Press: 53-78.

Öğün, B. 1978. Die Urartäischen Bestattungsbräuche. In: Dorner F.K, S. Şahin, E. Schwertheim & J. Wagner. Eds. Studien zur Religion und Kultur Kleinasiens. Festschrift für Friedrich Karl Dörner zum 65. Geburtstag am 28. Februar 1976. II. – Leiden, Brill: 639-678.

Özgen, E. 1984. The Urartian Chariot Reconsidered. II. Archaeological Evidence, 9th-7th Centuries BC. – Anatolica XI: 91-154.

Özgüç, T. 1969a. Altıntepe II-Mezarlar, Depeo Binası ve Fildişi Eserler. Tombs, Storehouse and Ivories. – Ankara, Türk Tarih Kurumu Basımevi.

Özgüç, T. 1969b. Urartu and Altıntepe. – Archaeology 22, 4: 256-263.

Parpola, S. 1987. The Correspondence of Sargon II. Part I. Letters from Assyria and the West. – Helsinki, Helsinki University Press.

Pfeiffer, R.H. 1967. State Letters of Assyria. A Transliteration and Translation of 355 Official Assyrian Letters Dating from the Sargonid Period (722-625 BC). – New York, American Oriental Society.

Piotrovskii, B.B. 1967. Urartu. The Kingdom of Van and its Art. – London, Evelyn, Adams & Mackay Ltd.

Piotrovskii, B.B. 1970. Karmir-Blur, Al'bom. – Leningrad, Izdatel'stvo "Avrora".

Rehm, E. 1997. Kykladen und Alter Orient. – Karlsruhe, Badisches Landesmuseum.

Salvini, M. 2001. The Inscriptions of Ayanis (Rusahinili Eiduru=Kai) Cuneiform and Hieroglyphic. In: Çilingiroğlu, A. & M. Salvini. Ed. Ayanis I. Ten Years Excavations at Rusahinili Eiduri-kai 1989-1998. – Roma, CNR Documenta Asiana: 285-288.

Salvini, M. 2006. Urartu Tarihi ve Kültürü. – İstanbul, Arkeoloji ve Sanat Yayınları.

Salvini, M. 2008. Corpus Dei Testi Uratei. Volume I-III. – Rome, Istituto di Studi Civilta Dell'e Egeo e Del Vicino Oriente.

Seidl, U. 1993. Urartian Furniture. The Furniture of Western Asia Ancient and Traditional. – In: Hermann, G. Ed. The Furniture of Western Asia, Ancient and Traditional. Papers of the Conference Held at the Institute of Archaeology, University College London, June 28 to 30. – Mainz, Philipp von Zabern: 181-186.

Seidl, U. 2004. Bronzekunst Urartus. – Mainz, Philipp von Zabern.

Sevin, V. 2007. Çavuştepe'den Kabartma Bezemeli Eşsiz Bir Tunç Eser. In: Metin, A., D.A. Meltem & P. Hakan Ed. Belkıs Dinçol ve Ali Dinçol'a Armağan/VITA Festschrif in Honor of Belkıs Dinçol und Ali Dinçol. – İstanbul, Graphis Matbaa: 721-727.

Taşyürek, O.A. 1975. Adana Bölge Müzesindeki Urartu Kemerleri. – Ankara, Türk Tarih Kurumu Basımevi.

Yıldırım, R. 1989. Urartu İğneleri. – Ankara, Türk Tarih Kurumu Basımevi.

Wartke, R.B. 1990. Toprakkale. Untersuchungen zu den Metallobjecten im Vorderasiatischen Museum zu Berlin. – Berlin, Akademie-Verlag.

CHARIOTS IN THE DAILY LIFE OF NEW KINGDOM EGYPT: A SURVEY OF PRODUCTION, DISTRIBUTION AND USE IN TEXTS

Ole Herslund

INTRODUCTION

The present paper consists of a philological examination of the evidence for chariots in the daily life of New Kingdom Egypt (1549-1069 BC), using a wide range of texts and genres. This examination focuses on chariots as a constituent of daily life in the New Kingdom, here understood in the broadest sense as the chariots in civilian contexts, rather than in the more frequently encountered context of warfare. The textual evidence for chariots outside battle inscriptions is, however, rare and derives from an uneven distribution of fragmentary tomb inscriptions and literary works, which makes synthesising the material in an overview challenging and possibly tentative. Nevertheless, by highlighting certain details, it is possible to gain some insights into a wide spectrum of the role of chariots in daily life through a series of socio-historical glimpses that shed light on chariot workers, craft specialisation and production, chariot distribution, chariot symbolism and meanings, private ownership, and the chariot's use in a civil context.

CHARIOT MATERIALS, WORKERS AND PRODUCTION

Most of our knowledge concerning chariot materials and production is derived from archaeological studies of them and their remains, coming from a primarily technological perspective (Herold, 2006; Littauer & Crouwel, 1985: 92-95; see also Sandor, this volume). To this can be added a number of New Kingdom reliefs in which the manufacturing of chariots is often found in connection with larger multipurpose workshops (Drenkhahn, 1976: 130-132; Herold, 2006: 51-78; Littauer & Crouwel, 1985: pl. LXXVI). Philological investigations into chariot workers and production have been limited to a single catalogue of New Kingdom titles of workers (Steinmann, 1980: 151) and a later, more thorough, collection of lexemes for chariot workers, materials and related actions (Hofmann 1989: 182-198).

The materials used in chariot manufacture represent the few references to chariots that are fairly specific in inscriptions and texts. This type of qualification of chariots through their constituent materials appears to carry two major connotations. The materials are either mentioned to emphasise the visual quality and splendour of a chariot, or, more frequently, to emphasise the high-priced nature of a chariot, which could be made from expensive and exotic materials. It is not uncommon to find references to both Egyptian and Asiatic chariots covered in gold or electrum (Davies, 1930: pl. XIII, XXII; Gardiner, 1937, 53; Säve-Söderbergh, 1957: pl. III; Sethe, 1907: 657-659, 663, 669, 690, 692, 704, 706, 712, 717, 809). A single example from Papyrus (P.) Anastasi IV (16, 9-10; Gardiner, 1937: 53) mentions how chariots could also be 'decorated with carved blossoms' and have 'joints (?)' (*tst*) made of ivory.

There are also a number of references to the different types of wood used for chariot construction. These lexemes for kinds of wood can be further qualified by their foreign place of origin, which thereby underline their cultural value and costly nature as imports. The types of wood include *br* wood (Gardiner, 1937: 53, 116), *dšr* wood (Gardiner 1937: 53), two Asiatic wood types called *ssnḏm* and *knkwt* (Sethe, 1907: 707), wood from Mitanni (Davies, 1930: pl. XXII), Nubian wood called *šnd.t kš* 'Kushite-Acacia (?)' (Säve-Söderbergh, 1957: pl. III) and *t3g3* wood from Egypt (Gardiner, 1937: 112, 116; Sethe, 1907: 707). Sadly, like most plant terminology, the ethnobiological semantics underlying these terms for types of wood remain largely unknown.

Given the technological knowhow required for building chariots as well as the fact that chariot production was dependent on state acquisitions of metals and wood, it is not surprising that we can identify dedicated chariot makers amongst the many groups of craft specialised people in the New Kingdom workforce. Chariot makers can be identified from a number of stelae and tomb inscriptions, which provide some socio-historical insights into the craft of a specialised group of people who built and performed maintenance on chariots.

In texts and inscriptions, chariot makers are labelled by the compound title *ḥmw-wrr.t* "Chariot Maker" (Schiaparelli, 1887: 290; Schneider, 1977: 13), with the variant *ḥmw mrkbt* from the 20th Dynasty (1187-1069 BC; Gardiner, 1947: 68*), ranked beneath a *ḥry ḥmw wrr.t* "Chief Chariot Maker" in some form of hierarchical organisation.

The earliest evidence for a dedicated chariot maker stems from a stela of the Amarna Period belonging to the "Chief Chariot Maker" Ptah-mai, which also shows how two of his sons Nakht and Rija worked as *ḥmw.w wrr.t* "Chariot Makers." Hence, we get a glimpse of the well-known anthropological phenomenon in which craft specialisation is made hereditary (Schiaparelli, 1887: 290). Only two additional New Kingdom occurrences of the title *ḥry ḥmw wrr.t* "Chief Chariot Maker" are known from the later 19th Dynasty (1298-1187 BC; Herold, 2006: 52-53; Schneider & Raven, 1981: 94).

At times chariot workers are simply referred to generically as *ḥmw.w* "craftsmen" (Fischer-Elfert, 1986: 227; Gardiner, 1937: 30), but in two instances we also find additional types of specialised craftsmen working on chariots. In one example a chariot is being repaired by both *ḥmw.w* "craftsmen" and *tbw.w* "leather workers" in the Satirical Letter of P. Anastasi I: "You make your way into the armoury; workshops surround you; craftsmen and leather-workers are all about you. They do all what you wish. They attend to your chariot, so that it may cease from lying idle" (Fischer-Elfert, 1986: 227). The miscellany text on the verso of P. Anastasi III is formed as an instruction given to a workshop with *ḥmw.w* "craftsmen", working on a *mrkbt*-type chariot, and *ḥmty.w* "metal smiths" working on a bronze clad *tprt*-type chariot (Gardiner, 1937: 30). Thereby, the terminology of the sources indicate that in addition to dedicated chariot builders, certain parts of the construction, or possible repair phases, required additional types of craftsmen with a specialised knowledge of specific materials and their properties.

In the List of People section of the Onomasticon of Amenemope we find the chariot makers listed after the *tbw.w* "leather workers" and *irw-tryn* "armourers", while the "chariot makers" themselves are followed by the *ḥmw.w-ʿḥ3.w* "weapon/arrow makers" and *ir.ty pdt.w* "bow makers" – in effect a small nomenclature of the personnel of the New Kingdom military industrial complex (Gardiner 1947: 68*).

We know from titles that an armoury was called a *ḥpš*, and in at least one instance from the 19th Dynasty we find a man who was both "Chief Chariot Maker" as well as "Overseer of a Workshop in the Armoury" called Kairy (Drenkhahn, 1976: 131-132; Herold, 2003; Quibell, 1912: pl. 76, 3; 78, 4). A reconstructed scene from his Saqqara tomb gives an insight into how the production of chariots could be set within a larger multifunctional armoury that, in addition to chariots, displays metal working and the production of projectiles, while rows of men in the lower registers bring forth bow and arrow quivers, swords, helmets, chariots and chariot parts (Herold, 2003: 198, Abb. 2). Hence, a variety of produce made by leather workers, bronze smiths and chariot workers, which the texts likewise point out, could all be integrated in work on chariots.

The hierarchical organisation of the workers, the workshop setting, the degrees of craft specialisation and the employment of expensive and imported materials are all indicative of the institutionalised nature of chariot production in New Kingdom Egypt.

DISTRIBUTION OF CHARIOTS

The written record also provides some insights into the distribution of chariots within Egyptian society that cannot be directly related to warfare or booty. This can be detected in a number of different texts, but no more so than in the context of gifts presented to the pharaohs on the occasion of accession to the throne, royal jubilees and new year's celebrations, in which not only the kings and their reigns got rejuvenated, but so did a whole range of royal and cultic statuary and equipment (Aldred, 1969).

In the Theban tomb of Amenhotep (TT 73), the High Steward of Hatshepsut, we find a chariot amongst the gifts presented to the pharaoh. It is labelled "great chariot of Kushite Acacia (?), wrapped with gold" (Säve-Söderbergh, 1957: 2, pl. III). The same theme of presenting gifts to the king appears in the Theban tomb of Kenamun (TT 9), High Steward of Amenhotep II, who lists a substantial quantity of objects, like statuary, collars, weapons, as well as ornamented horse covers and chariots. The inscriptions state that the goods were "the work of all craftsmen of the Delta Towns", thus produced in the north where Kenamun served as High Steward, but they were destined to become presents before the king in Thebes. The chariots are generically described as "being of silver and gold", but two chariots, one of which is named "The One of Syria" (*t3-m3w rn=s*), are specified as being made of wood brought from Nahrin. Thereby we can follow a supply line from the wood being cut and brought from Mitanni in Syria to the workshops in the Nile Delta and finally presented to the pharaoh in Thebes (Davies, 1930: 24, pl. XIII; XXII).

In the later Miscellany Text composed as an instruction to a chariot workshop (Gardiner, 1937: 30) the *mrkbt* "chariot" of the pharaoh is said to be constructed, or possibly repaired, for the feast of New Year's Day. In another instruction, likewise from the Ramesside Miscellanies, the scribe of the armoury Mahu commissions the scribe Pewehem to arrange the construction of chariots for the second celebration of the king's Heb-Sed (Gardiner, 1937: 4). Hence, the combination of texts, inscriptions and representations testify to the cultural significance of creating and presenting specially made coronation and jubilee chariots to the pharaoh.

A number of inscriptions from the 18th Dynasty (1549-1298 BC) describe how these golden vehicles could be used in both warfare (Sethe, 1907: 657-659, 663, 669, 690, 692, 704, 706, 712, 717, 809) and royal appearances (Kakosy, 1977: 58; Murnane & Van Siclen III, 1993: 86), and how gilded chariots could symbolically frame the king as a manifestation of the sun (see Calvert, this volume). On his Theban Victory Stele Amenhotep III is described as "The Beautiful God, Golden [Horus] shining on the chariot, like the rising sun" above a scene in which Asiatic enemies are crushed underneath his chariot (Petrie, 1897: pl. X). We find a similar statement about Akhenaton on the early Boundary Stelae of Amarna, though this time during a peaceful event: "[...] His Majesty, Live, Prosperity, Health, appeared on a great chariot of electrum, like Aton, when he rises in the horizon" (Murnane & Van Siclen III, 1993: 86). An inscribed whip handle belonging to Tutankhamun (JE 61995) shows how the event of the king appearing publically on a chariot was continuously equated to the sun in the post-Amarna Period: "He (the king) appears on his chariot (lit. horse) like Re, everybody gathers to see him" (Kakosy, 1977: 58; see Calvert, this volume).

PRIVATE OWNERSHIP AND DAILY USE OF CHARIOTS FROM A TEXTUAL PERSPECTIVE

Although the textual sources for private ownership and use of chariots are less informative for an overview than those derived from the pictorial and archaeological record, tomb inscriptions and literary works do provide additional glimpses into the role of the chariot. Returning to the tomb of Kenamun another reference to a chariot in an inscription can be found stating that it was given to Kenamun by the king as a reward (*ḥsiwt.w*), at some point during his career. The inscription mentioning this chariot appears in the context of a damaged depiction of a weeping Nephtys following a bier and a possible sacrifice and offering scene, so the chariot itself may have been depicted amongst the now vanished display of funerary equipment (Davies, 1930: 47).

Additional textual evidence about private ownership and use of chariots in daily life is limited in general, though the group of Ramesside Miscellany texts offer some glimpses of chariots in a daily life setting (Gardiner, 1937). The Miscellanies cannot be taken to be accurate historical documents, but there is no reason to think that they draw on anything other than what would have been recognisable imagery of elite life in Egypt for the reader, listener or copyist.

In the literary P. Anastasi III (6, 7-8; Gardiner, 1937: 27) we read how an army officer buys a chariot pole for 3 *deben* and a chariot for 5 *deben*. Janssen (1975: 329) remarks that these prices seem extremely doubtful, when compared to the price of a bed for instance, which ranged between 15 and 20 *deben*. Conversely, if the *deben* price is taken to refer to silver *deben*, to which the text makes no reference, the price of the pole seems unreasonably high (*Ibidem*).

It is the only attested price for a chariot from ancient Egypt and given the literary context we can only speculate as to the validity of the stated price level. There is, however, an interesting social dimension to the passage in P. Anastasi III (6, 7-8) in that it suggests that a chariot officer could be responsible for buying his own vehicle as noted by Caminos (1954: 98) and Kees (1933: 235, note 6). There is, however, reason to be cautious, as the Miscellany Text in question belongs to the group of texts in which scribes present a negative view of the army, its members and lifestyle. The officer is here portrayed as lacking skills for different aspects of his profession, so the circumstance that he should buy his own chariot could potentially signify a reduction of personal worth rather than a general picture of charioteers having to acquire their own vehicle. In any case, the passage in P. Anastasi III (Gardiner, 1937: 27) suggests that in addition to royal gifts of chariots to individuals, like the one given to the high steward Kenamun, it was possible to acquire chariots through private means.

In the so-called School Text of Papyrus (P.) Lansing we read how the scribe of the army and overseer of the cattle of Amun, Nebmare-nakht, called Raia, has built himself a richly furnished mansion owing to a successful scribal and teaching career. Raia's lavish elite residence is here described as having, among many other things, "...horses in the stable" and gardens that provide the wood for not only the construction of his boats, but also of a chariot (Gardiner, 1937: 111-112). The metonymy between ownership and an expensive vehicle to express a relatively abstract concept like 'success in life' is of course quite recognisable for us, when one thinks about the embodied status we associate with super sports cars.

Thus, literary texts and tomb inscriptions indicate that there were at least three ways in which elite people could acquire a chariot: as a royal gift or reward, a personally financed acquisition, or by having personal access to the relevant materials, facilities and required workforce. That some elite men in the Ramesside Period owned private chariots can also be discerned in a more indirect way through the generic dream literature and its topics where, according to the Beatty Dreambook, "should a man see himself in a dream yoking (?)/attaching a chariot, (then) It is Bad! (it means that) insults are hurrying against his very flesh" (Gardiner, 1935: pl. 7).

In addition to the well-known trope of the active and masculine pharaoh using his chariot for hunting, training and leisure purposes (Helck, 1955: 1279; 1957a: 1541; 1957b: 1739), the texts of the New Kingdom inform us also how chariots were simply used for personal transport over land (see also Köpp, this volume). This could be on short distances, as revealed by the Boundary Stelae of Akhenaton, where the king and his attendants drive around the royal city and desert plane, or the more long distance travelling of the *mhr* "messenger" traversing the mountainous and hostile landscape between Egyptian institutions and town centers in the Levant, as described in the Satirical Letter of P. Anastasi I. The Satirical Letter emphasises the knowledge required of the *mhr* "messenger" concerning the proper routes through the landscape, and failing to navigate correctly could result in being ambushed at night, or simply crashing the chariot in the dangerous, rocky terrain.

The motif of a chariot messenger moving swiftly through the landscape from waypoint to waypoint can also be found in the Ramesside Love Poems of Papyrus (P.) Chester Beatty I. These Love Poems (I-III) consist of metaphorical stanzas expressing the speed by which a man moves to his longing lover with 'chariot riding' and 'the gazelle' as sources for the 'speed' metaphors; the 'fastest vehicle' and the 'fastest animal' in Late Bronze Age Egypt.

Poem I is of particular interest, because in addition to the metaphorical relation between 'chariots' (source) and 'speed' (topic) we get a glimpse of a fast message system with a chariot rider moving between dedicated chariot stations with fresh horses. Hence the stanzas express not only the speed associated with chariot riding, but also the inherent limitation of chariot riding over distances as well as the physiology of the horses : "O! That you may come to your sister (*i.e.* female loved one) swiftly! Like a swift messenger of the king [...] all stables are held ready for him, he has horses at the stations. The chariot is harnessed in its place; he may not pause on the road" (Gardiner, 1931: pl. XXIXa).

Although featured in literary passages, the *mhr* "messenger" and *wpw.ty nsw.t* "Royal Envoy" (see also Abbas, this volume) moving on chariots between way points with stables and facilities, both seem to be indicative of a kind of New Kingdom institutionalised fast message system, based on chariots and dedicated way stations; a fast message system, which reminds one of the Pony Express of 19th century America. Though not concerned with an institutionalised fast message system as such, one can find an additional example of the trope of 'sending messages by chariot' in the Capture of Joppa on Papyrus (P.) Harris 500 (see also Manassa, this volume), where the general Djehuty dispatches a *kdn* "charioteer" to announce, deceitfully, to the besieged town that the Egyptians have surrendered (Gardiner, 1932: 84).

CONCLUSION

I have suggested here that in spite of the uneven distribution of an already fragmentary textual record concerning chariots in the daily life of New Kingdom Egypt, certain details in tomb inscriptions and literary works do provide glimpses into the meaning of chariots, their production and distribution, as well as personal ownership and use of chariots.

By focussing on the relatively few textual references to chariots in the daily life of the New Kingdom one encounters a range of topics, such as production, distribution, civilian use and certain meanings which the ancient Egyptians related to chariots, all of which possess a socio-historic dimension.

With regards to production, the evidence suggests that chariot workers were organised in some form of loose hierarchical organisation, and consistently in contexts where other craft specialists appear. The qualification of chariots in texts attests to the variety of materials used like wood, leather, and metals, some of which were of high value and imported into Egypt from faraway places. Furthermore, they all correlate to the textually identifiable craft specialists of chariot workers, leather workers and metal workers. Inscriptions also hint as to how the craft of chariot making could be passed on from father to sons. The Ramesside Onomasticon's listing of the chariot makers among other kinds of weapon makers, as well as Ramesside inscriptions and texts referring to chariot production and repair, situate chariot production within a larger institutionalised setting of a multifunctional armoury.

The inscriptions and texts concerned with the culturally significant event of presenting the king with golden chariots as parts of royal festivals provide us with further details concerning the imports of materials and institutionalised manufacturing of chariots. The chariots given to Hatshepsut and Amenhotep II by their high stewards are specified as being made of wood from Africa and Asia. The latter was brought to workshops in the Nile Delta, where the chariots were manufactured, before being shipped off to Thebes and presented before the king. The Miscellany Texts concerned with the production of chariots indicate that different types of chariots were manufactured within the same setting and show how the commission to the workshops went from a 'scribe of the armoury' to another scribe, who was then responsible for carrying out the task.

Members of the elite could earn their own chariots as royal rewards or gifts, like the one given by the king to Kenamun, while the Ramesside Miscellany Texts suggest that it was also possible for people with the sufficient resources to buy a chariot or have one made privately. In any case, the relatively frequent use of the 'chariot' as a topic in miscellanies, love poems and dream literature indicates that private ownership of chariots was perhaps not entirely uncommon among elite men in the civic sector of society.

Although a rare topic in texts, we find chariots in daily life contexts used for personal transportation in Egypt, but also in the rocky landscapes of the Levant. The textual sources indicate that chariots were used for both short distance travelling by the king and his courtiers as well as longer distance travelling by messengers and royal envoys when on the job. Long distance travelling in chariots, however, seems only to have been possible when moving between dedicated waypoints with fresh horses and repair facilities.

A few inscriptions and texts shed light on some of the multifaceted meanings the ancient Egyptians related and applied to chariots. The famous golden chariots of the pharaohs could serve to frame the king as a manifestation of the shining sun, or sun god, during public displays and appearances. Finally, the Ramesside Miscellany Texts and love poetry enable us to detect some deep rooted cognitive semantic structures relating to chariots, when we come across the chariot used either as a conceptual source to express the abstract notions of high status and a successful scribal career, or as source for textual stanzas evoking the embodied concept of moving with utmost speed in love poetry.

CITED LITERATURE

Aldred, C. 1969. The 'New Year' Gifts to the Pharaoh. – Journal of Egyptian Archaeology 55: 73-81.

Caminos, R.A. 1954. Late-Egyptian Miscellanies. – London, Oxford University Press.

Davies, N. de. G. 1930. The Tomb of Ken-Amun at Thebes. Volume I-II. – New York, Metropolitan Museum of Art.

Drenkhahn, R. 1976. Die Handwerker und ihre Tätigkeiten im alten Ägypten. – Wiesbaden, Harrassowitz.

Fischer-Elfert, H.-W. 1986. Die satirische Streitschrift des Papyrus Anastasi I. – Wiesbaden, Harrassowitz.

Gardiner, A.H. 1931. The Library of A. Chester Beatty. Description of a Hieratic Papyrus with a Mythological Story, Love-Songs and other Miscellaneous Texts. – London, Emery Walker, Ltd.

Gardiner, A.H. 1932. Late Egyptian Stories. – Bruxelles, Fondation Égyptologique Reine Élisabeth.

Gardiner, A.H. 1935. Hieratic Papyri in the British Museum. Third Series. Chester Beatty Gift. – London, British Museum Press.

Gardiner, A.H. 1937. Late Egyptian Miscellanies. – Bruxelles, Fondation Égyptologique Reine Élisabeth.

Gardiner, A.H. 1947. Ancient Egyptian Onomastica. Volume I. – London, Oxford University Press.

Helck, W. 1955. Urkunden der 18. Dynastie. Heft 17. Historische Inschriften Thutmosis' III und Amenophis' II. – Berlin, Akademie Verlag.

Helck, W. 1957a. Urkunden der 18. Dynastie. Heft 19. Historische Inschriften Thutmosis' IV. und biographische Inschriften seiner Zeitgenossen – Berlin, Akademie Verlag.

Helck, W. 1957b. Urkunden der 18. Dynastie. Heft 20. Historische Inschriften Amenophis' III. – Berlin, Akademie Verlag.

Herold, A. 2003. Ein Puzzle mit zehn Teilen. Waffenkammer und Werkstatt aus dem Grab des *Kyjrj* in Saqqara. In: Kloth, N., H. Altenmüller, K. Martin & E. Pardey. Eds. Es werde niedergelegt als Schriftstück. Festschrift für Hartwig Altenmüller zum 65. Geburtstag. – Hamburg, Helmut Buske Verlag: 193-202.

Herold, A. 2006. Streitwagentechnologie in der Ramses-Stadt. – Mainz, Philipp von Zabern.

Hofmann, U. 1989. Fuhrwesen und Pferdehaltung im alten Ägypten. – Bonn, Rheinische Friedrich-Wilhelms-Universität (Unpublished Ph.D dissertation).

Janssen, J.J. 1975. Commodity Prices from the Ramesside Period. An Economic Study of the Village of Necropolic Workmen at Thebes. – Leiden, Brill.

Kakosy, L. 1977. Bark and Chariot. – Studia Aegyptiaca 3: 57-65.

Kees, H. 1933. Ägypten. Kulturgeschichte des Alten Orients. – München, C.H. Beck'sche Verlagsbuchhandlung.

Littauer, M.A. & J.H. Crouwel. 1985. Chariots and Related Equipment from the Tomb of Tutankhamun. – Oxford, Griffith Institute.

Murnane W.J. & C.C. Van Siclen III. 1993. The Boundary Stelae of Akhenaten. – New York, Routledge, Chapman & Hall Inc.

Petrie, W.M.F. 1897. Six Temples at Thebes. – London, British School of Archaeology.

Quibell, J.E. 1912. Excavations at Saqqara (1908-1909, 1909-1910). The Monastery of Apa Jeremias. – Kairo, l'Institut Français d'Archéologie Orientale.

Säve-Söderbergh, T. 1957. Private Tombs at Thebes. – Oxford, Griffith Institute.

Schiaparelli, E. 1887. Museo Archaeologico di Firenze. – Roma, Antichità.

Schneider, H.D. 1977. Shabtis. An Introduction to the History of Ancient Egyptian Funerary Statuettes with a Catalogue of the Collection of Shabtis in the National Museum of Antiquities at Leiden. – Leiden, Rijksmuseum van Oudheden.

Schneider, H.D. & M.J. Raven. 1981. De Egyptische Oudheid. – Leiden, Staatsuitgeverij.

Sethe, K. 1907. Urkunden der 18. Dynastie. Abteilung IV. Band III. Heft 9-12. Historisch-biographische Urkunden. – Leipzig, J.C. Hinrichs'sche Buchhandlung.

Steinmann, F. 1980. Untersuchungen zu den in der handwerklich-künstlerischen Produktion beschäftigten Personen und Berufsgruppen des Neues Reichs. – Zeitschrift für Ägyptische Sprache und Altertumskunde 107: 137-158.

THE CHARIOT AS A MODE OF LOCOMOTION IN CIVIL CONTEXTS

Heidi Köpp-Junk

INTRODUCTION

As means of locomotion, mount animals, sedan chairs or chariots are known from ancient Egypt for overland travel (Köpp, 2008b, 401-412; Köpp-Junk, 2013: 6-9; 2014: 199-276). The oldest mode of travel, however, was simply to walk because it was the easiest and cheapest way to move, even though it was the slowest. The very reverse applies to the chariot. Compared to all other means of travel, except for horseback riding, the chariot was the fastest, but also the most expensive one. Besides the chariot, the owner has to purchase horses as well as have a personal staff for maintenance and care of both. Therefore, at the beginning of the 18th Dynasty (1540-1278 BC), only the king and a few high officials could afford them (Hofmann, 1989: 33). However, about 2,000 chariots are estimated for the Egyptian army of the 19th Dynasty (1278-1176 BC; Langenbach, 2009: 347). This figure provides indication of the increasing use of the chariot. How many additional chariots were privately owned is uncertain, but several tomb scenes as well as textual evidence from the New Kingdom show them as an obvious component of daily life as a mode of locomotion.

This contribution discusses the general use of chariots in civil contexts. Additionally, its radius of action with regards to overland travel is analyzed, as well as how chariots were transported by water. This is followed by on overview of the traveling speed of the vehicle.

THE CHARIOT AS A MODE OF LOCOMOTION IN CIVIL CONTEXTS

In ancient Egypt chariots were not used for the transport of loads, but only as a means of locomotion. Beside warfare they were used in civil contexts for hunting, sports, and also for travel (Köpp-Junk, 2014: 239-269; Powell, 1963: 165; Schulman, 1980: 144-146, 148).

The use of the Egyptian chariot in warfare is well-attested and often discussed (Littauer & Crouwel, 1979a; Schulman, 1963: 75-98; 1980: 105-153; Spalinger, 2003: 163-199; see also Spalinger, this volume) whereas the civil context has rarely been paid attention to (see Sabbahy, this volume).

Hunting Scenes

A number of hunting scenes displaying pharaohs on chariots are known, such as Tutankhamun chasing lions, ostriches, hyenas and gazelles as shown on the convex lid of the painted box from his tomb (Egyptian Museum, Cairo, JE 61467; Carter Number 21; Saleh & Sourouzian, 1986: No. 186). In Medinet Habu, Pharaoh Ramesses III (1185-1153 BC) is depicted in his chariot, hunting desert game, lions and other animals with bow and arrow (figure 1; Decker & Herb, 1994: pl. 184; Epigraphic Survey, 1930: pl. 35; Epigraphic Survey, 1932: pl. 116-117, 130). Furthermore, there is textual evidence. The Dream Stela of Thutmose IV (1398-1388; see Calvert, this volume) states that that the king went into the desert near Memphis to hunt lions and desert game from his chariot (Helck, 1957: 1541, lines 8-13). But not only the king used the chariot for hunting; in several scenes in Theban tombs (TT) from the 18th Dynasty it is attested for private persons as well (see *e.g.* TT 56 [Userhat], TT 84 [Iamunedje and Meri], TT 123 [Amenemhet]; Hofmann, 1989: 281-283, 354-356).

Sports

The sporting aspect of chariots plays a secondary role and is rarely evidenced. In the text on Amenhotep II's Great Sphinx Stela his skills in target shooting while speeding his chariot are praised (Helck, 1955: 1280, line 12-1281, line 7), which is further supported by a relief from the Karnak Temple, now in the Luxor Museum (Luxor Museum No. J 129; Decker & Herb, 1994: pl. 70, folding plate A, E 4-5). It shows Amenhotep II on his chariot, aiming with bow and arrow at a target made of copper. The same is described in the text on the Dream Stela of Thutmose IV (Helck, 1957: 1541, line 8-10). Chariot races, known from ancient Rome, are, as yet, unattested in Pharaonic Egypt.

Means of Travel

For the royal family and the elite in the New Kingdom, the chariot was the status symbol par excellence and the supreme mode of locomotion, both for private and public appearances and travel (Hofmann, 1989: 284-287, 326-332; Köpp-Junk, 2014: 239-269; Powell, 1963: 165; Schulman, 1980: 144-146, 148). Since the Predynastic Period (5000-3000 BC) and during the Old and Middle Kingdom (2663-2195 BC and (2066-1650 BC respectively), the carrying chair was the most prestigious mode of travel for the elite (Köpp-Junk, 2014: 234, 396). In the New Kingdom (1540–1078 BC) the carrying chair no longer appears as the preferred mode of transportation for the elite; instead, it is depicted only in cultuc context. The chariot replaced the carrying chair as the most prestigious method of locomotion of the elite in the New Kingdom. The importance of the chariot in civil contexts should not be underestimated, since it influenced daily life significantly, as scenes in the private tombs of Amarna show (see below and also Sabbahy, this volume). As Schulman (1980: 145) expressed somewhat provocatively, "its main non-military use was hardly anything else than serving as a taxi". Akhenaten went by chariot to inspect the boundary stelae (Helck, 1958: 1966: 14; 1982: 13; 1983: 7; 1986: 14) or to visit the temple (Amarna Tomb 5 [Pentu]; Davies, 1906: pl. 5). He also used it as the common mode of locomotion for royal family outings, as is shown in several tombs at Amarna (figure 2). A scene in the Amarna tomb of Panehesi (Tomb 6) shows Akhenaten and Nefertiti on a chariot ride, accompanied by high officials and the princesses following in their own chariots. Nefertiti drives herself; four of her daughters follow her without a charioteer, two in each chariot with the reins lying in the hand of one of them (Davies, 1905a: 18, pl. 13, 15-16). The same scenes appear in the tomb of Merire I (figure 4; Amarna Tomb 4; Davies, 1903: pl. 10 & 17). In scenes in the tombs of Ahmes (Tomb 3) and Mahu (Tomb 9) at Amarna, Nefertiti appears together with Akhenaten and a daughter as a three-

Figure 1. Pharaoh on his chariot, hunting desert game with bow and arrow. Temple of Medinet Habu. Photograph by S. Schips.

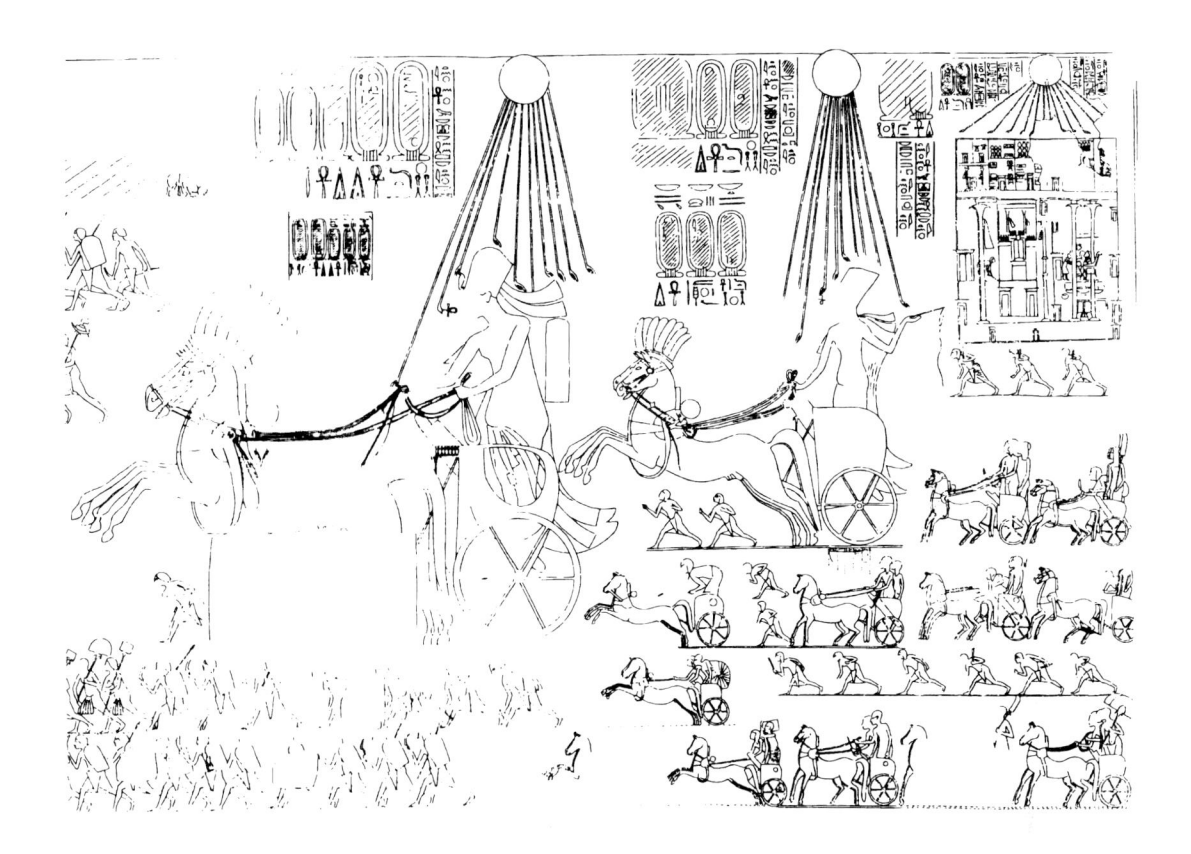

Figure 2. The chariot as the prestigious mode of locomotion. Akhenaten and Nefertiti on a ride in a chariot, accompanied by high officials and the princesses on chariots as well. Tomb of Panehesi. Amarna. 18th Dynasty. From: Davies (1905a: pl. 13).

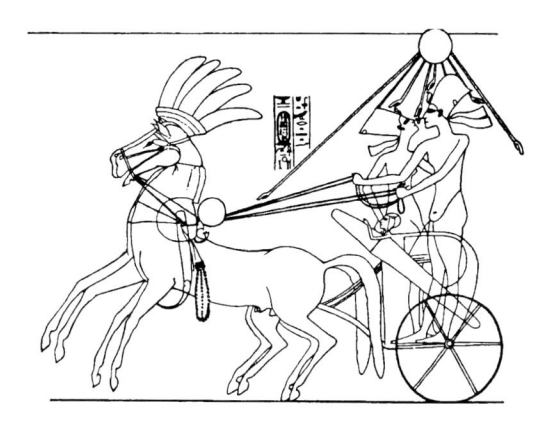

Figure 3. Nefertiti together with Akhenaten and a daughter. Tomb of Ahmes. 18th Dynasty. Amarna. From: Davies (1905b: pl. 32).

Figure 4. Nefertiti alone in a chariot. Tomb of Merire. Amarna. 18th Dynasty. From: Davies (1903: pl. 17).

some in the chariot (figure 3; Davies, 1905b: pl. 32 & 32A; Davies, 1906: pl. 12 C, 20, 41).

More textual evidence is provided in the literary text called the Tale of the Two Brothers in Papyrus (P.) d'Orbiney, dated to the 19th Dynasty (Wettengel, 2003: 43, 170, 272), which reports the king enjoying a short trip in a richly decorated chariot of pale gold, leaving his palace in order to see the Persea tree (P. d'Orbiney 17, line 4-5; Gardiner, 1932: 27, line 4-7).

Not only pharaohs, but also high officials used chariots in civil contexts for inspecting agricultural work (for example the tomb painting British Museum No. 37982; Davies & Gardiner, 1936: pl. 68), going to the palace (Amarna Tomb 9 [Mahu]; Davies, 1906: pl. 17), or taking captives to the vizier (Amarna Tomb 9 [Mahu]: Davies, 1906: pl. 26). To receive the Gold of Honor it was common practice to drive to the palace by chariot as well (Amarna Tombs 1 [Huya]: Davies, 1905b: pl. 17; 2 [Merire II]: Davies, 1905a: pl. 33; Hofmann, 1989: pl. 36; 7 [Parennefer]: Davies, 1908: pl. 4; 8 [Tutu]: Davies, 1908: 19-20; Hofmann, 1989: pl. 34-35; Theban Tomb (TT) 49 [Neferhotep]: Decker, 1984a: 1133, n. 9; Lacovara, 1997: fig. 34; Vandier, 1964: fig. 365). Several scenes show the tomb owner's return home after the audience given by the king (Hofmann, 1989: 284-285; Amarna Tomb 7 [Parennefer]: Davies, 1908: pl. 4-5; TT 41 [Amenemipet Ipy]: Hofmann, 1989: pl. 39), TT 23 [Thay]: Hofmann, 1989: 40). Besides, chariots served in private life as a mode of locomotion to attend a banquet (TT 75 [Amenhotep Sise]; Vandier, 1964: fig. 98) or visit a temple (Amarna Tomb 9 [Mahu]; Davies, 1906: pl. 18-19). The use of the chariot in the New Kingdom in civil context and its ubiquity becomes obvious from these scenes, and also from textual evidence. In the Ramesside Tale of Woe in Papyrus (P.) Pushkin, the protagonist Wermai complains that he was on his way afoot since his chariot and his horses had been stolen and without them he was forced to walk (P. Pushkin 127, col. 3, line 4-7; Caminos, 1977: 25, pl. 7).

No Exception to the Rule: Women in Chariots

The use of chariots as a mode of locomotion in civil context was not restricted to men; there is pictorial and textual evidence for women as well (in detail see Köpp, 2008a: 34-44; see also Sabbahy, this volume). For example, in the 18th Dynasty and more specifically, the Amarna Period, women (generally the queen and princesses) are shown driving or riding in chariots in pairs or alone (figure 3-4; Amarna Tomb 6 [Panehesi]: Davies, 1905a: pl. 13, 15-16; 4 [Merire I]: Davies, 1903: pl. 10, 17; 3 [Ahmes]: Davies, 1905b: pl. 32, 32A; 9 [Mahu]: Davies, 1906: pl. 12 C, 20, 41). One restored scene on a talatat block shows Nefertiti driving a chariot alone (Hoffmeier, 1988: 36, pl. 18), another one pictures her driver as well (Redford, 1973: pl. 9, 1). Yet another talatat block depicts two chariots containing pairs of women, escorted by a driver (Metropolitan Museum of Art, New York, Accession No. 1985.328.16). Possibly, they are Court Ladies rather than princesses as they do not seem to wear the princesses' typical side-locks, as shown in the scene from the Tomb of Panehesi (figure 2; Davies, 1905a: pl. 13). Furthermore, a very unusual scene from the tomb of Huy (TT 40) shows an oxen-drawn chariot with a Nubian lady as a passenger, accompanied by an Egyptian driver (Davies & Gardiner, 1926: pl. 27-28).

Beside the civil context there are depictions of women in chariots in martial situations as well. An ostracon from the 20th Dynasty (1176-1078 BC) shows a woman together with a driver (Egyptian Museum, Cairo, CG 25125), fighting with bow and arrow against an opponent. She is identified as a queen (Daressy, 1901: pl. 24; Peck & Ross, 1979: 158f., no. 90) or more specifically Tausret (Callender, 2004: 103-104). Another interpretation names her as the goddess Astarte (Houlihan, 2001: 120, fig. 132; Pomerantseva, 1992: 514, fig. 3; Wildung & Drenkhahn, 1984: 181, no. 89). In a scene in the temple of Edfu, dating to the Ptolemaic Period (310-30 BC), the goddess Astarte is depicted in a chariot. This time she is clearly identifiable by the

Figure 5. The goddess Astarte on a chariot. Temple of Edfu. Photograph by S. Schips

nearby inscription (figure 5; Chassinat, 1928: pl. 148; 1931: 113; Leclant, 1960: 54-62, pl. 4; Woytowitsch, 1995: fig. 725. For Astarte on horseback see Davies, 1953: pl. 3; Leclant, 1960: 1-67; Schulmann, 1957: 265, 269).

Textual evidence for women in connection with chariots in civil contexts is rather rare. In the text of P. d'Orbiney from the 19th Dynasty already mentioned previously there is a reference to a woman, following Pharaoh in her own chariot (P. d'Orbiney 17, line 4-5; Gardiner, 1932: 27, line 4-7). Moreover, on two of the chariots from the tomb of Tutankhamun his wife Ankhesenamun is mentioned (Decker, 1984b: 869-877). On chariot A3 two inscriptions include the text: "Great Royal Wife, Ankhesenamun, who lives" and "Great Royal Wife, his beloved, Ankhesenamun, who lives" (Littauer & Crouwel, 1985: 24). Two others are visible on chariot A1 and read "The Great Royal Wife, Lady of the Two Lands, Ankhesenamun, who lives" and "The Great Royal Wife, Lady of the Two Lands, Ankhesenamun, who lives for ever and eternity" (Littauer & Crouwel, 1985: 14). Due to these inscriptions Decker (1984: 875, 877) interprets Ankhesenamun as being a joint user of the chariot and sees it in context with the royal family outings known from Nefertiti and Akhenaten together in the chariot.

To analyze these data briefly: most belong to the reign of Akhenaten and Tutankhamun and are associated with the pharaoh. Their context is not martial, except for the ostracon with the shooting woman. Noticeable is the fact that the evidences for women in chariots increases in the Amarna Period, corresponding with the strengthened position of the women of the royal family in this period (Decker, 1984: 877). All in all, depictions and texts dealing with women in chariots – and incidentally, in carrying chairs as well – demonstrate that they used the same means of transport as men. Evidently, there were no gender-specific restrictions for female mobility with respect to means of transportation. The women used appropriate mode of transportation according to their elite social class (Köpp, 2008a: 41).

The pictorial and textual evidence quoted above shows that the chariot obviously combines different benefits for its user. Besides its advantage as military equipment during battle and its use in sport and hunting, it provides the owner with social status and prestige like a Mercedes limousine today. It is quite apparent that in the New Kingdom the chariot was used as a mundane mode of locomotion in the everyday life of the Egyptian elite, employed in a variety of situations.

LONG-DISTANCE TRAVEL

In the majority of cases, the distance covered by chariots is not explicitly mentioned. Nevertheless, there is evidence supporting the idea that the chariot was used for long journeys as well as short ones,[1] even in the desert.[2] This makes sense for the elite, since alternative modes of long-distance land travel are lacking, with the only other options being walking, or the redundant carrying-chair. Donkeys are seldom attested as riding animals in ancient Egypt, though it is assumed that on expeditions the leaders used donkeys for riding in the Middle Kingdom (Köpp-Junk, 2014: 206; Stadelmann, 2006: 301). Horse riding is rarely shown as well, though it was used when high speed tavel was needed such as for messengers.[3]

Sources for Overland Travel

Travels and travellers are mentioned in non-fictional and fictional texts, but traveling is not the core motif; it is mentioned only in passing, and the information is rather fragmentary. Sometimes only the destination or the starting point of a journey is mentioned in the inscription; very seldom both. Moreover, the means of transport or locomotion used on the voyage are rarely stated (Köpp-Junk, 2014: 275-282). But nonetheless there are rare examples of textual evidence for travel to faraway places in civil contexts by chariot. For example, in the Ramesside Papyrus (P.) Anastasi I (18, line 5-20, 6; 23, line 1- 24, 6; 25, line 8-26, 1; Fischer-Elfert, 1983: 123-130, 137-143, 146-147; 1986: 159-161, 196-203, 223-224) the use of chariots on long distance journeys is attested. Several foreign and distant locations, such as Hatti and Qadesh, are mentioned (P. Anastasi I 18, line 7-19, 4; Fischer-Elfert, 1986: 160). The route passes through very rough terrain (P. Anastasi I 19, line 2-6; 24, line 2-26, 6; Fischer-Elfert, 1983: 125-127, 141-148;

1986: 160, 203; Ritter, 1990: 61). Moreover, some expedition texts imply that chariots were also used in some of the expeditions to the Eastern Desert. An inscription on a rock stela from Kanais dating to the reign of Seti I (1276-1265 BC) alludes to the presence of His Majesty's charioteer *Iwny* (Kitchen: 1975: 304, line 1-3). A short text from the reign of Ramesses IV (1386-1377 BC) found in the Wadi Hammamat refers to the visit of the charioteer *Pn-iri-R'w-ms-sw* (Couyat & Montet, 1912: 108, Inscription No. 223). Another inscription of the same period relates to the largest known New Kingdom expedition to the Wadi Hammamat, consisting of 8,361 members. The text lists one royal chariot driver, 20 stable masters and 50 charioteers (Couyat & Montet, 1912: 37, Inscription No. 12, lines 14-16).

The chariot itself could be used as a mode of long-distance locomotion. Of course, on such trips the tread and the construction of wheel hub and axle are exposed to very high stress. But in case of deterioration or loss, replacement and wearing parts as well as spare wheels could be taken along; the latter is known from European bog finds (Hayen, 1989: 32). Therefore, the light-weight construction of the chariot does not contradict its use over long distances. But the use depends on the quality of the travelled route, that is, whether roadways existed or if the subsoil was appropriate enough on its own. Several kinds of tracks suitable for chariots are known from ancient Egypt, accommodating the use of the chariot on long-distance travel (Köpp-Junk, 2014: 88). Roadway construction was very sophisticated in Pharaonic times; many roads and paths have been found, especially in the desert, but within settlements as well (figures 8-10; *Ibidem*: 30-92). The traveller using the chariot benefited from these, since they made traveling more comfortable, releasing him from worrying about the unevenness of the ground or hidden surprises, like stones or small rocks. Additionally, the tracks functioned as a guide (*Ibidem*: 65-67): with their surface visible from far away, they ensured the correct path of the journey, and the traveller's safe arrival at his destination (*Ibidem*: 73-81). When no prepared roadways existed, the chariot was usable for cross-country driving on even ground that was not rugged or sprinkled with rocks and with an appropriate surface, for example, the area between Saqqara and the Bent Pyramid of Sneferu in Dahshur, where the desert consists of sand, scattered with small stones. Every now and then, areas of soft sand appear (figures 6 & 7).

However, the spoked wheels and the narrow treads of only two cm width (chariot A1 from Tutankhamun, Littauer & Crouwel, 1985: 16, and the chariot in the Museum of Florence, Decker, 1986: 41; Horn, 1995: 50) suggest that the chariot was not capable of being driven on uneven or rocky terrain at high speed. In the text of P. Anastasi, which vividly details the adversities a traveller has to face on a long distance journey, a chariot accident is reported when the horses bolted due to a poor driving surface (P. Anastasi I 25, line 8-26, 1; Fischer-Elfert, 1983: 146-147; 1986: 224-225). Moreover, it is described how the traveller passed rough terrain and climbed a mountain with the chariot being tied up by ropes. The text continues "Thy chariot rests upon thy shoulder" (Gardiner,

Figure 6. Desert near Dahshur, between the Mastaba el-Pharaon of king Shepseskaf and the Bent Pyramid. Photograph by H. Köpp-Junk.

1964: 21). Therefore referring to the text (P. Anastasi I 19, line 7-8; Fischer-Elfert, 1983: 127-128; 1986: 160, 167), on rough or rugged sections of the trail the chariot could be carried on the shoulder by the charioteer on short segments of impassable ground. The same is stated by Assyrian texts dating from Tiglath-Pileser I (1114-1076 BC) and Sanherib (705-681 BC; Richter, 2004: 512). Pictorial evidence also proves that Egyptian chariots were carried even on the shoulder of only one man (Brack & Brack, 1988: pl. 88). Of course this procedure was only applicable for very short segments of the whole travel route.

Another possible way of moving chariots is dismantling and transporting them on donkeys or ox-drawn wagons in rough terrain. Richter (2004: 512) assumes this mode of transportation for Assyrian chariots to reach far away battlefields, although there is no attested evidence for this as yet

Figure 7. Desert surface in Dahshur with areas of very soft sand and zones of sand scattered with pebbles. Photograph by H. Köpp-Junk.

Figure 8. Ways were built by clearing the track. The debris was removed and mounted on both sides of the trail, marking the direction and making it visible from and over long distances. The ground was leveled and the unevenness of the track, like small wadis, was filled with additional material such as earth and stone chips. The construction was similar to the building technique nowadays. Ways have an even, unplastered sand surface. The picture shows a modern way near Dahshur. Photograph by H. Köpp-Junk.

Figure 9. The oldest paved road attested in ancient Egypt is the Widan el-Faras Road, running nearly 12 km through the desert. This Old Kingdom road shows very different kinds of surfaces on its entire length. In this section it is plastered with sandstone slabs. Photograph by H. Köpp-Junk.

Figure 10. Section of the Widan el-Faras Road, covered with petrified wood. Photograph by H. Köpp-Junk.

from ancient Egypt. Transporting the disassembled chariots on donkey back would have the advantage that, due to the form of their hooves, they have an excellent foothold on hilly or uneven ground (Ohler, 1988: 35) and are therefore independent of roads and paths. The maximum carrying capacity of a donkey is about 150 kg in temperate climates (*Ibidem*: 35). However, the British Army manual from 1923, referring to long-distance travel, calculates the carrying capacity of donkeys at only 50 kg (Peacock & Maxfield, 2001: 297). These very differing figures demonstrate the fact that the carrying capacity was not only severely influenced by climate and temperature, but also by the duration of the journey. As the chariot in the Museum of Florence with only 24 kg[4] (Decker, 1986: 42) shows, an Egyptian chariot can weigh less than 30 kg, though depending on the type.[5] Therefore the transport of a disassembled Egyptian chariot by donkeys was theoretically possible, although it should be noted that the component parts are still a bulky freight, especially the wheels and the pole.

Apart from donkeys, it is conceivable that chariots could be transported on sledges or wheeled vehicles like carts and wagons. In contrast to donkeys, their use is essentially influenced by the condition of the travelled terrain, for they need solid ground or trafficable roadways. Moreover, it is to point out that, although sledges were used since the 1st Dynasty (2900-2720 BC), carts and wagons are very seldom attested in the New Kingdom; all in all hardly 10 wagons and even fewer carts are evidenced up to the 19th Dynasty (Köpp-Junk, 2014: 159-198).

Therefore, a combination of the several alternatives to cover long distances by chariot is possible: *i.e.* its use as mode of locomotion, being carried on short distances on the shoulder as proved from ancient Egyptian texts, or transported on the back of donkeys or oxen-drawn wheeled vehicles or sledges, which is theoretically possible but not attested yet. The destination, the quality of the traveling route, and the existence or length of impassable sections are the determining factors whether or in which combination these several possibilities were mixed.

Chariot Transport by Water

Often the full itinerary of a journey was a combination of sections travelled by land and by water. Texts and depictions reveal the transport of chariots by ship to cover segments of long-distance journeys by waterway, or just to cross the river Nile or a canal.

The Bentresh stela (Kitchen, 1979: 284-287) mentions that a statue of Khonsu was brought to Bakhtan on a large vessel, accompanied by five smaller boats, with chariots and horses being taken along for the outward journey that lasted for 17 months.

As well as rough terrain, crossing the Nile or a canal does not hinder the traveller from continuing his journey by chariot. In the story of the Doomed Prince it is stated that he was given a chariot including weapons before he ferried across the Nile to the east bank (Papyrus [P.] Harris 500 verso. 4, 13-5, 1; Gardiner, 1932: 2, line 14-16). Some scenes from New Kingdom tombs of the 18th Dynasty show the transport of chariots by ship in order to cross the river such as in TT 57 (Hofmann, 1989: pl. 70; Wreszinski, 1923: 207) as well as in TT 162 (Davies, 1963: pl. 18; Hofmann, 1989: pl. 69) and TT 324 (Davies & Gardiner, 1948: pl. 22, 23; Hofmann, 1989: pl. 72). In the tomb of Paheri in El Kab (Hofmann, 1989: pl. 68; Tylor & Griffith, 1894: pl. 3) two ships are shown, each transporting a chariot. So obviously the transport of horses and chariots by boat was common practice in order to continue the journey to its point of destination with a mode of locomotion appropriate to the traveller's social status (Hofmann, 1989: 289).

TRAVELLING SPEED

To calculate a day's journey for reaching the next water deposit or lodging place, traveling speed was of great importance. Naturally, this differed dramatically depending on the means of transportation, as well as other factors including the weather, terrain and the traveller's physical constitution. Walking in sand is more exhausting than on solid ground and influences the traveller's advancement considerably. For chariots, thin wheels like those found on Egyptian chariots are even more prone to sink into soft sand than wider ones. On sandy ground friction increases and is 30 times higher than on even terrain (Horn, 1995: 55), so the tensile strength increases as well. Thus, for the horses it is more exhausting to pull the chariot through sand than over solid ground, which affects the progress and the one day travel distance.

Information regarding the speed of overland travel is seldom provided by ancient Egyptian sources. By taking similar means of transportation and locomotion known from the Middle Ages, the modern era, and from contemporary practical experiments in temperate climates into account, the ancient Egyptian speed of travel can be estimated (Köpp, 2013: 21-22; Köpp-Junk, 2014: 347-363). On horseback, up to 4-7 km/h could be reached at walking pace, and 45-52 km/h at full gallop (Junkelmann, 1990: 46). Concerning the speed of Egyptian chariots, Hofmann (1989: 333-344) stated that the calculated breaking resistance of the chariots from the tomb of Tutankhamun lies between 40.1 km/h (chariot A5) and 87.4 km/h (chariot A3), at which speed the rim would break. A recent experiment with a replica of an Egyptian chariot gave a speed of 38 km/h over a distance of 1,000 m on modest ground with a driver of about 70 kg (Spruytte, 1977: 39). Therefore it seems to be realistic to suppose a maximum speed of about 40 km/h for Egyptian chariots. In order to facilitate a comparison to current conditions: at modern trotting races about 50-55 km/h could be reached (Hofmann, 1989: 334; Kemna, 1992: 366; Spruytte, 1977: 39). Nevertheless, these figures do not give a hint concerning the daily rate on long-distance travel on chariots, but refer to the maximum speed on short distances. Approximate values might be achieved by looking at the speed of ridden horses, which lies at 30-50 km/day (Köpp-Junk, 2014: 399). For horse-drawn freight wagons from the European Middle Ages 20-30 km/day are assumed (Denecke, 1987: 215), having, however, a much higher weight than an Egyptian chariot. To ascertain more definitive figures, further experiments with scientifically reliable replicas of Egyptian chariots are required.

CONCLUSION

On short distances the chariot was used in civil context like a modern high status, trendy sports car – not only as the fastest means of locomotion next to riding, but also a very highly valued one for both men and women. The chariot replaced the carrying chair as the most prestigious way to travel. This change is a very important fact in the development of the Egyptian traffic system from the Old Kingdom to the end of the New Kingdom: new means of transport and locomotion appeared, such as wagons, carts, horses and chariots, but they did not replace each other; they complement those already extant, like oxen, donkeys and sledges because of their different spheres of use. The replacement of the carrying chair by the chariot is the only one attested.

Apart from being a status symbol and object of prestige, chariots were used as a mundane mode of locomotion on short trips and long-distance journeys. Cross-country driving with chariots depended on the surface of the travelled routes. In the New Kingdom the technique of roadway construction had reached a very high level, supporting the use of chariots on long distances. Over unsuitable terrain with rough or hilly sections it could be transported by donkeys or vehicles or carried, depending on the length of the impassable section. Pictorial evidence shows that chariots were taken along on ships to continue the overland travel afterwards. The traveling speed depended on various aspects as to the quality of the tracks and the travelled terrain, the condition of the traveller and his team of horses, temperature and climate.

NOTES

1 Long-distance travels are defined here as journeys over greater intervals lasting more than one day. Accordingly, short trips cover less distance and take less time.

2 On desert travel and transport in Egypt in detail see Köpp (2013: 103-128).

3 On modes of transport and locomotion in detail see Köpp-Junk (2013: 92-275).

4 Herold points out that some pieces were not included during the restoration, which implies that the actual weight was somewhat higher. The replica of the *Roemer- and Pelizaeus-Museum, Hildesheim* has a weight of less than 30 kg as well (Herold, 2004: 126-127, 138).

5 For the surely heavier quadriga in the Museum August Kestner in Hannover see Köpp-Junk &

Loeben (2013: 174-175) and Littauer & Crouwel (1979b: 117-118).

CITED LITERATURE

Brack, A. & A. Brack. 1980. Das Grab des Tjanuni. – Mainz, Philipp von Zabern.

Callender, V.G. 2004. Queen Tausret and the End of Dynasty 19. – Studien zur Altägyptischen Kultur 32: 81-104.

Caminos, R.A. 1977. A Tale of Woe: Papyrus Pushkin 127. – Oxford, Griffith Institute.

Couyat, J. & P. Montet. 1912. Les inscriptions hiéroglyphiques et hiératiques du Ouâdi Hammâmât. – Le Caire, Institut Français d'Archéologie Orientale du Caire.

Chassinat, É. 1928. Le temple d'Edfou. Part 10,2. Mission Archéologique Française au Caire 27, 2. – Le Caire, Institut Français d'Archéologie Orientale du Caire.

Chassinat, É. 1931. Le temple d'Edfou. Part 6. Mission Archéologique Française au Caire 23. – Le Caire, Institut Français d'Archéologie Orientale du Caire.

Daressy, M.G. 1901. Ostraca. Catalogue Général des Antiquités Égyptiennes du Musée du Caire No. 25001-25385. – Cairo, l'Institut Français d'Archéologie Orientale.

Davies, N. 1903. The Rock Tombs of El Amarna. Part I. The Tomb of Meryra. – London, Egypt Exploration Fund.

Davies, N. 1905a. The Rock Tombs of El Amarna. Part II. The Tombs of Panehesy and Meryra 2. – London, Egypt Exploration Fund.

Davies, N. 1905b. The Rock Tombs of El Amarna. Part III. The Tombs of Huya and Ahmes. – London, Egypt Exploration Fund.

Davies, N. 1906. The Rock Tombs of El Amarna. Part IV. The Tombs of Penthu, Mahu and others. – London, Egypt Exploration Fund.

Davies, N. 1908. The Rock Tombs of El Amarna. Part VI. The Tombs of Parennefer, Tutu and Ay. – London, Egypt Exploration Fund.

Davies, N. 1923. Two Ramesside Tombs at Thebes. – New York, Metropolitan Museum.

Davies, N. 1953. The Temple of Hibis in el Khargeh-Oasis, Part III. – New York, Publications of The Metropolitan Museum of Art Egyptian Expedition 17.

Davies, N. 1963. Scenes from Some Theban Tombs. Private Tombs at Thebes IV. – Oxford Griffith Institute.

Davies, N. & A.H. Gardiner. 1926. The Tomb of Huy, the Viceroy of Nubia in the Reign of Tutankhamun. – London, Egypt Exploration Society.

Davies, N. & A.H. Gardiner. 1936. Ancient Egyptian Paintings. Part II. – Chicago, University of Chicago Press.

Davies, N. & A.H. Gardiner. 1948. Seven Private Tombs at Kurnah. – London, Egypt Exploration Society.

Decker, W. 1984a. Wagen. In: Helck, W. & W. Westendorf. 1984. Lexikon der Ägyptologie. Band VI. – Wiesbaden, Harrassowitz: 1130-1135.

Decker, W. 1984b. Die Inschrift auf dem Wagen des Tutanchamun. In: Junge, F. Ed. 1984. Studien zur Sprache und Religion Ägyptens. Band 1. Festschrift Wolfhart Westendorf. – Göttingen, Hubert & Co.: 869-877.

Decker, W. 1986. Der Wagen im Alten Ägypten. In: Treue, W. Ed. 1986. Achse, Rad und Wagen. – Göttingen, Vandenhoeck & Ruprecht: 35-59.

Decker, W. & M. Herb. 1994. Bildatlas zum Sport im Alten Ägypten. Corpus der bildlichen Quellen zu Leibesübungen, Spiel, Jagd, Tanz und verwandten Themen. – Leiden, Brill.

Denecke, D. 1987. Straße und Weg im Mittelalter als Lebensraum und Vermittler zwischen entfernten Orten. In: Herrmann, B. Ed. 1987. Mensch und Umwelt im Mittelalter. – Stuttgart, Fourier Verlag: 207-223.

Epigraphic Survey. 1930. Medinet Habu I. Earlier Historical Records of Ramses III. – Chicago, Oriental Institute of the University of Chicago Press.

Epigraphic Survey. 1932. Medinet Habu II, Later Historical Records of Ramses III. – Chicago, Oriental Institute of the University of Chicago Press.

Fischer-Elfert, H.W. 1983. Die satirische Streitschrift des Papyrus Anastasi I. Textzusammenstellung. – Wiesbaden, Harrassowitz.

Fischer-Elfert, H.W. 1986. Die satirische Streitschrift des Papyrus Anastasi I. Übersetzung und Kommentar. – Wiesbaden, Harrassowitz.

Gardiner, A.H. 1932. Late Egyptian Stories. Bibliotheca Aegyptiaca I. – Brüssel, Édition de la Fondation Égyptologique Reine Élisabeth.

Gardiner, A.H. 1964 [1911]. Egyptian Hieratic Texts. Series I: Literary texts of the New Kingdom Part 1: The Papyrus Anastasi I and the Papyrus Koller, together with the parallel texts. – Leipzig, Hinrichs.

Hayen, H. 1989. Früheste Nachweise des Wagens und die Entwicklung der Transportmittel. – Mitteilungen der Berliner Gesellschaft für Anthropologie und Ethnologie und Urgeschichte 10: 91-99.

Helck, H.W. 1955. Urkunden der 18. Dynastie: Historische Inschriften Thutmosis' III. und Amenophis II. Urkunden des ägyptischen Altertums IV/17. – Berlin, Akademie-Verlag.

Helck, H.W. 1957. Urkunden der 18. Dynastie: Historische Inschriften Thutmosis' IV. und biographische Inschriften seiner Zeitgenossen. Urkunden des ägyptischen Altertums IV/19-20. – Berlin, Akademie-Verlag.

Helck, H.W. 1958. Urkunden der 18. Dynastie: Inschriften von Amenophis III. bis Haremheb und ihrer Zeitgenossen. Urkunden des ägyptischen Altertums IV/22. – Berlin, Akademie-Verlag.

Herold, A. 2004. Funde und Funktionen - Streitwagentechnologie im Alten Ägypten. In: Fansa, M. Ed. 2004. Rad und Wagen. Der Ursprung einer Innovation im Vorderen Orient und Europa. – Mainz, Philipp von Zabern: 123-142.

Hoffmeier, J.K. 1988. The Chariot Scenes. In: Redford, D.B. Ed. 1988. The Akhenaten Temple Project 2: *Rwd-mnw*, Foreigners and Inscriptions. – Toronto, University of Toronto Press: 35-45.

Hofmann, U. 1989. Fuhrwesen und Pferdehaltung im Alten Ägypten. – Bonn, Rheinische Friedrich-Wilhelms-Universität.

Horn, V. 1995. Das Pferd im Alten Orient: Das Streitwagenpferd der Frühzeit in seiner Umwelt, im Training und im Vergleich zum neuzeitlichen Distanz-, Reit- und Fahrpferd. Documenta Hippologica. – Hildesheim, Georg Olms.

Houlihan, P.F. 2001. Wit and Humour in Ancient Egypt. – London, Rubicon Press.

Junkelmann, M. 1990. Die Reiter Roms. I. Reise, Jagd, Triumph und Circusrennen. – Mainz, Philipp von Zabern.

Kemna, C. 1992. Bemerkungen zu den Darstellungen der Wildeseljagd. – Turin, International Association of Egyptologists: 365-370.

Kitchen, K.A. 1975. Ramesside Inscriptions: Historical and Biographical. Part I. – Oxford, Blackwell.

Kitchen, K.A. 1979. Ramesside Inscriptions: Historical and Biographical. Part II. – Oxford, Blackwell.

Köpp, H. 2008a. Weibliche Mobilität: Frauen in Sänften und auf Streitwagen. In: Peust, C. Ed. 2008. Miscellanea in honorem Wolfhart Westendorf. – Göttinger Miszellen Beiheft 3: 34-44.

Köpp, H. 2008b. Reisen in prädynastischer Zeit und Frühzeit. In: Engel, E., U. Hartung & V. Müller. Eds. 2008. Zeichen aus dem Sand. Festschrift Günter Dreyer. – Wiesbaden, Harrassowitz: 401-412.

Köpp, H. 2013. Desert Travel and Transport in Ancient Egypt. An Overview Based on Epigraphic, Pictorial and Archaeological Evidence. In: Riemer, H. & F. Förster. Eds. 2013. Desert Road Archaeology in Ancient Egypt and Beyond. – Köln, Heinrich-Barth-Institut: 107-132 (In Print).

Köpp-Junk. H. 2013. Travel. In: Frood, E. & W. Wendrich. Eds. UCLA Encyclopedia of Egyptology. http://digital2.library.ucla.edu/viewItem.do?ark=21198/zz002gvznf.

Köpp-Junk, H. 2014. Reisen im Alten Ägypten. Reisekultur, Fortbewegungs- und Transportmittel in pharaonischer Zeit. – Wiesbaden, Harrassowitz (In Print. Note: the page numbers refer to the text of the manuscript submitted to the publishing house; they might at times differ from the printed version).

Köpp-Junk, H. & C.E. Loeben. 2013. Plaque avec représentations: char et hiéroglyphes. In: Andreu-Lanöe, G., S. Labbé-Toutée & P. Rigault. Eds. L'art du contour - Le dessin dans l'Égypte ancienne. Catalogue de l'exposition édité sous la direction de Guillemette Andreu-Lanoe. – Paris, Somogy: 174-175.

Lacovara, P. 1997. The New Kingdom Royal City. – London, Paul Kegan.

Langenbach, O. 2009. Aufbau und Organisation der ägyptischen Streitwagentruppe. In: Gundlach, R. & C. Vogel. Eds. 2009. Militärgeschichte des pharaonischen Ägypten. – Paderborn/München/Wien/Zürich, Ferdinand Schöningh: 345-358.

Leclant, J. 1960. Astarté à cheval d'après les représentations égyptiennes. – Syria 37: 1-67.

Littauer, M.A. & J.H. Crouwel. 1979a. Wheeled Vehicles and Ridden Animals in the Ancient Near East. – Leiden, Brill.

Littauer, M.A. & J.H. Crouwel. 1979b. An Egyptian Wheel in Brooklyn. – Journal of Egyptian Archaeology 65: 107-120.

Littauer, M.A. & J.H. Crouwel. 1985. Chariots and Related Equipment from the Tomb of Tutankhamun. – Oxford, Griffith Institute.

Ohler, N. 1988 [1986]. Reisen im Mittelalter. – München, Artemis.

Peacock, D.P.S. & V.A. Maxfield. 2001. Survey and Excavation at Mons Claudianus 1987-1993. Volume II: Survey and Excavation. – Le Caire, Institut Français d'Archéologie Orientale.

Peck, W.H. & J.G. Ross. 1979. Ägyptische Zeichnungen aus drei Jahrtausenden. – Bergisch-Gladbach, Lübbe.

Pomerantseva, N. 1992. The Sketches on Ostraca or "The Sheets of Sketch-book" of Ancient Egyptian Masters. In: Atti Sesto Congresso Internazionale di Egittologia I. – Turin, International Association of Egyptologists: 513-520.

Powell, T.G.E. 1963. Some Implications of Chariotry. In: Forster, J.L. & L. Alcock. Eds. 1963. Culture and Environment. Essays in Honour of Sir Cyril Fox. – London, Routledge/London, Paul Kegan: 153-170.

Redford, D.B. 1973. Studies on Akhenaten at Thebes. I. A Report on the Work of the Akhenaten Temple Projekt of the University Museum, University of Pensylvania. – American Research Center in Egypt 10: 77-94.

Ritter, T. 1990. *dr.wt*: der Speichenkranz des Wagenrades. – Zeitschrift für Ägyptische Sprache und Altertumskunde 117: 60-62.

Saleh, M. & H. Sourouzian. 1986. Die Hauptwerke im ägyptischen Museum Kairo. Offizieller Katalog. – Mainz, Philipp von Zabern.

Schulman, A.R. 1957. Egyptian Representation of Horsemen and Riding in the New Kingdom. – Journal of Near Eastern Studies 16: 263-271.

Schulman, A.R. 1963. The Egyptian Chariotry: A Reexamination. – Journal of the American Research Center in Egypt 2: 75-98.

Schulman, A.R. 1980. Chariots, Chariotry and the Hyksos. – Journal of the Society for the Study of Egyptian Antiquities 10, 2: 105-153.

Spalinger, A.J. 2003. The Battle of Qadesh: The Chariot Frieze at Abydos. – Ägypten und Levante 13: 163-199.

Spruytte, J. 1977. Etudes expérimentales sur l'attelage. Contribution à l'histoire du cheval. – Paris, Crépin Leblond.

Stadelmann, R. 2006. Riding the Donkey: A Means of Transportation for Foreign Rulers. In: Czerny, E., I. Hein, H. Hunger, D. Melman & A. Schwab. Eds. 2006. Timelines. Studies in Honour of Manfred Bietak. Part II. – Leuven, Peeters: 301-304.

Tylor, J.J. & F.L. Griffith. 1894. The Tomb of Paheri at El Kab. Wall Drawings and Monuments of El Kab. – London, Egypt Exploration Fund.

Vandier, J. 1964. Manuel d'archéologie égyptienne. Part IV. – Paris, Picard.

Wettengel, W. 2003. Die Erzählung von den beiden Brüdern: der Papyrus d'Orbiney und die Königsideologie der Ramessiden. – Freiburg, Universitätsverlag.

Wildung D. & R. Drenkhahn. 1984. Nofret Die Schöne. Die Frau im Alten Ägypten. – Mainz, Philipp von Zabern.

Woytowitsch, E. 1995. Die Wagen der Schweiz in der europäischen Bronzezeit. – Basel, Schwabe.

Wreszinski, W. 1923. Atlas zur altägyptischen Kulturgeschichte. Band 1, 2. – Leipzig, Hinrichs.

THE CHARIOT THAT PLUNDERS FOREIGN LANDS: 'THE HYMN TO THE KING IN HIS CHARIOT'

Colleen Manassa

INTRODUCTION

New Kingdom (1549-1069 BC) literature preserves a number of new genres of texts, ranging from love poetry and praise of cities to lengthy military compositions and works that can be classified as historical fiction (Manassa, 2010; Moers, 2010; Ragazzoli, 2008). The genre is itself not a fixed category of unchanging types of text, but rather reflects changes in society (Fowler, 1982: 170-183). Perhaps no New Kingdom genre better reflects societal – indeed technological – developments than the composition known as the Hymn to the King in His Chariot (also known as Poem on the King's Chariot). Prior to the adoption of the chariot into the Egyptian military during the terminal 17th and early 18th Dynasty, such a text could not have been composed. Furthermore, the frequent incorporation of foreign loan words into the Hymn to the King in His Chariot showcases the increasing cosmopolitanism of New Kingdom society, further reflected in contemporaneous literature (Spalinger, 2007: 151-152).

The present tripartite overview of the Hymn to the King in His Chariot will first describe the content of the two surviving exemplars of the text and their potential for understanding ancient chariot terminology and other parts of the royal panoply, and then examine the cultural significance of the texts as literature. The literary analysis will focus particularly on how paronomasia, a punning type of word-play, is used with technical terminology to create a work of art. The examination of the literary aspects of the text further exploits the intertextual relationship between the Hymn to the King in His Chariot and a work of historical fiction commonly called The Capture of Joppa. Finally, the present article examines several different festivals and events that possess aspects salient to the Hymn to the King in His Chariot and that may provide performative settings for the composition. Ultimately, focusing on these relatively murky texts may aid in additional identifications of obscure terminology and most importantly restore a work not commonly included within examinations and presentations of New Kingdom literature.

HYMN TO THE KING IN HIS CHARIOT: TECHNICAL ANALYSIS

The Hymn to the King in His Chariot is known from only two ostraca – Edinburgh O. 916 (now National Museum of Scotland A.1956.319) and O. Turin S. 9588 (formerly CG 57365). The Edinburgh ostracon was first included in Erman's collection of ancient Egyptian literature (1923), following an 1880 edition of the ostracon itself; the only other literary compilation to include the hymns is Bresciani (1999: 498-499). The *editio princeps* of the Turin ostracon was published by Černý (1927: 224-226), subsequently republished by Lopez (1982: pl. 112). The first philological edition of both ostraca appeared in 1933 by Dawson & Peet. In 1986, Schulman examined Egyptian technical terms for the chariot, including an analysis of the oft-attested loan words. However, as Schulman himself notes (1986: 19), his interests lay solely with the lexicographical analysis of the chariot's parts rather than a "literary, grammatical, or philological viewpoint." Hofmann (1989: 208-215) analyzed the components of the chariot in the hymns in the context of other texts that include technical chariot terminology. In 2008, Manley published another translation, which offers often unsubstantiated identifications of particular terms with specific aspects of chariot construction. Studies of the abundant loan words in the short hymns (Hoch, 1994; Jéquier, 1922; Meeks, 1997; Schneider, 2008; Ward, 1969) and an online compilation of previous commentaries by Popko (2012a; 2012b) represent the only other substantial scholarly treatments of these interesting compositions.

The two texts do not contain any overlapping passages, but the ostraca appear to represent different sections of a single, lengthier composition (Dawson & Peet, 1933: 168; Schulman, 1986: 19). Even if the two ostraca do not represent a single composition, they are certainly within the same genre. Although clearly poetic in form – as has long been recognized – the expected verse points are not present. The following translation and commentary focuses on the identification of each chariot part mentioned within the hymns, as well as any theological associations of the chariot (for an expanded philological analysis, see Manassa, Forthcoming a).

National Museum of Scotland A.1956.319 (formerly Edinburgh Ostracon (O.). 916)

Edinburgh O. 916 is now accessioned as National Museum of Scotland (NMA) A.1956.319 (Manley, 2008). The ostracon measures 21.6 cm high and 10.2 cm wide and contains fifteen lines of text on the recto and sixteen on the verso, all in black ink. The preserved text both begins and ends in the middle of a sentence, and one can only guess at the original length of the composition. The basic structure of the text consists of names of chariot parts or weapons associated with the chariot that are then described using metaphorical or punning statements. This structure is immediately apparent in the first lines of the recto:

[1][...]*m3* sees every foreign land,
> while (as for) its ram's [2]head–
> the two horns are iron.

The flo[3]or (*im*) of your chariot:
> gracious (*im3*) towards you do
> they become, [4]the (foreign) rulers.

The cab supports (ꜥ*dr*) of your cha[5]riot:
> those who terrify (ꜥ*rḏ.wt*) every
> foreign country.

The [6]rail (*ṯ3*) of your chariot:
> it takes away (*ṯ3y*)[7] the spirit and
> morale of the (enemy) troops.

The preserved text appears to begin in the middle of a word ending with –*m3*, followed by the phrase (*ḥr*) *m3* "sees". One can leave aside the highly obscure ram horns for now (see below), and focus instead on three uses of paronomasia in these lines that are characteristic of the hymns as a whole. The first feature that is immediately apparent is the use of loan words – and for the difficult translation of this text, recourse must be made to Semitic cognates. The following analysis of the three terms will suggest that they describe the main elements of the body of the Egyptian chariot, with each punning statement demonstrating how that part of the royal chariot acts towards the foreign lands.

The term *im* appears in another text that describes the technical aspects of chariot construction – Papyrus (P.) Anastasi IV, part of the large corpus of the Late Egyptian Miscellanies. In one text within P. Anastasi IV is a list of objects that must be prepared for the pharaoh's arrival, which include "beautiful chariots of berery-wood" with various gilded elements and other parts decorated with colored leather, rosettes, and semi-precious stones (Gardiner, 1937: 53). Within the description of the chariot is the following statement: "their *im* of weaving (*m sḫt*)" (Gardiner, 1937: 53; following Jéquier, 1922: 153-154). Although Caminos (1954: 214) disputes the reading 'weaving', no other term appears to fit the context, and the P. Anastasi IV passage would be a logical description of the woven floor of a chariot (Hofmann, 1989: 216; Schulman, 1986: 40). Interlaced leather straps were affixed to the lower wooden D-shaped floor of the chariot (figure 1). The identification of *im* as the entire floor of the chariot rests on the wood-determinative of

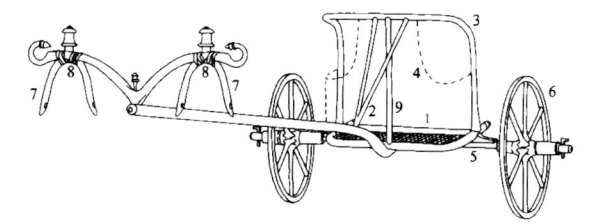

1. *im* "floor"
2. *ꜥdr* "front support"
3. *ṯꜣ* "rail"
4. *bt* "side"
5. *sd* "tail" (axle?)
6. *ḥꜣb* "tire"
7. *dr.wt* "yoke saddles"
8. *mḥꜣ* "bindings" (for yoke saddles?)
9. *ꜥmd* "front support"

Figure 1. Schematic rendering of an ancient Egyptian chariot, with potential identification of the parts of the chariot mentioned in the Hymn to the King in His Chariot. From (adapted): Herold (1999: pl. XXI).

the word in P. Anastasi IV and the leather determinative in NMA A.1956.319, which would encompass the D-shaped wooden piece of the floor as well as the leather straps that created the surface on which the charioteer (in this case the king) would stand.

Next are the *ꜥdr*, a term possibly related to the Semitic root for 'helper' (Darnell, 1986: 17-18; Fischer-Elfert, 1986: 204; Hoch, 1994: 88-90) that are said to 'terrify' – using another loan word (*ꜥrdt*; Hoch, 1994: 78-79) – the foreign lands. Schulman (1986: 30) interpreted the *ꜥdr* as yoke braces. However, since those are consistently made from leather, the identification does not fit with the wood determinative in NMS A.1956.319; furthermore, yoke braces are not a major part of the chariot equipment (for examples in two-dimensional depictions, see Manassa, 2002: 264). Alternatively, as Hoch (1994: 90) suggested, the *ꜥdr* could be the wooden supports that connected the body to the yoke pole, what Littauer & Crouwel (1985: 4) call the 'front supports'. Based on Hoch's reasoning, the *ꜥdr* could also incorporate the 'triple supports' of the front rail (*Ibidem*: 10-11). The 'front supports' are leather in the Florence chariot (Littauer & Crouwel, 1985: 105; Roberto Del Francia 2002: 26-27), but wood on several of Tutankhamun's chariots, and also appear to be wood from their depictions in reliefs of the Ramesside Period (*e.g.* Epigraphic Survey, 1930: pls. 9, 10, 16, *passim*). The supports that stretch between the siding of the chariot and the top rail in depictions of the royal chariot at Medinet Habu may represent another possibility for the identification of the *ꜥdr*-supports (*e.g.* figure 2; Epigraphic Survey, 1930: pls. 16, 17, 22, 23, 24 31, 32, 33, 35, 37, 38, 42; 1932: pls. 68, 70, 72, 73, 77, 87, 88, 90, 116). This feature of the chariot body appears as early as the reign of Thutmose III (Hofmann, 1989: 453, 455) and appears sporadically in depictions of royal chariots in the battle reliefs of Seti I (Epigraphic Survey, 1986: pls. 11, 28, 35). The *ꜥdr*-support would then be differentiated from the *ꜥmd*, which would be the main vertical support at the front of the body. However, without further documentation, one cannot precisely determine whether the *ꜥdr* supported different elements within the body, connected the body to the yoke, or encompassed both elements.

The *ṯꜣ* of the chariot, which Schulman (1986: 32-33) tentatively identified as the 'handgrip' may instead be the entire upper rail of the chariot body. This solves the problem that Schulman noted, which is that a chariot should have more than one handgrip (Manassa, 2002: 264) and here, the term *ṯꜣ* is singular. In Egyptian chariots, the rail was either one continuous piece attached to the floor of the chariot or two pieces precisely joined (Littauer & Crouwel, 1986: 9-10). In the chariot-manufacturing scene from the tomb of Puyemre (Theban Tomb [TT] 39; Davies, 1922: pl. 23), the rail is shown as a single horse-shoe-shaped element. This rail (*ṯꜣ*) is indeed what one would 'seize' (*ṯꜣy*) while driving or riding in the chariot, and seizing the 'morale and spirit' of the enemy troops can be illustrated quite dramatically in reliefs such as scenes from the Sety I (1296-1279 BC) battle reliefs (Epigraphic Survey, 1986: pls. 12, 13) and Ramesses III (1185-1153 BC) at Medinet Habu (*Ibidem*, 1932: pl. 73).

If properly identified, the three terms, *im*, *ꜥdr*, and *ṯꜣ* would describe three inter-connected parts: the floor, the body or front supports, and the rail, the three main structural components of the body (figure 1).

In each case, we see the chief literary device within The Hymn to the King in His Chariot: paronomasia. This form of word-play is often recognized in Middle Kingdom literature, but rarely appreciated in the corresponding corpus of New

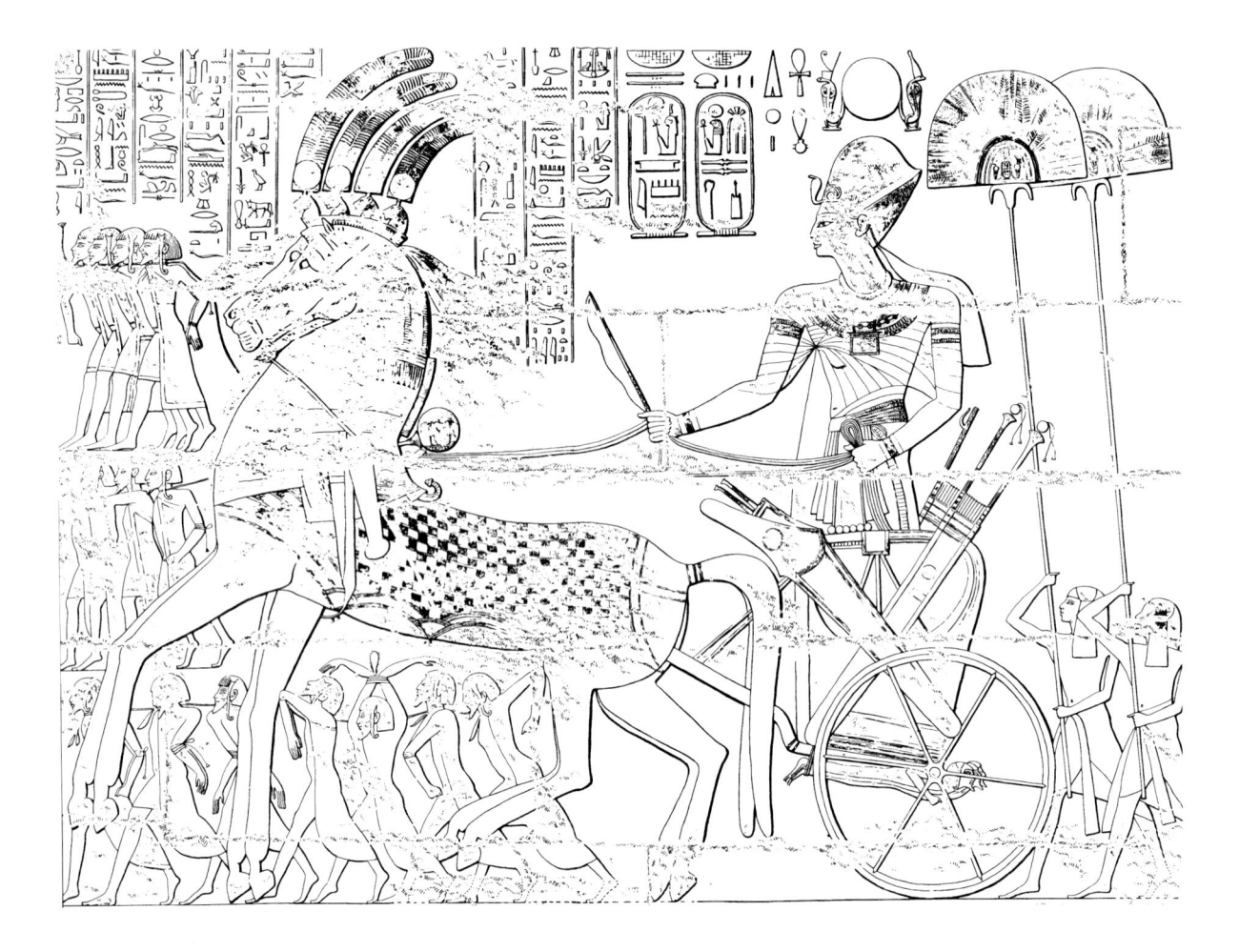

Figure 2. Ramesses III in his chariot returning from the first Libyan campaign. From: Epigraphic Survey (1930: pl. 24).

Kingdom texts (see further below). Placed within the corpus of New Kingdom hymns, The Hymn to the King in His Chariot represents an under-appreciated literary achievement of the Ramesside Period (1298-1069 BC).

The next portion of the poem appears to describe the siding of the chariot, and does not use a pun, but rather a mythological allusion:

The sides (*bt*) [8] of your chariot:
    Bata, lord of [9]Saka,
        while he is the staff of the son of Bastet,
        [10]as one exiled to every foreign land.

The term *bt* is probably related to Akkadian *bītu*, which can be used to describe a 'container, repository, or housing' (Oppenheim, 1965: 282), and Hoch (1994: 115) notes that the Amarna letters can use *bītu* to refer to a leather container. Schulman (1986: 40) is probably correct then, to equate the *bt* in The Hymn to the King in His Chariot with the wood and leather siding of the chariot. The sides are compared to Bata, among the more mysterious of divinities within the Egyptian pantheon. The toponym Saka can be equated with modern el-Qeis, between the Bahr Yusuf and the Nile just east of el-Bahnasa/Oxyrhynchus (Barbotin, 1999: 13-14). The appearance of Bata, Lord of Saka, in The Hymn to the King in His Chariot is interesting for its literary allusions, since a cycle of stories may have been composed around this figure (Barbotin, 1999). In the Tale of the Two Brothers, Bata is the protagonist – the younger brother, who, after being seduced by his elder brother's wife, flees to the Valley of the Pine, and after several mythologically charged episodes, reigns as Pharaoh of Egypt (Hollis, 2008; Wettengel, 2003). The 'exile' of Bata in the hymn and his self-imposed flight in the Tale of the Two Brothers may thus share a common mythological template. Furthermore, an Egyptian chariot is an object that, like the divinity Bata, travels to Syria-Palestine, and later returns in triumph.

The next section of the Hymn to the King in His Chariot in the Edinburgh ostracon details the weapons and other elements of the chariot's accoutrements. One can distinguish between organic, functioning parts of the chariot, and additional elements of the chariot's equipment that are not part of the actual 'machine' (Schulman, 1986: 20-21).

The spears (ẖmy.wt) of your <chariot>:
> [11]the steering oars (ẖmy.w) at the back of the foreign lands.

The javelin (niwy) of your chariot:
> [12]fear (nrw) of you has entered into them (the foreign lands).

The [13]dagger (ḥrp) of your chariot:
> [14]it terrifies (ḥri) those who are in your grasp,
> devouring the land of Kharu,
> carrying away [verso, 1]the land of Kush.

The sword (sf.t) of your [2]chariot:
> your strong arm cuts down (sft) the rebellious mountains;[3]
> and they fall to [4]pieces.

The four weapons mentioned in this section represent most of the chariot's panoply – the ꜥwn.t staff appears in the following section, and the Turin ostracon begins with the most distinctive chariot weapon of all: the bow. Of the four weapons, the identification of the ẖmy.wt is the most difficult, since it only occurs in one other context, namely a list of weapons in Papyrus (P.). Koller (Gardiner, 1937: 116-117): "Their chariots of berery-wood, filled with [all manner] of weapons of war: 80 arrows in their quivers, the hemyt-weapon, the mereh-lance, the herep-dagger, the sefet-sword."

The punning on the ẖmy.wt of the chariot led the author to create a further metaphor in which the foreign lands are a ship with Egyptian steering oars at their stern. The nautical imagery in this line of the hymn is prominent in several Egyptian literary works (Parkinson, 2012: 133-135, 208). The pharaoh can be the pilot of the 'ship of state', and the metaphor in the The Hymn to the King in His Chariot provides an interesting extension of the nautical metaphor to international relations. Like the preceding lines of text, the pun on the steering oar emphasizes Egypt's political domination of foreign territory without highlighting the violence and warfare that characterize most of the remaining lines of the hymn.

The other weapons mentioned in the Edinburgh ostracon are easier to identify, since they are well paralleled in other texts. Multiple javelins appear within the quivers of Ramesside chariots, with their distinctive decorative strap with ball (e.g. figure 2; Epigraphic Survey, 1986: pls. 3, 4, passim; 1930: pls. 9, 10, passim). The edged weapons use both foreign and Egyptian terms. According to Hoch (1994: 233-235), the ḥrp is a short-sword or dagger, which would contrast with the Egyptian sf.t, which in the Year 11 Libyan campaign of Ramesses III could be up to three cubits long (Manassa, 2003: 59-60). In war reliefs from Medinet Habu, Ramesses III attacks Libyans from his chariot, shooting arrows into the enemy horde, with a short sword tucked into his belt (figure 2; Epigraphic Survey, 1930: pl. 18).

The final section of the Edinburgh ostracon describes heterogeneous parts of the chariot, and the ostracon literally ends in the middle of a sentence:

The tail (sd) of your [5]chariot:
> you break through (sd) their (mountain) [6]passes.

The tire (h3b) of your chariot:
> [7]their backs are bent (h3b) to you because of (your) victories.

The ꜥrq of your chariot:
> you are wise (ꜥrq) like Thoth.

The ꜥwn.t-staff of your chariot:
> it plunders (ꜥwn) the distant foreign lands;
> it smites one, and a thousand fall, without an heir remaining.

The yoke saddles (lit. "hands" ḏr.wt) of your chariot:
> (they are) Anat and Astarte.

The mḥ3-bindings of your chariot:
> it binds (mḥ3) those who are evil.

As for the …

No convincing element has been identified as the tail of the chariot. Schulman (1986: 31-32) pointed to an element that sticks out from the back of Ramesses III's chariot in the lion hunting scene at Medinet Habu (Epigraphic Survey, 1930: pl. 35). However, the apparent 'tail' is just a continuation of the reins tied to the king's waist. Another element that sticks out from the rear of the floor of the body are enemies' heads that jut out from the back of the royal chariot in the battle reliefs of Seti I at Karnak (*Ibidem*, 1986: pl. 6, 31), Ramesses II at Abydos (Rommelaere, 1991: 95, fig. 64), and Ramesses III at Medinet Habu (Epigraphic Survey, 1930: pl. 24), but these are unlikely to be called 'tails'. Another tentative suggestion is to identify the *sd* with a fly-whisk, such as those found with Tutankhamun's chariots (Hofmann, 1989: 232-233; for the fly-whisks, see Littauer & Crouwel, 1985: 90-91).

Since the *sd* appears in conjunction with the *ḫ3b*-tire, the 'tail' may refer to the axle, since it is located at the very rear of the body, but this is only a tentative suggestion (for the possible identification of the term *m3wt* with axle, see Hofmann, 1989: 224-225). The term *ḫ3b* for 'tire' is not a foreign loan word (as in Hoch, 1994: 240), but rather derives from an Egyptian root for a curved element (Meeks, 1997: 46); the outer rim of the Egyptian chariot wheel consisted of several overlapping curved elements, making the rib determinative (Gardiner F42) particularly appropriate (Hofmann, 1989: 230-231).

The identification of the ʿ*rq* is problematic and proposals have ranged from Schulman's 'chariot box' (1986: 29-30) to Manley's 'quiver' (2008: 109). The latter should be dismissed, since the Egyptian term for quiver, *isp.t*, appears elsewhere in descriptions of chariots (as in P. Koller above; see also Hofmann, 1989: 218-219; Lesko, 2002a: 47). The identification of 'chariot body' rests on the determinatives – the leather sign and the hobble – but the lexeme that seems to be most appropriate to this context is ʿ*rq* 'to put on (clothing)' (Erman & Grapow, 1926: 211.19-23). Could this term refer then to the horses' housing? Either leather or cloth housings are possible and ubiquitous in depictions of royal chariot horses (Rommelaere, 1991: 118-119; compare the cloth example from the tomb of Tutankhamun, see Littauer & Crouwel, 1985: 88, pl. 62), and the hobble determinative might have been influenced by the common term ʿ*rq* 'fruit basket' that uses that determinative (Lesko, 2002: 74). However, this is simply a conjecture based on the elements of the chariot and tack preserved in two-dimensional depictions and archaeological evidence.

The ʿ*wn.t* is part of the chariot panoply, a type of wooden staff identifiable by its down-curving hand-guard; such staffs appear along with javelins in a large weapons' case next to the bow-case in the reliefs of Ramesses III at Medinet Habu (figure 2; Epigraphic Survey, 1930: pls. 9, 10, 18, 19, 24; 1932: pls. 70, 72, 77, 94, 116). Not only does the ʿ*wn.t* 'plunder (ʿ*wn*) the foreign lands', but the ʿ*wn.t*-staff, at least by the New Kingdom, is an import from lands as distant as Mitanni (Davies, 1941: pl. XIII). The statement 'it smites one and a thousand fall' may also be an allusion to the Ramesside story The Capture of Joppa, a significant intertextuality that will be addressed further below.

Next, the Edinburgh ostracon compares the 'hands' of the chariot to Astarte and Anat. Any identification of this element must take into consideration its mention in Papyrus (P.) Anastasi I (Fischer-Elfert, 1983: 142-143; 1986: 201-207):

Your chariot is upon its side; you fear to press your horses.
If it is thrown to the pit,
> your "hand" will lie exposed,
> your kushna fallen.
You unharness the team in order to repair the "hand," in the midst of the narrow pass.

The 'hand' is clearly an essential part of the functioning of the chariot, and one that requires the horses to be unharnessed before they can be repaired. Ritter (1990) suggested that the damaged 'hand' refers to a broken 'spoke'; since each spoke actually consisted of parts of two V-shaped objects (Rommelaere 1991: 92-93; Western, 1973: 91), a cupped hand and the spoke of an ancient Egyptian chariot could be visually equated. However, to repair a wheel, the horses would not necessarily need to be unyoked, although if not an emergency situation, such might have been desirable.

One of the most significant clues to the identification of the 'hands' is that they can appear either in the dual, as in the Edinburgh ostracon, or just one can be damaged, as in P. Anastasi I. Another indication of the function of the 'hand' of the chariot may appear in a slightly later passage in P. Anastasi I, where the broken chariot is being repaired (Fischer-Elfert, 1983: 148-149; 1986: 227-229 [with differing identification of the chariot parts]):

They shall repair your chariot, removing broken (parts),
> your pole (ꜥ) will be planed anew,
> then its yoke arms (dby.wt) attached,
> leather set down for its "hand" and ḫꜣ;
> they will prepare your yoke.

One of the most certain equations of chariot lexicography and chariot structure is that the ꜥ of the chariot is its main pole (Hofmann, 1989: 219-220; Schulman, 1986: 28). The 'hands' attached to the arm would fit an equation of the hands and the yoke saddles, as Schulman proposed (1986: 34). If the 'hands' of the chariot are the yoke saddles, then this would contrast nicely with the tail being the axle, since then we would have the front and the rear of the entire chariot structure respectively. The context of the chariot repair passage suggests that the 'hand' is related to the yoking system at the front of the pole, and the leather element could easily refer to the leather covering of the yoke saddles (compare Littauer & Crouwel, 1985: 28-29) or to the yoke saddle pad (Manassa, 2002: 264). The passage in P. Anastasi I also offers a solution for the singular use of 'hand' – perhaps the 'hand' is used to refer to the yoke saddle of the lead horse, while the ḫꜣ (related to the term for 'behind') may refer to the yoke saddle of the second horse of the team. Alternatively, the ḫꜣ could be a reference to the backing element, the looping piece of leather that depended from the base of the yoke saddles and prevented a horse from backing out of the yoke; these backing elements are well-attested in the pictorial record, and Littauer & Crouwel (1985: 28) note that slots through the heads of Bes on one pair of yoke saddles in the tomb of Tutankhamun are placed so that when added, the backing strap would look like Bes' tongue. While the identity of the ḫꜣ-element remains highly uncertain, the equation of the dr.wt-hands in the Edinburgh ostracon with the yoke saddles fits all of the available evidence. The yoke saddles literally hold on to the horses, sitting in front of the withers (Littauer, 2002), and as dual elements, the Edinburgh ostracon compares them to Astarte and Anat. Unmentioned by Schulman, however, is the iconographic evidence for the goddesses Astarte and Anat that further supports his argument for dr.wt as yoke saddles. A weapon-wielding Astarte appears on horseback in numerous Egyptian depictions of the goddess (Cornelius, 2004: 42-44; Rommelaere 1991: 136-138). Since the yoke saddles are the only elements that would ride atop the horse like the goddesses, identifying the 'hands' as yoke saddles creates a perfect metaphor with the two Asiatic goddesses.

The final preserved element of the chariot in the Edinburgh ostracon is the mḫꜣ-bindings that predictably 'bind' evil-doers. While the term mḫꜣ can refer to ropes and fetters in general (Lesko, 2002a: 201), following upon a possible mention of yoke saddles, these bindings could refer to the leather straps that hold the saddles to the yoke arms (tentatively proposed by Schulman, 1986: 41). Such straps do not survive well in the archaeological record, although the reconstructed examples of the Florence chariot show how the bindings functioned (Roberto Del Francia 2002: 30-31), and stone knobs from chariot yoke saddles from Per-Ramesses show further indirect evidence of binding the saddles to the yoke (Herold, 1999: 38-40).

Ostracon (O.) Turin S 9588

Excavated in Deir el-Medina by Schiaperelli in 1909, O. Turin S 9588 provides the only other surviving exemplar of the Hymn to the King in His Chariot (Černý, 1927: 224-226; Lopez, 1982: pl. 112). Paleographically, the ostracon dates to the 20th Dynasty (1187-1069 BC). Unlike NMS A.1956.319, O. Turin S 9588 refers both to objects that are part of the chariot or its panoply, as well as weapons held directly in the hand of the king. The overall hymnic structure is similar to the Edinburgh ostracon, however, and as mentioned earlier, both ostraca probably represent two parts of a single, lengthier composition.

[1]As for the bow which is in your hand:
> mꜣ.t of mnw.

As for the shield which [...] [2]on the nw.
As for the [3]tḫ of your chariot:
> the one who tramples (ḫnd) in Syria,
> the point of your lance (reaches) the end of every land.

As for the front support (ꜥmd) of your <chariot>:
> [4]you stand firm (ꜥmd) in Naharin,
> you destroy their towns.

As for the [...][5]of your chariot:
> Isis and Nephthys.

As for the staff (šbd.t) that is in your hand:
> <it> strikes (šbd); [6]they come on (their) knees,
> (saying that?) they will request peace because of your power.

As for the whip [7]that is in your hand:
> the horns of Horus, son of Isis;
> just as he [wreaks havoc] in the mountain of copper,
> so does he destroy [8]in Lebanon.

As for the ḥyry of your chariot:
> [9]the sky with its four [supports].

It has come (to an end).

The preserved text on the Turin ostracon consists of eight stanzas, divided evenly between objects held in the king's hand and additional parts of the chariot. While the king's panoply, bow, shield, shuba-staff, and whip, are easily identified, the chariot terminology of the Turin ostracon is even more obscure than that of the Edinburgh text. Despite the lingering obscurities within the text, one can confidently identify the object of the hymn as the king, as has been assumed in the foregoing analysis. The list of items in the Turin ostracon also finds a visual complement in the tomb of Qenamun, where a chariot being presented to the king is accompanied by a bow, shield, whip, and sword (Davies, 1930: pl. 22, see further below).

Schulman (1986: 46-49) suggested that the mention of the 'ram's horn' in the first line of the Edinburgh ostracon indicates that the person being addressed in these texts is the god Amun rather than the king. While the ram-headed standard preceding Ramesses III into battle (Epigraphic Survey, 1930: pl. 17) indicates that the chariot can be a divine mode of transport, no pictorial or textual evidence suggests that a fully-armed anthropomorphic Amun would ride in a chariot into battle. Furthermore, the 'ram head' mentioned in the first line of the Edinburgh ostracon is most likely a reference to the yoke-arms at the end of the chariot pole (Littauer & Crouwel, 1985: 4), rather than a divine standard riding within the chariot. In an exceptional scene, the god Montu rides in the chariot with Thutmose IV (Carter & Newberry: 2002: pls. 10-11), but the deity adopts a supportive role, wielding no weapons, while the pharaoh remains the active chariot warrior; textually other deities, such as Sekhmet (Kitchen 1977: 87), can appear within the chariot, but again the gods are alongside the king, rather than standing in lieu of the pharaoh. The only deity who routinely rides in and fights from a chariot is Horus-Shed, who can attack noxious creatures from a griffon-borne chariot on Third Intermediate Period through Late Period cippi (Berlandini, 1998 [noting rare cases where Bes also appears in the chariot]). While hymns to divine chariots exist in the corpus of Mesopotamian literature (Pongratz-Leisten et al., 1992; Salonen, 1951), all aspects of the Egyptian hymn to the chariot and its panoply point towards the king as the object of praise.

The first item of the royal panoply in the Turin ostracon is the bow, the chariot weapon par excellence. However, the metaphor in the hymn is obscure, particularly since mꜣ.t is a hapax legomenon (Hoch, 1994: 176). The shield (qrꜥ) uses the same root as qrꜥw "shieldbearer" (Ibidem: 298-301) part of the two-man crew of an ancient Egyptian chariot team (Spalinger, 2007: 176-177); the presence of a royal shield bearer does not appear within royal reliefs, but is prominent in the figure of Menna, Ramesses II's shieldbearer at Qadesh.

The hymn then returns to parts of the chariot with the tḫ that 'tramples' Syria and is compared with the 'point of a lance'. The term tḫ may be related to tḫr in P. Anastasi IV, which appears to describe the decorative leather siding of the chariot body (Gardiner, 1937: 53): "their tḫr like the color of red cloth, carved with rosettes". The relationship between the *tḫ/tḫr* and *bt* (defined as 'side' above) is uncertain – possibly the latter refers to the wooden framework of the sides, while the former describes the wood or leather decoration between the framework.

The paronomasia in the next line, "as for the front support (ʿmd) of your chariot, you stand firm (ʿmd) in Naharin", uses the Semitic root 'to support' (Hoch, 1994: 70); the ʿmd has been identified as the main support of the chariot body (Hofmann, 1989: 221; Schulman, 1986: 18), which may contrast with the ʿdr, the front support or smaller side supports (see above). The final three portions of the Turin ostracon include two additional royal objects, a shuba-staff and a whip, and another unknown part of the chariot. The determinative of *ḥyry* suggest another term for the leather bindings (Hoch, 1994: 223), and the comparison to the four supports of the sky may refer to the four separate reins (Hofmann, 1989: 229).

HYMN TO THE ROYAL CHARIOT: LITERARY ANALYSIS

From the texts themselves, one may next consider the literary and cultural context of the Hymn to the King in His Chariot. Although the chariot was rapidly incorporated into Egyptian military organization and royal ideology in the early 18th Dynasty (Spalinger, 2007: 1-24; Vernus, 2009) and had become an aspect of the divine, solar world by the end of that Dynasty (Darnell & Manassa, 2007: 78; Kemp, 1989: 276-279), the chariot retained foreign aspects. The complex construction of the chariot's wooden wheels, spokes, and hubs relied on foreign woods (Western, 1973). The foreign origin of woods is also attested textually. In the tomb of Qenamun, a chariot with an elaborately decorated bow-case is labeled (Davies, 1930: pl. 22): "the [first] chariot of his Majesty whose name is Tinetamu ('she of the Asiatics') whose wood was brought from God's Land in the foreign country of Naharin." TT 73 includes a depiction of a chariot whose wood was imported from the land of Kush (Säve-Söderbergh, 1957: pl. 3): "great chariot of acacia of wretched Kush, worked in gold." In the Hymn to the King in His Chariot, Naharin and Kush are among the foreign places conquered by the various elements of the chariot. Just as the names of the parts of the chariot are imported from abroad, so are the physical parts of the chariot; for an Egyptian, a foreign object being used to conquer a foreign land creates a poetry all of its own, and one can see this same literary device employed in contemporaneous narrative fiction.

The foreign loan-words within the Hymn to the King in His Chariot, while ponderous in the extreme for modern scholars, were for the ancient Egyptian scribe a way to craft poetry from exotica (Guglielmi, 1984: 495-496; Loprieno, 2000: 18-19). Paronomasia and other forms of word-play are a well-attested feature of Egyptian literature (Guglielmi, 1984; Loprieno, 2000; 2001: 129-158), and examples from Middle Kingdom literature are clearly part of 'eloquent speech'. Among the many possible examples, one may compare the punning speeches of the Eloquent Peasant, who may instruct an official thus: "If you go down to the Sea of Truth (*mꜣʿ.t*), you will sail on it with a true fair wind (*mꜣʿ*)" (Parkinson, 2012: 69-71). Such Middle Kingdom poetic extravagance deserves the attention it has received in the secondary literature, and a similar emphasis should be placed on the clever use of paronomasia with foreign loan words in the Hymn to the King in His Chariot.

Creating a pun between a loan word and Egyptian terms for domination linguistically 'conquered' Egypt's enemies – the Egyptians might use foreign words to name chariot parts, but each of those names proclaimed Egypt's inevitable victory. English translations of the text simply cannot capture the poetic achievement of the composition, and the lexicographical difficulties have led modern scholars to overlook the hymn's importance in Egypt's literary history. The unique composition is the literary embodiment of Egypt's empire, and an Egyptian who read this text probably could not look at a chariot without recalling the clever puns of the poem.

Foreign terms used within the context of paronomasia are not common within the corpus of New Kingdom literature, but a significant intertextuality exists between the Hymn to the King in His Chariot and the fictional tale The Capture of Joppa. Belonging to the small corpus of New

Kingdom historical fiction, The Capture of Joppa appears to derive from the same martial-themed scribal milieu as The Hymn to the King in His Chariot (Manassa, 2010; 2013). In the fragmentary beginning of The Capture of Joppa, the Egyptian general Djehuty is besieging the city of Joppa, and apparently meets the ruler in a tent outside the city walls. During the ensuing conversation, the ruler of Joppa asks to see the ꜥwn.t-staff of Pharaoh Menkheperre. Djehuty obliges the foreigner's request by striking him on the forehead with the very staff – an act that recalls royal smiting scenes. With the ruler of Joppa incapacitated, the Egyptian general then uses a stratagem to take the city. He has soldiers hidden in baskets and pretends to capitulate to the "Mistress of the Ruler of Joppa" telling her that the baskets are the first of the tribute of the surrendering Egyptian forces. The gates of the city are opened, and the Egyptians capture Joppa, enslaving all of its inhabitants and declaring victory in the name of Thutmose III.

Two aspects of the Capture of Joppa are particularly relevant to the Hymn to the King in His Chariot. First of all, the term for basket within the tale is not a usual Egyptian term, but rather a foreign (possibly Hurrian) loan word ṯḫbs(ti) (Hoch, 1994: 362-363; Manassa, Forthcoming b; Ward, 1989). Just as the foreign names of the chariot are used in the hymn to describe the destruction of the foreign lands, a foreign type of basket is used to capture an enemy city (Manassa, 2010: 255; 2013). The use of the ꜥwn.t-staff as a symbol of Pharaonic authority and its ability to 'plunder' a foreign land is identical in the Hymn to the King in His Chariot and the The Capture of Joppa. Djehuty smites the ruler on the forehead with the ꜥwn.t, in other words he smites one, and the entire city of Joppa is defeated – meaning a thousand fall. It is even possible that the statement in the Hymn to the King in His Chariot is an allusion to the story The Capture of Joppa.

Most significantly, the playfulness and humor within the The Capture of Joppa suggests that the otherwise ponderous loan words in the Hymn to the King in His Chariot are actually employed for their entertainment value. Both of the ostraca probably derive from Deir el-Medina, the Turin ostracon certainly so, and one cannot assume that the community of workmen had intimate knowledge of each part of a chariot. As the reader or member of the audience puzzled out the imagery, he was simultaneously entertained by the fact that each foreign aspect of the chariot defeats the foreign lands whence it comes. Despite the continued difficulties of rendering the Hymn to the King in His Chariot into modern languages, one should not underestimate its poetic or playful effect for its ancient audience.

HYMN TO THE KING IN HIS CHARIOT: PROPOSED SETTINGS

One final aspect of the hymn to consider is the potential setting for the Hymn to the King in His Chariot. Where and when might an audience have gathered in order to hear such a text recited? Other texts and depictions of chariots from a variety of New Kingdom contexts, including several that have already been quoted above in the discussion of technical terms, suggest three potential settings for the Hymn.

First is the coronation celebration, during which the so-called New Year's Gifts were presented (Aldred, 1969; Hartwig, 2004: 79-81). During the 18th Dynasty (and one can assume during the Ramesside Period as well), these 'gifts' presented to the king included elaborately decorated chariots, such as those in the tombs of Qenamun (Davies, 1930: pl. 22) and TT 73 (Säve-Söderbergh, 1957: pl. 3). As such products were being delivered, Egyptians may have recited how each part of the chariot contributed to the king's domination of his foes. Similar presentation scenes, in which foreigners themselves carry the exports from their region, ranging from natural resources to highly decorated chariots, may be another related setting for the Hymn to the King in His Chariot (Hartwig, 2004: 73-76). Changing decorum in New Kingdom tomb decoration means that Ramesside parallels for such scenes do not exist, but a lack of funerary depictions of the ritual does not imply their demise (compare the durbar ceremonies under Akhenaten and Tutankhamun, Darnell & Manassa, 2007: 125-131).

Contemporaneous with the ostraca attestations of the Hymn to the King in His Chariot is textual evidence indicating that chariots were presented during the royal jubilee. Papyrus (P.) Bologna 1094, part of the extensive corpus of the Late Egyptian Miscellanies, describes the manufacture of chariots for the second jubilee (Caminos 1954: 14-16; Gardiner, 1932: 4): "The scribe of the armory of pharaoh Mahu speaks to the scribe Pawehem [...] You should direct your attention to causing every commission to be carried out for the second jubilee, very excellently and with the strength of copper, in order to have made the chariots for the second jubilee."

The description of 'jubilee' chariots in P. Bologna 1094, a Memphite text probably dating to the reign of Merenptah (1212-1201 BC; Gardiner, 1932: XIII), resonates strongly with the Hymn to the King in His Chariot. The corpus of Late Egyptian Miscellanies includes not only praise of the king himself, but also praise of his residence (Ragazzoli, 2008), and it is possible that hymns relating to the royal panoply, particularly the king appearing resplendent in his chariot, were performed during jubilee festivities. Although not directly related to the jubilee festival, the use of chariots in the daily royal procession at Amarna and the inclusion of elaborately outfitted chariots at the Opet Festival during the reign of Tutankhamun (Epigraphic Survey, 1994: pls. 22 & 95) provide further possible festival contexts for the Hymn to the King in His Chariot.

Finally, annual celebrations of military victories or the pharaoh's arrival at a particular city could be additional occasions for the recital of texts such as those found on the Edinburgh and Turin ostraca. For example, Ramesses III decreed an annual festival for the celebration of his victories over the Libyans (Grandet, 1994: 246-247). Although Libya is not mentioned within the two preserved examples of the text, other examples of the genre may have been composed for such occasions; a work of historical fiction set during Merneptah's Libyan campaign was copied during Ramesses III's reign, and may have been commissioned for a similar festival celebration (Manassa, 2010: 258-259; 2013). The Late Egyptian Miscellanies provide evidence for the final proposed setting for the Hymn to the King in His Chariot. In P. Anastasi IV is an elaborate description of chariots with gilded pieces and other parts decorated with fine metals and precious stones (Caminos 1954: 201; Gardiner, 1932: 53). These lavish chariots appear to have been manufactured for the arrival of the pharaoh to a city that contained a Window of Appearance – perhaps even for a celebration or festival like those mentioned above. Other hymns are known to have been associated with the arrival of the newly-crowned pharaoh to Thebes (Fischer-Elfert, 1999), and in combination with the evidence for the New Year's Gifts mentioned previously, the Hymn to the King in His Chariot was likely composed for performance in a royal festival setting.

CONCLUSION

The Hymn to the King in His Chariot provides unique information regarding the technical terminology of an ancient Egyptian chariot, a hymnic complement to more sober lists of chariot parts found in P. Anastasi I and the Late Egyptian Miscellanies. The use of paronomasia to create statements about domination of foreigners and the grouping of the stanzas allows at least tentative identifications of various Egyptian terms and loan words with specific elements of an ancient chariot. The composition is a hymn, however, not a technical treatise, and one should not overlook its poetic structure and complexly constructed puns and mythological allusions. To summarize the literary merits of the Hymn to the King in His Chariot: just as the Egyptian armies conquered foreign lands, so did Egyptian poets use foreign words verbally to curb Egypt's foes.

CITED LITERATURE

Alred, C. 1969. The 'New Year' Gifts to the Pharaoh. – Journal of Egyptian Archaeology 55: 73-81.

Barbotin, C. 1999. Le papyrus Chassinat III. – Revue d'Égyptologie 50: 5-26.

Berlandini, J. 1998. Bès en aurige dans le char du dieu-sauveur. In: Clarysse, W. Ed. Egyptian Religion. The Last Thousand Years. – Leuven, Peeters: 31-55.

Bresciani, E. 1999. Letteratura e poesia dell'antico Egitto. Cultura e società attraverso i testi. – Turin, Einaudi.

Caminos, R. 1954. Late Egyptian Miscellanies. – Oxford, Oxford University Press.

Carter, H. & P.E. Newberry. 2002 [1904]. Tomb of Thoutmosis IV. – London, Duckworth.

Černý, J. 1927. Deux nouveaux fragments de textes littéraires connus depuis longtemps. – Revue de l'Égypte ancienne 1, 3/4: 221-226.

Cornelius, I. 2004. The Many Faces of the Goddess. The Iconography of the Syro-Palestinian Goddesses Anat, Astarte, Qedeshet, and Asherah c. 1500-1000 BCE. – Fribourg, Academic Press.

Darnell, J.C. 1986. The Harried Helper. pPushkin 127: 4, 15-16. – Göttinger Miszellen 92: 17-21.

Darnell, J.C. & C. Manassa. 2007. Tutankhamun's Armies. Battle and Conquest during Ancient Egypt's Late 18th Dynasty. – Hoboken, NJ, Wiley & Sons.

Davies, N. d. G. 1922. The Tomb of Puyemre at Thebes. – New York, Metropolitan Museum of Art.

Davies, N. d. G. 1930. The Tomb of Ken-Amun at Thebes. – New York, Metropolitan Museum of Art.

Davies, N. d. G. 1941. Syrians in the Tomb of Amunejeh. – Journal of Egyptian Archaeology 27: 96-98.

Dawson, W.R. & T.E. Peet. 1933. The So-Called Poem on the King's Chariot. – Journal of Egyptian Archaeology 19: 167-174.

Epigraphic Survey. 1930. Medinet Habu I. Earlier Historical Records of Ramses III. – Chicago, Oriental Institute of the University of Chicago Press.

Epigraphic Survey. 1932. Medinet Habu II. Later Historical Records of Ramses III. – Chicago, Oriental Institute of the University of Chicago Press

Epigraphic Survey. 1986. The Battle Reliefs of Sety I. – Chicago, Oriental Institute of the University of Chicago Press.

Epigraphic Survey. 1994. Reliefs and Inscriptions at Luxor Temple 1. The Festival Procession of Opet in the Colonnade Hall. – Chicago, Oriental Institute of the University of Chicago Press.

Erman, A. 1880. Hieratische Ostraka. – Zeitschrift für Ägyptische Sprache und Altertumskunde 18: 93-99.

Erman, A. 1923. Die Literatur der Aegypter. – Leipzig, J.C. Hinrichs.

Erman, A. & H. Grapow, Eds. 1926. Wörterbuch der ägyptische Sprache. Volume 1. – Leipzig and Berlin, Akademie Verlag.

Fischer-Elfert, H.-W. 1983. Die satirische Streitschrift des Papyrus Anastasi I. – Wiesbaden, Harrassowitz.

Fischer-Elfert, H.-W. 1986. Die satirische Streitschrift des Papyrus Anastasi. Übersetzung und Kommentar. – Wiesbaden, Harrassowitz.

Fischer-Elfert, H.-W. 1999. Die Ankunft des Königs nach ramessidischen Hymnen. – Studien zur Altägyptischen Kultur 27: 65-85.

Fowler, A. 1982. Kinds of Literature. An Introduction to the Theory of Genres and Modes. – Cambridge, Harvard University Press.

Gardiner, A. 1937. Late Egyptian Miscellanies. – Brussels, Édition de la Fondation égyptologique Reine Élisabeth.

Grandet, P. 1994. Le Papyrus Harris I. – Cairo, Institut Français d'Archéologie Orientale du Caire.

Guglielmi, W. 1984. Zu einigen literarischen Funktionen des Wortspiels. In: Studien zu Sprache und Religion Ägyptens, Band 1: Sprache. – Göttingen, Hubert & Co.: 491-506.

Hartwig, M. 2004. Tomb Painting and Identity in Ancient Thebes, 1419-1372 BCE. – Turnhout, Brepols.

Herold, A. 1999. Streitwagentecnologie in der Ramses-Stadt. Bronze an Pferd und Wagen. – Mainz, Philipp von Zabern.

Hoch, J. 1994. Semitic Words in Egyptian texts of the New Kingdom and Third Intermediate Period. – Princeton, Princeton University Press.

Hofmann, U. 1989. Fuhrwesen und Pferdehaltung im alten Ägypten. – Bonn, Rheinischen Friedrich-Wilhelms-Universität (Unpublished Ph.D dissertation).

Hollis, S.T. 2008. The Ancient Egyptian "Tale of the Two Brothers". A Mythological, Religious, Literary, and Historico-Political Study. – Oakville, CT, Bannerstone Press.

Jéquier, G. 1922. Matériaux pour servir à l'établissement d'un dictionnaire d'archéologie égyptienne. – Bulletin de l'Institut Français d'Archéologie Orientale du Caire 19: 1-271.

Kemp, B.J. 1989. Ancient Egypt. Anatomy of a Civilization. – London, Routledge.

Kitchen, K.A. 1977. Ramesside Inscriptions. Historical and Biographical. Volume 2. – Oxford, Blackwell Ltd.

Lesko, L. 2002. A Dictionary of Late Egyptian. – Providence, B.C. Scribe Publications.

Littauer, M.A. 2002. The Function of the Yoke Saddle in Ancient Harnessing. In: Rauwling, P. Ed. Selected Writings on Chariots, other Early Vehicles, Riding and Harness. – Leiden, Brill: 479-486.

Littauer, M.A. & J.H. Crouwel. 1985. Chariots and Related Equipment from the Tomb of Tutankhamun. – Oxford, Griffith Institute.

Lopez, J. 1982. Ostraca ieratici N. 57320 – 57499 Milan. – Cisalpino-La Goliardica.

Loprieno, A. 2000. Puns and Word Play in Ancient Egyptian. In: Noegel, S.B. Ed. Puns and Pundits. Word Play in the Hebrew Bible and Ancient Near Eastern Literature. – Bethesda, MD, CDL Press: 3-20.

Loprieno, A. 2001. La pensée et l'écriture: pour une analyse sémiotique de la culture égyptienne. – Paris, Cybele.

Manassa, C. 2002. Two Unpublished Memphite Relief Fragments in the Yale Art Gallery. – Studien zur Altägyptischen Kultur 30: 255-267.

Manassa, C. 2003. The Great Karnak Inscription of Merneptah. Grand Strategy in the 13th Century BC. – New Haven, Yale Egyptological Seminar.

Manassa, C. 2010. Defining Historical Fiction in New Kingdom Egypt. In: Melville, S.C. & A. Slotsky. Eds. Opening the Tablet Box. Near Eastern Studies in Honor of Benjamin R. Foster. – Leiden, Brill: 245-269.

Manassa, C. 2013. Imagining the Past. Historical Fiction in New Kingdom Egypt. – Oxford, Oxford University Press.

Manassa, C. Forthcoming a. The Hymn to the King in his Chariot: Paronomasia and Chariots in New Kingdom Literature.

Manassa, C. Forthcoming b. From Wool to Basketry: Materials, Contact Linguistics, and *tḥbs(t)* in Ancient Egyptian. – Lingua Aegyptia.

Manley, B. 2008. The King of Egypt Upon His Chariot. A Poem (Ostracon NMS A.1956.319). – Cosmos 24: 107-118.

Meeks, D. 1997. Les emprunts Égyptiens aux langues sémitiques durant le Nouvel Empire et la Troisième Période Intermédiaire. Les aléas du comparatisme. – Bibliotheca Orientalis 54, 1/2: 32-62.

Moers, G. 2010. New Kingdom Literature. In: Lloyd, A.B. Ed. A Companion to Ancient Egypt. – Malden, MA, Wiley Blackwell: 685-708.

Oppenheim, L. 1965. The Assyrian Dictionary of the Oriental Institute of the University of Chicago. Volume II. – Chicago, The Oriental Institute of the University of Chicago.

Parkinson, R.B. 2012. The Tale of the Eloquent Peasant. A Reader's Commentary. – Hamburg, Widmaier Verlag.

Pongratz-Leisten, B., K. Deller & E. Bleibtreu. 1992. Götterstreitwagen und Götterstandarten. Götter auf dem Feldzug und ihr Kult im Feldlager. – Baghdader Mitteilungen 23: 291-356.

Popko, L. 2012. oEdinburgh 916, Streitwagenhymnus. – Retrieved November 15, 2012, from: http://aaew.bbaw.de/tla/servlet/GetTextDetails?u=guest&f=0&l=0&tc=1039&db=0.

Popko, L. 2012. oTurin CG 57365. – Retrieved November 15, 2012, from: http://aaew.bbaw.de/tla/servlet/OTPassport?u=guest&f=0&l=0&oc=1040&db=0.

Ragazzoli, C. 2008. Éloges de la ville en Égypte ancienne, Histoire et littérature. – Paris, PUPS.

Raulwing, P. 2000. Horses, Chariots and Indo-Europeans. Foundations and Methods of Chariotry Research from the Viewpoint of Comparative Indo-European Linguistics. – Budapest, Archaeolingua.

Ritter, T. 1990. *dr.wt*: Der Speichenkranz des Wagenrades. – Zeitschrift für Ägyptische Sprache und Altertumskunde 117: 60-62.

Roberto Del Francia, P. 2002. Il carro di Firenze. In: Guidotti, M.C. Ed. Il carro e le armi del museo egizio di Firenze. – Florence, Giunti: 16-37.

Rommelaere, C. 1991. Les chevaux du nouvel empire égyptien: origines, races, hanachement. – Brussels, Connaissance de l'Égypte ancienne.

Salonen, A. 1951. Die Landfahrzeuge des alten Mesopotamien. Eine lexikalische und kulturgeschichtliche Untersuchung. – Helsinki, Suomalainen Tiedeakatemia.

Säve-Söderbergh, T. 1957. Four Eighteenth Dynasty Tombs. – Oxford, Griffith Institute.

Schneider, T. 2008. Fremdwörter in der ägyptischen Militärsprache des Neuen Reiches und ein Bravourstück des Elitesoldaten (Papyrus Anastasi I

23, 2-7). – Journal of the Society for the Study of Egyptian Antiquities 35: 181-205.

Schulman, A. 1986. The So-Called Poem on the King's Chariot Revisited. – Journal of the Society for the Study of Egyptian Antiquities 16: 28-35, 39-44.

Spalinger, A. 2007. Transformations in Egyptian Folktales. The Royal Influence. – Revue d'Égyptologie 58: 137-156.

Vernus, P. 2009. Réception linguistique et idéologique d'une nouvelle technologie. Le cheval dans la civilisation pharaonique. In: Wisa, M. Ed. The Knowledge Economy and Technological Capabilities, Egypt, The Near East and the Mediterranean, 2nd millennium B.C. - 1st millennium A.D. – Barcelona, Editorial Ausa: 2-47.

Ward, W. 1989. Egyptian *tḫbs*. A Hurrian Loan-Word in the Vernacular of Deir el-Medina. – Göttinger Miszellen 109: 73-82.

Western, A.C. 1973. A Wheel Hub from the Tomb of Amenophis III. – Journal of Egyptian Archaeology 59: 91-94.

Wettengel, W. 2003. Die Erzählung von den beiden Brüdern. Der Papyrus d'Orbiney und die Königsideologie der Ramessiden. – Fribourg, Academic Press.

A GLIMPSE INTO THE WORKSHOPS OF THE CHARIOTRY OF QANTIR-PIRAMESSE – STONE AND METAL TOOLS OF SITE Q I

Silvia Prell

INTRODUCTION

The excavations carried out by the Hildesheim Mission at site Q I from 1980 to 1987 allowed a unique insight into daily life, especially working life, in the residence of Ramesses II (1279-1212 BC), located in the Eastern Delta (figure 1). Site Q I is situated south of the modern village of Qantir (figure 2), not far away from site Q IV where the stables of the chariotry were unearthed in the 1990s (Pusch, 1999). The whole complex lies within a huge palace district as was posited by the results of a topographical survey conducted by Dorner (1996) and confirmed by magnetic surveys carried out by Becker and Fassbinder subsequently (Pusch *et al.*, 1999: 147).

The workshops that came to light in Q I were highly specialized and therefore the connected stone and metal tools excavated therein were an eligible subject for intensive analysis. This is a rare example when dynastic stone tools are given the attention they derserve. Particularly the macro-

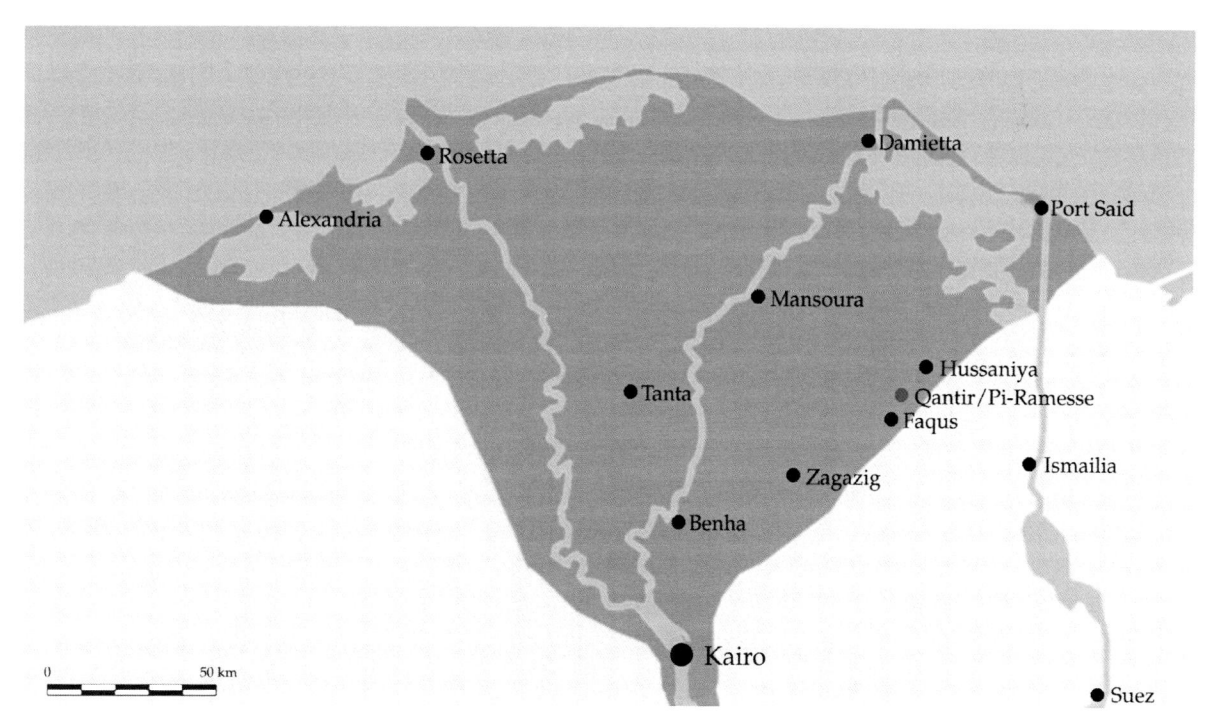

Figure 1. The location of Qantir-Piramesse in the Eastern Delta. From: Prell (2011: 17).

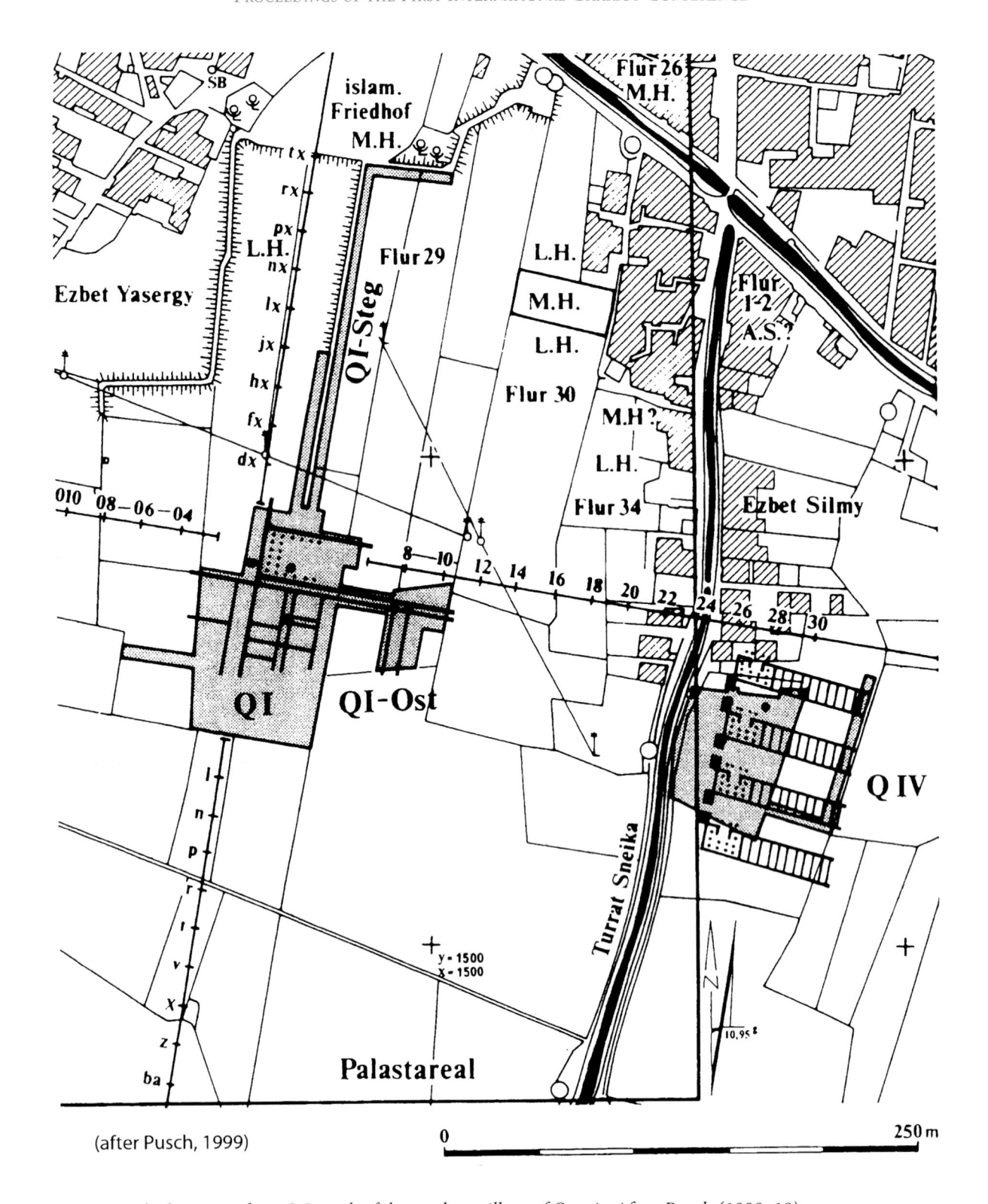

Figure 2. The location of site Q I south of the modern village of Qantir. After: Pusch (1999: 18).

lithics tools like pounders or grinders, commonly found during excavations of a settlement site, but largely neglected since the time of Petrie (1917; save for Amarna and Ain Asyl, Kemp & Stevens, 2010; Jeuthe, 2012 respectively), were studied. It is important to note that this category of tools, as well as microlithics (compare Tillmann, 2007) continued to be used in Egypt long after the invention of bronze tools.

SITE Q I

The site in question, Q I, can be subdivided into two main occupation phases. A foundry of industrial dimensions belonging to an earlier phase of occupation (Stratum B/3) has been unearthed in the north (Pusch, 1990: 75-100); affiliated workshops belonging to the foundry were attached in the south. This complex can most likely be connected to the construction of the new capital under Seti I (1296-1279 BC) and Ramesses II.

After the abandonment of the foundry, a court of considerable size was established on its former ground (figure 3). This court can be identified as belonging to the chariotry of the royal residence due to the presence of pieces of chariots made of stone and bronze (Herold, 1999; 2006) as well as horse hoof prints in the corresponding layers (Pusch, 1996: 134). The workshops formerly connected to the foundry remained in place, partly changed their layout (Prell, 2011: 170) and started to supply the garrison stationed at the site (Pusch, 1996: 133-140). The stratum in question was labelled B/2 and can be subdivided into at least two phases, B/2b and B/2a (Pusch, 1990: 100-102), which manifest themselves within the workshops by a functional change of certain parts of the complex (see below).

An analysis of the existing material provides insights into the organisation and assembly of a highly specialized workshop that is associated with the armed forces and under government control. This special context makes an intensive examination of the finds, especially the remaining tools, particularly important.

THE TOOLS

The majority of the tools from site Q I are different instruments made of stone. The classification itself was based exclusively on the available objects, initially without considering further parameters such as find spots and stratification. Four main groups stand out (Prell, 2011: 27-80): crushing, abrading, smoothing/polishing and grinding or grating tools, which can be subdivided further. Among the first group are several hammers of different shapes and materials, often with percussion marks on the surface, which are characteristic of their use. They can consist of simple pounders, made from boulders used as found (figure 4.1-3), but also several intentional shaped forms are known (figure 4.4-6). The

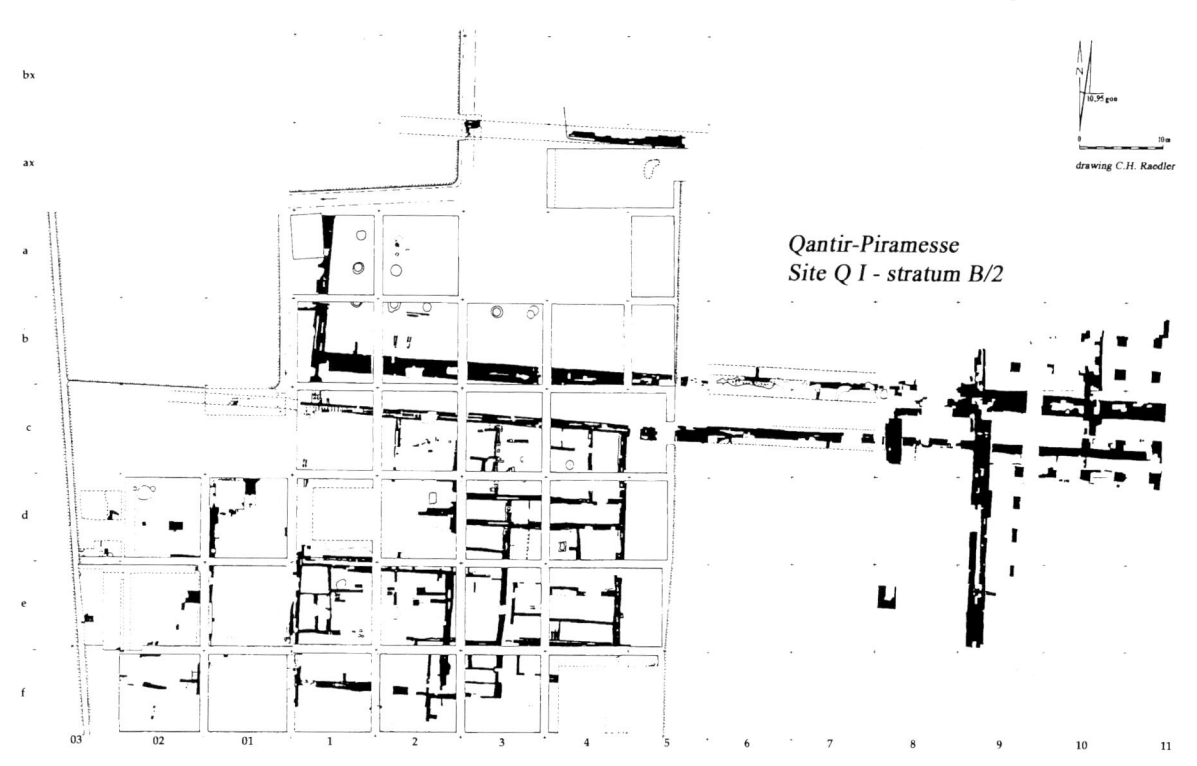

Figure 3. Site Q I, stratum B/2. From: Raedler (2007: 258).

1 pounder, silex, Inv.-Nr. 3860
2 pounder, agate, Inv.-Nr. 3878
3 pounder, limestone, Inv.-Nr. 3884
4 hammerstone, cubical, diorite, Inv.-Nr. 3888
5 hammerstone, wheel-shaped, quarzite, Inv.-Nr. 3901
6 hammerstone, spherical, diorite, Inv.-Nr. 3895

Figure 4. Examples of pounders and hammerstones. Scale bars in cm. Photographs by A. Krause.

second group consists of varying types of abrasive tools (figure 5), mostly made of quartzite and used to shape the manufactured piece, as well as whetstones, made of sandstone, which might additionally have been utilized for sharpening metal tools (figure 6). The third group is made up of polishing tools (figure 7), used to finalize the surface treatment. The latter group is, like the hammerstones, composed of simple boulders used as found, as well as intentionally shaped types (for very specialized polishing tools see below). The fourth group is composed of grinders (figure 8) and graters.

Additional tools are known that do not fit into the four main established groups. For example, pressure stones for a wooden drill (figure 9) prove that such drills had been used on-site, even if the organic components are not preserved in the wet soil of the Delta (Prell, 2011: 81-82). Working plates, anvils, stone bowls, mortars, a few tools made of pottery as well as pigments complete the picture (*Ibidem*, 2011: 87-101).

The above-mentioned groups frequently exhibit evidence of use as multi-purpose tools. Hammerstones are found to have surfaces with marks of abrasion (figure 10), an abrasion stone can have percussion marks from short-term use as a hammer, and a grinder can be utilized as a supplementary anvil. This multifunctional character complicates the process of identifying the specific branch of production for which certain tools were used. Unfortunately workshop scenes depicted in tombs cannot help here (Prell, 2011: 123-166), as a tool with comparable shape can for example be used for smoothing wood or embossing metal sheets or vessels (figure 11).

Furthermore, the distribution of stone tools on site does not help very much with the identification of the different branches of production located within the complex, as is visible on the overall plan (figure 12), which is not subdivided into the layers the tools were found in. Also the mapping subdivided into the distinct layers provides little additional information (Prell, 2011: 179-226) and does not link certain tools with special parts of the workshops. One should note that the considerable density of tools in the eastern section of the complex is due to the better preservation of structures in this part of the site. The concentration of tools found in huge pits in the court, which disturb this area, suggests that most of the tools found here are from a dump, rather than from a meaningful archaeological context.

Only one kind of stone tool found in site Q I can be tied to a special function – the tool used to smooth and polish arrowheads made of bone (Prell, 2011: 65-71). This connection was already made by Pusch (1990: 105) during excavations, based on the large amounts of waste, semi-complete and finished products found in a certain part of the complex, indicating a workshop manufacturing bone items.

Of those specialized items, two different kinds can be distinguished: polishing tools made of steatite with drill holes and/or semicircular grooves (figure 13 & 14), and slabs, which might or might not show grooves (figure 15). It is noteworthy that the latter are made of phyllite, a material which is not documented elsewhere in Egypt for any kind of object, except for only a few, unpublished examples of the same type of tool known from nearby Tell el-Dab'a. but deriving from uncertain contexts.

Contrary to the stone tools that were relatively numerous at site Q I, only a few metal tools came to light in the workshops (Prell, 2011: 102-122), most of which are proportionally small in size and represent miscellaneous metal implements, like chisels, styluses and punches (figure 16). The overall plan with the finds indicated in their original find spots (figure 17) clearly shows the paltry deposit of metal tools in comparison to the plentiful deposit of stone ones. Larger metal tools like adze blades or saws, whose use at site Q I can be proven by the appearance of saw-marks on numerous bone artefacts (*Ibidem*: 103), are not found at all and were, due to their value, most likely removed by the craftsmen in the course of the abandonment of the workshops (for a few bigger metal items see *Ibidem*: 116-120).

Metal tools were often found together with bronze arrowheads and other small metal objects, such as nails, shafts, wire or pieces of sheets, also in small hoards, so that one can consider them as items kept for recycling. Together with the lack of bigger metal implements it seems most likely that after the abandonment and re-location of the workshops, tools and raw materials were moved out in an organized way; even the well-preserved stone tools were apparently taken along (Prell, 2011: 254).

1 abrasive stone, quartzite, Inv.-Nr. 3953
3 abrasive stone, quartzite, Inv.-Nr. 3960
5 abrasive stone, quartzite, Inv.-Nr. 3963
2 abrasive stone, quartzite, Inv.-Nr. 3956
4 abrasive stone, quartzite, Inv.-Nr. 3966
6 abrasive stone, quartzite, Inv.-Nr. 3982

Figure 5. Examples of abrasive stones. Scale bars in cm. Photographs by A. Krause.

1 whetstone, sandstone, Inv.-Nr. 4000
3 whetstone, sandstone, Inv.-Nr. 4017
5 whetstone, sandstone, Inv.-Nr. 4024
2 whetstone, sandstone, Inv.-Nr. 3999
4 whetstone, sandstone, Inv.-Nr. 4020
6 whetstone, sandstone, Inv.-Nr. 4009

Figure 6. Examples of whetstones. Scale bars in cm. Photographs by A. Krause.

1 polishing pebble, flint, Inv.-Nr. 4169	2 polishing tool, shist, Inv.-Nr. 4106
3 polishing pebble, quartz, Inv.-Nr. 4178	4 polishing tool, diorite, Inv.-Nr. 4098
5 polishing pebble, agate, Inv.-Nr. 4192	6 polishing tool, diorite, Inv.-Nr. 4105

Figure 7. Examples of polishing pebbels and tools. Scale bars in cm. Photographs by A. Krause.

1 grinding stone, granite, Inv.-Nr. 4043
2 grinding stone, quartzite, Inv.-Nr. 4044
3 grinding stone, quartzite, Inv.-Nr. 4049
4 grinding stone, quartzite, Inv.-Nr. 4052

Figure 8. Examples of grinding stones. Scale bars in cm. Photographs by A. Krause.

Consequently, the metal objects are not necessarily found in their original place of use, but might have been discarded in a pile, or abandoned as they broke, which makes their attribution to a specific production branch even more difficult than was the case for the stone tools.

With a few exceptions, the distribution of the tools within the complex displays no noteworthy concentrations that link certain tools to specific parts of the workshops. But after combining all the information available, including the archaeological evidence, raw materials, unfinished and finished products, it becomes apparent that some parts of the workshop can be associated with certain branches of production (Prell, 2011: 227-238).

WORKSHOP

A workshop belonging to the foundry (stratum B/3) is found in the better preserved northeast of the building complex, where the finds and features, like small hearths and water basins, point to bronze casting on a small scale (Prell, 2011: 173-176; 215-218). After the abandonment of the foundry and the erection of the courtyard (stratum B/2b), a larger modification was carried out in the eastern building complex. A wing of storerooms was installed in the central part of the edifice. At the same time, a pillared building was erected in the southwest (*Ibidem*: 170). In stratum B2/b indications for the following production branches can be found (*Ibidem*: 227-233): small-scale hot metalworking in the northeast and processing of cold metal in the south (figure 18). Scales of armour lances and arrowheads made of bronze point to the production of offensive and defensive armament, and some bronze knobs also suggest the manufacture of chariots. Sheets of gold were used to decorate the products (Herold, 1999: 41-47). The western rooms are pretty much destroyed, but the presence of scrapers made of broken pottery connects them to leather working, as tools like these are hallmarks of such an activity (Raedler, 2007: 49). Whetstones suggest the employment of larger bronze tools such as cutting knives, while pigments provide evidence for the colouring of finished products. Due to the scales and the complete process of scale armour assembly, as well as the scrapers that were employed to scrape the skin's hypoderm, one can assume that the processing of hides and bronze used for body armaments took place here.

The pillared edifice contains soil layers rich in humus along with a large amount of bone waste as well as roughly shaped objects made of bone, mostly semi-finished bone pins. This building can thus be identified as a bone workshop, where mainly bone arrowheads were fabricated. The specialized polishing stones (see above) also predominantly derive from here. Many artefacts made from flint, especially sickle blades, originating in the pillared building indicate woodworking as well, maybe even the manufacture of complete sickles as pointed out by Tillmann (2007: 77-78). Above all, the manufacture of complete arrows can be assigned to this building, a fact suggested by the presence of arrowheads made of materials other than bone together with the assumable processing of wood and reed. The manufacture of bows might have taken place in the same neighbourhood, but cannot be definitively localized. The western building complex, which is badly preserved, is associated with hot metal working and presumably delivered, among other things, bronze arrowheads to the pillared building.

At the beginning of stratum B/2a, the complex of workshops undergoes larger alterations (Prell, 2011: 171-172). The processing of hot metal in the northeast is now abandoned and a scribe's office, furnished with limestone architecture, is added (figure 19). A shield mould for the metal fittings of a Hittite Figure-of-Eight-Shield made of limestone and found *in situ* in this stratum reveals that the metal parts for shields were now being manufactured here (Pusch, 1990: 103-104; 2004: 242-246).

The absence of pottery scrapers to the west of the office makes it clear that the skin processing had been given up. The continuing use of pigments and whetstones speaks, however, of a general retention of the craft. Maybe shield coverings made of leather were fabricated here now, which were, unlike the leather scales of the body armor, not made from rawhide (Hulit, 2006: 102-103). The architecture of the pillared building is slightly altered during a renovation, but its specialization is maintained. Except for the on-going production of arrows (and bows), wooden shields might have also been produced here at this time as flint implemets are still found

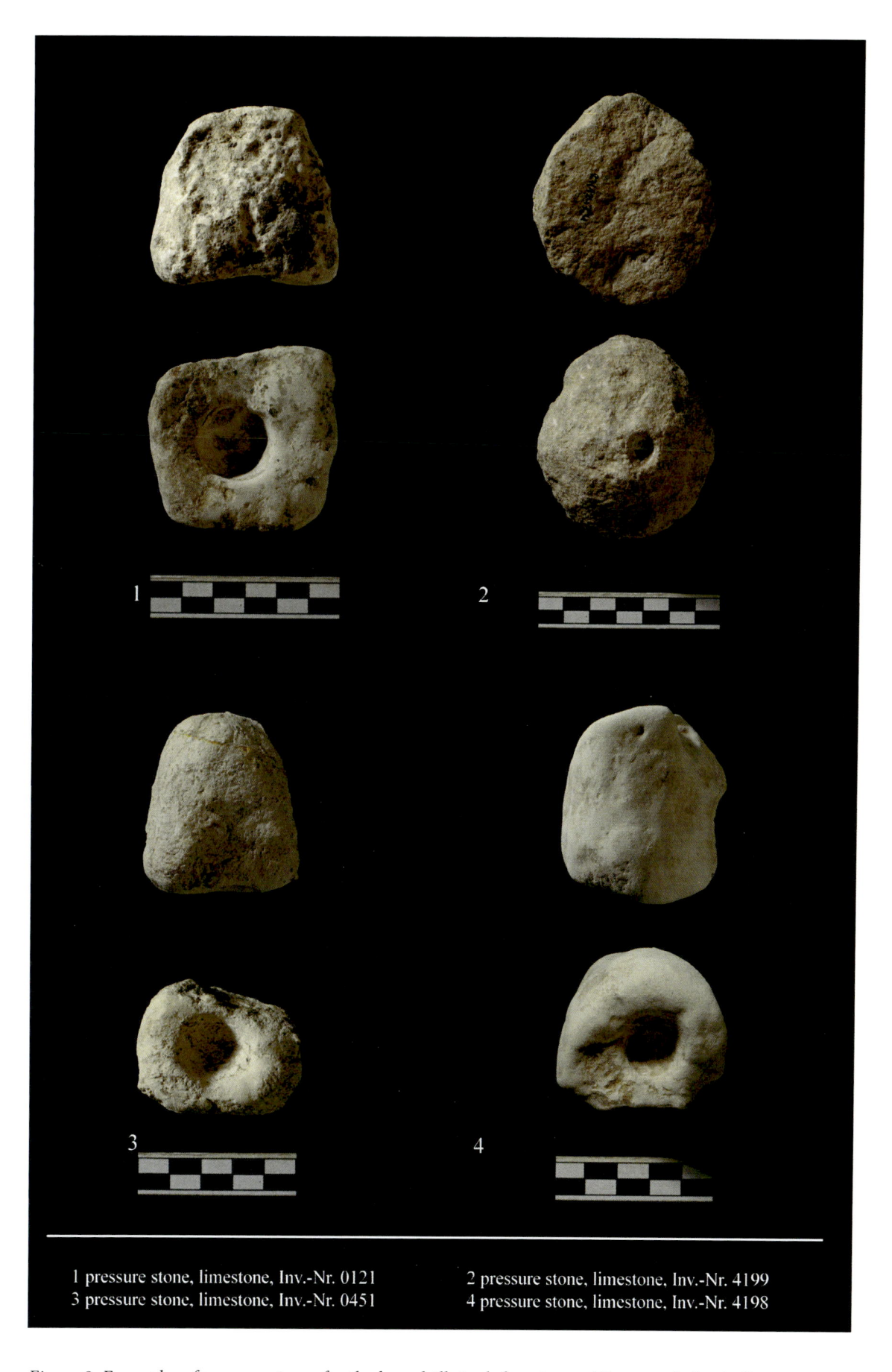

1 pressure stone, limestone, Inv.-Nr. 0121
3 pressure stone, limestone, Inv.-Nr. 0451
2 pressure stone, limestone, Inv.-Nr. 4199
4 pressure stone, limestone, Inv.-Nr. 4198

Figure 9. Examples of pressure stones for the bow drill. Scale bars in cm. Photographs by A. Krause.

Figure 10. Hammerstone Inv.-Nr. 3931 with surface showing marks of abrasion. Scale bar is 5 cm. Drawing by A. Klang.

here. The workshop complex to the west retains its involvement with hot metal processing.

The different workshop areas function together as an assembly line for producing different kinds of armaments, which is particularly true for the metal workshops. However, scales of armour and yoke saddle knobs made of bone prove that the bone workshop also worked with other branches of production and was not confined only to the manufacture of arrowheads. Based on the few chariot parts that were found in the workshops themselves (Herold, 2006: 41), the fabrication and repair of complete chariots cannot be assumed in the excavated part of the workshops. The bronze chariot parts, however, suggest that complete chariots were produced nearby. It is important to note that the workshops unearthed in the southern part of site Q I only represent a small portion of a much larger complex of different workshops that were organised as an artisan's quarter within the palatial district. Consequently, one cannot assume that the excavated area represents all the craft activities associated with chariotry.

CONCLUSION

The exposed part of the workshops can be identified with the *khepesh*, the armoury of the garrison, as also displayed in New Kingdom tombs (Prell, 2011: 155-160) such as Puyemre (Theben Tomb [TT] 39), Hepu (TT 66) or Menkheperrasonb (TT 86). As an establishment run by the state and belonging to the palace workshops, it was subject to strict administration and organisation, as well as concerned with the supply

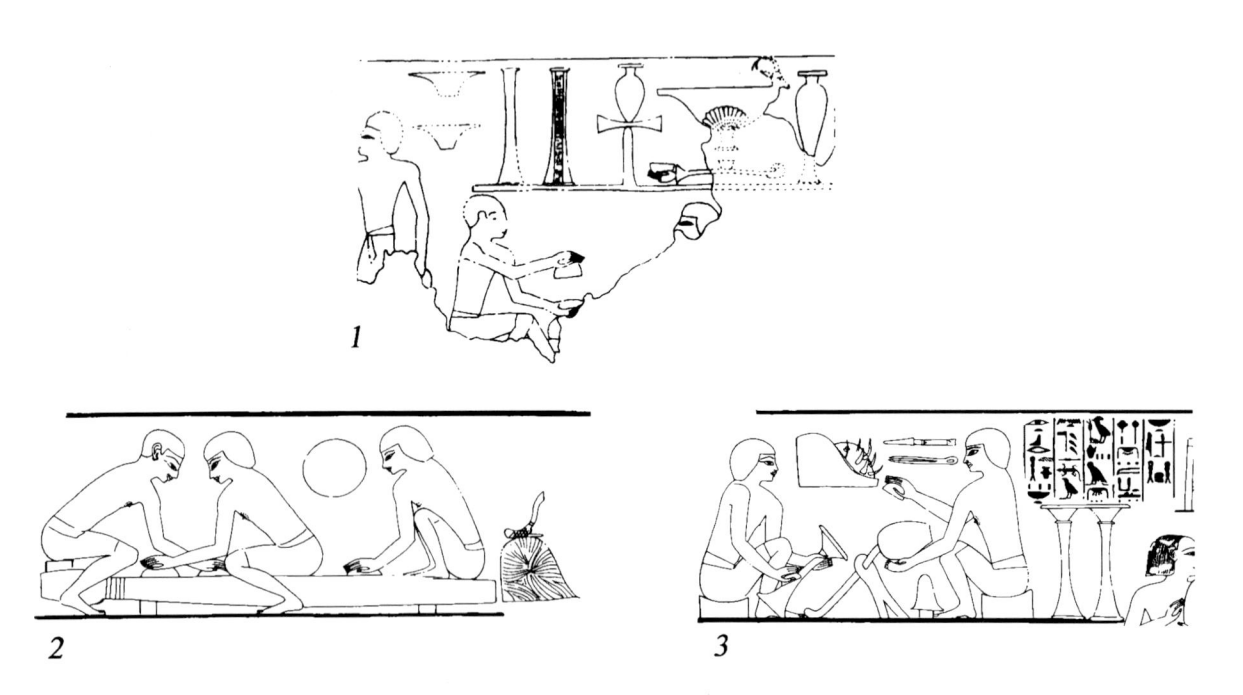

Figure 11. Tools of comparable shape are used for 1) Embossing metal sheets; 2) Smoothing wood; 3) Embossing metal vessels. From: Herold (2006: 61); Davies: (1943: pl. LIII) & Davies (1943: pl. LV) respectively.

Figure 12. Distribution of stone tools in site Q I. From: Prell (2011: 179).

Figure 13. Specialized polishing tools Inv.-Nr. 4138, 4136, 4145, 4140 made of steatite for arrow heads made of bone. Scale bars in cm. Photographs by A. Krause.

of raw materials and the transportation, storage and distribution of manufactured products (Herold, 2003). Thus, it does not seem astonishing that after the workshops were abandoned, the raw materials as well as the tools were taken to a new domain, in a relocation that one can assume was organized; certainly, the absence of larger metal tools as well as intact and well-preserved stone tools suggests such a course of action.

CITED LITERATURE

Dorner, J. 1996. Zur Lage des Palastes und des Haupttempels der Ramsesstadt. In: Bietak, M. Ed. Haus und Palast im Alten Ägypten. Denkschriften der Österreichischen Akademie der Wissenschaften 14. – Wien, Austrian Acadamy of Science Press: 69-71.

Herold, A. 1999. Streitwagentechnologie in der Ramses-Stadt. Bronze an Pferd und Wagen. Forschungen in der Ramses-Stadt 2. – Mainz, Philipp von Zabern.

Figure 14. Polishing tool Inv.-Nr. 4138 and arrow head Inv.-Nr. 0446. Photograph by A. Krause.

Figure 15. Polishing slab Inv.-Nr. 4118 and arrow head Inv.-Nr. 0126. Scale bar in cm. Photograph by A. Krause.

Figure 16. Chisels Inv.-Nr. 0424, 4572 and stylus Inv.-Nr. 4578. Scale bar in cm. Photographs by A. Krause.

Herold, A. 2003. Ein Puzzle mit zehn Teilen. Waffenkammer und Werkstatt aus dem Grab des *Ky-jrj* in Saqqara. In: Kloth, N. Ed. Es werde niedergelegt als Schriftstück. Festschrift für Hartwig Altenmüller zum 65. Geburtstag. – Hamburg, Helmut Buske Verlag: 193-202.

Herold, A. 2006. Streitwagentechnologie in der Ramsesstadt. Knäufe, Knöpfe und Scheiben aus Stein. Forschungen in der Ramses-Stadt 3. – Mainz, Philipp von Zabern.

Hulit, T. 2006. TutAnkhamun's Body Armour: Materials, Construction, and the Implications for the Military Industry. In: Dann, R.J. Ed. Current Research in Egyptology V. Proceedings of the Fifth Annual Symposium University of Durham 2004. – Oxford, Oxbow Books: 100-111.

Kemp, B. & A. Stevens. 2010. Busy Lives at Amarna: Excavations in the Main City (Grid 12 and the House of Ranefer, N49.18). Volume II. The Objects. – London, Egypt Exploration Society/Amarna Trust: 401-447.

Jeuthe, C. 2012. Balat X. Ein Werkstattkomplex im Palast der 1. Zwischenzeit in Ain Asyl. – Le Caire, Institut Français d'Archéologie Orientale

Petrie, W.M.F. 1917. Tools and Weapons. – London, Constable & Co LTD.

Prell, S. 2011. Einblicke in die Werkstätten der Residenz. Die Stein- und Metallwerkzeuge des Grabungsplatzes Q I. Forschungen in der Ramses-Stadt 8. – Hildesheim, Gerstenberg Verlag.

Pusch, E.B. 1990. Metallverarbeitende Werkstätten der frühen Ramessidenzeit in Qantir - Piramesse/Nord. Ein Zwischenbericht. – Egypt & Levant 1: 75-113.

Pusch, E.B. 1996."Pi-Ramesses-Beloved-of-Amun, Headquarters of thy Chariotry." - Egyptians and Hittites in the Delta Residence of the Ramessides. In: Eggebrecht, A. Ed. Pelizaeus-Museum Hildesheim Guidebook. The Egyptian Collection. – Mainz, Philipp von Zabern: 126-144.

Pusch, E.B. 1999. Vorbericht über die Abschlußarbeiten am Grabungsplatz Q IV 1997. – Egypt & Levant 9: 17-37.

Pusch, E.B., H. Becker & J. Fassbinder. 1999. Palast - Tempel - Auswärtiges Amt?- Oder: Sind Nilschlammauern magnetisch zu erfassen? – Egypt & Levant 9: 135-153.

Pusch, E.B. 2004. Piramesse-Qantir. Residenz, Waffenschmiede und Drehscheibe internationaler Beziehungen. In: Petschel, S. & M. von Falck. Ed. Pharao siegt immer. Krieg und Frieden im Alten Ägypten. – Bönen, Druckverlag Kettler: 240-263.

Raedler, Ch. 2007. Geräte aus Keramik in der spätbronzezeitlichen Ramsesstadt. Die Schaber der Werkstätten des Grabungsplatzes Q I. In: Pusch, E.B & M. Bietak. Ed. Die Keramik des Grabungsplatzes Q I. Teil 2. Schaber - Scherben - Marken. Forschungen in der Ramses-Stadt 5. – Hildesheim, Gerstenberg Verlag: 14-266.

Tillmann, A. 2007. Neolithikum in der späten Bronzezeit. Steingeräte des 2. Jahrtausend aus Auaris-Piramesse. Forschungen in der Ramses-Stadt 4. – Hildesheim, Gerstenberg Verlag.

Figure 17. Distribution of metal tools in site Q I. From: Prell (2011: 212).

production branches stratum B/2b

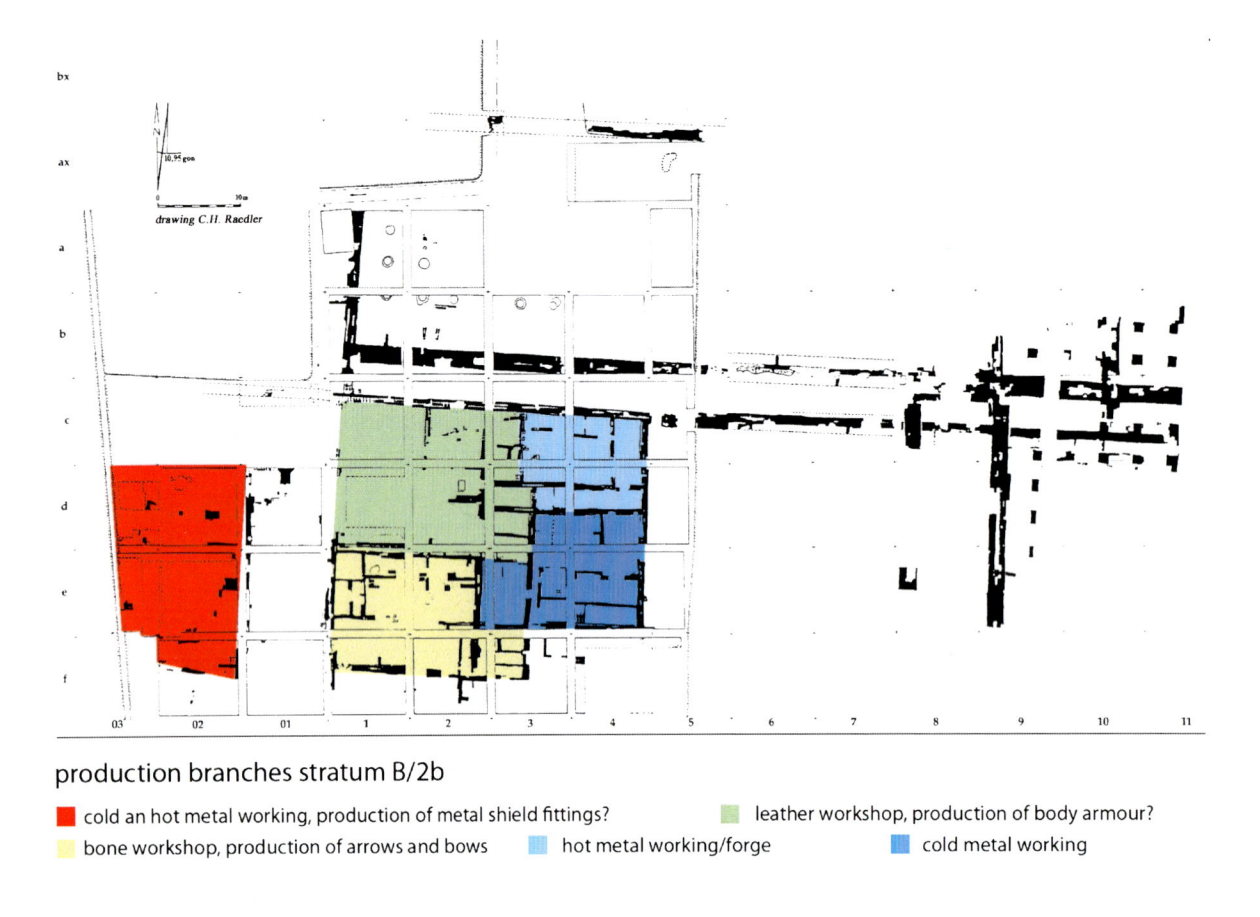

- 🟥 cold an hot metal working, production of metal shield fittings?
- 🟩 leather workshop, production of body armour?
- 🟨 bone workshop, production of arrows and bows
- 🟦 hot metal working/forge
- 🟦 cold metal working

Figure 18. Established production branches in excavated area in stratum B2/b. From: Prell (2011: 233).

production branches stratum B/2a

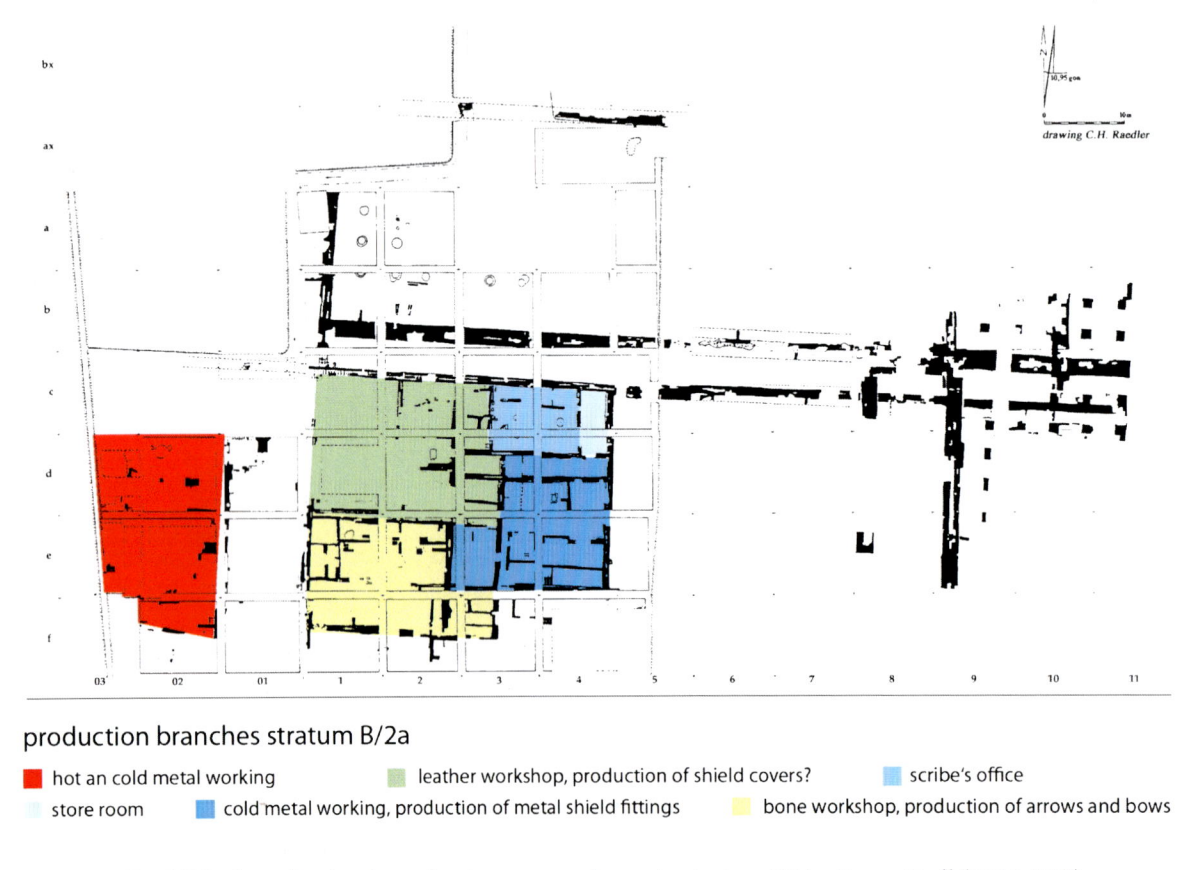

- 🟥 hot an cold metal working
- 🟩 leather workshop, production of shield covers?
- 🟦 scribe's office
- ⬜ store room
- 🟦 cold metal working, production of metal shield fittings
- 🟨 bone workshop, production of arrows and bows

Figure 19. Established production branches in excavated area in stratum B2/a. From: Prell (2011: 237).

WAGONS AND CARTS IN THE 3RD MILLENNIUM BC SYRIAN JAZIRAH: A STUDY THROUGH THE DOCUMENTATION

Mattia Raccidi

INTRODUCTION

The first information related to wheeled vehicles in the ancient Near East dates back to the end of 4th millennium BC (ca. 3200-3100 BC). Proto-cuneiform signs from Uruk IVa (Green & Nissen, 1987: 220) representing sledges and wheeled (or rollers) vehicles, the so-called 'sledge cars', are the oldest examples of land vehicles in the ancient Near East (Littauer & Crouwel, 1979: 13). Contemporary representations of sledges come from Arslantepe/Malatya (seal impression; Frangipane, 1997: fig. 16, 1) and from Iran (steatite plaque; Herzfeld, 1934: 223).

The vehicles represented by these signs were probably the forerunners of the 3rd millennium BC wagons: the famous 'battle car' found in the royal cemeteries at Ur (Woolley, 1934), Kish (Langdon, 1924) and Susa (De Mecquenem, 1943), all dated to about 2600 BC and represented on the Standard of Ur, also found in the royal cemetery. Indeed, from the 3rd millennium BC wagons and carts spread throughout Mesopotamia and Syria.

The acme of this diffusion, documented by an increase in the references related to wheeled vehicles, may be placed in the Syrian Jazirah during the period of the so-called Second Urban Revolution (Akkermans & Schwartz, 2003). Through the analysis of the different categories of documentation it was possible to identify various types of vehicles as well as diverse functions. The primary distinction between carts (two-wheeled vehicles) and wagons (four-wheeled vehicles) has been attested in the main categories: models, glyptic and written sources.

Wheeled vehicles also had a leading role in this society, insomuch as, in the early 2nd millennium BC, Hammurabi of Babylon reminds an ambassador of Zimrî-Lîm of Mari that donkeys and wagons were the strength of his land (Charpin *et al.*, 1988: 390-393).

Therefore, the main aim of the present contribution is the analysis of the documentation related to wagons and carts from the major 3rd millennium BC sites of the Syrian Jazirah, in order to better understand their role and their functions within this society.

In this paper the regional Jazirah periodization as presented in the volume edited by Lebeau (2011) is used.

THE JAZIRAH AND THE 3RD MILLENNIUM BC

Geography

Jazirah is the Arabic word for 'island', which can be the area comprised between two main rivers (figure 1). Thus, geographically the Syrian Jazirah is bordered by the Euphrates and by the Syrian/Iraqi and Syrian/Turkish borders. This area is crossed by two important rivers, tributaries of the Euphrates: the Balikh (west) and the Khabur (East). Precisely the Upper Khabur basin is the area of primary focus for this communication.

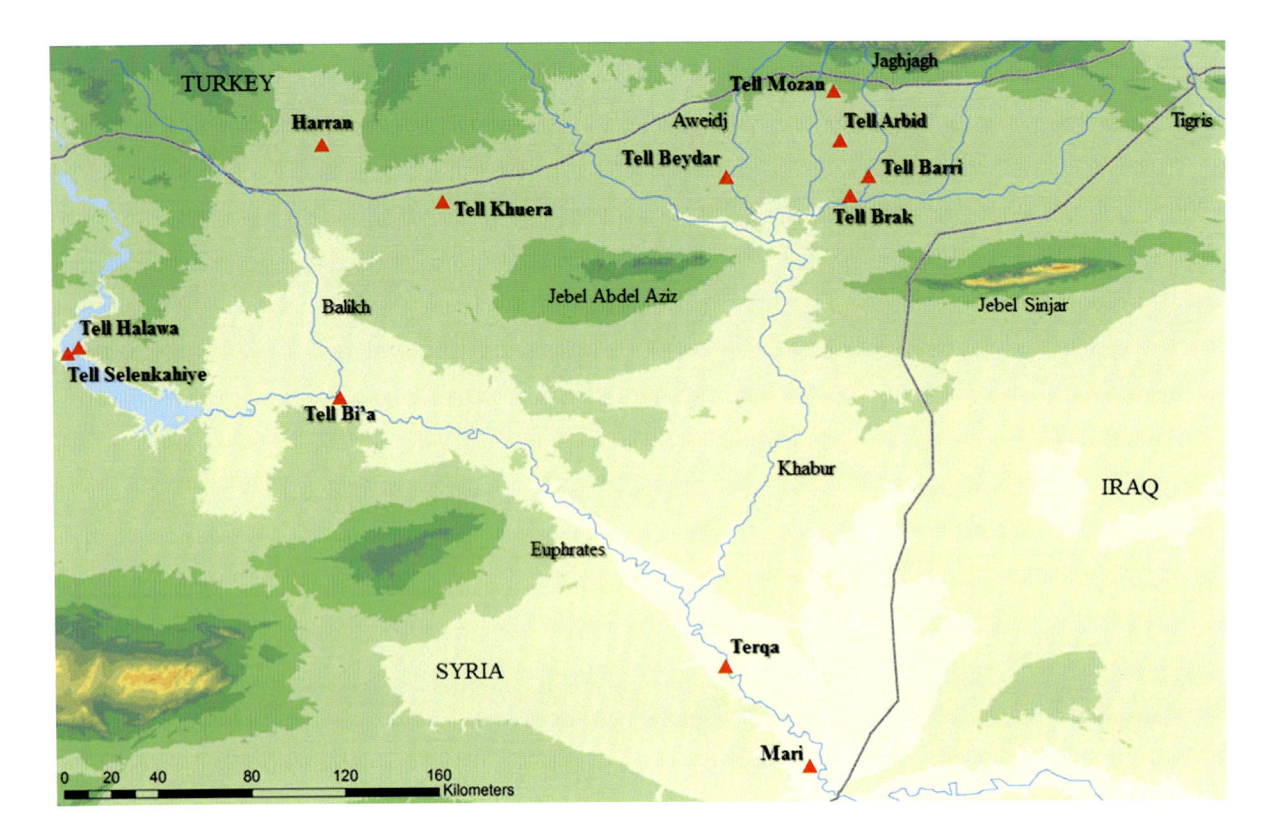

Figure 1. The Syrian Jazirah and the sites mentioned in the article. Map by M. Raccidi.

The upper Khabur basin, also known as the Khabur Triangle, was a very fertile area, still considered the bread-basket of Syria. Dry-farming had been assured by a high annual rainfall and by numerous tributaries, such as Radd, Jaghjagh, Khanzir, Aweidj and Jarrah. Another strong point of this region was the geographic location: being close to the mountains of Tauro, it was a fundamental area to control the traffic that connected Turkey to Assyria and southern Mesopotamia.

The Beginning of 3rd Millennium BC: Ninevite V Period (2900-2500 BC)

After the collapse of the Uruk system, at the end of the 4th millennium BC, in north-eastern Syria a regional culture emerged, the so-called Ninevite V culture (corresponding to Early Jazirah I-IIIa). The term derives from a type of pottery, painted or incised with geometric patterns, found for the first time by Mallowan, in 1931, in the fifth layer of deep sounding at Nineveh.

The Ninevite V period was characterized by rural settlements with little or no evidence of monumental architecture, elite art, or writing. Among these villages of the upper Khabur, the largest sites were: Tell Brak (ancient Nagar), Tell Mozan (ancient Urkesh), Tell Leilan (ancient Shekhna; in the Early 2nd millennium BC Tell Leilan was named Shubat-Enlil by Shamshi-Adad I). These sites were the main centers of the region throughout the 3rd millennium BC.

The first evidence of wagons dating to this period comes neither from written sources nor seals or seal impressions since there were no written records at the time, and the glyptic evidence was limited to geometric motifs. Thus, the earliest attestations of wheeled vehicles were terracotta models. Further evidence related to wheeled vehicles belongs to this period: the recent discovery at Mari of the impression of two wheels imprinted in the bitumen.

The Mid-3rd Millennium BC: Second Urban Revolution (2500-2350 BC)

Starting from the mid-3rd millennium (Early Jazirah IIIb) many urban centers with monumental architecture, elite art and written records appeared in Syria. The main examples were Ebla in western Syria and Mari in southern Syria. The sites of the upper Khabur basin were no exception to this urbanization. New settlements appeared while others expanded: especially, the main sites of the region, Tell Brak, Tell Leilan and Tell Mozan, reached the size of c. 100 ha.

In the region west of upper Khabur, which is relatively dry, a type of settlement characterized by a circular concentric plan, appeared. These sites, designed *Kranzhügel*, are typical phenomenon of the Second Urban Revolution, the largest and famous are Tell Khuera (known as Harbe by the Middle Assyrian period) and Tell Beydar (ancient Nabada). Given their position, in a relatively dry region, it has been suggested that their main economic occupation was linked to animal breeding and to the commercial trade. Indeed, as suggested by Lebeau & Sulaiman (2005: 25) "The mention of professional cartwrights at Tell Beydar and the abundance of chariots and wagons representations, either covered or not, in the local glyptic, as well as the frequent mention of the visits payed by the *en* – i.e., the Lord of Nagar – at Tell Beydar: all these elements suggest that the site had an important function as a caravan trade station in an area that was ideal for equid breeding, and at a time very close to the beginning of the horse domestication".

The period of the Second Urban Revolution coincides with the acme of the presence of wheeled-vehicles documentation. Models become a common category in the terracotta assemblages from many sites, and new types and new decorations appear. A large assemblage of seal impressions representing wheeled vehicles in warfare, worship or hunting scenes, come from Syrian sites, mainly from Tell Beydar. Written records from Ebla and Tell Beydar mention craftsmen specialized in cart and wagon construction as well as materials for the construction and use of these vehicles, especially textiles, and draft animals (mainly donkeys).

The Akkadian Empire and the End of the 3rd Millennium BC (2350-2000 BC)

During the last quarter of 3rd millennium BC (Early Jazira IV-V) urban societies of Syria were first subjugated by the southern Mesopotamian state of Akkad and later knew a period of crises and, to some extent, the collapse of urbanization.

Wheeled vehicles documentation in the last quarter of the 3rd millennium BC is mainly characterized by terracotta models that preserve types and varieties of decorations of the previous period, in addition to some seal impressions, mainly from Tell Brak.

THE WHEELED VEHICLES DOCUMENTATION

Four categories of wheeled vehicles documentation have been recognized and analyzed (figure 2).

1) Models;
2) Glyptic – two-dimensional art;
3) Written sources;
4) Full-size vehicles.

The first category, models, is the most prevalent example of wheeled vehicles. As mentioned above, these become common in the mid-3rd millennium BC terracotta assemblages, although the earliest examples have been attested from the Ninevite V period (2900-2500 BC) onwards. This category provides important information on the different types of vehicle and their widespread use.

Glyptic representations and written records have a limited chronological and geographical distribution. However, at Tell Beydar an important corpus of tablets and seal impressions related to wheeled vehicles has been found. Both categories provide information on types and functions of vehicles. The most famous example of two-dimensional art is the Standard of Ur with its shell inlays representing war wagons. Similar figures come from the Ishtar and Ninni-Zaza temples as well as from the pre-Sargonic palace of Mari.

Finally, no full-size vehicles have been found in Syrian Jazirah. However, the so-called Mari Wheels have been included in this category.

Models

The oldest examples of models from Syrian Jazirah date to the Early Jazirah II (2700-2600 BC). In this period mainly two-wheeled models have been attested (Bollweg, 1999: type II; Pruß, 2011: type C 04; Raccidi, 2012: type I). The first examples of ter-

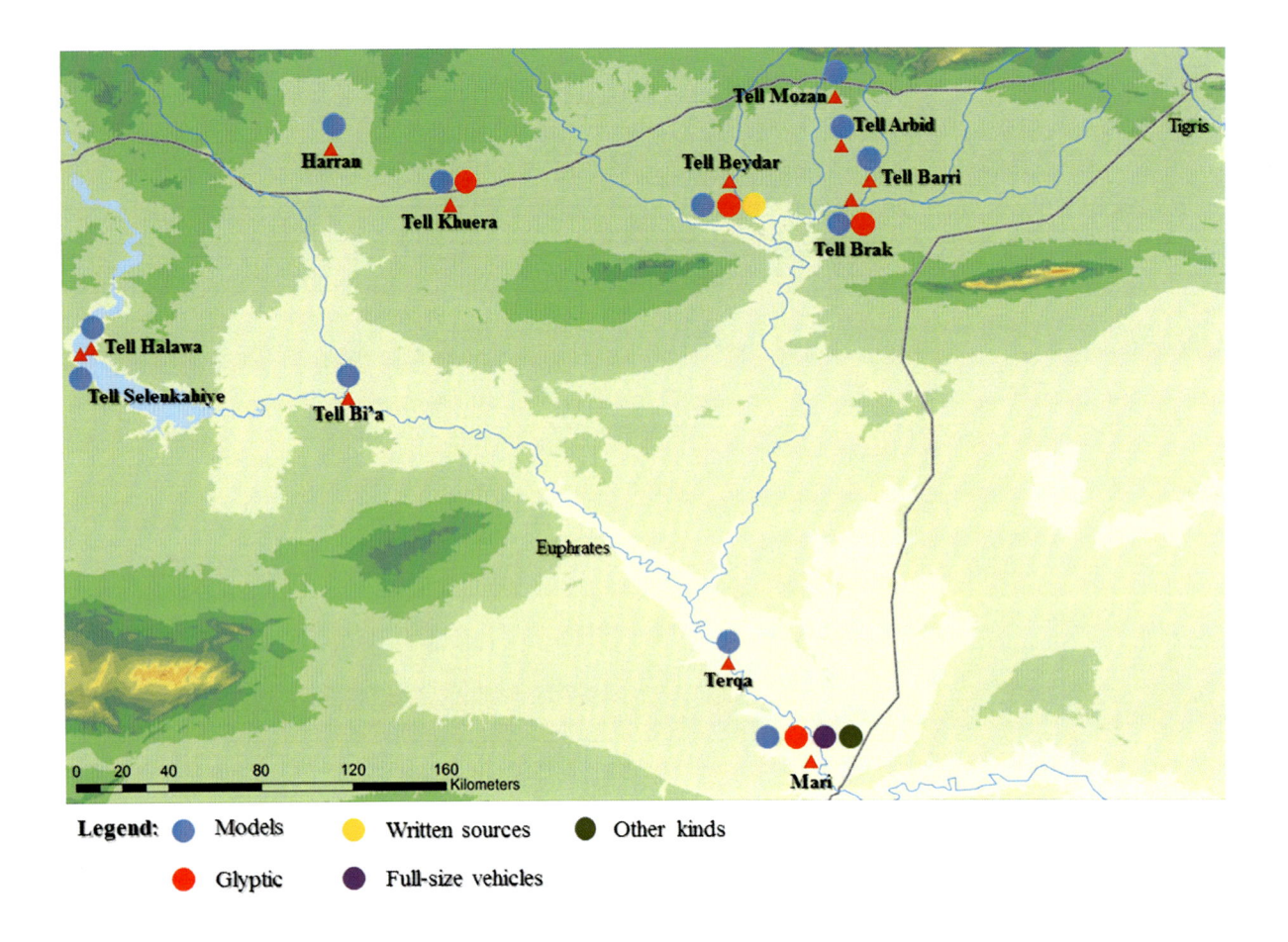

Figure 2. Distribution of wheeled-vehicles documentation categories in the 3rd millennium Syrian Jazirah sites. Map by M. Raccidi.

racotta models of carts from southern Mesopotamia date back, slightly earlier, to the beginning of 3rd millennium BC (c. 2900-2800 BC) (Bollweg, 1999: Type VI; Littauer & Crouwel, 1979: 'straddle car'). The Syrian Jazirah carts have two main features: a basically trapezoid front shield, with its upper part usually rounded and a platform body without seat, sometimes surrounded by a narrow frame. Very few examples have incised decoration, which appear mainly on the front shield.

These early examples have been found at Tell Brak (Matthews, 2003: fig. 5.79, no. 17), Tell Beydar, Tell Khuera (Pruß, 2011: 245) and Tell Arbid (Raccidi, 2012: 613). Models from Tell Arbid have two important peculiarities: they all have been found in cultic contexts (Sector W: Bielinski, 2012; Raccidi, 2012: 618) and are all made of a specific fabric: dark brown clay, low fired and with very few inclusions.

Only three fragments of wagons date back to the Early Jazirah II. Two fragments come from Tell Brak (Oates, 2001: fig. 487, nos. 21-22) and one from Mari (Margueron, 2004: fig. 79), all these specimens belong to tilted vehicles. Tilted vehicles are usually four-wheeled wagons with an open front, and often with a decorated cover. The two axles are usually tubular and attached under the body: in some cases the axles are pierced through the base. On the front, vertical lugs, from one to three, form the common towing system. This contrasts with the hole for the draught pole, which is common in the other types. In many cases the tilt has an incised decoration; the most common patterns are geometrics motifs: zigzag, herringbone or grid. Two types of tilted wagon models have been differentiated on the basis of their construction technique: hand-made with body and U-shaped cover (figure 3B) and those in which the body and cover merge seamlessly in the form of a vase (figure 3A).

Although first examples from Tell Brak date back to the Early Jazirah II, these models became common in the northern Mesopotamian sites assemblages starting from the mid-3rd millennium BC,

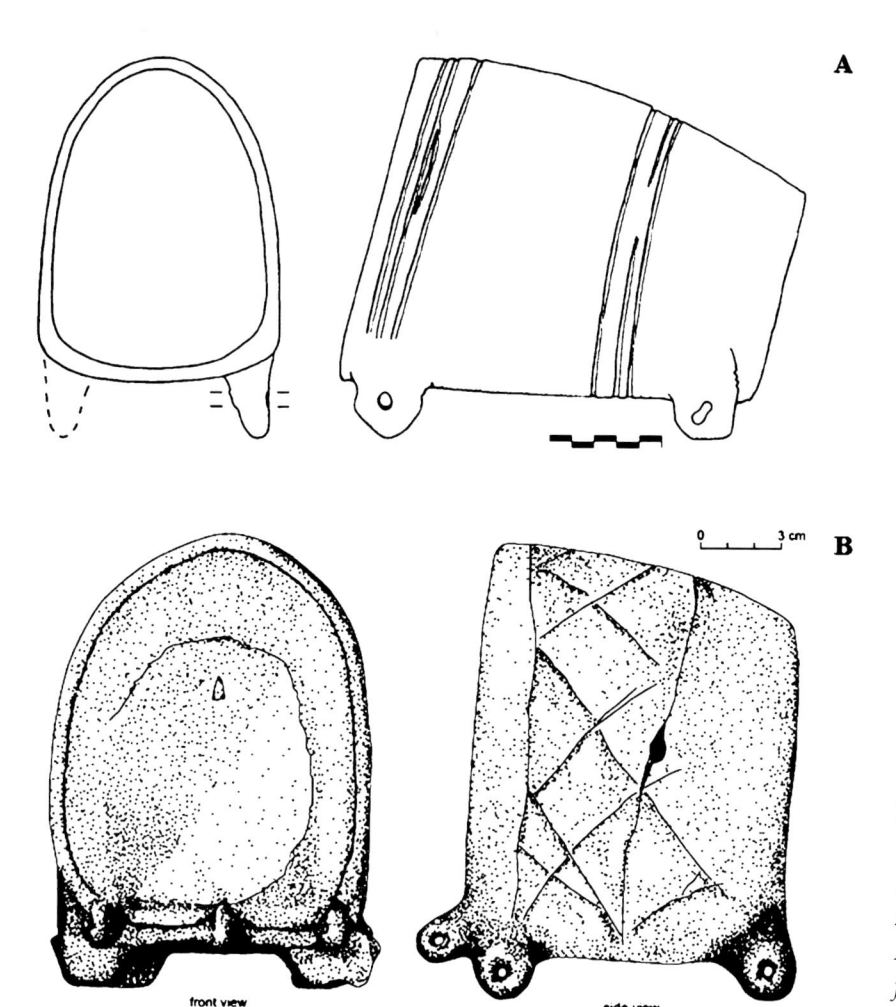

Figure 3. Models of covered vehicle. A) Tell Brak. From: (Oates, 2001: fig. 487: no. 25,3. TB.83.6); B) Tell Arbid. From: Raccidi (2012: fig. 6. ARB '03 SD 36/65 - 36-1).

and are found at many sites, such as Tepe Gawra, Tell Arbid, Tell Barri, Tell Bi'a and Tell Selenkahiye (Bollweg, 1999: 29-30: Type XII; Pruß, 2011: 246: Type C08; Raccidi, 2012: 611-613: Type VI).

A general increase in quantity and types of models has been attested from the second half of the 3rd millennium BC, with models of wheeled-vehicles becoming a common category of the Syrian Jazirah terracotta assemblages. Both, cart and wagon models have been attested at many sites in a period that ranges from the mid to the end of 3rd millennium BC (Early Jazirah IIIb-V).

Models of wagons without coverage emerge for the first time during this period. Three main types have been attested: the first (figure 4A) have a deep rectangular box-body and a high front shield. They have been attested in the period Early Jazirah IIIa-IV (2600-2170 BC) (Bollweg, 1999: 28: Type XI; Pruß, 2011: 244: Type C 01; Raccidi, 2012: 610: Type V 'flat base').

The two axles, often pierced through the base, are in the frontal and rear parts. Outside the body, in the rear, there is a footboard, a trapezoidal appendix used in the full-size wagons to carry a second standing person, as shown on the Standard of Ur, while the charioteer, holding the reins, stood on the front, protected by the shield. Actually, these models, the so-called 'battle car', closely resemble the wagons depicted on the Standard. They are usually decorated with incised lines on the shield (X-shaped pattern) and on the box (vertical lines pattern), and sometimes human figures were applied on the shields. Moreover, the upper part of the shield is most often horn-shaped. They are common in the assemblages of sites of the western Jazirah and middle-Euphrates region, for example at Tell Khuera (Orthmann, 1995: figs. 17, nos. 25-26; 35, nos. 9-12; 71, nos. 53-55; 72, nos. 56, 59-62; 89, no. 10), Tell Halawa (Neufang & Pruß, 1994: fig. 51, nos. 79, 81) and Tell Bi'a (Miglus &

Figure 4. Models of wagon. A) Tell Khuera. From: Orthmann (1995: fig. 71: no. 55,4. TCH.90.F.566); B) Tell Brak. From: Oates (2001: fig. 487: no. 12. TB.5114).

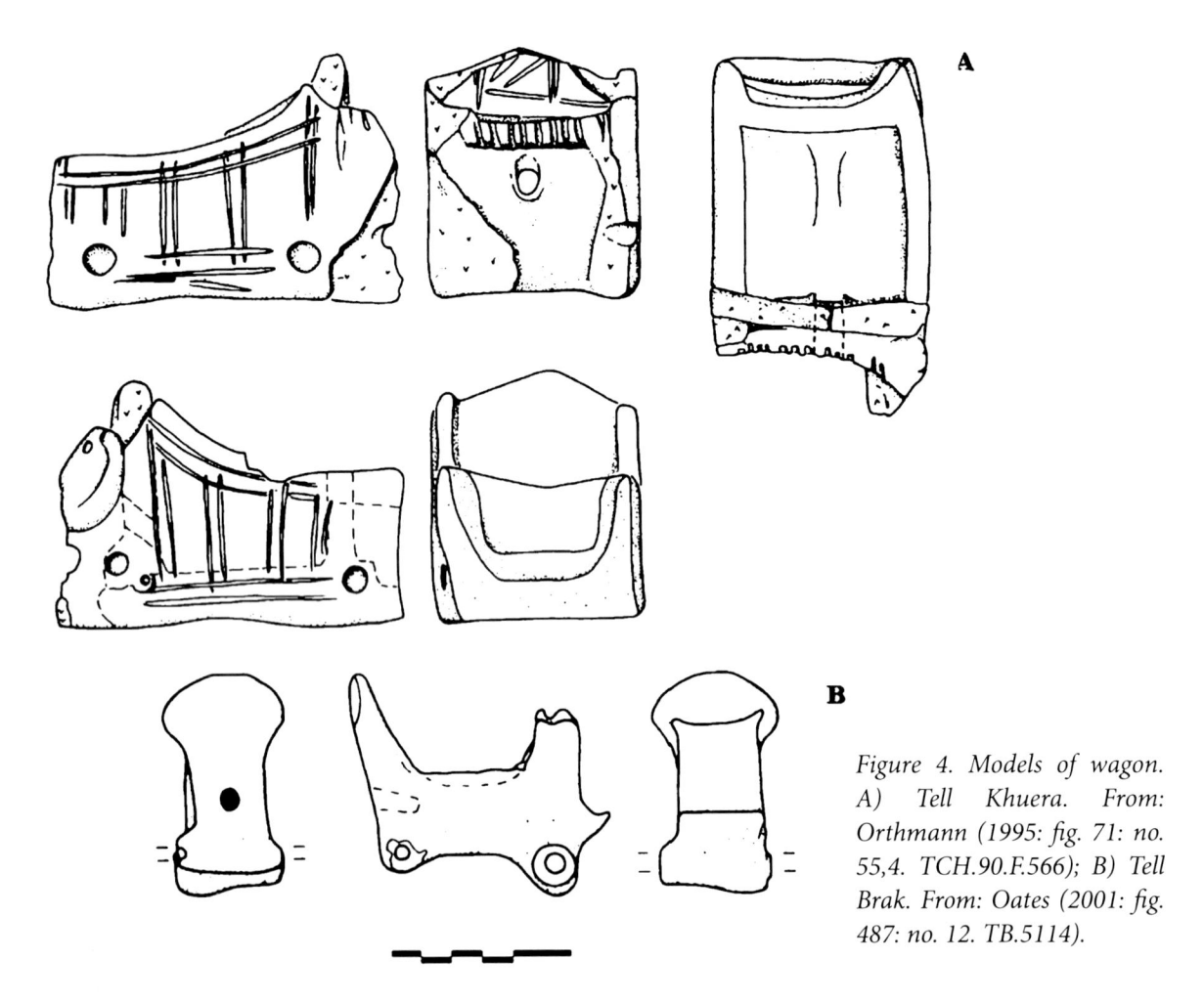

Strommenger, 2002: pls. 21, nos. 10-12; 39, no. 9; 43, no. 22; 46, no. 3; 48, nos. 27-28; 91, nos. 43, 46; 95, nos. 22-26).

In the eastern Jazirah sites the second type of wagon models predominates (figure 4B). These models have a rectangular and narrow box-body, characterized by shallow frames, and a more or less broad seat in the rear (Bollweg, 1999: 24-27: Types VIII, X; Pruß, 2011: 244: Type C 03; Raccidi, 2012: 610: Type V 'rounded base'). The frontal shield, sometimes slightly oblique, is often decorated with incised X-shaped or vertical lines patterns or with impressed dots. In some cases both decoration techniques are used. The frontal and rear axles are, almost always, cylindrical-shaped and protrude from the body and in the rear there is the footboard. These models have been found at many sites of the eastern Jazirah, such as Tell Arbid (Raccidi, 2012: fig. 5), Tell Barri (Pecorella & Pierobon Benoit, 2008: 47) and Tell Brak (Oates, 2001: fig. 487, nos. 12-15).

The third type of models has a rectangular and narrow platform-body without a seat in the rear (Bollweg, 1999: 25-26: Type IX; Pruß, 2011: 244: Type C 02; Raccidi, 2012: 610: Type IV). This type, as the previous one, has been attested between Early Jazirah IIIa and Early Jazirah V (2600-2000 BC). The platform-body has very shallow frames but, more frequently, has no frame at all. The frontal shield is oblique and decorated like that of the previous type. The frontal axle, pierced through the base in the same way as the rear axle, slightly protrudes frontally. In the rear there is always a footboard. These models, as the previous ones, are found in the terracotta assemblages of eastern Jazirah sites; but some specimens have been found at Tell Arbid (Raccidi, 2012: fig. 4), Tell Barri (Pecorella & Pierobon Benoit, 2005: 52) and Tell Beydar (Pruß, 2011: pl. 4, no. 4).

Models of tilted wagons increase between the mid and the end of the 3rd millennium BC. They are common in upper Mesopotamian sites while, surprisingly, there are no traces of these models in southern areas. Some examples come from Tepe Gawra (Speiser, 1935: Pl. XVI c), Tell Brak (Oates,

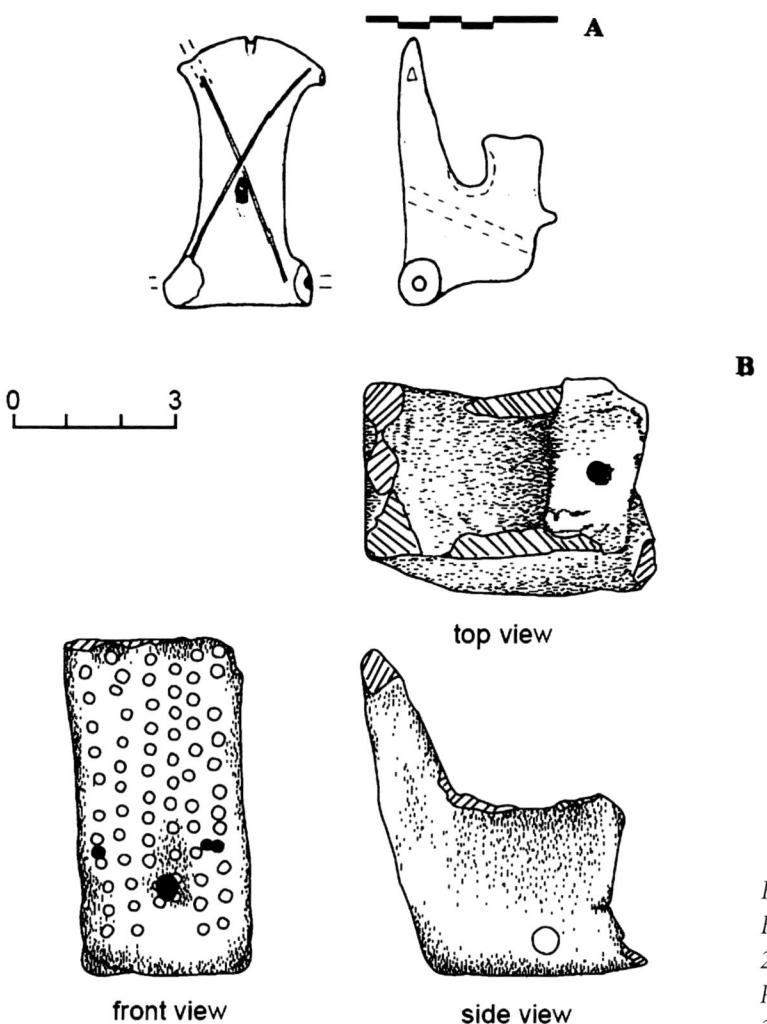

Figure 5. Models of cart. A) Tell Brak. From: Oates (2001, fig. 488: no. 27,3. TB.1349); B) Tell Arbid. From: Raccidi (2012: fig. 2). ARB '05 SD 35/65 - 16-1).

2001: fig. 487, nos. 18, 23-26), Tell Arbid (Raccidi, 2012: fig. 6), Tell Barri (Pecorella, 1995: 32), Tell Bi'a (Strommenger & Kohlmeyer, 1998: pl. 162, nos. 1-7) and Tell Selenkahiye (Liebowitz, 1988: pl. 32, no. 1; Van Loon, 2001: pl. 6.8 b).

Regarding two-wheeled models, two different types emerge. The first and most common type has a short rectangular platform-body, sometimes slightly concave, a high frontal shield and a seat in the rear (Bollweg, 1999: 19-21: Type IIIb; Pruß, 2011: 245: Type C 05-06; Raccidi, 2012: 608-609: Type III) (figure 5A). The platform-body in some cases has very shallow frames. The axle, usually under the front, is sometimes seen under the middle and, less frequent, under the rear part of the model. The high frontal shield is commonly decorated with X-shaped incised lines and its upper part is horn-shaped. It can be divided into three different types:

1) Separated/pierced horns-shaped;
2) Separated horns-shaped;
3) Unified horns-shaped.

In the rear section there is the seat and very frequently the footboard. This type of models is common through the second half of the 3rd millennium BC, especially during the first quarter (Early Jazirah IIIb-IV; 2500-2170 BC). Examples are known from Tell Brak (Oates, 2001: fig. 302b), Tell Arbid (Raccidi, 2012: fig. 3), Tell Beydar (Lebeau & Suleiman, 1997: pl. 1.1) and Tell Melebiya (Lebeau, 1993: pl. 90, no. 1).

The second type of two-wheeled models has a rather deep box-body with high frontal shield (Bollweg, 1999: 22-23: Type IV; Raccidi, 2012: 606-607: Type II) (figure 5B). In the rear there is a footboard and in some cases a seat or a simple frame. The axle is under the central part of the body, usually tubular-shaped, but sometimes it pierces into the base. The upper part of the frontal shield has the common form described above and it is usually decorated with the X-shaped incised lines but also with impressed dots. These dots can be on the shield on the frames or on the seat of the model. Models of this type are less frequent compared to the previous types: examples are known from Tell Arbid (Raccidi, 2012: fig. 2), Tell Khuera (Orthmann, 1995: fig. 71, no. 51), Tell Bi'a (Bollweg, 1999: figs. 16-17) and Tell Selenkahiye (Van Loon, 2001: pl/ 6.8 c).

Glyptic – Two-Dimensional Art

Seals or seal impressions representing wheeled vehicles date back mainly to the second half of the 3rd millennium BC. These representations come from both, southern and northern Mesopotamia but, unfortunately, a rather significant number are unprovenanced. The main Syrian Jazirah sites with wheeled vehicles representations are Tell Beydar, Tell Brak, Tell Khuera and Mari. All impressions from these sites show wagons, while some of these, notably from Tell Beydar, represent tilted vehicles as well.

Although the majority of these representations date to the Early Jazirah IIIb-V periods, corresponding to the second half of the 3rd millennium BC, the first example in glyptic art dates back to the Early Jazirah I (2900-2700 BC) and comes from Tell Khuera (Moortgat & Moortgat-Correns, 1976: figs. 22a-b). The representation is very stylized and in a single register. The wagon has a platform body without seat in the rear. The frontal shield, undecorated, is horn-shaped in its upper part. The standing charioteer holds the reins of a single draught animal. In front of the wagon is a group of four animals: a dog, surmounted by a scorpion, a gazelle and a deer, before whose face an unidentified plant is depicted. The scene, given the presence of wild animals and the absence of weapons, has been interpreted as a hunting scene (Jans & Bretschneider, 1998: 169).

Starting from the mid-3rd millennium BC the most important assemblage of wheeled vehicles representations in glyptic art come from Tell Beydar (Jans & Bretschneider, 1998). At least eight impressions belong to this assemblage, although some of them are very small fragments and only a part of the vehicles is recognizable. The bests preserved are the impressions *bey*. 1 (Jans & Bretschneider, 1998: figs. 11-12, pl. I *bey*. 1) and *bey*. 2 (Jans & Bretschneider, 1998: fig. 13, pl. *bey*. 2).

The first impression, *bey*. 1 (figure 6A), is divided into two registers, in the upper one a war scene where a wagon is represented. The seat and the horn-shaped upper part of the frontal shield are represented. The seated charioteer holds the reins of a single draught animal, although more detailed representations suggest that the vehicle should be pulled by a team of four. To complete the 'wagon group' a fallen enemy is represented upside down in front of the draught animal. This standardized representation of the fallen enemy, upside down in front or between the paws of the draught animals, is a typical feature of the wagon representations in the warfare scenes of the period, and is found, for example at Tell Brak, Mari, Ur, Kish and Abu Salabikh. In front of the 'wagon group' there are six fighting human figures, two of them are kneeling and hold a shield or a bow in their hands. The lower register has a wagon scene too but in this case a tilted vehicle is represented. According to Jans & Bretschneider (1998: 162) the scene has been interpreted as cultic. Nadali (2009), however, proposed that the scene represents a siege. The center of the register is occupied by a rectangular structure decorated with two X-shaped bars. Three human torsos protrude from the top. Most likely, the structure is a temple or an altar. On the left side, there is a tilted wagon, the pole and the reins of the vehicle, facing upwards, placed on the structure. Beneath the vehicle a kneeling figure raises one arm, the same gesture that is repeated by two standing figures in flounced skirts behind the wagon. On the right side, a standing person is transported on a vable platform, flanked by two standing figures in flounced skirts that raise the arm.

This seal impression from Tell Beydar can be compared to those found at Mari belonging to king Ishqi-Mari (Bretschneider et al., 2009). They have much closer parallels with the Syrian seal housed in the Louvre Museum (Collon, 1987: fig. 722).

The second seal impression from Tell Beydar (figure 6B) is still divided into two registers and represents a tilted wagon in a cultic/ritual scene. On the left side of the upper register there is an en-

Figure 6. Seal impressions representing wheeled vehicles. A:) Bey. 1. From: Jans & Bretschneider (1998: pl. I, Bey. 1); B) Bey. 2. After: Jans & Bretschneider (1998: pl. I, Bey) 2); C) Ishqi-Mari Seal 1. From: Bretschneider et al. (2009: fig. 1).

throned figure, most likely the ruler, holding a cup and, behind him, a standing figure with a kind of palm-leaf fan. In front of the ruler stands a cup-bearer with a jar and a tilted wagon carrying two human torsos pulled by two human figures. Given the cultic nature of the scene, the figures inside the vehicle can be interpreted as divine statues. In the lower register crossed animals and human figures are represented.

The seal impressions of Ishqi-Mari (figure 6C) dates between the end of Early Jazirah IIIb and beginning of Early Jazirah IV (c. 2350-2250 BC), and, as previously said, they share similarities with the Beydar impression, although some important peculiarities can be observed. The composition of both Mari impressions are very similar – in fact, they differ only in minor details. As the Beydar example, they are divided into two registers. In the lower one, warfare actions with wagons are represented. These scenes, as well as the whole impression, are more detailed than the examples from Beydar. The vehicles have a seat or a high frame in the rear; the decorations on the sides and on the frontal shields are clearly visible. In the former there are vertical grooves while on the shields there are the common X-shaped bars. Moreover, the upper part of the shields is horn-shaped and the quiver with javelins is attached on the front. In both impressions, above the vehicles box, there are upside down heads(?) instead of charioteers. The vehicles are pulled by equids with the usual fallen enemies beneath their hooves. Finally, in front of the wagon there are the traditional groups of fighting human figures.

In the upper registers ritual scenes are shown. Ishqi-Mari, holding a mace, is enthroned and behind him stands a servant holding a fan, and a hero (Master of the Animals) holding two lions. In front of Ishqi-Mari astral signs and symbolical animals are represented. The most important novelty, which makes these impressions unique, is the presence of the cartouche with the name of the king.

At least six seal impressions representing wagons come from Tell Brak and date to the Early Jazirah IV (2350-2170 BC) (Buchanan, 1966: fig. 292; Matthews, 1991: figs. 6, 11; Matthews et al., 1994: figs. 1-3). During this time, Tell Brak was under the control of the Akkadian Dynasty, the king Naram-Sin built his palace there, and thus the site became the administrative center of the region. The impressions are standardized and very stylized, the best preserved showing the wagon type with a seat at the rear and a frontal shield with horn-shaped upper part (wagon type 2 described above). The vehicles are driven by seated charioteers, with a second person usually standing on the footboard. The vehicles are pulled by a single draught animal, an equid, with the fallen enemy beneath its hooves.

The most famous example of two-dimensional art is the Standard of Ur, found in the royal cemetery and representing the so called 'battle car'. Other representations are on the so-called Vultures Stele of Eannatum of Lagash (Littauer & Crouwel, 1973), on a votive plaque from Ur (Woolley, 1934) and on two vases in scarlet ware, one from Khafaja and one from Susa (Nagel, 1964).

In the Syrian Jazirah, once again, the site of Mari provides some examples belonging to this category, although very limited. They are mother of pearl inlays of wheels, carts and wagons, very similar to those of the Standard of Ur, dating to the second half of the 3rd millennium BC (c. 2500-2300 BC). The inlays certainly belonged to a type of elite art given the attention to detail, and because they have been found respectively in the Ishtar temple (Parrot, 1956: pl. LVI), in the Nini-Zaza temple (*Ibidem*, 1967: pl. LXV) and in the pre-Sargonic palace (Parrot, 1969: fig. 10; 1970: pl. XIV. 3).

A fragment of a cart with a decorated box body and a tripartite lenticular disk-wheel come from the Ishtar temple. Another fragment shows two heads of harnessed donkeys. The Nini-Zaza temple has returned the highest number of wheeled vehicles inlays, such as tripartite lenticular disk-wheels, frontal shields decorated with X-shaped bars and horn-shaped upper part, two-wheeled cart with box body and some fragments of a 'battle car', as well as examples with a fallen enemy between the draught animals paws, the standing charioteer and the second standing soldier. Finally from the pre-Sargonic palace mainly tripartite lenticular disk-wheels are recovered. Some of these have a saw-toothed crown along the circumference. Since this feature is visible also in the copper model of cart from Tell Agrab (Frankfort, 1943: pls. 58-60) it could be representing the copper nails that have been found in the wheels from Kish (Langdon, 1924) that were used to strengthen the wheel.

Written Sources

Written sources related to wheeled vehicles in 3rd millennium BC Syrian Jazirah are very limited and essentially concentrated in the site of Tell Beydar. From 1993 more than 200 administrative tablets dating to the Early Jazirah IIIb (2500-2350 BC) have been found at the site. The texts mainly provide information on the economic activities such as production and distribution of grain, organization of labor and management of herds. Explicit references to types of wagon, and their functions are not found in these texts, although professional cartwrights (nagar ^{giš}gigir) are mentioned. This means that wheeled vehicles were probably used regularly in daily life activities. Moreover, plowing teams composed by four draft animals (oxen or asses) are frequently cited in the texts (Sallaberger, 1996: 82). As suggested by Widell (2003: 719), since ethnographic evidence shows that a plowing team was usually composed by two animals, the Beydar 'teams' might have been used for pulling wheeled vehicles rather than plows.

Finally, Beydar tablets record a number of journeys of the Lords of Nagar (Tell Brak) to Nabada (Tell Beydar) and neighboring settlements. The visits had mainly economic and political purposes, since Nabada was one of the main sites under the control of the Nagar rulers. However, despite this focus, the shrines of the city and of the neighboring settlements were visited nonetheless. In the texts the allocation of fodder for the donkeys of the Lords of Nagar during these visits are mentioned. It is possible that, given the large number of animals (up to 50), some of them were used in teams of four for pulling the wagons of the rulers.

A contemporary source of information is the archive of Ebla. Ebla, along with Nagar and Mari, was one of the main centers that dominated northern Mesopotamia during the mid-3rd millennium BC. In the economic texts from its archive four terms, used to identify different types of wheeled vehicles, have been attested (Conti, 1997: 23-71):

giš gígir-II: This was the most common reference; it has usually been interpreted as 'two-wheeled cart';
giš gígir-IV: Less common than the previous one; it has been interpreted as 'four-wheeled wagon'. When specified it is drawn by oxen;
giš É × GÍGIR (giš gígir – é): It has been interpreted as 'covered wagon' and usually assigned to important personalities;
giš gígir-sum: This is the less common type in the Ebla texts, known also in the pre-Sargonic Mesopotamia and interpreted as 'carrying wagon'.

Given their economic nature, the Ebla texts often refer to construction materials of wheeled vehicles, such as wood and textiles. In particular, wool was divided into good and bad qualities, it was assigned to the construction of the giš É × GÍGIR (giš gígir – é) and probably used for covering. It was also assigned for the construction of the other types of vehicle (Conti, 1997: 33-34).

Full-Size Vehicles

Unfortunately no full-size vehicles comparable to those found at Ur, Kish and Susa have been found in Syrian Jazirah. However, the relevant discovery at Tell Hariri/Mari of the impression of two wheels imprinted in bitumen opened new horizons in the information regarding the diffusion of wheeled vehicles in this region (Butterlin & Margueron, 2006; Margueron, 2004; 2010).

The wheel marks were found during the excavation seasons of 2002-2003, in level C (phases 3-5) of chantier L, belonging to the first settlement at Mari, the so-called Ville 1, founded in 2900 BC. Both wheels were found in the same structure but in different rooms. Moreover, *roue* 1, the best preserved one, was on the floor of phase 4 while *roue* 2 was on the floor of phase 5. Although no wood traces remained, the very thin mark on the bitumen had preserved many details. The wheel was a tripartite lenticular disk-wheel with a diameter of 61 cm, the center had a domed hub of 18 cm in diameter and projecting for about 3 cm, with a central hole of c. 3 cm. The wheel was composed of three elements: a central plank 22 cm wide, 61 cm long and two crescent-shaped planks, both 19 cm wide, 54 cm long. *Roue* 1 was lying on the floor of locus 406, one of the ancillary rooms surrounding the courtyard of the building, to the west. Close to the wheel, to the north, there was a donkey skeleton stretched along the western wall of the room, while to the south there were fragments of large vessels and a number of bronze tools.

The second wheel was in a room smaller than locus 406, and located on the opposite side of the central courtyard. Though in worse condition than the other wheel, it was still possible to recognize the circular shape, which had a radius of 31 cm. It means that *roue* 2, being circa 62 cm in diameter, was of the same size of *roue* 1. As in the previous case, there were abundant ceramic objects and bronze tools on the floor of the room.

Although this find represents an isolated case in the Syrian Jazirah, thus far, the discovery of the Mari wheels remains an important piece of evidence. In fact, the wheels are the oldest evidence in the ancient Near East, dating back at least to 2850 BC (the specimens from southern Mesopotamia date back only to 2600 BC), and furthermore, they are the first evidence found in a production context instead of a funerary one. Unfortunately, no traces of vehicles have been found to go with the wheels.

CARTS, WAGONS AND THEIR FUNCTIONS

Wheeled vehicles in the Syrian Jazirah made their first appearance during the first centuries of the

3rd millennium BC, as confirmed by the imprints of wheels found at Mari. These early vehicles were probably two-wheeled, though it is not possible to be certain given the lack of documentation. Two types of carts are essentially attested: those with platform-body and those with box-body. Although there are no emphasized chronological and geographical distribution differences between the two types, the first turns out to be more common.

Few fragments of tilted wagons confirm the presence of four-wheeled vehicles during the Ninevite V period (c. 2900-2500 BC). These vehicles, which spread through northern Mesopotamia and Syria only, may have a different origin than the later wagons that clearly recall the southern Mesopotamian 'battle car'. It is possible that, given their limited distribution, covered wagons were brought by Anatolian or Trans-Caucasian populations (Moorey, 2001: 347). Indeed, a well-preserved example, although slightly later (mid-2nd millennium BC), has been found in the Lchashen necropolis (Grygorian, 2010) in Armenia and a bronze model of this type comes from southern Anatolia (Kulakoğlu, 2003).

The relationship between the two main types of wagons, however, is totally different. In fact, as observed especially in the category of models, wagons without seat and similar to the southern Mesopotamian 'battle car' spread primarily in the Balikh and middle-Euphrates region while those with shallow frames and a seat in the rear spread in the north-eastern Jazirah, especially in the Khabur region. This different geographical distribution has no chronological basis, since both types have been attested simultaneously from the mid to the end of the 3rd millennium BC. Regarding the real reasons of this different distribution one can offer a few assumptions. One such can be linked to the cultural and political relations at the beginning of 3rd millennium BC. In fact, the sites of the middle-Euphrates and Balikh Valley regions had close connections to those of southern Mesopotamia especially through the key-site of Mari. Given these connections, it is possible that the southern Mesopotamian 'battle car' spread throughout the middle Euphrates and Balik Valley regions rather than in the Khabur region, where wagons may have had a different evolution.

In the three categories aforementioned (models, glyptic and written sources) a different relation between carts and wagons has been noted. In the case of models, carts and wagons, they all have similar attestations, with a slight predominance in the first group (see the case of Tell Arbid: Raccidi, 2012: figure 7). In the case of glyptic art, however, wagons clearly predominate, while this relationship is totally reversed in the written source, where carts are the most common type of vehicles attested. These relations can suggest different functions of the wheeled vehicles. Indeed, glyptic representations that may be considered elite art almost exclusively represent wagons and tilted wagons in warfare or religious contexts. This seems to be confirmed by the Ebla texts in which covered vehicles are often assigned to high status personalities. Moreover, wagons were probably used by the Lords of Nagar during their visits to Nabada.

Functions of a more quotidian use cannot be excluded for wagons, as well as for carts (which in the Ebla texts are the most frequently mentioned). One of the main activities in which they might have been involved was agricultural production: in a text of early 2nd millennium BC, the so-called 'Farmer's Instructions' (Civil, 1994), wagons were linked to the transportation of barley from the fields to the threshing floor (*Ibidem*: 33):

91 Establish properly your paths.
92 Your wagons should be in working order.
93 Feed (well) the wagon's oxen.
94 Let your prepared threshing floor rest for a few days.

Although the majority of the fragments that make up the text come from the southern Mesopotamian city of Nippur and are dated to the first centuries of the 2nd millennium BC, they remain an important source of information about the use of the wagons in agricultural activities in the ancient Near East, including the 3rd millennium BC Jazirah.

CONCLUSION

Though it would be misleading to explain the phenomenon of the evolution and diffusion of wheeled vehicles in the 3rd millennium BC Syrian Jazirah in the absence of more precise documentation, the data just presented provide a valuable starting point for this purpose. Through their analysis it is possible to suggest several points:

The society of the Syrian Jazirah during the first centuries of 3rd millennium BC was fertile ground in which, for the first time, the idea and reality of wheeled vehicles spread. The innovation, most likely, came from southern Mesopotamia, passing through the key-site of Mari, although an Anatolian or Trans-Caucasian influence in the evolution and spread of certain types cannot be excluded.

The origins and trajectories of diffusion of wheeled vehicles remain a highly debated topic. They may be summarised into three hypotheses:

- A single origin in Mesopotamia (Sherrat, 2006);
- A single origin in the region north of the Black Sea (Matuschik, 2006);
- Two origins: one in Mesopotamia and one in the region north to the Black Sea (Vosteen, 2006).

From the firsts and relatively few examples during the Ninevite V Period, carts and wagons became a common category during the second half of the 3rd millennium BC, as proven by the increase in the documentation and dissemination. This outcome was probably supported by the environmental conditions of the Syrian Jazirah landscape that were eminently suitable for wheeled transport. The landscape of the Syrian Jazirah was almost completely flat, semi-arid and with poor vegetation, and thus suitable for wheeled vehicles – much more so than the southern Mesopotamian, that, although flat, is marked by large marshlands.

Van Liere & Lauffray (1954), Wilkinson (1993; Wilkinson *et al.*, 2010) and Ur (Ur, 2003; 2009; 2011), recognized dark linear lines in the landscape of this region, the so-called 'hollow ways', that have been interpreted as modern remains of ancient tracks or paths, produced by the continuous passage of human, animal and vehicle traffic. Moreover, Ur & Wilkinson (2008: fig. 6), in the area around Tell Beydar and in the surroundings of Tell Brak, noted a close connection between hollow ways and sites of the second half of the 3rd millennium BC. Thus, the period of maximum use of the hollow ways has been identified between the mid of 3rd and the beginning of 2nd millennium BC (Wilkinson *et al.*, 2010: fig. 13).

These features as well as the increase in the documentation related to wheeled vehicles, and consequently the spread of wagons and carts in Syrian Jazirah, seem to be the result of the favorable social, political, and economic conditions, provided by the Second Urban Revolution from the mid till the end of 3rd millennium BC.

CITED LITERATURE

Akkermans, P.M.M.G. & G. Schwartz. 2003. The Archaeology of Syria. From Complex Hunter-Gatherers to Early Urban Societies (c. 16,000-300 BC). – Cambridge, Cambridge University Press.

Archi, A. & M. Biga. 2003. A Victory over Mari and the Fall of Ebla. – Journal of Cuneiform Studies 55: 1-44.

Bielinski, P. 2012. Tell Arbid 2008-2009. Preliminary Report on the Results of the Thirteenth and Fourteenth Seasons of Polish-Syrian Excavations. – Polish Archaeology in the Mediterranean 21: 511-536.

Bollweg, J. 1999. Vorderasiatische Wagentypen im Spiegel der Terrakottaplastik bis zur Altbabylonischen Zeit. – Freiburg, Universitätsverlag.

Bretschneider, J., G. Jans & A.S. Van Vyve. 2009. War of Lords. The Battle of Chronology. – Ugarit Forschungen 41: 5-28.

Buchanan, B. 1966. Catalogue of Ancient Near Eastern Seals in the Ashmolean Museum. Volume I. Cylinder Seals. – Oxford, Clarendon Press.

Butterlin, P. & J.-Cl. Margueron. 2006. Deux roues à Mari et le problème de l'invention de la roue en Mésopotamie. In: Pétrequin, P., A.M. Pétrequin & R.M. Arbogasr. Eds. Premiers chariots, premiers araires: la diffusion de la traction animale en Europe pendant les 4. et 3. millénaires avant notre ère. – Paris, Centre National de la Recherche Scientifique: 317-328.

Charpin, D., F. Joannès, S. Lackenbacher & B. Lafont. 1988. Archives Épistolaires de Mari I/2, Archives Royales de Mari XXVI. – Paris, Editions Recherche sur les Civilisations.

Civil, M. 1994. The Farmer's Instructions. A Sumerian Agricultural Manual. – Barcelona, Editorial Ausa.

Collon, D. 1987. First Impressions. Cylinder Seals in the Ancient Near East. – London, British Museum Publications.

Conti, G. 1997. Carri ed equipaggi nei testi di Ebla. In: Fronzaroli P. Ed. Quaderni di Semitistica 19. – Firenze, Università di Firenze: 23-71.

De Mecquenem, R. 1943. Fouilles de Suse. – Mélanges de la délégation de Perse 29: 3-161.

Frangipane, M.A. 1997. 4th Millenium Temple Palace Complex at Arslantepe-Malatya. North-South Relations and the Formation of Early State Societies in the Northern Regions of Greater Mesopotamia. – Paleorient 23, 1: 45-73.

Frankfort, H. 1943. More Sculpture from the Diyala Region. – Chicago, Oriental Institute Publications.

Green, M.W. & H.J. Nissen. 1987. Zeichenliste der archaischen Texte aus Uruk. Archaische Texte aus Uruk 2. – Berlin, Mann.

Grygorian, A. 2010. Findings from the Bronze Age Burial Mounds in Armenia IV-I Millennia B.C. from the Collections of the Hystory Museum of Armenia. – Yerevan, History Museum of Armenia.

Herzfeld, E. 1934. Aufsätze zur altorientalischen Archäologie. – Archäologische Mitteilungen aus Iran 6: 111-223.

Jans, G. & J. Bretschneider. 1998. Wagon Representations in the Early Dynastic Glyptik. They Came to Tell Beydar with Wagon and Equid. – Subartu 4, 2: 155-195.

Kulakoğlu, F. 2003. Recently Discovered Bronze Wagon Models from Şanliurfa, Southeastern Anatolia. – Anatolia 24: 63-77.

Langdon, S. 1924. Excavations at Kish. The Herbert Weld and Field Museum of Natural History Expedition to Mesopotamia. – Paris, Geuthner.

Lebeau, M. 1993. Tell Melebiya. Cinq campagnes de recherches sur le Moyen-Khabour (1984-1988). – Leuven, Peeters.

Lebeau, M. 2011. Associated Regional Chronologies for the Ancient Near East and the Eastern Mediterranean. Volume I. Jezirah. – Turnhout, Brepols.

Lebeau, M. & A. Suleiman. 1997. Tell Beydar. Three Seasons of Excavations (1992-1994). A Preliminary Report. – Turnhout, Brepols.

Liebowitz, H. 1988. Terracotta Figurines and Model Vehicles. – Malibu, Undena Publications.

Littauer, M.A. & J.H. Crouwel. 1973. The Vulture Stele and an Early Type of Two-Wheeled Vehicle. – Journal of Near Eastern Studies 32: 324-329.

Littauer, M.A. & J.H. Crouwel. 1979. Wheeled Vehicles and Ridden Animals in the Ancient Near East. – Leiden, Brill.

Margueron, J.-Cl. 2004. Mari métropole de l'Euphrate au IIIe et IIe millénaires av. J.-C. – Paris, Picard.

Margueron, J.-Cl. 2010. L'adoption de la roué et les débuts de la civilisation urbaine. In: Becker, J., R. Hempelmann & E. Rehm. Eds. Kulturlandschaft Syrien. Zentrum und Peripherie. – Münster, Ugarit-Verlag: 331-347.

Matthews, D. 1991. Tell Brak 1990. The Glyptic. – Iraq 53: 147-157.

Matthews, R.J. Ed. 2003. Excavations at Tell Brak. Volume 4. Exploring an Upper Mesopotamian Regional Centre, 1994-1996. – London, British School of Archaeology in Iraq.

Matthews, R.J., W. Matthews & H. McDonald. 1994. Excavations at Tell Brak. – Iraq 56: 177-194.

Matuschik, I. 2006. Invention et diffusion de la roué dans l'Ancient Monde: L'apport de l'iconographie". In: Pétrequin, P., A.M. Pétrequin & R.M. Arbogasr. Eds. Premiers chariots, premiers araires: la diffusion de la traction animale en Europe pendant les 4. et 3. millénaires avant notre ère. – Paris, Centre National de la Recherche Scientifique: 279-298.

Miglus, P.A. & E. Strommenger. 2002. Tall Bi'a/Tuttul. VIII. Stadtbefestigungen, Häuser und Tempel. – Saarbrücken, Saarbrücker Druckerei und Verlag.

Moorey, P.R.S. 2001. Clay Models and Overland Mobility in Syria, c. 2350-1800. In: Meyer, J-W., M. Novák & A. Pruß. Eds. Beiträge zur Vorderasiatische Archäologie. – Frankfurt, Johann Wolfgang Goethe-Universitat, Archäologisches Institut: 344-351.

Moortgat, A. & U. Moortgat-Correns. 1976. Tell Chuera in Nordost-Syrien. Vorläufiger Bericht über die siebte Grabungskampagne, 1974. – Berlin, Gebr. Mann.

Nadali, D. 2009. Representations of Battering Rams and Siege Towers in Early Bronze Age Glyptic Art. – Historiae 6: 39-52.

Nagel, W. 1964. Djamdat Nasr-Kulturen und Fruhdynastische Buntkeramiker. – Berlin, Verlag Bruno Hessling.

Neufang, B. & A. Pruß. 1994. Wagenmodelle. In: Meyer, J.W. & A. Pruß. Eds. Die Kleinfunde von Tell Halawa A. – Saarbrücken, Saarbrücker Druckerei und Verlag: 156-180.

Oates, J. 2001. Equid Figurines and Chariot Models. In: Oates, D., J. Oates & H. McDonald. Eds. Nagar in the Third Millennium B.C. Excavations at Tell Brak 2. – London, British School of Archaeology in Iraq: 279-293.

Orthmann, W. 1995. Ausgrabungen in Tell Chuera in Nordost-Syrien I. Vorbericht über die Grabungskampagnen 1986 bis 1992. – Saarbrucker, Saarbrucker Druckerei und Verlag.

Parrot, A. 1956. Le Temple d'Ishtar. – Paris, Gauthner.

Parrot, A. 1967. Le Temple d'Ishtar et de Ninni-Zaza. – Paris, Gauthner.

Parrot, A. 1969. Le fouilles de Mari, dix-septième campagne (autumne 1968). – Syria XLVI: 191-208.

Parrot, A. 1969. Le fouilles de Mari, dix-huitième campagne (autumne 1969). – Syria XLVII: 226-247.

Pecorella, P.E. 1995. Tell Barri - Kahat. Relazione preliminare della campagna del 1995. – Firenze, Firenze University Press.

Pecorella, P.E. & R. Pierobon Benoit. 2005. Tell Barri - Kahat. La campagna del 2002. Relazione preliminare. – Firenze, Firenze University Press.

Pecorella, P.E. & R. Pierobon Benoit. 2008. Tell Barri - Kahat. La campagna del 2003. Relazione preliminare. – Firenze, Firenze University Press.

Pruß, A. 2011. Figurines and Model Vehicles. In: Lebeau, M. Ed. Associated Regional Chronologies for the Ancient Near East and the Eastern Mediterranean. Volume I. Jezirah. – Turnhout, Brepols: 239-254.

Raccidi, M. 2012. Chariot Terracotta Models from Tell Arbid. – Polish Archaeology in the Mediterranean 21: 605-623.

Sallaberger, W. 1996. Grain Accounts. Personnel Lists and Expenditure Documents. – Subartu 2: 89-106.

Sherrat, A. 2006. La traction animale et la transformation de l'Europe néolithique. In: Pétrequin, P., A.M. Pétrequin & R.M. Arbogasr. Eds. Premiers chariots, premiers araires: la diffusion de la traction animale en Europe pendant les 4. et 3. millénaires avant notre ère. – Paris, Centre National de la Recherche Scientifique: 329-360.

Speiser, E.A. 1935. Excavations at Tepe Gawra I. – Philadelphia, University of Pennsylvania Press.

Strommenger, E. & K. Kohlmeyer. 1998. Die Altorientalischen Bestattungen, Ausgrabungen in Tall Bi'a/Tuttul. I. – Saarbrücken, Saarbrücker Druckerei und Verlag.

Ur, J. 2003. CORONA Satellite Photography and Ancient Road Networks. A Northern Mesopotamian Case Study. – Antiquity 77: 102-115.

Ur, J. 2009. Emergent Landscapes of Movement in Early Bronze Age Northern Mesopotamia. In: Snead, J.E., C. Erickson & W.A. Darling. Eds. Landscapes of Movement. Paths, Trails, and Roads in Anthropological Perspective. – Philadelphia, University of Pennsylvania Museum Press: 180-203.

Ur, J. 2011. Urbanism and Cultural Landscapes in Northeastern Syria. The Tell Hamoukar Survey, 1999-2001. – Chicago, Oriental Institute Publications.

Ur, J. & T.J. Wilkinson. 2008. Settlement and Economic Landscapes of Tell Beydar and its Hinterland. – Subartu 21: 305-327.

Van Liere, W. & J. Lauffray. 1954. Nouvelle prospection archéologique dans la Haute Jezireh syrienne. – Les annales archéologiques de Syrie 4, 5: 129-148.

Van Loon, M. 2001. Selenkahiye. Final Report on the University of Chicago and University of Amsterdam Excavations in the Tabqa Reservoir, Northern Syria, 1967-1975. – Istanbul, Nederlands Historisch-Archaeologisch Instituut te Istanbul.

Vosteen, M.U. 2006. Une double invention. Véhicules à roués at traction animale. In: Pétrequin, P., A.M. Pétrequin & R.M. Arbogasr. Eds. Premiers chariots, premiers araires. La diffusion de la traction animale en Europe pendant les 4. et 3. millénaires avant notre ère. – Paris, Centre National de la Recherche Scientifique: 239-246.

Widell, M. 2003. Some Observations on the Administration, Agriculture and Animal Management of Tell Beydar. – Ugarit-Forschungen 35: 717-733.

Wilkinson, T.J. 1993. Linear Hollows in the Jazira, Upper Mesopotamia. – Antiquity 67: 548-562.

Wilkinson, T.J., C. French, J. Ur & M. Semple. 2010. The Geoarchaeology of Route Systems in Northern Syria. – Geoarcheology 25: 745-771.

Woolley, C.L. 1934. The Royal Cemetery. Ur Excavations II. – London, The Trustees of the Two Museums.

DEPICTIONAL STUDY OF CHARIOT USE IN NEW KINGDOM EGYPT

Lisa Sabbahy

INTRODUCTION

The chariot appears in Egypt by the end of the Second Intermediate Period (1650-1549 BC), when the Theban kings of the 17th Dynasty have begun to battle the Hyksos ruling in Lower Egypt (Schulman, 1980; Shaw, 2001). Once the chariot is introduced, it is used extensively throughout the period of the New Kingdom, particularly by the king. Its use is initially limited to military purposes, but eventually high officials also use chariots in both official capacities and hunting. By the time of the later 18th Dynasty (1549-1298 BC), during the Amarna Period, royalty, both male and female, use chariots in processions to and from palaces and temples. Female use of chariots, both as driver and occupant, is extremely restricted, however, and, for the most part, limited to the Amarna Period. By the later New Kingdom, the Ramesside Period (1298-1069 BC), chariots are limited to royal scenes of warfare and hunting.

DEPICTIONS OF HUNTING AND WARFARE

The earliest chariot evidence is textual, such as in the autobiographical inscription of Ahmose son of Ebana, who mentions "following the chariot of His Majesty", in the reign of Ahmose (1549-1524 BC; Sethe, 1961: 3,6). Representational evidence is more limited, however. There are fragments of battle scenes from Ahmose's temple at Abydos, but it is not clear from the fragments of bridled horses and chariots whether or not the chariots belong to the Hyksos or the Egyptians (Harvey, 1998: figs. 76-79). There are also similar fragments of scenes, for example, horse hooves and a chariot wheel, from the funerary temple of Thutmose II (1491-1479 BC), either built or finished by Thutmose III (1479-1424 BC) on the West Bank of Thebes (Bruyère, 1926: pls. II-IV). But again, it is not clear that these are Egyptian chariots, rather than those of the foreigners that they are fighting.

A fragment of a hunting scene is preserved in the Theban tomb of User (TT21), reign of Thutmose I (1503-1491 BC; Davies, 1913: pl. XXII). The fleeing animals, shot with arrows, are preserved, but only part of the wheel of the chariot pursuing them is. The first complete hunting scene is that in the tomb of Userhet (TT56), reign of Amenhotep II (1424-1398 BC; Beinlich-Seeber & Shedid, 1987: pl. 12). Userhet stands in the chariot, reins tied around his back, shooting arrows at the fleeing desert animals.

Userhet's stance in his chariot is modeled on that of king Amenhotep II. On a red granite block from Karnak, now in the Luxor Museum (J. 129), the king is galloping in his chariot, while shooting arrows at a copper ingot, with the reins tied around his waist (Romano, 1979: fig. 53). A close parallel to Amenhotep II's target shooting scene is the later scene showing king Ay (1333-1328 BC) shooting at a similarly shaped target (Davis, 1912:127). This scene is on a small piece of gold foil, found in the Valley of the Kings and now in the Egyptian Museum, Cairo (JE

57438), and may have originally decorated the end of a quiver. In the scene, the target is on the top of a pole, which has two foreigners tied to it, and two more are kneeling in front with their hands up in adoration of the king. Ay is in the chariot alone, pulling back his bow, with the reins tied around his waist.

After Amenhotep II, the next known hunting scenes are those of king Tutankhamun (1335-1325 BC). For the most part his hunting scenes are on objects from his tomb, but there are also two blocks found in the 9th Pylon at Karnak preserving parts of a bull-hunting scene attributed to Tutankhamun (Lauffray, 1979: pl. 120; Sa'ad, 1975: pl. 34), and other blocks possibly show a desert hunt (Eaton-Krauss, 1983; Johnson, 1992: 17). Both the obverse and reverse of Tutankhamun's bow-case depict the king in his chariot, reins tied behind his back, shooting at fleeing desert game (McLeod, 1982: pls. 9 and 14). One side of Tutankhamun's fan (Carter Number 242) represents him shooting ostriches in the same manner (Houlihan, 1986: fig. 1), and on the other side he drives his chariot behind the bearers taking back the kill (Edwards, 1978: 110-113). The lid of his painted box (Carter Number 21) has two parallel scenes of hunting game in the desert. The king is again alone in his chariot, shooting with the reins tied behind his back (Edwards, 1978: 76-77).

After Tutankhamun's hunting scenes, the next known royal scenes of hunting from a chariot are those of king Ramesses III (1185-1153 BC) at Medinet Habu. He is shown shooting desert game, with the reins tied around his waist (Epigraphic Survey, 1932: pl.116). The king spears the lions and bulls, again with the reins tied around his waist. In the lion-hunting scene the torso and arms of the king are twisted around to spear behind him, while his bottom half and the reins stay in place, facing front (Epigraphic Survey, 1930: pl. 35). In the bull-hunting depiction, as the king spears the bulls, he steps over the front rail of the chariot with his left leg, putting his foot down on the chariot pole (Epigraphic Survey, 1932: pl. 117), still with the reins around his waist.

It has been suggested that tying the reins around the waist is merely artistic license so that the king can be shown alone in the chariot; no one could actually drive a chariot in this position. But as seen in Userhet's tomb, he is also shown this way. Did royal artistic license extend to the elite as well? Looking at other chariot scenes with archers gives further evidence.

In the Battle of Qadesh, two men are shown in each Egyptian chariot; there is a shield-bearer and an archer (figure 1). The shield-bearer holds the shield with one hand, and holds onto the chariot with the other. Occasionally his free hand reaches out and holds the reins that are tied around the archer's waist while he is shooting. Another scene from the Qadesh battle shows the royal princes arriving in chariots. Each prince drives the horses while also holding his bow in one hand. A shield-

Figure 1. Shield-bearer and archer. Abu Simbel Great Temple. After: Oriental Institute P2345, Photographic Archives, Nubia. Drawing by L.D. Hackley.

Figure 2. Prince following Ramesses II into battle. Abu Simbel Great Temple. After: Oriental Institute P2419. Photograpic Archives Nubia. Drawing by L.D. Hackley.

bearer is also with each prince in the chariot, and helps with the reins (figure 2).

In the poem about the battle, Ramesses II refers several times to his charioteer and shield-bearer (Lichtheim, 1976: 68-70). In the action described in the poem, it is clear that wielding the shield to protect the king is this man's main responsibility, but obviously, he could help drive as well. In all of these examples, the archer drives the chariot, but when busy shooting, ties the reins around his waist. This would not only keep the horses steady, but would help the archer balance, and prevent him from falling out of the back of the chariot (Crouwel agrees with this, Personal Communication, 2012). It seems possible, therefore, that an archer hunting in a chariot, could do so alone with the reins tied around his waist.

CHARIOTS WITH BOUND CAPTIVES

The upper part of a granite block in the Egyptian Museum, Cairo (JE 36360) depicts Amenhotep II victorious, presenting tied up captives to the god Amun (Zayed, 1985: pls. 1-2). It was found in the 4th Pylon of Karnak in 1904, and may have come from the same monument as the granite block in the Luxor Museum that depicts Amenhotep II target shooting, discussed above. In the lower part of the scene, the king ties up captives, and then, mounted on a chariot, leads them away. The king also has three captives on the back of his chariot horses, two tied to the front of the chariot and one tied on his back on the chariot pole (figure 3).

A very similar scene is found on a limestone stela from the mortuary temple of his grandson, king Amenhotep III, which was later reused in the mortuary temple of king Merenptah (1212-1201 BC; Petrie, 1896: pl. X). The upper and lower parts of the stela are each divided in half by the scenes. In the top half, figures of Amun stand back-to-back in the center of the stela, while the king on one side offers a figure of Ma'at to him, and on the other side, jars of wine. Below, there are two back-to-back figures of the king in a chariot. On the viewer's right, the king drives over foreigners from the south, although the lower part of this scene with the horses' legs is missing. On the left he drives over foreigners from the north, although the body of the chariot, and those of the horses are broken away. It is clear on the right side, however, that four captives are tied and seated on the chariot horses, while another is tied kneeling on the chariot pole. A sixth face can be seen protruding from the bottom front of the chariot (Saleh & Sourouzian, 1987: Obj. No. 143).

Figures tied to royal chariots are not seen often after this. Johnson (1992: 29) suggests that the depiction of prisoners on the chariot horses was somewhat awkward, and so the scene was 'discontinued'. There are some Ramesside examples, but they only have

Figure 3. Amenhotep II with captives. After: Abdel Hamid Zayed, in: Posener-Krieger (1985: pl. 1). Drawing by L.D. Hackley.

figures tied under the chariot, not on any other parts. A good example of this is the triumphal return of Ramesses III from his Libyan campaign. Three Libyans are tied under the base of his chariot, heads facing to the back (Epigraphic Survey, 1930: pl. 77). Many more bound captives walk in front of, and beside the king's chariot, but only these three are actually attached to the chariot.

DEITIES AND CHARIOTS

The present author had expected to find a fair number of chariots depicted in association with deities, but actually these scenes are quite rare. The most famous is undoubtedly the scene on the right exterior side of the chariot of Thutmose IV (1398-1388 BC), found in his tomb in the Valley of the Kings (Carter & Newberry, 1904: pl. 10; see also Calvert, this volume). The king is shown driving his chariot, reins around the waist, and shooting arrows into a mass of dead and fleeing enemy chariots. Beside the king in his chariot, and helping him shoot, is the god Montu, hawk-headed and wearing a disk and feathers on his head. The god is placed just behind the figure of the king, but set a bit farther back, so that the figures overlap. The king is in front and also taller, so it is clear he is the main figure. The inscription in front of the king states that he is 'beloved of Montu' (figure 4).

There is an interesting detail on the body of the chariot. The head and neck of a small duck or goose (see Calvert, this volume) is shown at the very bottom of the side of the chariot, just above the spoke of the wheel that is parallel with the base of the chariot. There is at least one other example of some type of small figure in that position. Part of a limestone block from the Great Temple at Amarna in the Ashmolean Museum, Oxford (1927.4087) depicts a chariot wheel with a small kneeling, captive figure in the same position at the bottom of the body of the chariot, just visible above and in front of the axel

Figure 4. Thutmose IV and Montu. After: Carter, in: Carter & Newberry (2002: pl. 10). Drawing by L.D. Hackley.

(Whitehouse, 2009: 75.). There might be another example of this type of kneeling figure on a talatat block from Karnak (Ertman, 1998: 59-60). Tutankhamun's chariot A1 seems to have had a bronze snake attached to the lower right corner of the chariot, and it might have been a similar type of object such as the duck or bound figure, with an amuletic or protective purpose (Littauer & Crouwel, 1985: pl. XII). Crouwel agreed with this interpretation at the conference, although this is still debated (Salima Ikram, Personal Communication, 2013; see also Calvert, this volume). These small figures are perhaps related to small heads of foreigners, which can be found as decoration on the top of the chariot's linchpins, and again serve as symbolism of the king's destruction of the enemies of Egypt (Ritner, 1993: 130-131). This type of decorated linchpin appears first in the Amarna Period, on a talatat from the Great Aten Temple at Amarna (Aldred, 1973: 151). They are common on chariots in the royal military scenes of the 19th (1298-1187 BC) and 20th Dynasties (1187-1069 BC; Epigraphic Survey, 1986: pls. 5, 10, 22, 35; Epigraphic Survey, 1930: pls. 21, 30, 31). The small head can also be shown being bitten by a lion whose head is on top of it (Epigraphic Survey, 1930: pl. 17).

Another deity depicted in a chariot is the god Shed, the 'protector' or 'savior', who is known beginning in the 18th Dynasty (Brunner, 1983: 547-9).

A small limestone fragment from the Amarna Period preserves the figure of a nude young man with a side lock, in a chariot with reins around his waist, pulling back a bow (Brooklyn Museum Acc. No. 36.965). Brunner (1984: 49-50) has identified the figure as Shed, rather than as a young prince, such as Tutankhamun. Indeed, there are other depictions of Shed from Amarna on stelae from the tomb chapels east of the Workman's Village (Peet & Woolley, 1923: 97, pl. XXVIII).

The only other association of a deity with a chariot is the standard of Amun set up in a chariot leading Ramesses III's campaign against the Libyans (figure 5). The chariot is driven by one of the royal princes, and the king follows along behind, driving his own chariot. The two chariots are exactly the same size, and the king and the god's standard are exactly the same height. The inscription accompanying the standard's chariot reads in part: "Words spoken by Amon-Re, king of the god's: Behold, I am before you, my son…I open for you the ways of the Tjemehu" (Epigraphic Survey, 1930: pl. 17).

AMARNA PERIOD CHARIOT SCENES

In the Amarna Period a number of new and unusual chariot scenes appear. In the talatat blocks

Figure 5. Standard of Amun in a chariot. After: Epigraphic Survey (1930: pl. 17). Drawing by L.D. Hackley.

Figure 6. Akhenaten with stepping-stool. After: D.B. Redford, in: Redford (1976: pl. 12). Drawing by L.D. Hackley.

from Karnak, a partially restored scene depicts king Akhenaten (1352-1335 BC) stepping into his chariot with the help of a stool (figure 6). This is the first known scene of a king mounting his chariot, and one that will be repeated numerous times in Ramesside temple relief scenes of the king setting off on campaign (Epigraphic Survey, 1930: pl. 16), and returning in victory to Egypt (Epigraphic Survey, 1986: pl. 35).

Another development in the Amarna Period is the appearance of female members of the royal family in a chariot with the king, or else in their own chariot accompanying him. Although this type of scene appears in the Karnak talatat, it is much more common in Amarna tomb scenes depicting royal processions in the city. In a reconstructed scene based on Karnak talatat blocks TS 1465 and TS 1441, the king, in a large chariot, is followed by the queen, driving alone in a chariot, about 40% of the size of the king's (Hoffmeier, 1988: pl.18). If the restoration is correct, this is the "first example in art of a queen driving a chariot" (Hoffmeier, 1988: 36). In another scene, the king and queen are together in a chariot. The king is driving, followed by three small registers of attendants in chariots. An interesting detail is that the queen's right hand holds onto a handle on the side bar of the chariot (Redford, 1988: pl. 37). Chariot handles for passengers only seem to be depicted in the Amarna Period (Hoffmeier, 1988: 39), the same period in which females are often seen in chariots, so perhaps handles and female use of chariots are related (see also Manassa, this volume). There is at least one instance in the Amarna Period, however, of a male holding onto a handle; see the discussion of the stela of Any below.

In the rock cut tomb of Ahmes (T3) at Amarna, there is a badly preserved scene depicting Akhenaten, Nerfertiti and one of their daughters, together in a chariot driven by the king (Davies, 1905c: pl. 35a). There is no evidence of royal daughters associated with chariots in the Karnak talatat, so this is the earliest example of a royal daughter in a chariot. The king faces forward, and the queen, slightly in front of him and on his far side, turns to face him. The Aten is directly above them, and one ray holds an ankh-sign between their faces. The princess stands in the very front of the chariot with just her head over the bar, while her left arm rests on the quiver.

The tomb of the Aten priest, Meryre (T4), has a procession scene with the king driving a large chariot, and the queen behind driving a much smaller one. Behind that, two much smaller registers show their daughters and attendants in chariots (Davies, 1905a: pl.10). The first group in each of the two small registers is a chariot with two princesses. One drives, holding the reins and whip, while the other stands beside her, right hand grasping a handle on the bar of the chariot, and left arm around her sister. Behind each chariot with the princesses are three chariots with attendants. Each chariot is driven by a charioteer, who is depicted on the far side of the chariot, hunched over as he protrudes from a kind of cabin, separating him from the two attendants. Each attendant holds a tall feather fan in her right hand, and holds onto a handle on the chariot with her left hand.

Figure 7. Princesses and attendants. After: Davies (1905b: pl. 15). Drawing by L.D. Hackley.

The partition separating the driver from the other occupants of the chariot is not depicted in other scenes of attendants. A somewhat similar processional scene is in the tomb of Panehsy (T6). This time one small chariot with princesses, and attendants following, is behind the queen, and another is in the register just below her chariot (figure 7). As in the tomb scene just discussed above, one princess drives and another stands beside and behind her. The attendants are two to a chariot, and the charioteer is hunched over driving, but clearly not separated by a partition. A talatat block found at Hermopolis has a similar grouping of attendants (Cooney, 1965: 57), with the driver leaning forward on the far side, but clearly there is no partition separating him from the attendants.

In the Ramesside Period young princes are also depicted in chariots with attendants. In the scenes of Ramesses II at the temple of Beit el-Wali, dating to the 13th year of the reign of his father Seti I (1296-1279 BC), and carved while Ramesses was still prince, his first born son, Amenherwonemef, and his fourth son, Khaemwaset, are shown in two small registers behind their father's large chariot, as he drives into and shoots fleeing Nubians (Ricke *et al.*, 1967: pl. 8). The princes both stand holding on to the side and front of the chariot, while a charioteer drives. The older of the princes must have been five years, and his younger brother four years old at the time (Kitchen, 1982: 40).

ELITE CHARIOT USE FOR OFFICIAL PURPOSES

High officials of the New Kingdom are depicted making use of chariots for important occasions in their professional life. One such occasion is that of the king rewarding them with a gold collar. Scenes depicting this in private tombs are known from the reign of Thutmose IV in the 18th Dynasty to the reign of Ramesses IX (1123-1104 BC) in the 20th Dynasty (Binder, 2008). Twelve tombs, from the Amarna Period to the 19th Dynasty, include the official's use of a chariot as part of the occasion.

During the Amarna Period, rather than a single scene of the gold collar being given by the king to the official, the occasion becomes a sequence of scenes. The rock cut tomb of Meryre II (T2) at Amarna contains a good example of the scene sequence in the rewarding of the gold collar (Davies, 1905b: pl. 33). Meryre is standing under the Window of Appearance while king Akhenaten leans over and hands him down a gold collar. Other gold collars are already around his neck. In the register just below this, Meryre, greeted by cheers, returns to his waiting chariot. Then in the lowest register, Meryre is driven home in his chariot amid a jubilant crowd. Meryre stands in the chariot holding the side and front of the bar of the chariot, while a charioteer drives.

A much simpler version of the scene is depicted on the stela of Any, found at Amarna (Freed, 1999: 173). Any is shown being driven by a charioteer. He stands, wearing four gold collars, holding a handle on the left side of the chariot, and resting his right hand on the bar of the chariot. In the inscription above him, it states: "I come in peace as the favored one of the king".

The Collar of Gold scene in the Theban tomb of Neferhotep (TT49), dating to the reign of king Ay near the end of the 18th Dynasty, is perhaps the most interesting of all these scenes.

Figure 8. Neferhotep and his family after being honored (TT 49). After: Davies (1933: pl. 2). Drawing by L.D. Hackley.

It gives us an example of the fact that, although royal females used chariots, when a chariot was the conveyance of choice, its use does not seem to have extended to non-royal females. Neferhotep is seen below the Window of Appearance, having been given the collar of gold (Davies, 1933: pl.1). Then he is seen driving away in his chariot, in the same pose as Meryre II, with a charioteer doing the driving. In the scene in the registers above this, the queen gives Neferhotep's wife a gold collar from her own Window of Appearance. The wife turns to go, and is escorted away by an attendant who takes her arm. She does not share her husband's chariot, nor does she have her own (figure 8). In fact, the present author has not been able to find any depiction of a non-royal female in a chariot.

Officials also used chariots in their work. The earliest complete, surviving New Kingdom scenes featuring chariots are actually non-royal and non-military. The tomb of Renni (T7) at El Kab, dating to the reign of Amenhotep I (1524-1503 BC), shows Renni's chariot parked in the field, as part of a harvest scene (Tylor, 1900: pl. II). Beginning in the reign of Amenhotep I, in the early 18th Dynasty, there are scenes of a chariot standing empty in the fields, often with a servant, probably the chariot driver, either holding the reins, or sitting in the chariot, waiting. This type of chariot scene appears in tombs of officials connected to grain, such as that of Nebamun, probably from the reign of Thutmose IV, who was the scribe of the grain accounts of Amun. There is a beautiful fragment from his tomb in the British Museum, London depicting two chariots waiting by a sycamore tree (Parkinson, 2008: 110). Nearby, although not completely preserved, officials are measuring the fields of grain.

In other work scenes the official is actually in his chariot. For example, in the Theban tomb of Amenmose (TT89), who had a long career spanning from the reign of Thutmose III to that of Amenhotep III, he is depicted with his soldiers, leaving the shore of the Red Sea where the Puntites have brought him exotic goods (Davies *et al.*, 1941: pl. 25) His figure is broken away, but the horses and chariot are preserved. The Chief of Police at Amarna, Mahu, is depicted in his tomb taking part in the capture of three criminals, and having them taken to the vizier (Davies, 1905d: pl. 26). He drives up on his chariot, reaching out with his left hand to pull on the reins along with his charioteer (figure 9).

Figure 9. Mahu chasing criminals. After: Davies (1905b: pl. 26). Drawing by L.D. Hackley.

RAMESSIDE VARIATIONS IN ROYAL WAR AND HUNTING SCENES

In the extensive military scenes on mortuary temple walls in the Ramesside Period, a number of new details appear in chariot scenes. One is the motif of the smiting king, stepping over the front bar of the chariot and onto the chariot pole. The earliest evidence known for this is in the scenes from the reign of Seti I of the 19th Dynasty. In his battle against the Libyans depicted at Karnak Temple, Seti has caught a Libyan by the neck with his bow, and is stepping and swinging with his *khepesh* sword (Epigraphic Survey, 1986: pl. 28).

There is a similar scene in the temple of Beit el-Wali, carved in year 13 of Seti I, while Ramesses was still crown prince. Ramesses II steps onto the chariot pole while grasping his bow and the hair of two Bedouins in one hand, swinging his *khepesh* with the other (Ricke *et al.*, 1967: pl. 13). The latest known example of this scene is on an ostracon from the reign of Ramesses IV (1153-1146 BC) of the 20th Dynasty (Heinz, 2001: 323). The king is stepping onto the chariot bar while grasping foreigners with his left hand. His right arm is down by his side, and it is not clear if he is holding anything in it.

Another type of scene that first appears in the Ramesside Period is that of the king watching the "counting of the hands" after a battle. One way in which the king can be depicted in such a scene is sitting backward in his chariot (figure 10). The first completely preserved example of this is Ramesses II after the Battle of Qadesh (Desroches Noblecourt

Figure 10. Ramesses III seated backwards in a chariot, counting trophies. After: Epigrapic Survey (1930: pl. 76). Drawing by L.D. Hackley.

et al. 1971: pl. III, d). The king sits backward in his chariot, while piles of hands are counted in front of him (see also Calvert, this volume). There is also a fragmentary scene like this from Abydos, but only the chariot wheel with the king's feet can still be seen in front of the piles of hands (Naville, 1930: pl. 21). The latest depiction of this scene appears to be that of Ramesses III after his first Libyan battle (Epigraphic Survey, 1930: pl. 23). On the south wall of the second court, Ramesses III sits backward in his chariot in front of four registers: three with prisoners and piles of hands, and one with prisoners and a pile of phalli (figure 10).

CONCLUSION

The use of the chariot in ancient Egypt, other than by chariot divisions in the army, was limited to royalty and nobility. Chariots were expensive. They were made by specialists from partially imported materials (Littauer & Crouwel, 1985: 92-95; see also Herslund, this volume), and were pulled by horses that had been specifically trained to do so. For these reasons, chariots were a status item owned by a limited few. Kings of the New Kingdom used chariots and were depicted doing so. With few exceptions, only in the Amarna Period were royal females shown in and also driving chariots. In the 18th Dynasty nobility were shown in chariots, but their female relatives never were. Afterwards, in the Ramesside Period, elite tombs were decorated only with religious scenes, so we do not have much pictorial evidence for non-royal chariot use at that time. In conclusion, chariot use in the ancient Egyptian New Kingdom extended to royalty and nobility, but only among royalty, and their attendants in the Amarna Period, did females use the chariot.

CITED LITERATURE

Aldred, C. 1973. Akhenaten and Nefertiti. – New York, The Brooklyn Museum.

Beinlich-Seeber, C. & A.H. Shedid. 1987. Das grab des Userhat (TT 56). – Mainz, Philipp von Zabern.

Binder, S. 2008. The Gold of Honour in New Kingdom Egypt. – Oxford, Aris and Phillips Ltd.

Brunner, H. 1983. Sched. In: Helck, W. & E. Otto. Lexikon der Ägyptologie. Band V: 547-549. – Wiesbaden, Harrassowitz.

Brunner, H. 1984. Kein Amarna-Prinz, sondern ein Gott. – Göttinger Miszellen 78: 49-50.

Bruyère, B. 1926. Fouilles de Deir el Médineh. – Cairo, Fouilles de l'Institut Français du Caire.

Carter, H. & P.E. Newberry. 2002 [1904]. The Tomb of Thoutmosis IV. – London, Duckworth Press.

Cooney, J.D. 1965. Amarna Reliefs from Hermopolis in American Collections. – Brooklyn, The Brooklyn Museum.

Davies, N. de G. 1905a. The Rock Tombs of El Amarna. Volume I. The Tomb of Meryra. – London, Egypt Exploration Fund.

Davies N. de G. 1905b. The Rock Tombs of El Amarna. Volume II. The Tombs of Panehesy and Meryre II. – London, Egypt Exploration Fund.

Davies, N. de G. 1905c. The Rock Tombs of El Amarna, Volume III. The Tombs of Huya and Ahmes. – London, Egypt Exploration Fund.

Davies, N. de G. 1905d. The Rock Tombs of El Amarna. Volume IV. The Tombs of Penthu, Mahu and Others. – London, Egypt Exploration Fund.

Davies, N. de G. 1913. Five Theban Tombs (Being Those of Mentuherkhepeshef, User, Daga, Nehemawäy and Tati). – London, Egypt Exploration Fund.

Davies, N. de G. 1933. The Tomb of Nefer-hotep at Thebes. Volume II. Plates in Folio. – New York, Publications of the Metropolitan Museum of Art.

Davies, N.M. & N. de G. Davies. 1941. The Tomb of Amenmose (No. 89) at Thebes. – Journal of Egyptian Archaeology 26: 131-136.

Davis, T. 1912. The Tombs of Harmhabi and Touatankhanou. – London, Constable and Co.

Desroches Noblecourt, Ch., S. Donadoni & E. Edel. 1971. Grand temple d'Abou Simbel: la bataille de Qadech. – Cairo, Centre d'etudes et de documentation sur l'ancienne Égypte.

Eaton-Krauss, M. 1983. Tutanchamun als Jäger. – Göttinger Miszellen 61: 49-50.

Edwards, I.E.S. 1978. Tutankhamun. His Tomb and Its Treasures. – New York, Metropolitan Museum of Art.

Epigraphic Survey. 1930. Medinet Habu. Volume I. Earlier Historical Records of Ramses III. – Chicago, Oriental Institute of the University of Chicago Press.

Epigraphic Survey. 1932. Medinet Habu. Volume II. Later Historical Records of Ramses III. – Chicago, Oriental Institute of the University of Chicago Press.

Epigraphic Survey. 1986. Reliefs and Inscriptions at Karnak. Volume IV. The Battle Reliefs of King Seti I. – Chicago, Oriental Institute of the University of Chicago Press.

Ertman, E. 1998. Akhenaten's Use of Bound Foreign Prisoners in Chariot Scenes: A Commemoration of Specific Events or the King Victorious? – Annales du Service des Antiquités de l'Égypte 73: 51-60.

Freed, R. 1999. Pharaohs of the Sun. – Boston, Museum of Fine Arts.

Harvey, S. 1998. The Cults of King Ahmose at Abydos. – Pennsylvania, University of Pennsylvania (Unpublished Ph.D dissertation).

Heinz, S. 2001. Die Feldzugsdarstellengun des Neuen Reichs. Eine Bildanalyse. – Vienna, Österreichischen Akademie der Wissenschaften.

Hoffmeier, J. 1988. The Chariot Scenes. In: Redford, D.B. Ed. Akhenaten Temple Project. Volume II. *rwd-mnw*, Foreigners and Inscriptions. – Toronto, University of Toronto Press.

Houlihan, P. F. 1986. The Birds of Ancient Egypt. – Warminster, Aris and Phillips.

Johnson, W.R. 1992. An Asiatic Battle Scene of Tutankhamun from Thebes: A Late Amarna Antecedent of the Ramesside Battle-Narrative Tradition. – Chicago, University of Chicago, (Unpublished Ph.D dissertation).

Kitchen, K. 1982. Pharaoh, Triumphant. The Life and Times of Ramesses II. – Warminster, Aris & Phillips Ltd.

Lauffray, J. 1979. Karnak d'Égypte: Domaine du divin. – Paris, Editions du Centre National de la Recherche Scientifique

Lichtheim, M. 1976. Ancient Egyptian Literature. Volume. II. The New Kingdom. – Berkeley, University of California Press.

Littauer, M.A. & J.H. Crouwel. 1985. Chariots and Related Equipment from Tutankhamun's Tomb. – Oxford, Griffith Institute.

McLeod, W. 1982. Self Bows and Other Archery Tackle from the Tomb of Tutankhamun. – Oxford, Griffith Institute.

Naville, E. 1930. Details releves dans les ruines de quelques temples égyptiens. – Paris, P. Geuthner.

Parkinson, R. 2008. The Painted Tomb Chapel of Nebamun: Masterpieces of Ancient Egyptian Art in the British Museum. – Cairo, American University in Cairo Press.

Peet, T.E. & C.L. Woolley. 1923. The City of Akhenaten. Part I. – London, Egypt Exploration Society.

Petrie, W.M.F. 1896. Six Temples at Thebes. – London, Bernard Quartich.

Redford, D.B. 1976. Akhenaton Temple Project. Volume I. Initial Discoveries. - Toronto, University of Toronto Press.

Redford, D.B. 1988. Relief Scenes, Mainly from the *rwd-mnw*. In: Redford, D.B. Ed. Akhenaten Temple Project. Volume II. *rwd-mnw*, Foreigners and Inscriptions. – Toronto, University of Toronto Press.

Ricke, H., G.R. Hughes & E.F. Wente. 1967. Beit el-Wali Temple of Ramesses II. – Chicago, Oriental Institute of the University of Chicago Press.

Ritner, R. 1993. The Mechanics of Ancient Egyptian Magical Practice. – Chicago, Oriental Institute of the University of Chicago Press.

Romano, J.F. 1979. The Luxor Museum of Ancient Egyptian Art. Catalogue. – Cairo, American Research Center in Egypt.

Sa'ad, R. 1975. Fragments d'un monument de Toutânkhamon retouvés dans le IXe pylone de Karnak. – Karnak 5: 93-109.

Saleh, M., & H. Sourouzian. 1987. Official Catalogue. The Egyptian Museum Cairo. – Mainz, Philipp von Zabern.

Schulman, A.R. 1980. Chariots, Chariotry and the Hyksos. – Journal of the Society for the Study of Egyptian Antiquities 10: 105-154.

Sethe, K. 1961 [1927]. Urkunden der 18. Dynastie. – Berlin, Akademie-Verlag.

Shaw, I. 2001. Egyptians, Hyksos and Military Technology: Causes, Effects or Catalysts? In: Shortland, A. Ed. The Social Context of Technological Change: Egypt and the Near East, 1650-1550 BC. – Oxford, Oxbow Books: 59-72.

Tylor, J.J. 1900. Wall Drawings and Monuments of El Kab. – London, Bernard Quaritch.

Whitehouse, H. 2009. Egypt and Nubia in the Ashmolean Museum. – Oxford, Ashmolean Museum.

ART AND IMPERIAL IDEOLOGY: REMARKS ON THE DEPICTION OF ROYAL CHARIOTS ON WALL RELIEFS IN NEW-KINGDOM EGYPT AND THE NEO-ASSYRIAN EMPIRE

Arianna Sacco

INTRODUCTION

The goal of the present paper is to examine how chariots, and in particular royal chariots, are depicted in war scenes on wall reliefs both in New Kingdom Egypt, mostly representative by examples from 19th (1549-1298 BC) and 20th Dynasty (1298-1069 BC), and in the Neo-Assyrian Empire (934-609 BC). Chronologically, the present discussion encompasses both the Late Bronze Age (ca. 1550-1070 BC) and Iron Age (ca. 1100-600 BC), geographically, the study focuses on Egypt and Northern Mesopotamia.

Firstly, in the present work, the focus will be on similarities and differences between the two cultures in the depiction of royal chariots in war reliefs. The features of the royal chariots, how they are depicted, and how they changed in the course of time will be examined.

Secondly, the contribution of the royal chariots to the figurative composition and overall meaning of the war reliefs in the two empires will be analysed. To achieve this, the general iconography of the scenes in question will be studied and the representation of royal chariots with the depiction of non-royal chariots will be compared.

Thirdly, the paper will examine the differences and similarities in the meanings and messages conveyed by the representation of royal chariots in the war reliefs in the two aforementioned cultures, as well as who the intended audience was of the reliefs, and on which occasions they saw them. This will be achieved not only by using the above-mentioned analyses, but also by contextualizing them. The present author defines contextualizing as examining the kind of buildings in which the reliefs were originally found, the architectural unit in which they were located and the historical period during which they were made.

The comparisons allow one to identify how chariots contributed to propaganda in reliefs in two different Near-Eastern empires, which worked in fairly similar ways, and based themselves on the institutions of royalty and army (and clergy, but this is beyond the topic of the present work). The changing role of the chariots evolved from a period in which they actually had an important role to play on the battlefield, to a period in which they largely functioned as status symbols.

Despite clear differences between the Egyptian and Assyrian kingdoms, there are also similarities. In both cases, one is dealing with empires in whose main cities war scenes are widely depicted in wall reliefs. These reliefs are clearly propagandistic in nature and are always favourably disposed towards the king and his armed forces. Among the latter, chariots and charioteers are given the most vital role in these scenes and the emphasis is mostly placed on the kings in their royal chariots.

A key difference between the iconography of the two empires, as will be shown later, lies in the perceived value attached to regular charioteers and the king. Indeed, in Egypt the significance of the king is far greater than that attached to the bulk of the charioteers and other soldiers, while in Mesopotamia this difference is not as profound.

COMPARING EGYPT AND ASSYRIA

The Egyptian New Kingdom covers the Late Bronze Age (Bryan, 2000; Van Dijk, 2000), when chariots were an important part of contemporary armies (Fields, 2006: 16-19; Healy, 1992: 21-24; Littauer & Crouwel, 1979: 90-94; McDermott, 2004: 129-130; Moorey, 1986: 203-208; Schulman, 1963: 84-86). However, the Neo-Assyrian Empire dates to the full Iron Age, when true cavalry had substituted chariotry as an important part of the army and chariots were instead used to emphasize social status (Healy, 1991: 20-21; Littauer & Crouwel, 1979: 134-139; Nobel, 1990). But how did this effect the role of the chariot as element of the propaganda machine?

From a political point of view, the imperialistic agendas of the Assyrians and the Egyptians differed. The former was surrounded and had also been dominated by militarily strong peoples such as Babylonia, which took power in Assyria in ca. 1756 BC (Collins, 2008: 18-20; Healy, 1991: 3-6), and Mitanni *c.q.* Hurrians, who took power in Assyria during the 15th century BC (Healy, 1992: 12-14). This may have caused the Assyrians to heavily emphasize their military power in art and gave birth to a military and imperialistic mentality, where attack was considered the best form of defence in the face of conquest.

In Egypt, the situation was different, largely due to the fact that Egypt itself was relatively isolated. The Egyptians had to deal with trouble created by other foreign peoples such as the Nubians and the peoples of Syria-Palestine, as shown for example by the fortresses constructed in Nubia. Before the Third Intermediate Period (1064-656 BC), the 15th or Hyksos Dynasty (1650-1535 BC) had been the first foreigners to rule Egypt for some time. They managed to control Lower Egypt during the Second Intermediate Period (1650-1549 BC).

As a result, Egypt's imperialism was of a somewhat different character than that of Assyria. Not fuelled primarily by fear of conquest, but rather by imperialistic ambition, it was the kings of especially the 19th and 20th Dynasties, with their military backgrounds, that were a driving force behind Egypt's imperialism (Spalinger, 2005: 178-180). This means that they tended to present themselves primarily as aggressive military leaders or warlords (Healy, 1992: 17; McDermott, 2004: 89; Spalinger, 2005: 70, 171-172). New, successful conquests served to legitimize these rulers and emphasize their power in the face of rival that might also aspire to power (Spalinger, 2005: 173-176).

Furthermore, Egypt's imperialistic ambitions may also have sprung from the cohesion and confidence in the army created during the Theban reconquest (Spalinger, 2005: 47-48), which unified Egypt again after the divisions of the Second Intermediate Period and gave rise to the New Kingdom itself. This reconquest was started by Seqenenre Taa II (1558-1553 BC) and Kamose (1553-1549 BC), the last kings of the 17th Dynasty, and completed by Ahmose (1549-1524 BC), founder of the 18th Dynasty (Bourriau, 2000: 197-203; Healy, 1992: 7-9; McDermott, 2004: 88-89; Spalinger, 2005: 1-6 and 19-24). The main aim of these campaigns was to unify Egypt again and expel the foreign rulers. Its ultimate success demonstrated the capabilities and the qualities of the Egyptian army and of the people fighting in its ranks, which also lead to establishing the basis for imperialism.

Part of this surge in imperialism can also be attributed to the adoption of new instruments of war, namely the composite bow (Cotterell, 2004: 57-59; McDermott, 2004: 150-157; Moorey, 1986: 208-210; Partridge, 2002: 42-46; Shaw, 1991: 42-44) and the chariot (Fields, 2006; Littauer & Crouwel, 1979: 69-70; Partridge, 2002: 60-74). Both of these tools were probably acquired from the Hyksos, thereby levelling the playing field between Egypt and their Near Eastern rivals (Cotterell, 2004: 89-92; Fields, 2006: 14-15; Healy, 1992: 5-7; Littauer & Crouwel, 1979: 75-76; Moorey, 1986: 196-203, 211-212; Shaw, 1991: 39-42; Spalinger, 2005: 6-19). In this way, the Egyptians for the first time truly modernized their military equipment, not only by adopting new weaponry (such as the aforementioned composite bows), but improving it as well (the chariot is a good example, *cf.* Sandor, this volume). This allowed the Egyptians to defeat the Hyksos (Spalinger, 2005: 19), to better defend themselves against foreign attacks in general, and to expand into Asia (*Ibidem*, 2005: 48-52).

Last, but not the least, it should be mentioned that Egypt and Assyria differed with respect to the nature of kingship. In Egypt, the king was the incarnation of a god, the son of a god made flesh. Still, the lineage of a king was important too, so that a Dynasty such as the 19th and the 20th, not originating directly from the royal family, constantly had to strive for the support of the other gods, mostly Amun (McDermott, 2004: 135-137; Spalinger, 2005:75-76; Van Dijk, 2000: 305-307), and also to emphasize their right to their political rivals.

However, in Assyria, the king was an emissary and intermediary of the gods, working for, blessed by, and legitimized by them (Collins, 2008: 9; 2010: 182-186; Healy 1991: 4-5; Paley, 1976: 20-24). This was far more so the case in Assyria than in Egypt. In other words, the Assyrian king was the earthly hand of the gods, whose will he strove to accomplish by engaging in building activities and the management of irrigation channels, as well as by performing ritual duties in the temples. He was also blessed by the gods whenever he was granted military victories. In Assyria too, lineage was important, and kings not deriving directly from the ruling family – such as was probably the case for Sargon II (722-705 BC; see Healy, 1991: 28-32, 45) – had constantly to prove their might and defend their claims to the throne.

However, there were also similarities between New-Kingdom Egypt and the Neo-Assyrian Empire. In both empires, the king, the temple administration and the soldiers – who may or may not have been part of a standing army – were key constituent elements of their own identities. And it is perhaps because of this, as well as because of the interrelations with foreign leaders, that propaganda was necessary to the kings. Representation of war scenes on wall reliefs, recalling recent military conquests and showing the might of the king and his army, as well as the favour of the gods, were also meant to show the image of the king as a just, fierce and strong ruler who respected the wishes and expectations of the larger administrative and religious system (Grimal, 1986: 3-5, 717-722).

In both empires, in a more or less strict form, foreign territories were also considered the property of the king, and the acquisition of new territory was considered a royal duty. That is to say, both in Egypt and Assyria, the power of the ruler was considered to extend across all the lands, without borders. Particularly in Egypt, the identification of the king with the god Ra made his conquests a symbolic act of recreating the universe.

Finally, in both empires we are dealing with river cultures that emerged and developed in river valleys and where the development of chariots would have been helped also by the relatively flat landscape. Of course, the presence of one or more major rivers would have favoured the use of a fleet over other terrestrial means, such as chariots. This is, for example, the case for Egypt before the contact with the Hyksos. For domestic purposes, waterways could be used to reach areas swiftly with boats. But when these empires had to reach beyond their borders, they needed to travel by land. The Egyptians therefore had to rely on a purely land-based army when they got entangled in foreign affairs, such as with their neighbours in Syria-Palestine. The Assyrians had to move across land when they wished to deal with their neighbours in the north.

EGYPTIAN RELIEFS FEATURING CHARIOTS

From Egypt, the building with the largest number of war reliefs is the complex of temples dedicated to Amun at Karnak. Here, the campaigns of Seti I (1309-1291 BC) in Palestine, Syria and Libya and against the Hittites are represented on the external northern wall of the Hypostyle Hall (Healy, 1992: 48, 50; Spalinger, 2005: 198-201, figs. 12.1 & 12.2; Stevenson-Smith, 1958: 222-223). The king is shown in different contexts and poses. He is shown in his chariot setting off for war, with his horses slowly moving at a walk or a trot, or attacking the enemy, with galloping and rampant horses, or standing and smiting the enemies with a spear. In Near Eastern campaigns in Palestine, Syria and the land of Hatti, Seti is accompanied by other, significantly smaller Egyptian chariots, and all of them shoot arrows using composite bows, while against the Libyans, the king is the only one shown in a chariot, using not the bow and arrow, but instead spears and the *khepesh*. Possibly, the latter is because the Libyans used less complex weapons than those employed by the Egyptian and other Near Eastern peoples; beating them with more advanced equipment would

Figure 1. Karnak, temple of Amun. Hypostyle Hall, external northern wall. Seti I against Libyans. Drawing by J. Brouwers and A. Sacco. After: Healy (1992: 50); Spalinger (2005: fig. 12.1).

have made the victory appear far more easy and thus less glorious.

Furthermore, in the campaigns of Seti I in Palestine and Syria, the Egyptians are shown attacking walled and fortified cities surrounded by water courses and trees, as well as other chariots, and when shown fighting against the Hittites, the Egyptians fight against the enemies chariots. In all these compositions, the enemies are shown falling and being run over by the Egyptian chariots. It can be noticed, as in the battle against the Hittites (Spalinger, 2005: fig. 12.2), that some enemies escape on galloping horses and are followed and hit with arrows fired by the Egyptian king in his chariot. These horses probably have been detached from their chariots, which are also shown being chased by the Egyptian king in the same scene and killed eventually.

The Hypostyle Hall of the temple of Amun at Karnak also contains the campaigns of Seti I's son and successor, Ramesses II (1290-1224 BC), in Palestine and Syria (depicted on the external southern wall), as well as those of his son Merenptah (1212-1201 BC) against the Libyans and the Sea People and in Palestine (Spalinger, 2005: 242-243, figs. 14.1a & 14.2b). Here it can be seen that the king is represented in his chariot charging with rampant horses against walled and fortified cities, as well as against enemy chariots very similar to the Egyptian ones, using both the bow and arrows and the spear, the latter probably used after having fired all of the arrows, for more dramatic strikes or for closer combat. This time, though, the Egyptian soldiers are not depicted in chariots, but assaulting the walls using ladders, or fighting in ranks as infantry against the enemies. The king is also depicted walking and smiting the enemies with the *khepesh*, and the enemies are represented, as usual, falling under the Egyptian attack.

In addition, war reliefs representing chariots are found in the temple of Luxor (Healy, 1992: 54; Spalinger, 2005: 221-226, figs. 13.6a & 13.6b), where the Battle of Qadesh is shown on the external walls of both towers of the first pylon. Other battles of Ramesses II in Palestine and Syria are depicted on the external wall of the western tower of the second pylon, and on the external walls of the first portico. Egyptian chariots are shown in orderly rows with galloping horses, sometimes following the chariot of the king, and are often accompanied by the Egyptian infantry, which is shown in tight orderly ranks. However, the enemies are represented in disorder and chaos and, as in the other reliefs, are shown falling as a result of the Egyptian assault and are being overrun: this is how the Egyptians typically depicted their enemies. As in the aforementioned reliefs, the king is also shown charging against enemies and even enemy cities in his chariot, walking on top of fallen enemies and shooting arrows into fortified cities.

Other war reliefs with chariots are found at Ramesses II's temple in Abydos (Spalinger, 2005: 217-218, 221-226, figs. 13.2-13.5), where the Battle of Qadesh is again represented, similar to the ones previously described, as well as Ramesses II's battles in Syria and Canaan. In the latter, the king is depicted driving over the enemies with the chariot or walking on enemies and attacking a fortified city.

Other war reliefs with chariots are found in Nubia, in the Great Temple of Abu Simbel, where on the right wall of the Hypostyle Hall the Battle of Qadesh is again depicted (Spalinger, 2005: 221-226; Stevenson-Smith, 1958: 216-217), while on the left wall of the Hypostyle Hall battles of Ramesses II against the Libyans, against Nubians and against various groups in modern-day Syria are shown. The Battle of Qadesh is depicted in the same manner as in Ramesses' Abydos temple, even though its execution is coarser, while an additional image shows the king walking on Libyan enemies and killing them with a spear. In Syria, he is depicted attacking fortified cities on a chariot, followed by Egyptian chariotry in close order. In the battles against the Nubians, special emphasis is put on the Egyptians' victorious return with prisoners and booty.

More war reliefs with chariots attacking Nubians are found in the temple at Beit el-Wali, where Ramesses II's campaigns against Libyans and Nubians and in Syria are depicted. The king is shown in the chariot with galloping horses attacking the masses of Libyan enemies, as well as killing the captured enemy, while other prisoners are carried away by the crown prince. Similarly, the king is shown charging the masses of Nubians in a chariot with rampant horses, while in the case of the Syrians, the king is depicted walking on these enemies and attacking a city. In the representations of the campaigns in Syria-Palestine, fortified walled cities are emphasized. No doubt, this kind of city was a major feature of that area. Iconographically speaking, the emphasis placed on a well-prepared and equipped enemy would have made the victory seem more glorious. The Nubians, on the contrary, where less well-equipped than the Syrian peoples and used mostly bows and arrows. So, the representation of the king in the chariot shooting arrows would have been a proper one to show a balanced fight rather than a far too easy – and therefore less glorious – overwhelming Egyptian victory.

War reliefs with chariots are also depicted in the Ramesseum, where battles in Syria-Palestine and the Battle of Qadesh are represented on the southern tower of the first pylon, on the right wall of the first hall, and on the western wall of the northern tower of the second pylon (Michalowski, 1969: pls. 548-552; Spalinger: 221-226, fig. 13.1 & 13.7; Stevenson-Smith, 1958: 217). The depictions are similar to the ones of the Battle of Qadesh found in the temple of Luxor, with additional depictions of the Egyptian camp, of the king in his chariot attacking the disordered enemies, and of the Egyptian chariots fighting against the Hittite enemies in their chariots. The Hittite chariots are, as in the previous reliefs, represented in a similar way to the Egyptian ones. The main difference lies in the fact that they have a three-man crew, none of which appear armed with the bow. The similarities in the chariots probably derive from the fact that both Egyptians and Hittites chariots were based on the same Near-Eastern prototypes; the three-man crew is probably a genuine detail observed by the Egyptians on the battlefield.

Finally, war reliefs with chariots are found in the temple of Ramesses III (1185-1153 BC) at Medinet Habu, where wars against the so-called Sea Peoples are shown (Healy, 1992: figs. on pages 58-59 & 61; Michalowski, 1969: pl. 122 & 553-558; Partridge, 2002: 269-272; Spalinger, 2005: 255-256, figs. 13.8, 15.1 & 15.2 on pages 225 & 251-252; Stevenson-Smith, 1958: 224-225). Also, on the external northern wall and on the left wall of the second court, the first Libyan expedition of Ramesses III is depicted.

Figure 2. Abu Simbel, Great Temple. Hypostyle hall, left wall. Ramesses II against Syrians. Drawing by J. Brouwers. After: Photographs from http://www.crooktree.com/).

On the left wall of the first court the second Libyan expedition of Ramesses III is represented (Partridge, 2002: 267-268; Spalinger, 2005: 256-258). Finally, both on the external northern wall between the first and the second pylon and on the western wall of the northern tower of the first pylon Ramesses III's battles and conquests in Syria are represented (Partridge, 2002: 272-273). Here, as in the previous reliefs, the king is depicted in his chariot with galloping horses, holding bow and arrow and once also with the *khepesh*, and attacking fortified cities or masses of foes, as well as walking on enemies. In one of these scenes, his chariot is shown being taken care of by Egyptian soldiers. The king is accompanied, as in the aforementioned examples, by orderly ranks of Egyptian chariots and foot-soldiers. As in the other war reliefs, the enemies are shown disordered and smashed, the complete opposite of the state of the Egyptian army.

RELIEFS WITH CHARIOTS FROM ASSYRIA

From Assyria, reliefs with chariots are found in the Northwest Palace of Nimrud, where campaigns of Ashurnasirpal II (883-859 BC; Healy, 1991: 7-10) are depicted in room B or throne room, east wall of room G, east and west walls of room H, east wall of room L and in the west wing (Asher-Greve & Selz, 1980: 12-30; Barnett, 1970: 12-16; Cohen & Kangas, 2010: 50-85; Collins, 2008: figs. on pages 32-61; ; Gadd, 1934: 55-58, 60; Meuszyński, 1981: 22-24, pls.

1 & 2; Nobel, 1990: 63; Paley & Sobolewski, 1987: 78-79, pl. 5). The reliefs show the setting off for war and reaching the cities, as well as the pursuit of the fleeing enemy. Some reliefs also depict the aftermath and include prisoners. In battle scenes, the Assyrians are shown fighting in their chariots but, most of all, are shown assaulting the fortified walls of the enemy city. The walls are sometimes surrounded by water courses, in which Assyrian soldiers are shown swimming, even underwater, to reach the enemy walls. Assaults of the cities include archers shooting arrows while protected by shield-bearers. They also feature siege machines and ladders, as well as instruments used to breach the foundations. The king is shown standing and assaulting the city using bow and arrows.

Other Neo-Assyrian war reliefs with chariots are found in the Southwest Palace of Nimrud where, in the only room that has been found (Barnett, 1970: 21; Barnett & Falkner, 1962: 23-30, 36-42, pls. LXVIII-LXXI, LXXXI-LXXXIII, CXVI-CXVII, Collins, 2008: 63-70), campaigns of Ashurnasirpal II, the campaigns of Tiglath-Pileser III in Urartu and in Asia Minor, as well as campaigns of Esarhaddon (680-669 BC; Healy, 1991: 47-50) are represented in the entrance F and on the walls F and R. The army is shown marching off to battle. Also shown is the actual battle, the punishment of the enemy and the return with booty and prisoners. Chariots are always shown in these kinds of scenes and are also depicted in combat, sometimes driving over enemies. However, in the scenes, the assault of the walls by archers coupled with shield-bearers and soldiers on

Figure 3. Nimrud, Northwest Palace. Ashurnasirpal II at war. Drawing by A. Sacco. After: Meuszyński (1981: Tafel 2 B4-B3 upper line).

ladders as well as siege machines, is emphasized, as in the above-mentioned reliefs. Soldiers fighting on galloping horses with spears are also represented, as well as the Assyrian camp.

Other examples of war reliefs with chariots are found in the Central Palace in Nimrud (Asher-Greve & Selz, 1980: 30-48; Barnett & Falkner, 1962: 7-19, pls. XV-XVI, XLIII-XLIV; Gadd, 1934: 62-64, pl. VIII; Nobel, 1990: 63-65), where campaigns of Tiglath-Pileser III (745-727 BC; Barnett & Falkner, 1962: pl. XVI-XXV; Healy, 1991: 17, 24-28) in Babylonia, in Syria and against the nomadic tribe of the Qedarites, in the northern part of the Arabian peninsula, are depicted. Unfortunately, the conditions in which they were found do not allow reconstruction of their position in the palace. In these scenes sieges of fortified towns with archers firing arrows are represented, as well as images of the Assyrian camp. The cities are surrounded by water courses or moats, showing people rowing away and escaping. The scene of the campaign against the Qedarites shows a chariot attacking, with horses in full gallop, and passing over the camel of a defeated enemy. The relief showing the campaign in Syria depicts chariots riding over beheaded enemy corpses.

More war reliefs with chariots are found in the palace of Sargon II (721-705 BC; Lion, 1994; Michel, 1994) in Khorsabad (Botta, 1972: 118-133, 136-147, 159-161, pls. 52-77, 85-101, 139-143; Gadd, 1934: 64-65; Loud, 1936: 65-67, 79-80), on the base of the throne, on the northern and southern walls of room II, on the northern and southern walls of room V, on the walls of room XIII (all small rooms on the northern edge of the palace), in the inner part of door H leading to room II, and in the inner part of the doors leading to room V. Very famous are the reliefs depicting his campaign in Urartu (Guichard, 1994; Parayre, 1994). We see archers, protected by shield-bearers, attacking fortified cities located on hills, soldiers who try to enter these cities using ladders, soldiers on horses or chariots shooting arrows and passing over the corpses of the enemy. The king is shown charging the enemy in his chariot and passing over the corpses and cut-off heads of fallen foes.

Finally, war reliefs with chariots are found in the North Palace of Nineveh, where campaigns of Ashurbanipal (669-627 BC. Barnett, 1976: 5-7; Healy, 1991: 50-54) are depicted in rooms F-I, K-M, as well as in the courts J and O and on the upper floors of rooms S, T, V (Barnett, 1970: 30-34; 1976: 39-48, 54-60, pls. XVI-XXXVIII, LX-LXIX; Collins, 2008: 106-141; Gadd, 1934: 72-76; Nagel, 1967: 18-26; pls. 2-8, 11-12; Nobel, 1990: 65-66). The highlight of these reliefs is the representation of the Battle of Til-Tuba, on the banks of the river Ulai, against the Elamites guided by Te-Umman (depicted also in room XXXIII) in Sennacherib's Palace (also referred to as the Southwest Palace; room XXXIII was on the southern edge of the palace) in Nineveh (Barnett, 1970: 23-30; Barnett et al., 1998, 94-97, pls. 286-320; Collins, 2008: 100-105; Gadd, 1934: 70-72, pl. IX, XVII; Nagel, 1967: 27-39, pls. 9-10, 13-15, 17-18, 20-21). In these reliefs, we see both the actual battle, as well as the return of the victorious king and his army, accompanied by the spoils of war. Assyrian chariots are shown fighting against the enemy in their chariots, while towns are being assaulted, as in the previous examples, by archers protected by shield-bearers, and soldiers trying to breach the foundations of the walls. Comparable to the previously described scenes, men on horses are shown fighting, and Assyrian foot-soldiers are depicted

Figure 4. Nineveh, Southwest Palace. Chariot of Ashurbanipal. Drawing by Arianna Sacco. After: Nagel (1967: Tafel 13.2 lower line).

operating in close order. Here too, people are rowing across the water. Corpses of soldiers and their equipment float in the water. Enemies are depicted getting punished, or otherwise begging for mercy from the Assyrian king.

As a general observation, later Neo-Assyrian war reliefs show more details, not only in the kinds of elements added to the scenes, such as more elaborate vegetation and animal life, but also in the details added to every element: the armour, the branches and leaves of the trees, and the way that water is represented in the water courses).

ANALYSIS OF THE DESCRIBED RELIEFS

As far as the royal chariot is concerned, in Egyptian reliefs it can be easily distinguished from other chariots due to its large size; as always, the king is represented larger than any other figure. In addition, the king is always accompanied both by the solar disc, sometimes with uraei, and the divine symbol of Horus, Nekhbet, Mut or Montu. Examples include the many depictions of Ramesses II in the reliefs showing the Battle of Qadesh. Furthermore, the king always wears the uraeus, the Blue Crown or the Atef Crown. The king is always alone in his chariot, not only on the battlefield, but also in scenes preceding and following the main battle. During combat, the king has the reins tied around his hips. The non-royal Egyptian chariot always had a two-man crew, consisting of a charioteer and an archer (Schulman, 1963: 87-88), also on the battlefield.

In the Assyrian reliefs the king is, as usual, neither represented larger than the other figures, nor is he alone in his chariot, but with two other persons, namely a charioteer and a soldier armed with a sword (Barnett & Falkner, 1962: 36-37; Paley, 1976: 29-39). The royal chariot can be distinguished by the king's regalia and accoutrements, such as the *polos* (hat), long beard and hair, and the presence of the symbol of the god Ashur (which is the upper part of the anthropomorphic god shooting an arrow and framed by a circle featuring two wings and the tail of a bird), which can be considered analogous to the winged uraeus. Furthermore, the royal chariots are the only ones in which the shield-bearer carries a parasol when the chariot is not engaged in battle.

In both empires, royal and non-royal chariots share the same features in the periods under examination: the vehicles do not appear to be very different from regular chariots. In Egypt, they have low, open sides and are open at the back with the side rail curving downwards, while the wheels are represented as being very light and equipped with six spokes during the whole period here examined (*e.g.* Cotterell, 2004: 92-96; Fields, 2006: 15-16; Littauer & Crouwel, 1979: 78-81; McDermott, 2004: 130-132; Partridge, 2002: 65-68). On the side of the chariot, visible to the viewer of the relief, a quiver and bow-case are shown, usually crossing each other. Two horses always pull the chariot (Littauer & Crouwel, 1979; 82-84); they do not wear any protection, but sometimes sport headdresses. The horses are controlled by means of nose bands and two reins connected to a yoke, which in turn is connected to a pole that goes beneath the floor of the chariot (*Ibidem*: 84-90). Thus, the king is always alone in his chariot, whereas normal chariot crews consist of two people, sometimes accompanied by a runner. The latter serves as support for the crew of the chariot, helping and defending the crew in the event that they would fall off from the chariot, or defending the crew of the chariot from enemy attacks in case the chariot stopped for whatever reason. Reasons for the chariot stopping could include injuries sustained by one or both horses, or severe damage to the chariot (Fields, 2006: 18-19; McDermott, 2004: 130).

In Assyria, the chariots have tall, closed sides and are open at the back with the side rail curving downwards (Littauer & Crouwel, 1979: 101-110). Towards the end of the Neo-Assyrian Empire the rail is completely square, especially during the reign of Ashurbanipal, 669-627 BC (Collins, 2008: 97-99; Nagel, 1967: 40-49). The wheels are represented with thick felloes and become progressively bigger, and with thicker felloes, in time; they have six spokes in the reliefs of Ashurnasirpal II (883-859 BC), from the Northwest Palace of Nimrud, and of Esarhaddon (680-669 BC), from the Southwest Palace of Nimrud. The wheels have eight spokes in all the other reliefs, such as in those from the Central Palace of Nimrud and from Nineveh. Inside the chariot, we often see a spear, while on the sides two crossed quivers can be found (as during the reigns of Ashurnasirpal II, and Esarhaddon), or no quivers (as during the reigns of Tiglat-Pileser III, 745-727 BC, and Ashurbanipal, 669-627 BC; Barnett & Falkner, 1962: 39). Usually two horses pull the chariot, but chariots pulled by three horses are found during the reign of Ashurnasirpal II and Sargon II (721-705 BC; Littauer & Crouwel, 1979: 110-115), as it can be seen in the reliefs from the Northwest Palace of Nimrud and in the reliefs from the palace of Sargon II in Khorsabad. The horses are controlled through snaffle-bits (Littauer & Crouwel, 1979: 115-134), as well as through two or three reins for each hand of the charioteer – depending on the number of horses – and by an added pole, apart from the draft pole. It should be noticed that the pole is very wide and elaborate, except during the reigns of Tiglat-Pileser III and of Sargon II.

The horses wear embellishments and protections on their heads, backs and sides, though during the reign of Ashurnasirpal II (Collins, 2008: 29-32) and Ashurbanipal there wear fewer of these. Usually, in all Assyrian reliefs examined, there are three persons in the chariot: the charioteer (who holds the reins and controls the chariot), the archer (who shoots his arrows at the enemies and can be armed also with a sword), and a third soldier (who usually is in the rear of the chariot and can also be equipped with a sword). On some reliefs, though, as in the ones from the Northwest Palace of Nimrud and from the room II of Sargon II's palace in Khorsabad (Botta 1972: 118-133, pls. 52-77), the crew consists of two soldiers. Furthermore, it should be noted that outside of battle, the chariot crew sometimes consists of just the charioteer, with the horses led by one or two warriors on foot. Chariot soldiers differ in their accoutrements; some wear simple clothes, while others are equipped with scale armour and helmets. This variation can perhaps be attributed to the country of origin of these soldiers.

Concerning the context of the war reliefs with chariots, and the kind of scenes represented in them, it can be first noted that in Egypt such reliefs are located in temples, also on external walls, such as on the northern and southern external walls of Karnak (where campaigns of Seti I, Ramesses II and Merenptah are represented) and on the external walls of the towers of the first pylon of the temple of Luxor (where the Battle of Qadesh is represented). They include the departure of the king with the army, the true battle and the return, with the punishment of the enemy and, most importantly, his presentation with the rest of the booty to Amun (Partridge, 2002: 242). It is in these kinds of scenes that the crown prince is depicted (*Ibidem*: 260-261; Spalinger, 2005: 71), for example while tying up prisoners. This offers the opportunity to show the crown prince as taking part in battle, though not among the rank-and-file, to emphasize both the special ties with his father, the king (whom he would eventually succeed), and the accomplishments of his career in the army before ascending the throne.

In Assyria, by contrast, war reliefs with chariots are located in the royal palaces, mainly in the throne room and in the rooms around it. The major courts of the palace had war reliefs too, where they would have been more impressive than in the other rooms, because they would have been more illuminated. These reliefs include, apart from the true battle, also the moments of preparation for it as well as the moments after it when the defeated enemy is punished, pays his respects to the king or is taken away from his land. Moreover, it should be added that also other kinds of reliefs involving chariots are found in the palaces; they include hunting scenes, scenes in which the king is accompanied by genies and other supernatural creatures, or feature celebrations, as for example the founding of a new capital. On the contrary, in the temples only reliefs that are supernatural and religious in nature can be found.

CONCLUSION

The ongoing nature of the research allows for the following preliminary conclusions. Both in Egypt and in Assyria the chariot reliefs aim at emphasizing the strength and value of the king. In Egypt, they underscore the strength and the importance of the king; indeed his duty is to vanquish his enemies and to establish, in this way, order over chaos, and ensure justice (Spalinger, 2005: 77-78). Victory demonstrates that the king enjoys the favour of the gods, especially Amun, and thus legitimizes his right to rule as a god himself. In Assyria, the reliefs emphasize the favour and the right to power that the king receives from the gods, and his role as their earthly intermediary.

But there are also differences in how the kings are depicted in the Egyptian and Neo-Assyrian reliefs. The main difference lies in the relationship between the king and his army in battle scenes. In the Egyptian reliefs, both in the represented scenes (and in the texts, although beyond the topic of the present work), the emphasis is clearly placed on the king, who is credited with decisive influence in battle. By contrast, in the Assyrian reliefs, the king does not appear to be greatly emphasized relative to the Assyrian army as a whole (Collins, 2008: 25). Note, however, that in the texts accompanying the reliefs the king claims to act on his own, but with the help of the god.

Comparing the Egyptian and the Assyrian war reliefs that contain images of chariots, it must be pointed out the difference in the kind of building on which they are located. In Egypt, the scenes are found in temples, while in Assyria they are located in palaces, so in more secular locations. This probably derives partially from the intended audience for the reliefs. On the Egyptian side, the audience likely included the gods, members of the royal court and of the clergy, to which the king had to show his power and the fulfilment of his duties. Furthermore, it was meant to satisfy their expectations, to create consensus and to dissuade any attempt at conspiracy. For the Assyrian reliefs, the main audience would have consisted of local Assyrian nobles, who would have been dissuaded to take up arms against their king by the latter's military prowess being demonstrated. Moreover, the viewer would have been foreign visitors or foreign members of the court, and the purpose of the reliefs was probably to prevent rebellion or refusal to pay tribute (Porter, 2010: 143; Russell, 1991: 223-262).

The difference in the location of the reliefs in the two empires derives probably also from the importance that Amun had acquired in Egypt during the New Kingdom. Thus, the Egyptian kings decided to put the reliefs in the temples to dedicate and to offer in a certain way the victories to Amun, as also the booty was offered to him (possibly, in the reliefs since earlier periods). Of course, few Egyptian palaces have been recovered to compare with the Assyrian ones. In Assyria, on the contrary, the urge of dedicating the victory to a specific god was less significant: it was considered enough to deposit only a part of the booty in the temple. Furthermore, the different character of kingship in Egypt and Assyria no doubt had a part to play. As already mentioned, in Egypt the king had a divine nature and this would make a temple the natural place to depict reliefs commemorating the king's achievements, while in Assyria, the king was a human mediator whose depictions were best served in secular locations, such as palaces.

Finally, depictions of the Egyptian king fighting in a chariot date from a time when the chariotry was one of the constituent elements of contemporary armies, so the true engagement of the king in battle and his military abilities are emphasized in the iconographic sources. The Assyrian reliefs belong to an age when true cavalry had largely displaced chariotry. The chariot instead was now largely a prestige object that emphasized an exalted social position (Nobel, 1990: 62, 68). Hence, the Assyrian depictions of the king fighting in a chariot served more to underline his status as the highest ranking member of society, rather than reflect his actual military prowess on the battlefield.

During the Late Bronze Age, chariotry was a major part of the armies of the ancient Near East, including Egypt. In the Iron Age, there was a shift from chariotry to true cavalry. We see this, for example, in the army of the Neo-Assyrian Empire, where the large numbers of chariots had been mostly replaced by armed men riding on horseback. Horseback riding is already attested in reliefs. However, these were used mostly for ancillary actions such as reconnaissance and for carrying messages (Schulman, 1957).

Only in the Iron Age does true cavalry (*i.e.*, men fighting from horseback) appear (Drews, 2004: 1-3). Initially, horses are paired on the battlefield as if still yoked to a chariot, with one horseman holding the reins of another man's horse while the latter shoots arrows at the enemy. Such scenes are shown on Neo-Assyrian reliefs (such as the reliefs of Ashurnasirpal II from the Northwest Place of Nimrud, the Arabian campaign of Tiglat-Pileser III, represented in the Central Palace of Nimrud, or in his Urartean campaign, represented in the Southwest Palace of Nimrud, or in the reliefs of Ashurbanipal in the North Palace of Nineveh).

Eventually, these pairs of horsemen are replaced by solitary cavalrymen operating independently. However, the chariot still remained an object of status for the elite in both military (not only in the actual battle but also in the moments before and in the parades after) and non-military contexts, such as hunting by the king.

This present preliminary analysis aimed at showing how chariots functioned symbolically and practically in two different, yet comparable Near Eastern empires, namely New Kingdom Egypt and the Neo-Assyrian Empire. These two civilizations have been selected, since a study of the use of chariots in both illustrates the changing role of the chariot from the Late Bronze Age to the Iron Age. The study clearly shows that the chariot had a significant role in both empires. They enhanced the status of the king and the elite. However, in the Neo-Assyrian Empire, the chariot played a more subservient role than in New Kingdom Egypt.

More specifically, in New Kingdom Egypt, during the Late Bronze Age, the chariot was used to emphasize the strength and military skill of the king only in actual combat. The chariot *was* therefore the means that allowed the king to show his strength and bravery; the reliefs suggest that he won the battles singlehandedly, with his army presented as minor participants. However, in the Neo-Assyrian Empire, during the Iron Age, the chariot figured as a prestige item of both the king and his army and did not emphasize the king only; on the contrary, the use of the chariot itself in battle was not emphasized and was not used to present the king as more courageous and strong than the rest of the army.

CITED LITERATURE

Asher–Greve, J.M., & G.J. Selz. 1980. Genien und Krieger aus Nimrūd: neuassyrische Reliefs Assurnasirpals II. und Tiglath-Pilesars III. Archäologische Sammlung der Universität Zürich. – Zürich, Archäologisches Institut der Universität Zürich.

Barnett, R.D. & W. Forman. 1959. Assyrische Palastreliefs: Auswahl der Abb. und Aufnahmen von Werner Forman. – Praag, Artia.

Barnett, R.D. & M. Falkner. 1962. The sculptures of Aššur-Nasir-Apli II (883-859 B.C.), Tiglath-Pileser III (745-727 B.C.), Esarhaddon (681-669 B. C.) from the Central and South-West Palaces at Nimrud. – London, Trustees of the British Museum.

Barnett, R.D. 1970. Assyrian Palace Reliefs. – London, Trustees of the British Museum.

Barnett, R.D. 1976. Sculptures from the North Palace of Ashurbanipal at Nineveh (668–627 B.C.). London, Trustees of the British Museum.

Barnett, R.D., E. Bleibtreu, G. Turner & D. Collon. 1998. Sculptures from the Southwest Palace of Sennacherib at Nineveh. – London, British Museum Press.

Botta, P.E. & E.N. Flandin. 1972. Monument de Ninivé. – Osnabrück, Biblio Verlag.

Bourriau, J. 2000. The Second Intermediate period (c. 1650-1550 BC). In: Shaw, I. Ed. The Oxford History of Ancient Egypt. – Oxford, Oxford University Press: 172-206.

Bryan, B.M. 2000. The 18th Dynasty before the Amarna Period (c. 1550-1352 BC). In: Shaw, I. Ed. The Oxford History of Ancient Egypt. – Oxford, Oxford University Press: 207-264.

Caubet, A. Ed. 1995. Khorsabad, le palais de Sargon II, roi d'Assyrie. – Paris, Documentation française.

Cohen, A. & S.E. Kangas. 2010. "Our Nineveh Enterprise". In: Cohen, A. & S.E. Kangas Eds. Assyrian Reliefs from the Palace of Ashurnasirpal II: A Cultural Biography. – Hanover, Trustees of Dartmouth College: 1-85.

Collins, P. 2008. Assyrian Palace Sculptures. – London, British Museum Press.

Collins, P. 2010. Attending the King in the Assyrian Reliefs. In: Cohen, A. & S.E. Kangas. Eds. Assyrian Reliefs from the Palace of Ashurnasirpal II: A Cultural Biography. – Hanover, Trustees of Dartmouth College: 181-197.

Cotterell, A. 2004. Chariot: The Astounding Rise and Fall of the World's First War Machine. – London, Pimlico.

Drews, R. 2004. Early Riders: The Beginnings of Mounted Warfare in Asia and Europe. – New York/London, Routledge.

Fields, N. 2006. Bronze Age War Chariots. – Oxford/ New York, Osprey Publishing.

Gadd, C.J. 1934. The Assyrian Sculptures in the British Museum. – London, Trustees of the British Museum.

Guichard, M. 1994. La Huitième Campagne de Sargon. – Les Dossiers d'Archéologie hors-série 4: 38-43.

Guidotti, M.C. & V. Cortese. 2002. Antico Egitto: arte, storia e civiltà. – Firenze, Giunti Editore.

Healy, M. 1991. The Ancient Assyrians. – Oxford/ New York, Osprey Publishing.

Healy, M. 1992. New Kingdom Egypt. – Oxford/ New York, Osprey Publishing.

Lion, B. 1994. Sargon et sa Dynastie. – Les Dossiers d'Archéologie hors-série 4: 8-11.

Littauer, M.A. & J.H. Crouwel. 1979. Wheeled vehicles and Ridden Animals in the Ancient Near East. – Leiden, Brill.

Loud, G. & C.B. Altmann. 1936-1938. Khorsabad. – Chicago, University of Chicago Press.

McDermott, B. 2004. Warfare in Ancient Egypt. – Stroud, Sutton publishing.

Meuszyński, J.1981. Die Rekonstruktion der Reliefdarstellungen und ihrer Anordnung im Nordwestpalast von Kalhu, (Nimrūd): Räume: B.C.D.E.F.G.H.L.N.P. – Mainz, Philipp von Zabern.

Michalowski, K. 1969. The Art of Ancient Egypt. – London, Thames & Hudson.

Michel, C. 1994. L'Assyrie de Sargon. – Les Dossiers d'Archéologie hors-série 4: 4-7.

Moorey, P.R.S. 1986. The Emergence of the Light, Horse-Drawn Chariot in the Near-East c. 2000-1500 B.C. – World Archaeology 18.2: 196-215.

Nagel, W. 1967. Die neuassyrischen Reliefstile unter Sanherib und Assurbanaplu. – Berlin, Bruno Hessling.

Nobel, D. 1990. Assyrian Chariotry and Cavalry. – State Archives of Assyria Bulletin 4.1: 61-68.

Paley, S.M. 1976. King of the World: Ashur-nasir-pal II of Assyria 883-859 BC. – New York, Brooklyn Museum.

Paley, S.M. & R.P. Sobolewski. 1987. The Reconstruction of the Relief Representations and Other Positions in the Northwest-Palace at Kalkhu (Nimrud) II. – Mainz, Philipp von Zabern.

Paley, S.M. & R.P. Sobolewski. 1992. The Reconstruction of the Relief Representations and Other Positions in the Northwest-Palace at Kalkhu (Nimrud) III. – Mainz, Philipp von Zabern.

Parayre, D. 1994. Splendeurs et menaces de l'Ourartou. – Les Dossiers d'Archéologie hors-série 4: 32-37.

Parrot, A. 1961. Il mondo della figura: gli assiri. – Milano, Feltrinelli Editore.

Partridge, R.B. 2002. Fighting Pharaohs: Weapons and Warfare in Ancient Egypt. – Manchester, Peartree.

Porter, B.N. 2010. Decorations, Political Posters, Time Capsules, and Living Gods: The Meaning and Function of the Assyrian Palace Carvings. In: Cohen, A. & S.E. Kangas. Eds. Assyrian Reliefs from the Palace of Ashurnasirpal II: A Cultural Biography. – Hanover, Trustees of Dartmouth College: 143-158.

Pritchard, J.B. Ed. 1954. The Ancient Near East in Pictures Relating to the Old Testament. – Princeton, Princeton University Press.

Russell, J.M. 1991. Sennacherib's Palace without Rival at Nineveh. – Chicago, The University of Chicago Press.

Salvini, M. 1995. Sargon et l'Urartu. In; Caubet, A. Ed. Khorsabad, le palais de Sargon II, roi d'Assyrie. – Paris, Documentation française: 133- 157.

Schulman, A.R. 1957. Egyptian Representations of Horsemen and Riding in the New Kingdom. – Journal of Near Eastern Studies 16.4: 263-271.

Schulman, A.R. 1963. The Egyptian Chariotry: A Reexamination. – Journal of the American Research Center in Egypt 2: 75-98.

Shaw, I. 1991. Egyptian Warfare and Weapons. – Princes Risborough, Shire Publications.

Shaw, I. 2000. Egypt and the Outside World. In: Shaw, I. Ed. The Oxford History of Ancient Egypt. – Oxford, Oxford University Press: 308-323.

Spalinger, A.J. 2005. War in Ancient Egypt: The New Kingdom. – Malden MA, Blackwell Publishing.

Stevenson-Smith, J. 1958. The Art and Architecture of Ancient Egypt. – Harmondsworth, Penguin Books.

Taylor, J. 2000. The Third Intermediate Period (c. 1069-664 BC). In: Shaw, I. Ed. The Oxford History of Ancient Egypt. – Oxford, Oxford University Press: 324-363.

Van Dijk, J. 2000. The Amarna Period and the Later New Kingdom (c. 1352-1069 BC). In: Shaw, I. Ed. The Oxford History of Ancient Egypt. – Oxford, Oxford University Press: 265-307.

Vogel, C. 2010. The Fortifications of Ancient Egypt: 3000–1780 BC. – Oxford, Osprey Publishing.

CHARIOTS' INNER DYNAMICS: SPRINGS AND ROTATIONAL INERTIAS

Bela I. Sandor

INTRODUCTION

The safety, comfort and performance characteristics of a chariot depend on the vehicle's structural dynamics, which is a function of materials, geometry of components, and joint systems. Two areas are covered: spring systems and wheel structures. Every chariot has many springs, with a wide range of elastic properties. Leather is found as a tension spring in the yoke traces and in floor mats. The pole acts as a bending-and-torsion spring. The front floor bar acts as a bow spring, and also as an elastic warping element involved in the torsion of the pole. The subassembly comprising the axle, pole, yoke, pole-tail socket, and front floor bar is a shock-absorbing anti-roll mechanism, as long as the horses are running upright.

Wheel structures represent difficult design compromises in order to minimize the washboard effect, to provide spoke strength in compression, to resist bending in cornering maneuvers, and to minimize both the linear and rotational inertias in order to achieve high acceleration. The concept of rotational inertia leads to a fresh view of the advantages and disadvantages of using iron tires and nave hoops in racing, as hinted in a crash scene in the Lyon Circus Mosaic; the conclusion is in favor of not using any iron in a high-performance racing chariot.

CONTRASTING CHARIOT DESIGNS IN TECHNICAL RESEARCH

The Wetwang Celtic chariot (figures 1, 2 & 16) is peculiar in appearance, relatively primitive, cart-like, and, as is the case with other Celtic chariots, little known, in comparison with the more famous Egyptian and Roman ones. Its similarities and differences to the others are surprisingly useful in technical research of spring systems and wheel structures; the latter because of its surviving iron hoops.

Springs in Chariots

Contrary to common belief, even those held by many experts of ancient vehicles, all chariots contain springy elements, because wood and leather are not rigid. The only question that one could raise about such elements is one related to the spring constant, or stiffness, of each component, which depends on the property of the material (elasticity, which is independent of geometry), and the object's geometry and specific loading (Sandor, 1978). The Wetwang chariot, for example, shows a body with a rather heavy, stiff frame, centered and directly mounted on the axle. Such a mounting is excellent for balance on the axle, with negligible loading by the riders' weight on the horses. On the other hand, this central, neutral location of the body makes for a harsh ride, especially if the floor consists of

Figure 1. Wetwang Celtic chariot replica demonstrated at the British Museum, London. The driver stands over the axle, in the neutral but unsprung pole position, so the horses do not feel the rider's weight. © The Trustees of the British Museum, London.

Figure 2. Wetwang chariot body, alternative design. Note the heavy and rigid body frame, central axle position, and iron tire. © The Trustees of the British Museum, London.

boards, instead of a leather matting. The much earlier Tutankhamun-class chariot (Sandor, 2004; eight full vehicles of essentially similar design; covered by Littauer & Crouwel, 1985) appears only slightly different from the Celtic ones, but in fact, it is quite different and better in both spring systems and wheel construction. Figure 3 shows several of the springs of the Tutankhamun-chariot schematically.

The leather yoke traces of the chariot act as 'tension-only' springs; they stabilize the yoke and smooth out small unevennesses in the pull of the horses. The length of these lines varies a great deal from one chariot to another, depending on the attachment point on the pole. It is noteworthy that the spring action depends linearly on the length of the line, with the longer ones appearing to be softer, because the elongation under a given tensile load is directly related to the length (Sandor, 1978: 40); for example, a trace of length 2L stretches twice as much as a trace of identical cross-section but length L,

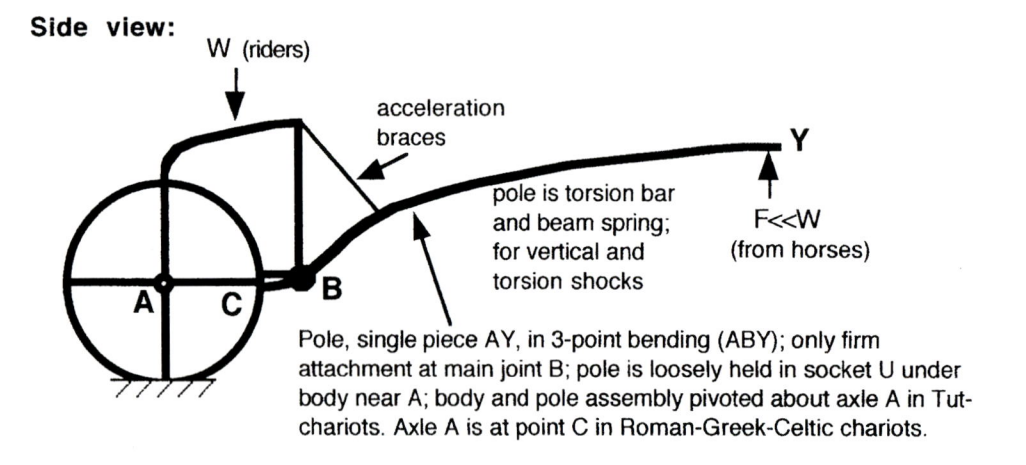

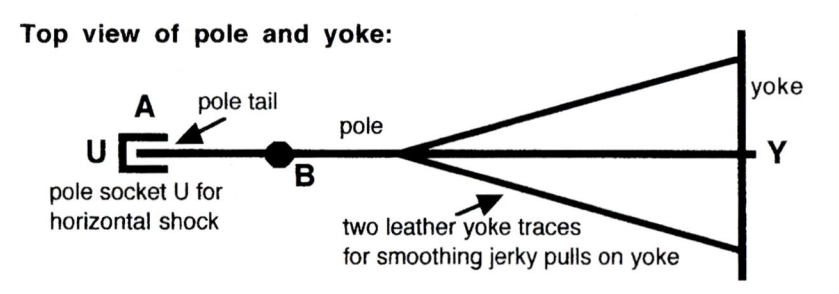

Figure 3. Schematic views of a chariot's main features. Diagram by B.I. Sandor.

under the same force. The yoke itself is a short beam spring that bends under the pulls of the horses and the leather traces; it may be considered as a relatively stiff spring. Another subtle spring is the pair of acceleration braces that connect the pole to the middle of the breastwork/belly-bar. The obvious function of these braces, which are normally sticks of wood, good for tension and compression (rarely of leather strips, which only have tension capability), is to fortify the upper structure of the body in the event a rider grabs the belly-bar during sudden accelerations. A less obvious but useful role of these braces is to create an essentially triangular, springy truss structure consisting of the pole segment, the belly-bar and its vertical support column (at point B in figure 3), and the two wooden braces, which can resist tension or compression. The entire pole itself is a complex spring: a beam in bending like a leaf spring in cars, or a torsion spring with the main loading provided by the yoke and the axle, with additional torsion contributed by the out-of-plane warping of the front floor bar. The analysis and discussion of this warping behavior and its consequences in structural dynamics are advanced topics in engineering, far beyond the scope of this paper. Easier to understand is the leaf-spring action of the pole in this particular configuration, where the axle is at the rear of the chariot body; the ancients certainly understood this fairly well, as illustrated in figure 4.

The key to figure 4 is visualizing the pole as it becomes a spring when a person steps on the chariot and moves forward toward the horses. In other words, the pole is not yet activated as a spring when the person is standing over the axle, because the axle can carry all his weight. As the person moves forward, the load on the axle is reduced, while the load on the horses increases. The precise distributions of these loads for any particular pole and its loading position are readily calculated using the method of static equilibrium. Normally, the extra load on the horses is small, less than 5% of the rider's weight on each, though it could contribute to their fatigue. The great advantage of the rear-axle configuration (figure 3) is the resulting superior suspension system with a softer ride than possible with the centrally located axle (figure 2). The softer ride is enhanced by the damping (friction; vibration decay; energy absorption) as the harness rubs and presses on the soft bodies of the horses. Note that, in apparent contradiction, a stiff suspension is desired for the uncomfortable but relatively short rides in racing cars and chariots for stability and precise handling at high speeds.

In addition to the pole being a bending and torsion spring, it is also part of the spring system based on the bow-like flexing of the D-shaped front floor bar, illustrated in figures 5 and 6. The small back-

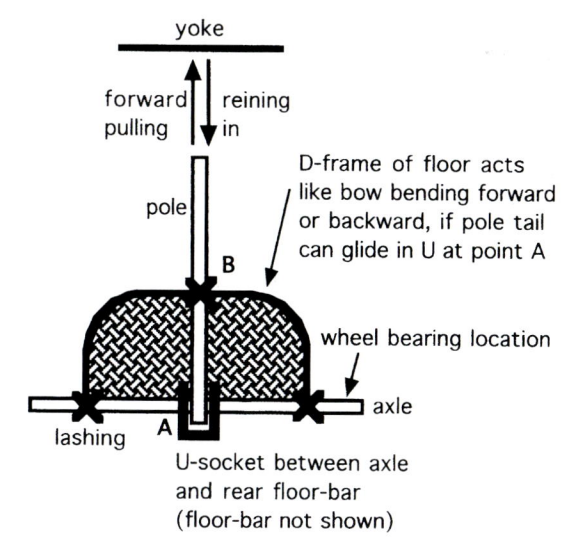

Figure 5. Bow-spring schematic. Diagram by B.I. Sandor.

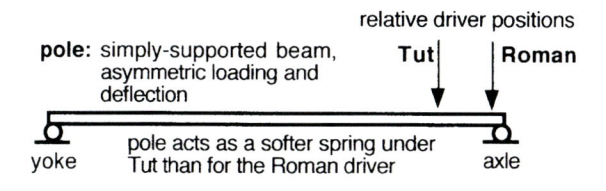

Figure 4. Activation schemes of pole spring in Egyptian vs. Roman chariots. Diagram by B.I. Sandor.

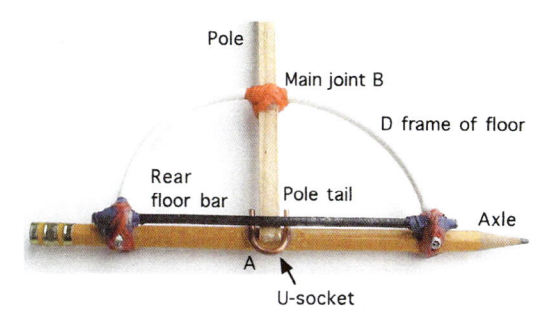

Figure 6. Bow-spring model; closeup of flat pole-tail loosely fitted in its socket on axle. By B.I. Sandor (2003).

and-forth movements of the pole are caused by fluctuations in the force applied by the horses, and by the wheels hitting ruts and rocks. The bow spring, lashed to the pole, softens these jerky motions, and the pole tail sliding and rubbing in its axle socket provides damping. The flat pole tail between the axle and the rear floor bar resists any twisting action by the pole, keeping the axle mostly horizontal whenever a wheel hits a bump and would tend to bounce into the air (Sandor, 2004). These stabilization features of the chariot (bow-spring and anti-roll mechanism) provide a combined action for the comfort and safety of the riders. There is only one other similar mechanism known, the trapezoidal pole-tail nesting in the Tiber bronze model of a Roman racing chariot (Sandor, 2012).

Composite Axle

The spring action of the axle should be considered with a new interest, regarding the discrete rawhide or leather thongs connecting the axle and the rear floor bar found on most of the Egyptian chariots (figures 7 & 8). Occasionally they are absent because of degradation over time, or rough handling, but still their traces can be found. The thongs, some stiffened by gesso and gold, have been documented from the earliest photographs of the Egyptian chariot equipment found (for examples see Littauer & Crouwel, 1985: 14, 21, 25, 27, 56; pls. II, IV, VIII, XIV, XVI, XXVII, XXVIII, XXX, LVI, LXVIII, LXIX).

Three purposes for the thongs are identified in this paper, although not all of them were likely as being intentional. The first and simplest reason is to secure the chariot body to the axle, but it should be noted that some axles have more thongs for that purpose than strictly necessary (eight axle thongs on chariot A6, Littauer & Crouwel, 1985: Plate LVI). Secondly, the thong arrangements effectively create a composite axle. In this, the load is applied from the pole tail to the axle, but also shared by the

Figure 7. Composite Tutankhamun-axle with thong (vertical dark element in center) between rear floorboard and axle. Egyptian Museum, Cairo (July 2012). Photograph by B.I. Sandor. Courtesy of the Ministry of State for Antiquities/Egyptian Museum Auhorities.

Figure 8. Composite Tutankhamun-axle, three thongs shown, to the right of the pole tail; Robert Hurford's reconstruction for NOVA TV documentary, Cairo (July 2012). Photograph by B.I. Sandor.

rear floor bar through the vertical connections. In other words, the composite axle acts as a single but flexible element. It may be called a proto-I-beam, with the round axle as the lower flange, the rectangular floor bar as the upper flange, and the short and fairly stiff rawhide bundles as a discontinuous vertical web. Such a beam has a good strength-to-weight ratio, but its pros and cons are not simple to analyze. This unique example should be further investigated, applying numerical, computerized engineering models (Finite Element Method). A third possible function for the axle thongs is to assure containment of the flat pole tail in the axle socket. This function could allow a little twisting of the pole tail within the socket (slightly pushing the axle and the rear floor bar further apart), but suppressing that twisting in a flexible, shock-absorbing fashion; this would enhance the soft response of the chariot during bumpy rides. This complex concept also needs further study and critical assessment.

Some of the chariot springs can be easily demonstrated with the aid of small flexible models, such as the bending of the D-frame in figure 6, or the more complete model in figure 9, where the pole can be bent and twisted, in addition to pulling on the D-frame. It is best to make such models highly flexible, so that the deformations are exaggerated and visible; this is in contrast to the typical com-

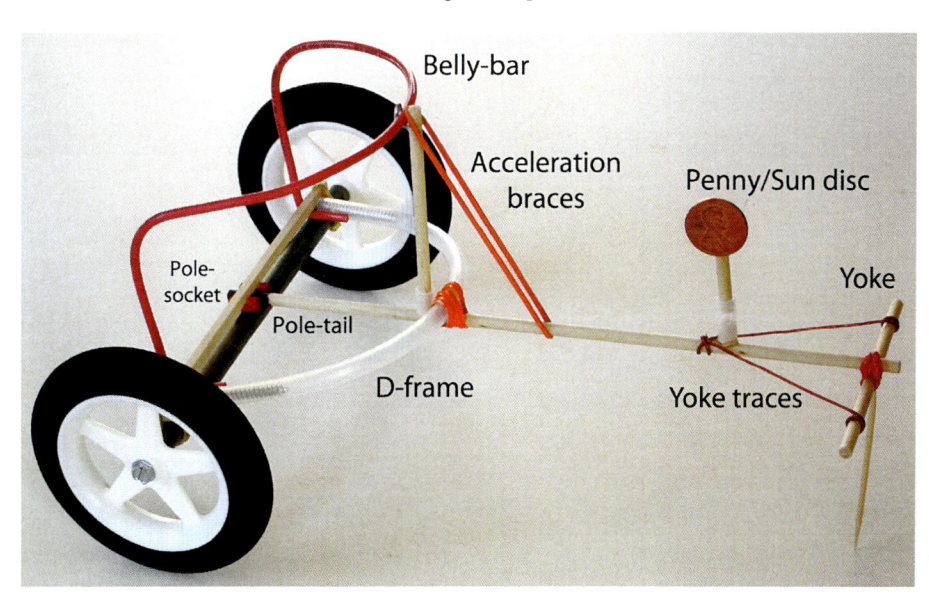

Figure 9. Hand-size flexible model of a Tutankhamun-chariot. B.I. Sandor (2011).

mercial chariot models made of hard plastic that are too stiff for such demonstrations.

On the whole, the suspension systems of a safe and minimally comfortable real chariot must have some purposely designed flexible components, such as the pole and the D-frame, and some of the rawhide-lashed joints are desirably 'squeaky' in their frictional, shock-absorbing behaviors.

Wheels

In contrast to suspension systems, a good wheel must be as rigid as possible, and there is much evidence that the ancients were constantly struggling to satisfy this eternally difficult requirement (the fundamental problems were not alleviated until the advent of pneumatic tires and modern materials).

Perfection in wheels is elusive, as seen in the statue of Jupiter holding a magnificent wheel (figure 10). This wheel is ordinary and familiar to us in its size, proportions, and number of simple spokes; it seems equally ready for a load of grain and a high-speed race in the circus. Indeed, it would be top-notch in a race for multipurpose vehicles. For a thoughtful designer, however, this is not a perfect wheel because it is the result of many difficult compromises; it may fail under a large load of bricks, and while it could be used in a race, it would be unlikely to win against the most sophisticated specialized machines. Several major issues for comprehensive wheel design and analysis are presented in figure 11. It should be noted that other concerns, such as those regarding material quality and environmental factors, may also be relevant.

Some of the conflicting requirements are easy to appreciate, such as the need for a large and strong wheel is contrary to achieving low weight. Others

Tutankhamun-wheel: *Rosetta Wheel*

For deciphering ancient conceptual vehicle designs

Major categories (w/nonlinearities, abstractions, conflicts):

1. **Diameter** should be large for rolling on soft or rough ground.

2. **Weight** should be small for economy (cost of fabrication; horsepower needs), and good performance (acceleration; sustained high speed).

3. **Weight distribution: rotational inertia** should be low for high acceleration.

4. **Spokes: bending and buckling strengths** should be high for safety.

5. **Rim stiffness** should be high to minimize washboard effect and assure vibration tolerance.

6. **Joint integrity** (time- and cycle-dependent) should be high for durability.

Figure 11. Crucial but conflicting requirements for a well-designed wheel. Many difficult compromises must be made, to this day.

Figure 10. Jupiter holding a fine example of a multipurpose wheel; a good transportation wheel, but a little heavy and large for circus racing. Photograph by B.I. Sandor. Courtesy of Musée Calvet, Avignon (Inv. G 136A).

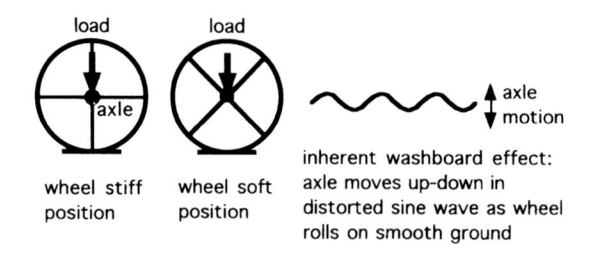

Figure 12. Washboard effect of a non-rigid rim. Diagram by B.I. Sandor.

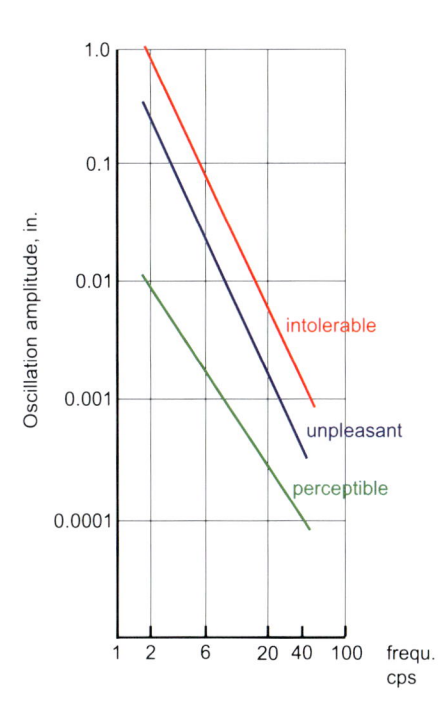

Figure 13. Vibration tolerance as function of oscillation amplitude and frequency. Diagram by B.I. Sandor.

Figure 14. Well-made bronze wheel eliminates washboard effect, with penalties of huge cost, weight and rotational inertia. Côte-St-André bronze-wood wheel of a ritual wagon (solar cult). These wheels were made whole, in the lost-wax casting process. Photograph by B.I. Sandor. Courtesy of Musée Gallo-Romain de Lyon-Fourvière.

are subtle; for example, high-strength spokes must be firmly nested in a massive and rigid hub of adequate length (Sandor, 2012) to resist side loads in cornering, and to prevent the loosening of spoke joints. Such hubs are heavy, with significant rotational inertias. Joint integrity and durability are enhanced by the use of metal tires, but these have large weight and rotational inertias. An unusually difficult design issue is the matter of rim stiffness, as seen in the conceptual diagram of the washboard effect (cyclic vertical motion of the axle caused by the bending of weak rims with not enough spokes), figure 12, and the corresponding human response to vibrations (figure 13).

The author demonstrates the mechanical cause of the washboard effect by using a hand-held flexible model wheel (of appropriately exaggerated rim flexibility) in the NOVA TV documentary Building Pharaoh's Chariot, that originally aired on PBS on February 6, 2013. In a real chariot the rim deflections are not noticeable, but they tend to adversely affect the quality of the ride.

One way to look at this problem is that a flexible rim makes the wheel springy, but this is a very bad spring for a chariot because it generates vertical vibrations even on smooth roads. This is worse if the overall suspension system is not able to sufficiently alleviate the wheel vibrations transmitted to the riders. It is remarkable that even very small oscillation amplitudes are felt by humans, especially in the frequency range typical of chariot wheels running at normal speeds.

Innumerable efforts have been made to solve the washboard problem (Sandor, 2004), none entirely satisfactory. A robust and elegant solution is in the large category of bronze wheels (figure 14), found in chariots and wagons in many countries, over centuries: the Carpathian-Rhône-Rhine-Etruscan wood-metal wheels (Emiliozzi, 1997; Piggott, 1983; Tarr, 1969). The sturdy metallic wheels served the needs for prestige, strength and durability, with no washboard effect, but at great penalties in cost, weight and rotational inertia.

Inevitably, an intermediate solution was found in eliminating most of the metal except the crucial iron tires and nave bands (Sandor, 2012). Excellent examples are the Celtic chariots (Brown *et al.*, 2007). The proportions of the Celtic wooden wheels with iron tires and nave bands are now well-established as illustrated in figures 15 and 16.

Figure 15. Celtic wheel's iron tire (5 kg) and nave band, with soil impressions of wood, from Garton Station (BM Nos. 1985 03-05 15 [tire], and 1985 03-05 19 [nave band]). Photograph by B.I. Sandor. Courtesy of the British Museum, London.

The iron in these wheels is useful with the tire consolidating the large number of spokes (diameter similar to the Tutankhamun-wheel's size), reducing wear on the rim and increasing its stiffness, and the nave bands protecting the hub against splitting. There is still a substantial disadvantage with the amount of metal (about 5 kg each tire) that adds to the total vehicle weight and high rotational inertia of the wheels. In other words, the Celtic example cannot be a good racing wheel, which of course was not the intended function of that vehicle.

The entire proportions of a fine Roman racing chariot are known from a small bronze model found in the Tiber (figure 17), now in the British Museum, London. It is instructive to compare this to those of the Tutankhamun-chariot (figure 18). This permits one to notice several advantages of this Roman vehicle in racing, such as the ability to accelerate with small wheels at high rates and to maneuver in chaotic situations by making the chariot as short and narrow as possible, retaining sufficient stability (Sandor, 2012). In other words, optimum design of wheels for high acceleration (from the starting gate and after every turn) and agility by having small overall size on crowded race tracks is necessary for winning races.

Two important and related issues require thoughtful consideration: wheel diameter and iron tires. Clearly, iron tires are potentially useful for wheels of any size, but they are not absolutely necessary for all situations. For example, many Egyptian wheels had wooden tires, and some had leather tires (figures 19 & 21). Leather is sufficient for wheel consolidation, and has the advantages of being light weight and easily applied; its main disadvantage is

Figure 16. Wetwang chariot reconstruction. © The Trustees of the British Museum, London.

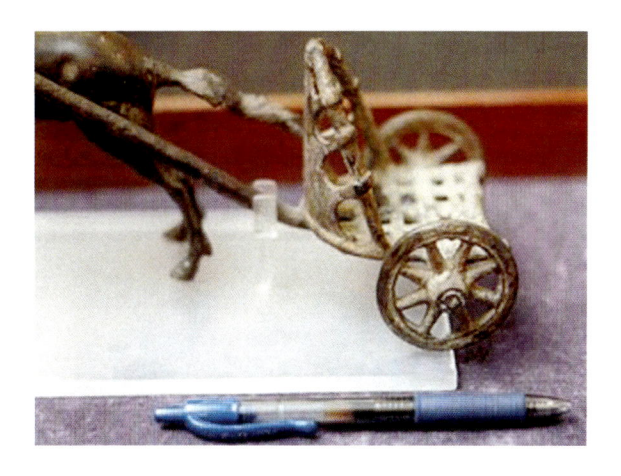

Figure 17. Bronze model of a Roman racing chariot. (BM GR 1894.10-30.1, Bronze 2694). Photograph by B.I. Sandor. Courtesy of the British Museum, London.

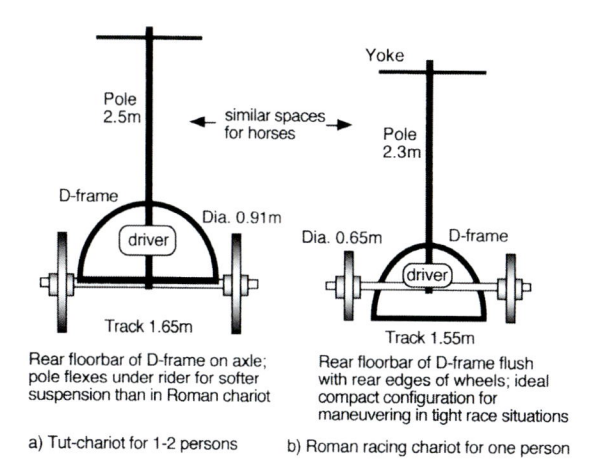

Figure 18. Comparison of Tutankhamun-chariots with Roman racing chariots. Diagram by B.I. Sandor.

lack of durability in comparison with iron. Leather tires may last up to a few tens of kilometers on non-abrasive ground (Robert Hurford, Personal Communication 2012). Anecdotally, some American pioneer wagons had leather tires, which means that they were still used in the 19th century.

The requirement for high acceleration is most important in racing, and this is where wheel size and shape optimization are critical. In fact, the greatest fundamental advantage of a spoked wheel was the greatly reduced mass and corresponding linear inertia, and the reduced rotational inertia. The latter is an abstract but important physical concept with a minor mathematical complexity. Minimizing rotational inertia is not important for a peasant cart or a stage coach, the only vehicles that Isaac Newton could see,

Figure 19. Leather tire on Tutankhamun chariot A5. Note the flat pole tail on the axle at upper right. Photograph by R. Hurford. Courtesy of the Ministry of State for Antiquities/National Military Museum, Cairo.

Figure 20. Shape-optimized wheel of a model of Roman racing chariot (BM GR 1894.10-30.1, Bronze 2694). Photograph by B.I. Sandor. Courtesy of the British Museum, London.

heaviness') as stated by Sandor (1987: 384): "For an infinitesimal mass element, its rotational inertia with respect to the axis of rotation is defined as the mass times the square of its nearest distance to that axis. For a rigid body, its rotational inertia is the summation of all of its elemental inertias".

Of course, Newton would have understood both the nonlinearity of the concept and the simple mathematical formulation instantly, if somebody had told him, or if he had to analyze a variety of fast-accelerating bodies. Remarkably, some ancient engineers understood, not the precise formula, but the facts that there is a rotational inertia, and that material far out on a wheel has a much greater effect on wheel accelerations than the same amount of material closer to the axis. Thus, a wheel was useful with just four thin spokes and a thin rim; more spokes were added later to reduce the washboard effect, incurring extra mass. Wheels with large rotational inertias (with much metal, large diameter, and many spokes) are shown in figures 14-16. Excellent examples of ancient wheels with reasonably minimized rotational inertias are seen in figures 19-21. Of these, the wheel of Tutankhamun-chariot A5 and the wheel from the Yuya-Tjuiu chariot in the Egyptian Museum in Cairo (JE 51188; Lit-

which is the reason he missed out on defining it (this was done in the 1730's by Leonhard Euler, a Swiss mathematician). This is crucial for racing wheels. To understand ancient wheels (or, say, bicycle wheels), it is necessary to have an appreciation of this special kind of inertia (which some ancient engineers might have called 'rotational

Figure 21. Three-layer leather tire on small wheel of Yuya-Tjuiu chariot in the Egyptian Museum, Cairo, similar in diameter and low rotational inertia to the Tiber wheel, figure 20. Photograph by B.I. Sandor. Courtesy of the Ministry of State for Antiquities/Egyptian Museum Authorities.

tauer & Crouwel, 1985) are good because of their leather tires, which provide sufficient consolidation of components at very low total mass, adequate for short runs. The Tiber wheel is superb because of its small size and excellent mass distribution with shape-optimization; the tapered spokes are needed for resistance to side loads. It is possible that extremely thin iron tires of small diameter were occasionally used in Roman racing chariots, as part of the evolution of wheel making.

Yuya-Tjuiu Chariot as a Racer

Considering the eight figures of 14-21, an interesting result emerges: the strong possibility that the Yuya-Tjuiu chariot was a representative of the earliest dedicated racing chariot, or a personalized, gilded version of such a vehicle. This finding is based on the fundamental concept that a wheel's diameter and stability factor (track width/diameter) define two essential qualities of a racing machine, from chariots to cars, as stated in figure 22.

It is true that all of Tutankhamun's chariots could be considered good for racing, better than the much later Celtic chariots (*cf.* figure 1). However, the diagram of figure 22 shows that the Yuya-Tjuiu chariot, regardless of what animals were used to pull it, is much closer in wheel design features to the fully optimized, dedicated Roman racing machines, than to the rest of the Tutankhamun-chariots. In addition to the two main factors for racing

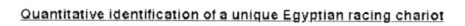

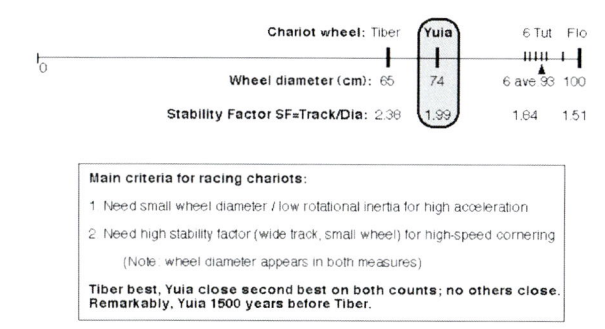

Figure 22. Geometry-based arguments for Yuya-Tjuiu chariot being a fine racing machine, technically in the same class as the Tiber model. 'Flo' represents the Florence chariot. Diagram by B.I. Sandor.

(figure 22), it is apparent that the Yuya-Tjuiu wheels have very low rotational inertias (having a light rim, six short and thin spokes, and no structural metal), perhaps even lower inertias than those of the top-notch Roman racers.

The arguments for the Yuya-Tjuiu racer can be taken further to elucidate the presence or absence of iron tires in Roman racing chariots. According to the theory, iron tires are good for making a strong and durable wheel, but not necessarily good enough to win a race against chariots with no iron (Sandor, 2012). This theory is supported by evidence gleaned from the Lyon circus mosaic (figures 23 & 24) in the Musée Gallo-Romain de Lyon-Fourvière.

It is clear from this mosaic that its creator understood all aspects of circus racing, and that the

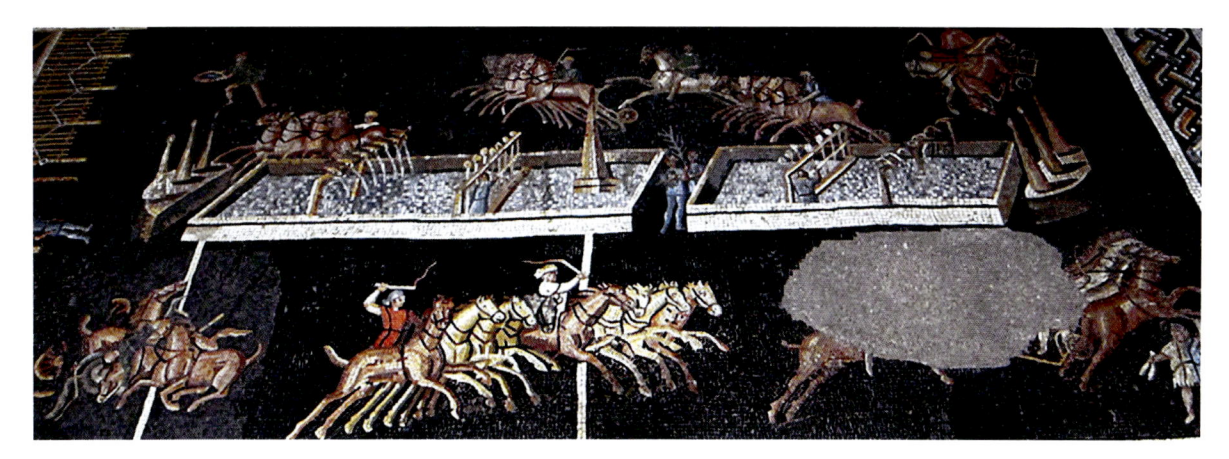

Figure 23. Lyon mosaic of a Roman racing event. Sparsor (water boy) in upper left, at an optimum position for him. Two crashes in progress: upper right, coming out of turn; lower left, coming out of turn; both in the most likely, theoretically predictable, places for a wheel to disintegrate. Photograph by B.I. Sandor. Courtesy of the Musée Gallo-Romain de Lyon-Fourvière.

meticulous details of the image are realistic. Thus, it is fair to say that (re: figures 23 & 24 – in the absence of such a highly regarded, significant component as an iron tire) there was no iron tire on this particular failed wheel (figure 24). This was a risk taken by the racing team, fully aware of the dangers of the low structural integrity of wheels made without iron tires, but hoping to win the race on fine wheels aimed to achieve high acceleration.

CONCLUSION

In summary, the inner dynamics of chariots is a complex subject that has two major categories: suspension systems and rotational inertias. A well-designed suspension system for the safety and comfort of the riders consists of springs (for a chariot, mainly the pole in bending and torsion, and the D-shaped front floor bar in bending and warping), and shock absorbers/dampers in rawhide or leather bindings. To minimize rotational inertia (needed for high acceleration), a wheel should have as little mass far from its axis as possible – a very difficult requirement because of the washboard effect that occurs with wheels with thin rims. A massive hub, and spokes tapered from the hub, however, are necessary to resist side loads in cornering. These basic requirements for a racing machine are best exemplified in the Tiber model and the Yuya-Tjuiu wheels. Thus, iron tires were probably mostly avoided in Roman racing as evidenced by the Lyon mosaic, while rawhide tires were possibly employed sometimes to consolidate the wheels.

CITED LITERATURE

Brown, F., C. Howard-Davis, M. Brennand, A. Boyle, T. Evans, S. O'Connor, A. Spence, R. Heawood & A. Lupton. 2008. The Archaeology of the A1 (M). – Oxford, Oxbow Books.

Emiliozzi, A.E. 1997. Carri da guerra e principi Etruschi. – Rome, Bretschneider.

Littauer, M.A. & J.H. Crouwel. 1985. Chariots and Related Equipment from the Tomb of Tutankhamun. – Oxford, Griffith Institute.

Piggott, S. 1983. The Earliest Wheeled Transport. – Ithaca, NY, Cornell University Press.

Sandor, B.I. 1978. Strength of Materials. – Englewood Cliffs, NJ, Prentice-Hall.

Sandor, B.I. 1987 [1983]. Engineering Mechanics. Statics and Dynamics. – Englewood Cliffs, NJ, Prentice-Hall.

Sandor, B.I. 2004. The Rise and Decline of the Tutankhamun-Class Chariot. – Oxford Journal of Archaeology 23, 2: 153-175.

Sandor, B.I. 2012. The Genesis and Performance Characteristics of Roman Chariots. – Journal of Roman Archaeology 25: 475-485.

Tarr, L. 1969. The History of the Carriage. – New York, Arco Publishing Co.

Figure 24. Wheel fragments at crash site in lower left of the Lyon circus mosaic. The remaining pieces are visible outside this image area (further off from the upper right). No iron tire is seen, in line with the theory that the best racing chariots had no metal components in order to have the lowest possible total weight and rotational inertia, at the risk of catastrophic fracture of the wheel. Photograph by B.I. Sandor. Courtesy of Musée Gallo-Romain de Lyon-Fourvière.

AN ALTERNATIVE THEORY FOR 'BIT-WEAR' FOUND ON THE LOWER SECOND PREMOLAR OF THE BUHEN HORSE

Yukiko Sasada

INTRODUCTION

The Buhen horse, which was found by Emery in 1958, had a significant impact on Egyptology because it is believed to be the earliest remains of a domesticated horse found in an ancient Egyptian site (Raulwing & Clutton-Brock, 2009: 6). The reason that it was believed that the Buhen horse was domesticated was because of the presence of apparent 'bit-wear' on the lower second premolars of the horse's skull (figure 1), which according to Raulwing & Clutton-Block (2009: 16-18, 24-32) provided evidence of domestication.

The skeletal remains of the Buhen horse is believed to date to Middle Kingdom Egypt (2066-1650 BC), around 1675 BC, and if authenticated by

Figure 1. The Buhen horse with wear on the lower second premolar. © Natural History Museum, London.

C14 dating, it would have placed the existence of a domesticated horse in Egypt significantly earlier than the Second Intermediate Period (1650-1549 BC), the times during which scholars had previously believed that domesticated horses had been introduced into Egypt (Clutton-Brock, 1992: 84). Unfortunately, however, C14 dating was not conclusive, and therefore the age of the Buhen horse remains speculative. Nevertheless, based on stratigraphic data, Emery (1965: 107) had suggested that the horse died in 1675 BC when the Buhen fortress was stormed. This date is still a matter of ongoing discussion since it was first suggested by Emery in 1959 (Raulwing & Clutton-Brock, 2009: 14-16, 22-24).

The question of whether or not a domesticated horse existed in 1675 BC is not the focus of this paper, although it is possible that the Buhen horse was domesticated based on the simple fact that the animal was found within the ramparts of the Buhen fortress. Rather, the question this paper addresses is whether it is reasonable and plausible to use the existence of apparent 'bit-wear' on the lower second premolars as credible evidence of domestication of equids in Egypt. We know that bits were already in use in the Near East in 1675 BC, based on Oren's discovery of the remains of a donkey with a metal bit in Tel-Haror that was dated between 1750 BC to 1650 BC (Littauer & Crouwel, 2001: 329, Oren, 1997: 265). The question is whether a bit can indeed cause wear on the lower second premolars such as was seen in the case of the Buhen horse, and if not, what alternative causes may have been responsible for the wear.

BIT-WEAR

The theory of a bit causing wear on the premolars was first suggested by Bökönyi (1968: 50) while working on the remains of horses found in an Iron Age site in Magdalenska gora in Slovenia. He found two horses with wear on the lower second premolars and suggested that this was caused by a) pulling of reins and a bit being pressed against the teeth and b) the horses chewing on the bit (*Ibidem*: 50). Since then, there have been several studies to investigate presence of bit-wear in domesticated horses and several scholars, including Clutton-Brock, have applied this theory to horses found in other archaeological sites. Unfortunately, the definition of bit-wear is not clearly defined in the literature, and two different theories have emerged.

The first theory was put forward by Brown & Anthony (1991; revised in 1998) based on comparing modern domesticated horses with feral ones. They believed that the bit-wear identified in the domesticated horses that they studied was caused by chewing on the bit and therefore, they focused their studies on the wear found on the occlusal surface of the lower second premolar teeth. The main criteria they used to identify bit-wear were significant occlusal wear and/or a significant bevel measurement. In a later study by Bendrey (2007; 2011), however, this theory was challenged. Bendrey believed that the bit was unlikely to cause occlusal wear as horses rarely chewed on the bit. Instead, he came up with an alternative theory that the bit could come into contact with the anterior edge of the lower second premolars, causing recognizable changes to the enamel surface of the tooth that could be used as evidence of bit-wear.

In this paper, both of these theories are challenged and the concept of bit-wear is revisited by asking two fundamental questions:

1) Can a bit really cause wear on the lower second premolars as suggested;
2) Does it occur in every horse which is bitted?

In order to understand the concept of bit-wear, a basic understanding of the following is crucial: the anatomy of the horse's mouth; how a bit is designed and fitted into the mouth; and how a rider or driver (in the case of a chariot) uses it to control the horse. A horse's teeth are divided into two sections: incisors in the front and premolars and molars in the back (figure 2). There are three premolars and three molars in each molar arcade and collectively they are called the 'cheek teeth'. The incisors are used for cutting grass during grazing, while the cheek teeth are used for mastication of grass and continually wear down through the horse's life, exposing the reserve crown.

Some scholars in the past, like Bökönyi (1968), have confused the first cheek tooth with the first premolar. The first premolar is in fact a residual tooth that is often not present, or if present, is small

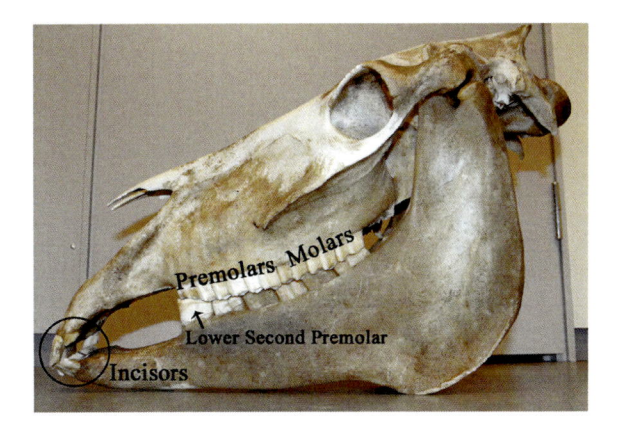

Figure 2. Anatomy of the equine mouth demonstrating the upper and lower molar arcades. Photograph by Y. Sasada.

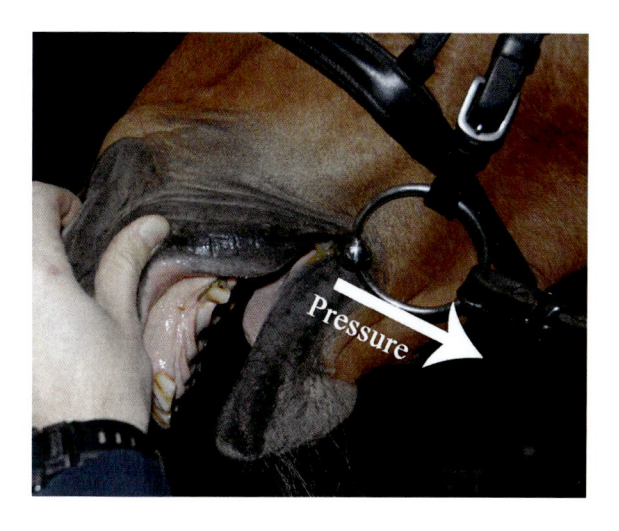

Figure 3. Downward pressure of a correctly placed bit when under tension from the reins. Photograph by Y. Sasada.

and has no function in mastication. It is in fact the second premolar that is the first cheek tooth in each molar arcade and is the tooth that is affected by bit-wear. Bits work by exerting pressure and leverage inside the horse's mouth (figure 3). The idea is that, by moving away from the discomfort of the pressing bit, the horse moves in the direction the rider or driver wants to go. The bit itself consists of a mouthpiece and rings or shanks that attach the bit to the bridle and reins. Now, bits are usually composed of metal, although the first bits were probably made of organic materials such as leather, cord or wood (Drews, 2004: 73-75). There is evidence of metal bits being used in the Near East is as early as the 17th century BC, although it could have been used ever earlier (Littauer & Crouwel, 2001: 329-336).

The bridle has the role of positioning the bit in the correct position in the mouth and holding it in place. The reins are then attached to the rings or shanks of the bit so that the rider or driver can communicate with the horse. When a bridle is correctly fitted, the reins are loose and are only tensioned to place pressure and leverage on the mouth when used for communication. The correctly fitted bit should be set in the interdental space and the bit should rest on the tongue and the bars on either side of the mouth. Depending upon the type of bit used, pressure is then placed on the tongue, the bars and the roof of the mouth to communicate or control the horse. As seen in figure 4, a correctly positioned bit lies between the incisors and cheek teeth and is nowhere near the second premolars.

In a living horse, the horse's lips are located in front of the second premolars. A correctly fitted bit should thus sit just behind the edge of the lips in the interdental space, and create one or two wrinkles at the edge of the lip (figure 5). When the bridle has been fitted too tightly, then the lip is being pulled backwards due to the tension of the bit, making the horse uncomfortable (figure 6). Due to the existence of the tongue, it is highly unlikely that the bit will hit the premolars when used correctly, unless the bit is poorly fitted, in which case the horse is able to move the bit backward with his tongue so that it comes into contact with the cheek teeth. This may cause enamel wear on the anterior edge of the second premolars as Bendrey (2011: 2989) has suggested; and in some cases, the horse may even chew on the bit, causing wear on the occlusal surface of the second premolars as Brown & Anthony have suggested. This is very rare, however, and in most cases when people talk about a horse 'grabbing the bit in its teeth' they actually mean that the horse tenses its lips and mouth against the bit to ignore the rider's commands, rather than actually getting the bit between their molars.

X-rays of a horse's head with a bit fitted correctly in the mouth illustrates this clearly. Figure 7 and 8 show the position of two different types of bits that have been properly fitted when the head is in a normal position while figure 9 depicts a horse with the head extended with the rein under tension. In either position, the bit is nowhere near the second

Figure 4. A correctly fitted bit with molar teeth superimposed. Photograph by Y. Sasada.

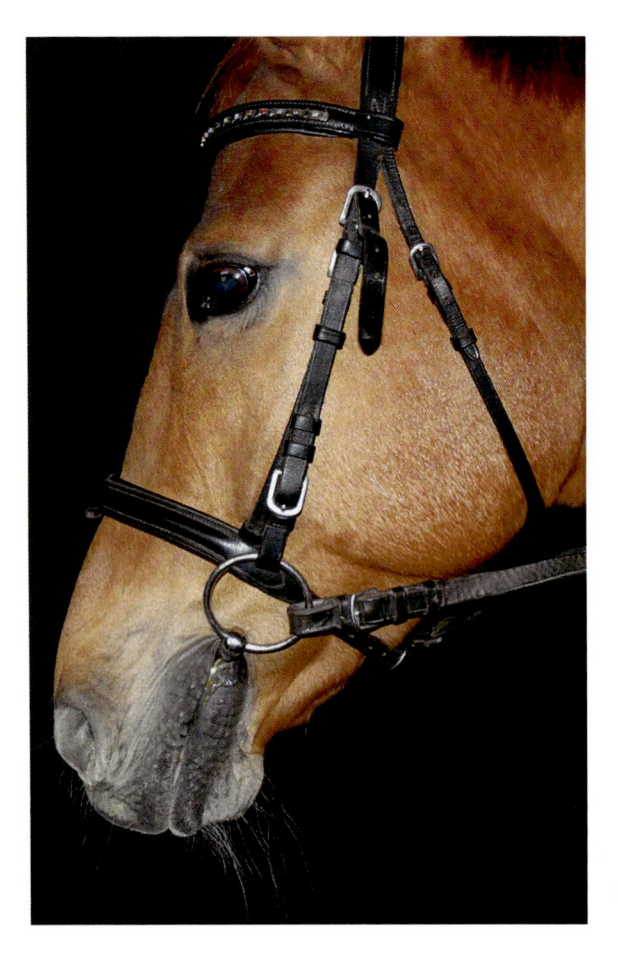

Figure 6. A bridle fitted too tightly. Photograph by Y. Sasada.

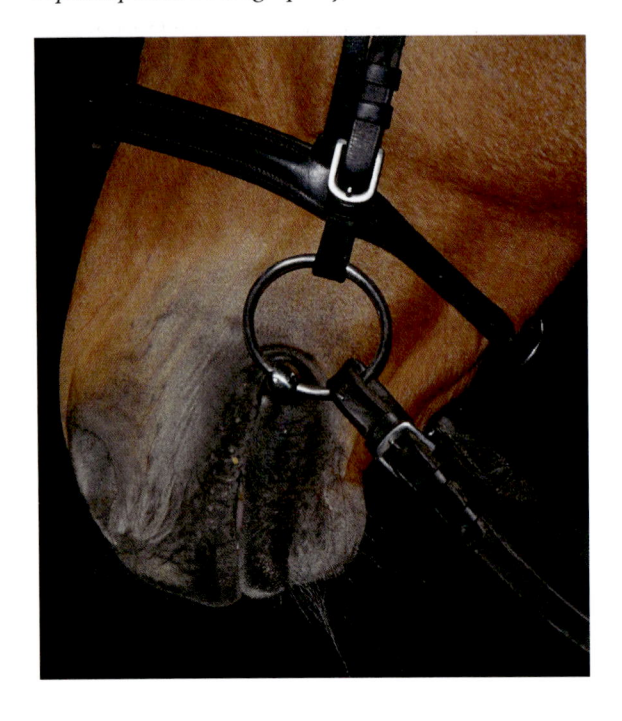

Figure 5. A correctly fitted bit. Photograph by Y. Sasada.

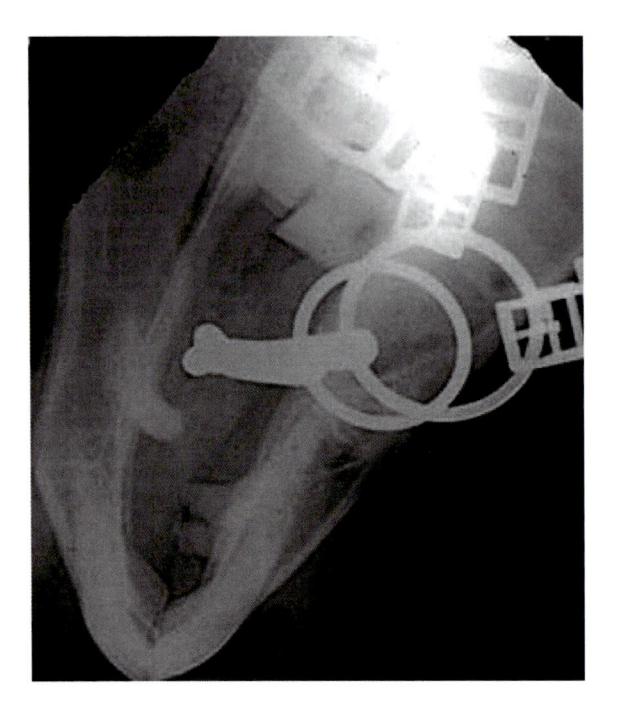

Figure 7. Lateral radiograph of the head of horse wearing a snaffle bit under rein pressure (broken mouthpiece). Photograph by D.G. Bennett.

premolars, but rather, it is placing pressure on the tongue and bars as it is designed to do.

More commonly, an improperly fitted bit or poor riding technique causes injuries to the tongue and other soft tissues of the mouth rather than second premolars. This is because the rider imparts a

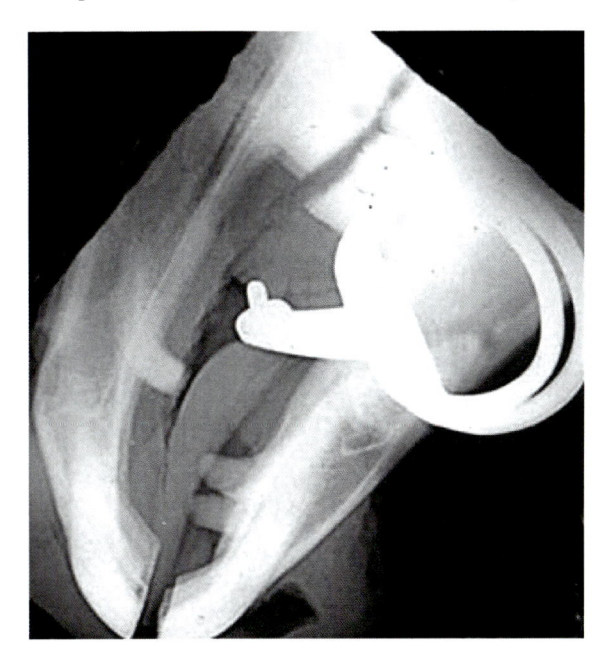

Figure 8. Lateral radiograph of the head of a horse wearing a snaffle bit under rein pressure (linked mouthpiece). Photograph by D.G. Bennett.

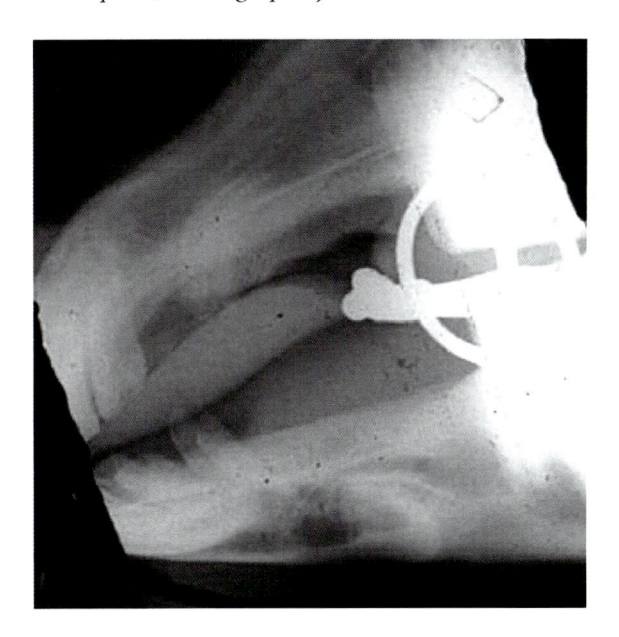

Figure 9. Lateral radiograph of the head of a horse a wearing snaffle bit under rein pressure (broken mouthpiece, nose extended). Photograph by D.G. Bennett.

downward force on the mouth when the reins are pulled rather than a backward force onto the second premolars. This downward force causes trauma to the tongue and soft tissues of the interdental space (figure 10) and in some severe cases, may even cause damage to the bone. It thus stands to reason that ancient Egyptians would have rapidly modified the design of their bits and bridle systems to prevent such injuries occurring, as an improperly fitted bit would have prevented the horse from performing the tasks that they were asked to do, and in the case of war, this could well have proved fatal to both horse and rider.

Many horsemen (and scholars) believe that when the bit is pulled by placing tension on the reins, it hits the lower second premolars, causing damage to the teeth. Because of this concern, horsemen will often have their horses 'bit seated'. Bit seating is an old term used to describe the rounding of the second premolars on the upper and lower arcades, resulting in a small groove in the front of the teeth (figure 11). It is thought by advocates of bit seating that the bit will actually rest in this area and prevent damage to the teeth. However, if the bit is resting in a bit seat, the horse's bridle is not fitted properly. What the bit seat is actually intended to do is prevent the bit pinching the delicate soft tissues of the mouth against the sharp enamel edges of the second premolars, thus preventing injuries and providing more comfort to the horse.

As mentioned earlier, Brown & Anthony (1998) believe that bit-wear is caused by a horse chewing the bit and therefore, they focused on the wear

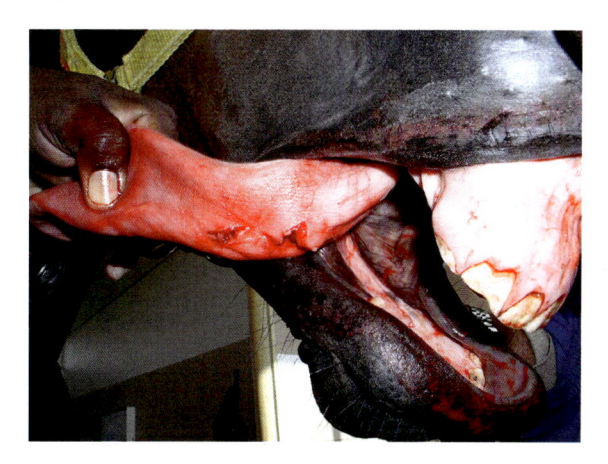

Figure 10. Trauma to the tongue caused by a bit. Photograph by M. Hewetson.

found on the occlusal surface of the teeth in their study. They took casts of the lower second premolar of 52 modern domestic horses and 20 modern feral horses and studied them for evidence of bit-wear. The criteria they (*Ibidem*: 340) used to identify bit-wear in their study population were "(1) significant "a" wear, and/or (2) a significant bevel measurement" to identify bit-wear on a horse older than three years old. Significant 'a' wear was defined by a loss of 50% or more of the occlusal enamel of the first cusp and a significant bevel measurement was defined as 3.15 mm or more. According to their study, over 90% of the frequently bitted modern horses exhibited evidence of bit-wear and the one horse which did not show any wear was dismissed as "she simply did not chew the bit" (Brown & Anthony, 1998: 336).

In a later paper, however, Bendrey (2007: 1037) challenged these results and the criteria that Brown & Anthony had used to identify bit-wear. Bendrey argued that significant occlusal wear and bevel measurements can also be caused by dental hooks on the upper premolars. This is a condition in which the upper and lower teeth are not aligned and the anterior portion of the second premolars are not in wear, causing overgrowths or 'hooks' which then cause corresponding wear on the lower second premolars similar to those which had been reported by Brown & Anthony as evidence of bit-wear (figure 12). They had not looked at the upper premolars in their study and thus Bendrey argued that the uneven wear observed on the lower second premolars in their study could have been due to dental hooks and not bit-wear as they had suggested. Brown & Anthony (1998: 332) comment that "the upper premolars were not studied partly because it proved impossible to make casts of the upper teeth on live animals unless they were fully sedated and lying down". Without a study of the upper premolars, however, it would be incorrect to accept their definition of what constitutes bit-wear, as it is impossible to rule out dental hooks as cause of the wear, particularly when considering that in a bad case of dental hooks, the bevel measurement can easily be larger than 3.15 mm.

Bendrey, on the other hand, has his own theory as to what constitutes bit-wear. He did not believe that chewing of the bit could cause wear but rather, he (2011: 2989) has suggested that during the use of a bit, "the bit can come into contact with the anterior edge of the lower second premolars and can cause recognisable changes to the enamel and dentine of the tooth". Therefore, he states, that instead of the bevel measurement, the criteria for evidence of bit-wear should include a height of enamel exposure in excess of 5 mm; anterior exposure greater than any exposure on the lingual or buccal side of the tooth; and the form of exposure should be an approximately parallel-sided band (Bendrey, 2007: 1040).

Bendrey worked on equid skeletons with known life histories held at various museums. He studied 32 working horses and 28 non-working horses. Out of the 28 non-working horses, three had evidence of bit-wear and were considered false positives. In the group of 32 working horses, however, only 18 (56%) had evidence of enamel or dentine wear suggestive

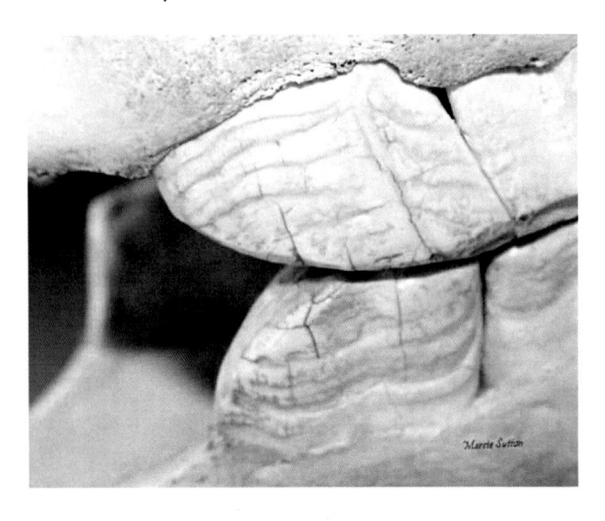

Figure 11. Bit-seat. Photograph by M. Sutton.

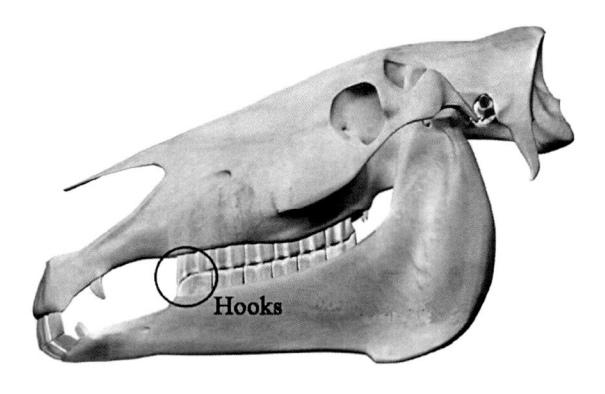

Figure 12. Hooks on anterior edge of the second premolars. Courtesy of Glacier Veterinary Service, LLC.

of bitting (Bendrey, 2007: 1038-1044). Bendrey explained the high percentage of false negatives in his study by the fact that the older horses in the study had insufficient height in their lower premolars for accurate measurements of height of enamel/dentine exposure (*Ibidem*:1042).

POSSIBLE ALTERNATIVE CAUSES OF THE WEAR

After studying the theories relating to bit-wear that have been put forward by Brown & Anthony, and later by Bendrey, it has become evident that they are both flawed due to the fact that they did not attempt to include the upper and lower set of premolars when formulating their theory. Any study that attempts to characterize bit-wear in horses should include a close study of both the upper and lower premolars, as the bit is just as likely to strike the upper premolar as it is the lower premolar. Furthermore, examination of the upper and lower premolars in the same horse will enable us to differentiate dental problems such as dental hooks and wave mouths (a wave-like pattern of wear, see below) from occlusal wear caused by biting.

Consequently, in order to investigate this problem, the author will study X-rays of 100 horses' heads to characterize bit-wear and determine just how prevalent this problem is. The population of horses for this study will be diverse due to the fact that the X-rays used will be those taken at equine veterinary hospitals for dental examinations. For a dental examination, X-rays will be taken from both the left and right sides of the horse and by studying them, the author will be able to identify whether the horse has wear on the second premolars and also suggest possible causes for the wear.

In conclusion, if it was not the bit that caused the abnormal wear on the lower second premolar of the Buhen horse, what then could have caused it? When studying the images of the Buhen horse, focus has always been placed on the lower second premolars, rather than commenting on the entire set of molars as a functional unit. Considering the age of the Buhen horse at the time of its death, 19 years old, and the wave-like appearance of the molar arcades, old age should be considered as an alternative cause for the apparent wear on the lower second premolars (figure 13). Therefore, an alternative theory is that it was caused by wave mouth that is often associated with old age. It is well-described in the veterinary literature that some horses may develop an abnormal pattern of wear on their molars. It can been seen in figure 14 that in the case of a wave mouth, both the upper and lower cheek tooth arcades are worn to form a wave like pattern (Baker & Easley, 2005: 113, 240-241, 346). This may cause abnormal occlusal wear on the lower second premolar, giving the appearance of bit-wear.

There is also a possibility that the tooth was damaged since the entire frontal region of the skull was badly crushed and was reconstructed in 1959 (Clutton-Brock, 1974: 90). Further detailed studies on the skull will be necessary to determine this but unfortunately no one has been able to examine the skull since it was returned to the authorities of Sudan in 1976 (the present author is currently in contact with

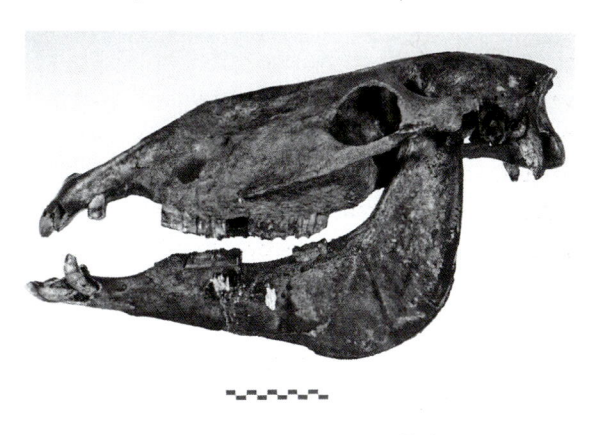

Figure 13. The skull of the Buhen horse. © Natural History Museum, London.

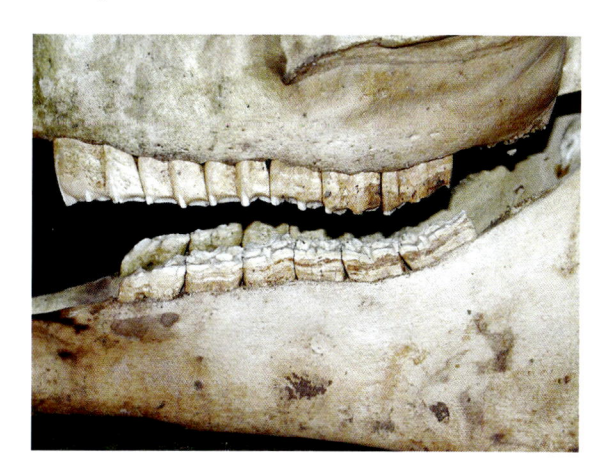

Figure 14. Wave mouth. Courtesy of Equine Dental Services.

the curator at the Sudan National Museum in order to locate the Buhen horse for further examination).

It is important when one is studying equine teeth that one should always look at them as a set rather than focusing only on one part. It is definitely possible that a bit causes wear on the second lower premolar teeth of horses, but in order to determine this conclusively, one should study both the upper and lower second premolars to exclude matching patterns of wear which could suggest other dental problems.

CITED LITERATURE

Anthony, D. W. & D. Brown. 1991. The Origins of Horseback Riding. – Antiquity 65: 22-38.

Baker, G. J. & J. Easley. Ed. 2005. Equine Dentistry 2nd Edition. - Edinburgh, Elsevier Saunders.

Bendrey, R. 2007. New Methods for the Identification of Evidence for Bitting on Horse Remains from Archaeological Sites. – Journal of Archaeological Science 34: 1036-1050.

Bendrey, R. 2011. Identification of Metal Residues Associated with Bit-Use on Prehistoric Horse Teeth by Scanning Electron Microscopy with Energy Dispersive X-ray Microanalysis. – Journal of Archaeological Science 38: 2989-2994.

Bökönyi, S. 1968. Mecklenburg Collection. Part I. Data on Iron Age Horses of Central and Eastern Europe. – Bulletin of the American School of Prehistoric Research 25: 3-71.

Brown, D. & D. Anthony. [1991] 1998. Bit Wear, Horseback Riding and the Botai Site in Kazakstan. – Journal of Archaeological Science 25: 331-347.

Clutton-Brock, J. 1992. Horse Power: A History of Horse and Donkey in Human Societies. – London, Natural History Museum Publications.

Drews, R. 2004. Early Riders: The Beginnings of Mounted Warfare in Asia and Europe. – London, Routledge.

Littauer, M.A. & J.H. Crouwel. 2001. The Earliest Evidence for Metal Bridle Bits. – Oxford Journal of Archaeology 20, 4: 329-338.

Oren, E.D. 1997. The "Kingdom of Sharuhen" and the Hyksos Kingdom. In: Oren, E. Ed. The Hyksos. New Historical and Archaeological Perspectives. – Philadelphia, The University Museum: 253-283.

Raulwing, P. & J. Clutton-Brock. 2009. The Buhen Horse. Fifty Years after Its Discovery (1958-2008). – Journal of Egyptian History 2: 1-106.

EGYPTIAN CHARIOTS: DEPARTING FOR WAR

Anthony Spalinger

INTRODUCTION

In a previous discussion attempts were made to employ certain New Kingdom (1549-1069 BC) temple scenes in order to establish some type of paradigmatic arrangement concerning their use within the forward march and ensuing battles of pharaoh (Spalinger, No Date). At that time the Qadesh conflict of Ramesses II (1279-1212 BC) and Muwatallis (1295-1272 BC) was the main interest. Now, however, a return to the tactical disposition of the elite chariotry at the point of departing for a campaign and during the march to battle is perused. The resulting face-to-face melee of war will be avoided and the complex issue of pictorial trustworthiness can be kept aside for most of the discussion even though that issue, a thorny one, shall not be ignored (Spalinger, 2011). Fortunately, the detailed study of Heagren (2010) is available now, whose opening chapter on the logistics of war, 'Battlefield Tactics', will provide the interested reader with more than sufficient information that relates to this discussion.

In the well-known Late Egyptian Story of The Doomed Prince the author required certain key elements of presentation when he drew up his hero (Heagren, 2010: 83-86; Liverani, 2004). Certain it is that the characteristics of all of the protagonists in this narrative, from low to high, were chosen from a rather limited template. The obvious cases of internal characterization were not included, and literary scholars have known the reasons for this for many years owing to the lack of internal charactizeration.

Yet, what is given to us needs to be reviewed once more, if only because the account, set in an earlier period of time than its redaction, indicates the desired requirements of certain New Kingdom warriors as well as their presence abroad in Asia. To the knowledge of the present author the only detailed approach that comes to the heart of the matter is that of Liverani and even there he was interested in the literary aspects, call them topoi, that are present in the statue record of king Idrimi (1500 BC; Dietrich & Loretz, 1981; Greenstein & Marcus, 1976; Liverani, 2004; Oller, 1989 – though missing the point of literary and folktale analysis). Even here, however, a mere contrastive analysis bore fruit, thus indicating that perhaps – and that word will have to be discarded at a later date – it is worthwhile to retrace the Egyptian concept of the elite chariot warrior, the *snni*, for yet another time in order to elucidate further his role in the proceedings.

The hidden role of the prince is of less interest because this key theme is connected with the young man's eventual success in Mitanni despite all of the odds being against him (Spalinger, 2007). That is to say, the 'stock' nature of the protagonist includes, actually visually in the hieratic as well as in the account itself, the royal nature of the main actor. But the progression through space and time is not at all parallel to that of an Egyptian monarch's. This is to be expected, as the hieratic story is not an account of war. Moreover, it is only on the battlefield that we meet Pharaoh as a 'true' chariot warrior, at least in the written reports of the New Kingdom. Elsewhere, and referring to the visual representations of campaigns, the king is depicted going to war in a chariot, fighting before the citadel-tell of the enemy, his later departure and return in a chariot. Hence, contrary to the literary accounts, the pictorial corpus stresses more of the mobile nature of the Late Bronze Age's military system.

In the Doomed Prince the young man asks his father to be 'released' from his villa and be allowed to do what he wishes; the future is in the hand of god. Note immediately that he is given a yoked chariot with an assistant as well as war material. Why was this done? Evidently, to satisfy the plot which had to be set up and prepared in stages long before the actual narrative was composed. Equally important, however, is the role of the prince. Disguised, he must nonetheless possess a superior bearing, one that might be challenged at home or abroad but, more significantly, he has to be accepted in his status by all foreigners as reflecting a superior class. The hero is not a diplomat or messenger, a *wpwtiw*. Nor, in fact, does he represent any Egyptian administrator in the New Kingdom, either at home or in Syro-Palestine.

As with Idrimi, the prince is in exile, albeit self-composed and desired. With his hound, the young man lives the life – somehow – of an elite Egyptian warrior of the New Kingdom. His immediate environment is Asia, and the historical setting is in the latter half of the 18th Dynasty (1549-1298 BC). Was the peaceful nature of this era purposely chosen to highlight the protagonist's successful career abroad? Note that unlike the 'standard' cases of royal marriage in Egypt, it is the Egyptian prince who married into the family of the Asiatic ruler and not a princess who came to Egypt in order to become the king's minor queen. Yet at the minimum, it is clear that the prince is traveling as a charioteer, a *snni*, and that his royal status remains hidden. Independent of his false words to the other princes of Syria, the depicted situation reflects the military role of the *snni*, the charioteer *par excellence*, and this aspect fits into the Egyptian military system of the second half of the 18th Dynasty and not into the era of the 19th Dynasty (1298-1187 BC; Gnirs, 1996: 19-31; Lopez, 1969: 10-11; Yoyotte & Schulman, 1964: 59-62, 155). Yet his role was not that high in the armed vehicular sector of the New Kingdom army, and became a synonym for the title "Shield Bearer", *qrʿw*. It is well-known that the research of Yoyotte & Lopez on these military titles stressed the necessity of examining the literary and historical aspects of each Egyptian reference. They specifically separated the Doomed Prince from contemporary Ramesside texts, but even there observed some peculiarities in the famous Qadesh Poem (Yoyotte & Lopez, 1969: 11, referring to the Qadesh Poem, a major literary narrative, P[oem section] 88-89 and 198-199; Kitchen, 1979: 32-33, 63-64).

The prince also has his assistant. As he must have a role in the chariot as well as his servant, surely he is the driver. Yet this conclusion does not seem *not* to fit into the expected three words associated with the chariotry (Yoyotte & Lopez, 1969: 10-11). The term *snni* disappears in the first half of the 19th Dynasty in the context of contemporary non-literary texts. The "Shield Bearer", *qrʿw*, which is a common *terminus technicus* in the later Ramesside Period (1298-1069 BC), is combined with the final term *kḏn*, the latter being reserved, in its most common locus of designation, to the driver of the chariot. Yoyotte & Lopez (1969: 10-12) stressed two sections in the Qadesh Poem where the older term *snni* was synonymous with *qrʿw*. As they pointed out with perfect clarity, because only two men operated an Egyptian chariot, these three terms need better analysis, synchronically as well as diachronically. We must separate parade functions, for example, from activities on a campaign. If on a march, Yoyotte & Lopez (1969: 10-12) concluded that one man drove and the other was the "Shield Bearer". This is a rational and simple method of explaining the two roles of chariot men. But in the course of a battle the division aforementioned between a *kḏn* and a *qrʿw* were not the same as before. In battle, the driving became less important than protecting the archer, which is to say that the role of a *kḏn* was transformed. *Snni* became equivalent to *qrʿw*, but earlier in 18th Dynasty the system of organization was simpler or, better to say, less differentiated.

Here is the development as adumbrated by Yoyotte & Lopez. It best explains the relatively high role that the Doomed Prince possessed if we place him, as this author feels is correct, to the 18th Dynasty:

A) First Phase: *snni* is the basic term, and could be augmented by simple additions such as 'superior', *ḥri* (Gnirs, 1996: 55; Schulman, 1964: 60, 156; Yoyotte & Lopez, 1969: 11).
B) Amarna Period: *kḏn* is introduced; and so by the
C) Ramesside Period (19th Dynasty, first half): there are now the 'drivers', the *kḏn*, as well as the "Shield Bearers" the *qrʿw*. The designation *snni* thus was extinct by the reign of Ramesses II, except in contexts that were mainly literary.
D) Ramesside Period (19th Dynasty, second half-20th Dynasty): *qrʿw* is the ordinary and lower title associated with the chariot warriors.

The Doomed Prince's dog may be seen as a possible war topos, or at least reflecting power and aggressive behavior, and its image we find beautifully recorded at Beit el-Wali where the young Ramesses II is ready to dispatch his Libyan enemy with the assistance of his dog, Anath is a Defender (Fischer, 1973; 1977). Naturally, the animal has a role to play in the narrative. Is the canine not one of the threats to the prince? But its presence as a traveling companion for a charioteer can also be linked with warfare, as can hunting.

How the prince reached the king of Naharain is not important to the text. Note, however, that he attains a goal that is not geographically Asia but instead personal. That is to say, the physical location of the princess matters less than the eventual success of the prince, which is immediately followed by tribulations. The kingdoms and empires are private holding of a great leader. The prince will lie to the assorted princes of Khor. The protagonist has no interest or foreknowledge of the daily proceedings in Naharain but is well-treated by the other princes of Syria. The list of activities ends with the prince's assistant, the chariot driver (Gardiner, 1932: 2a, note to 5,1, with regard to Peet's restoration *iw[.tw ḥr dit wʿ n sḏmw m]-sȝ=f*). Note that with the word *sḏmw*, 'subordinate/inferior', or better 'servant', we are certainly not in the Ramesside Period; neither does this descriptive reference indicate any specific role in the handling of horses and chariots. Indeed, there is no other role for him. The narrative simply labels the man as a *šmsw*.

The false statement of the prince that he was the son of a charioteer from Egypt, *ink šri wʿ n snni n pȝ tȝ n Kmt* (Gardiner, 1932: 3.16-4.1, 5.4-5 [lines 5,11 and 6,9]), is not significant to the king of Naharain. Rather, the ensuing lie that our hero gave surrounds his flight from Egypt owing to the presence of a stepmother is significant.

The prince's assistant, his *šmsw* (Gardiner, 1932 e.g.: 2.16 [line 5,1-restored]), fulfills the same role as the high-ranking military cadres of the New Kingdom did. Amunemheb under Thutmose III (1479-1424 BC), for example, adds the common phrase of 'following' (*šmsw*) his lord at his footsteps whether they be in the north or south (Gnirs, 1996: 27, 43, 51-53, 149-150; Habachi, 1957: 99-100; Redford, 1967: 57-58, 60; Yoyotte & Lopez, 1969: 5). He also remains always in the 'following', *šmsw*, of his lord. Yet this detailed biography and other, more abbreviated ones, avoids the personal chariot interest of the key military elite personages. In the earlier case of Ahmose son of Ebana, this soldier was living in a period where the naval orientation of the ships' crews had begun to diminish rapidly, and thus we do not find him reflecting most of the strong attitudes later associated with the king's chariotry. He may have been the 'first' of the army (Sethe 1907a: 7.7) but his war record is laconic with respect to chariots.

The military *šmsww*, as Faulkner (1953: 38-39) first specified, seem not to have been deeply involved in warfare (Yoyotte & Lopez, 1969: 10). Faulkner (1953: 38) translated the term as 'retainer', one that fits well within the history of the Doomed Prince. But it is evident that, at least from the reign of Thutmose III, and to the present author considerably earlier, this designation refers to troops who accompanied their lord in a campaign. Later, following Černý (1947: 57) – who also pointed out that in the Middle Kingdom the *šmsw* were armed 'retainers' – as well as Yoyotte & Lopez (1969: 10), these *šmsw* were also couriers and dispatch riders. It should thus be clear that the prince's retainer had a military role to play even if we do not hear of it. The most recent discussion of the personages associated with the word *šmsw* is by Gnirs (1996: 51-53). She usefully refers to two cases in Ramesses II's Qadesh Poem (P[oem] 33 & 82). The second is extremely useful because it tells us that when the Hittite chariots reached the pharaoh's camp, they hemmed in the king's 'followers'. Hence, this account reinforces our expectations concerning the 'intimate' nature of this personal group of bodyguard warriors. Gnirs regarded them as "members of the royal guard". There are also references to a *ḥri šmsw* to be noted (Gnirs, 1996: 55; Yoyotte & Lopez, 1969: 10). However, even the Sherden, who were given special places in camp and guarded the tent of Ramesses, did not belong to this select group.

Yet a military foreign *šmsw* would have been branded in Egypt when the end of campaigning or military duty took place. In this case does the papyrus account (Papyrus [P.] Anastasi V) assume that these 'assistants' or 'followers' were foreigners captured perhaps abroad, and thus placed in temples for occupation tasks (Caminos, 1954: 230, note on line 7.6; Gardiner, 1937: 59)? The references supplied by Caminos are overwhelming and appear, at first, to suppose that the Anastasi reference implies chariot warriors as well as infantrymen. If so, then does this Ramesside source another piece of underpinning to the conclusion that the 19th and 20th Dynasty military *šmsww* were different than those of the 18th? But the previous data were solely concerned with Egyptian natives who were *šmsw* in the war machine. On the other hand, we can perhaps see more clearly a further reason why the role of these 'followers' was strikingly different in Ramesside Period from earlier times. Namely, carried over or developed from the original designation for close helpers or assistants and without any specific role in warfare, the technical designation now included a personal connection in battle.

BACKGROUND DATA

Consider now two key documents. Thutmose III wholeheartedly demonstrates in his well-produced and cleverly oriented document of the Megiddo campaign an identical absence of continual direct references to chariots in his army (Redford, 2003). But at least, as with Amunemheb's private narration in Theban Tomb [TT] 85 (Sethe, 1907a: 890.10: *šms.n[=i] nb=i r nmtwt=f,* and 892.17 - *iw.i m šmswt=f*), he provides enough information to enable us to view his personal connection to his monarch. In the first account the king received the complaints of his high officials that the chariots will have to be dismantled if the Aruna Pass is taken. At this juncture the well-known account indicates that horse will have to follow horse and so forth. This automatically implies that the chariots, hitherto protecting the wings and the front/rear of the infantry, would not be of any use here. It may in fact have been the case that Thutmose's elite commanders preferred not to get caught in a defile where their superiority of vehicles was not at all important. Indeed, note the equally attentive words of those men: "shall our advance guard be fighting while [the rear guar]d is standing here in Aruna, unable to fight" (Sethe, 1907a: 650.5-7). In other words, the final section of the king's army was thus not ready for military disposition even though Thutmose III had left the pass and was protecting the front portion, presumably setting up his chariot protection once more.

We can also see that, independent of whether we wish to follow Redford (2003: 14-15) in his rather free restorations, that these officials explicitly urged their perspective upon the king insuring that he wait for the entire soldiery to come through the Aruna Pass. But within seven hours or so the Egyptian army had come to the bank of the Qina Brook. By this time it can be assumed that the army was re-established into its traveling dispositions. On the following day (or two days thereafter) Thutmose is described as being at the head of his army and in a chariot.

Here, though, it will be necessary to refer to Thutmose IV's Konosso inscription owing to its somewhat detailed presentation of a royal arm (Beylage, 2002: I 29-37; II 580-588; Helck, 1957: 1545-1548.6). A preliminary study was presented by Yoyotte & Lopez, and this author has retraced their investigations recently (Yoyotte & Lopez, 1969: 5; see also Bryan, 1991: 333-334). The Duties of the Vizier provide an excellent parallel to this narrative concerning how the army progressed south into Nubia (Boorn, 1988: 34 for *m itrti*; Černý translated that passage in his personal copy of Caminos, 1954, as "in two rows"; note that the date for the Duties is late Middle Kingdom). The king, Thutmose IV (1398-1388 BC), must be traveling south in his falcon boat and at the head of his flotilla. But there are corps of soldiers marching on both sides of the Nile. These men, simple footsoldiers and not chariotry elite men, were located at a distance in order to protect the entire army from possible molestation but not destruction. How could a land based Nubian army capture the Egyptian armada? According to the account:

"Proceeding after this by his majesty in order to overthrow the one who reached (= attacked) him in Nubia,
who was/he being powerful in his ship [of gold ?] as Re when he placed himself in the morning barque; and his sails were colored red and green; his teams of horses (= charioteers) were front-line assault troops escorting him, and his infantry (*mšꜥ*) were with him;
the elite infantry (*nḫtw-ꜥ*) were in two rows with recruits (*nfrw*) on his two sides,
and the ship was prepared with his 'followers' (*šmsw*)."

The term *nfrw* probably does not mean 'elite troops' as Schulman wanted (Gnirs, 1996: 10, note 45 and 71; Schulman, 1964: 20-21; Yoyotte & Lopez, 1969: 5), as indicated by the crucial phrases on the statue of Amunhotep Son of Hapu: *ṯs.n=i ḏ3mw nw nb=i* and *ṯs.n=i* [*nfrw*] (Helck, 1958: 1820.19, 1821.9). The first men are better translated 'young'/'youths' whereas the second are now understood to be 'recruits'. Faulkner (1953: 44) understood the *ḏ3mw* as 'troops'.

This progress was by water and still took place within Egyptian territory, and in Upper Egypt. The disposition of the march is revealing although one might question its pace owing to the fact that Thutmose subsequently put to shore at Edfu for the local feast of Tityou – he appears to have had time on his hands. However, in Nubia the monarch crossed over into the eastern desert and traversed the wadis therein. But it is the arrangement of this 18th Dynasty army that is of interest for the present work. Note the arrangement of the account. The elite troops preceded the harder working infantry. In fact, the former are described by means of their horses, an interesting use of metonymy.

A recent use of this text by Manassa (2007: 307) is worthwhile to cite in the same context. When the king, Thutmose IV, was ready to prepare for battle, the account states: "Meanwhile, actively giving his attention to his rearguard, without slackening, without straying (?) upon the mountains without delay, with each of the soldiers in his following". One can see a bit of the Egyptian army 'on the road', and also witness the king's attention to his rearguard.

The duality so well-represented by the bicolored sails of the king's ships is equally represented in the description, one that indicates a left and a right hand side of the advancing troops. Yoyotte & Lopez (1969: 5) noted the direction of interest: from outside inwards. We thus progress from the stalwart guard of chariots to the infantry. The latter are definitely assumed to have been 'covered' by these moving vehicles. Indeed, as it has been noted frequently, the Ramesside depictions of war specifically located the footsoldiers *within* a surrounding guard of charioteers. Indeed, it is not said that the infantry were 'with him'?

Closer yet are the best footsoldiers of the pharaoh. Note that these are not the charioteers. The men 'strong of arm' were placed in two rows with the equally tough *nfrw* right next to the king. Since the latter remains in his chief ship, can it be assumed that these two special infantry corps traversed the two sides of the Nile? Finally, we arrive at the innermost section of the army. Here, the king's 'followers', are mentioned. Note once more the common term *šmsw*, one that must not be misunderstood as a simple or general term Medinet Habu has a very useful passage when the king hunts lions (Edgerton & Wilson, 1936: 40; Kitchen, 1983: 31.11). There, Ramesses is praised by his 'personal guard' (the *šmsw*), as well as others: 'the soldiers (*mšꜥ*) are happy, officials (*srw*) rejoice and the guard (*šmsw*) exclaim to heaven'.

The scholarly issue in which this text was brought to bear concerns the term *nfrw*. Yoyotte & Lopez (1969: 5) preferred the term 'recruits', although both noted that Schulman's (1964: 20-21) reasonable conclusion that special types of footsoldiers and charioteers reflected the intended definitions in the heyday of the Egyptian Empire of the New Kingdom. Most certainly, we can allow the obvious coincidence of the *nfrw* with the Na'arn can be allowed. The latter is simply the West Semitic equivalent of the former. But Yoyotte & Lopez were essentially correct in noting that these men were recruits. Indeed, they followed the older analysis of Faulkner (1953: 44) at this point. His useful Hatshepsut (1472-1457 BC) example divided the army into marines and land warriors, perhaps reflecting the earlier and possibly the still persistent system of internal organization. Be that as it may, the recruits or *ḥwnw nfrw* are divided into footsoldiers who are archers, thus elite men on land, as well as the sailor-soldiers who have clubs and axes. The difference here may reflect the specific duty roster or even the specific roles that this duality entails; namely, that in the flotilla, the recruits kept their clubs and axes but on land used bows and arrows. Finally, note that Gnirs (1996: 10, note 71 and 45) prefers to see the scribes who were connected with these *nfrw* as 'muster' or 'inspector' scribes, even though the exact meaning appears to be blurred here.

It was Schulman's (1964: 16) contention that "the chariotry was an arm separate from the infantry" and he included all of the 18th Dynasty although there is no direct evidence for this. Yet he (*Ibidem*: 14) partly qualified this statement earlier by maintaining that, at least in the reign of Amenhotep III (1388-1348 BC), the chariotry was "conceived as a separate entity". Nowhere did he and indeed, no further Egyptologist as well, argue apodictically for the exact size of a platoon or squadron of chariots. True, Schulman (*Ibidem*: 26-29) felt that a 'company' (*s3*) of infantry came to 50 men even if it were a tactical rather than an administrative unity. Faulkner (1953: 45) argued for 200. Yoyotte & Lopez (1969: 7-8; Spalinger, In Press), argued for one officer over 25 men – the *ḥri pdt qrꜥw* above the 25 *rmṯ pdt qrꜥw*. Crucial to his argumentation was the further piece of information that the Egyptian term for 'company' was never employed to designate a specific body of chariots (Spalinger, In Press). But special promotions could occur, as the infrequent references of the *idnw* of the chariotry indicate. Amenemhab, and it is to be suspected that Ahmose son of Ebana too, were promoted to this level owing their person success in war.

Let us not forget that the *idnw* could be subordinate to the commander of the infantry or of the chariotry, although others seem to have been directly connected to the pharaoh (Yoyotte & Lopez, 1969: 7-8). Some of them were as 'lieutenants' serving their ruler, and others, the majority, were high officials, but still below the *imi-r mšꜥ* in the infantry and the *imi-r t-nt-ḥtri* of the chariotry. Gnirs (1996: 29-35) translates and understands the title *idnw n ti-nt-ḥtri* as a '*Feldmarschall*'. Although the word has no direct equivalent in English – 'field marshal' will not do. Gnirs refers back to some 16th century AD German references. The word, however, remains associated with the second half of the 19th century AD, Prussian and German in particular. In the Onomasticon of Amunemope there are scattered references of listings that appear to help us a bit in this matter (Berlev, 1992: 112-114; Gardiner, 1947; Yoyotte & Lopez, 1969: 6). The passages are (Gardiner, 1947: 24*-25*, 27*-29*, 112*-113*; Gnirs, 1996: 207; Schulman, 1964: 8-9, 123-124; Yoyotte & Lopez, 1969: 6-7):

87-89	94-98	234-237
imy-r mšꜥ	*imy-r ssmwt*	*ṯsw pdt*
sš mnfꜢit	*idnw t-nt-ḥtri*	*mnfꜢit*
idnw pꜢ mšꜥ	*kḏn*	*t-nt-ḥtri*
	snnj	
	ṯꜢi srit	

In Passage 94-98 Gardiner correctly saw that Amunemope passed to the equid ranks in the New Kingdom army owing to the first reference. The men in Passage 94-98, whom this author assumes to be somewhat inferior to those of Passage 90-93 in so far as a general is listed among the former, have the chariots division neatly summarized from top to bottom. In Passage 234-237 the infantry and chariotry follow upon the marshal of the host (Yoyotte & Lopez, 1969: 7).

This triple division is not that challenging, or even disconcerting, to interpret. The first seems securely based upon the infantry and the second the chariotry. Granted that the "Standard Bearers" should belong to both sectors. Note the older term *mnfꜢit* used at the start (Gnirs, 1996: 12-17). Yoyotte & Lopez (1969: 9) were correct to see that term, originally purely referring to mustered expedition men, as archaizing or, possibly, used in a recherché fashion as its typical of all too many literary writers, ancient Egyptian or modern. The final section presents the infantry before the chariotry, as always, but at the top are very important men, clearly the 'leaders' of both major divisions of an Egyptian army.

At Luxor, there is a useful parallel to the Onomastica evidence (Abd el-Razik, 1975; Berlev, 1992: 113; Gnirs, 1996: 15-16; Kitchen, 1979: 608.8-14; 1999: 408-409: 129; Spalinger, 2010: 427, note 7).

The order is exactly parallel to that presented in the latter, thus indicating a common time frame or époque into which these military officials lived and operated, it was not the 18th Dynasty. The equivalences are:

Onomastica	Luxor
imy-r mšʿ	*imy-r mnfȝit*
sš mnfȝit	
	ḥri pḏt = "Commander of Archers" (Gnirs, 1996: 10).

According to Gnirs (1996: 10-11), the *ṯsw pḏwt*, whom Schuman (1964: 7) labeled "Group Marshals" were the men who actually led their troops in battle. She paid more attention to the effective organization of the chariotry (Gnirs, 1996: 17-34). It was in the late 18th Dynasty that the data become more complex and detailed (Yoyotte & Lopez, 1969: 11 on the *kḏn*). Such references include Gnirs' "Field Marshals", the rank of the "First *kḏn* of His Majesty", and the *idnw* of the chariotry. The title "Overseer of Horses" (Gnirs' 'marshal') first appears under the reign of Thutmose III. Royal "Masters of the Stables" were common enough from the middle to the end of this period; only later such men who were connected to private stables (of officials). It may be for this reason that the commonplace extended epithets associated with warriors of the 18th Dynasty had no references to horses or chariots. The very common phrase "following his lord" has already been mentioned. At this point the further remarks of Gnirs (1996: 27-28) are useful to consult because she observed the presence of another typical passage associated with the military officers: "who fought on his two feet", with another variant, *iri rdwi n ḥm=f*. Evidently, the concept was restricted to footsoldiers and not to chariots. However, was it extended to all warriors and thus was not restricted to the infantry? That is to say, *šms ḥm=f* or *ʿr rwdi=f(i)* etc. might have been taken over, at an early date, and applied to the charioteers. Minmose's career, for example, indicates his loyalty to Pharaoh but avoids specificity relating to his exact role in the army of Asia. If the *Feldmarschall*'s position was well-defined by the reign of Amenhotep III – Gnirs' terminology is used here – so too was that of the marshal, except that the latter had already become a regular member of Egypt's army at an earlier time.

It will be interesting to contrast two Late Egyptian Miscellany tractates in order to demonstrate the conflicting feelings of the later epoch of the Ramessides with respect to charioteers (Spalinger, 2006: 5-50). Papryus [P] Anastasi IV says it all when it comes to the status and importance of the chariot. If one 'pleases' Amun then all will be successful in life. This deliberate turn to the importance of the clergy as a career, and not merely to Amun from pure pietistic bases, is what mattered, not the overt use of the chariot as a status symbol. This can also be found at an earlier time in the scenes of the court at Amarna, where not merely do the king's daughters have themselves propelled in the great open spaces, but likewise military men not at war. Moreover, see the reference to 'steeds of Khor', thereby indicating not only the foreign original for the chargers, but also the emphasis placed on their exotic nature, one perfectly suitable to an economy based on conspicuous consumerism.

The antithesis to this aspect is presented in one of the most interesting anti-military tractates of these Miscellanies. As P. Anastasi III, lines 6.8-10, was given an exemplary philological analysis by Fischer-Elfert (1983), attention shall be oriented to a different side of things. It is true that the chariot warrior is represented, and the 'attack' is very unlike those devoted to mere footsoldiers. Nevertheless, the title *snni ti-nt-ḥtri* already represented the later Ramesside understanding of the old term *snni*. What, precisely, are the scribal complaints? Horses he does not own, but rather obtains them from the royal stables, again indicating the near monopoly that the 'state' had upon the animals. They must be obtained from a 'military camp' because the young man wished to be a military charioteer. As for the chariot itself, the prospective elite soldier must pay for them via his mother's father. The strident nature of the diatribe is evident, and even though it is unique among the scribal anti-military tractates, it cannot be said to reflect the actual condition of any member of the warrior elite. This is despite the association of charioteers with the king that is so evident in the Qadesh Poem wherein Ramesses states that he earlier had "let them go back to their towns" thereby indicating the end of some military service for the nonce (Kitchen, 1979: 59.11-15 [P 184]).

QADESH ACCOUNTS

As a test of these so-far general notions of the worth of charioteers taken from the Egyptian accounts rather than a conclusion, easy to make, drawn from technical superiority of the chariots, a brief look at the Qadesh accounts will help further to orientate. Right at the beginning the introductory encomium to the king recognizes the expected army divisions into infantry and the corps of military vehicles (Kitchen, 1979: 10.1-4 [P 22], 10.5-10 [P 23]):

A) who saves his infantry (*mšˤ*) on the day of fighting; the great protector of his chariotry (*nt-ḥtri*)
B) who brings back his 'followers' (*šmsw*) and rescues his host (*mnf3it*).

Once more the preferred duality so beloved of the Egyptians can be observed. The first part moves from the lower to the higher (*cf.* P 25, 74, 90, 113-114, 117, 145 Hittites, 224, 240, 323, and 323) whereas the second treats the king's more intimate warriors and regular troops differently. See as well data from the Medinet Habu accounts (Kitchen, 1983: 22.8-9 [Year 5 Text] – *mnf3it* followed by *ssmwt*, 28.9-10, 28.15 (restored) – both *mšˤ* and *nt-ḥtrw*; *mnf3it* followed by *t-nt-ḥtri*, 40.10-11 [Year 8 Text], 61.1-2 [Year 11 Text]). This material indicates that the lengthy narratives, true literary accounts, used the more 'elegant' or 'classical' word *mnf3it* instead of the standard *mšˤ*.

And in the penultimate reference of the Poem the 'leaders' of both sections of the king's host are indicated. The former presents the standard arrangement, also known to us from an account of Seti I (1296-1279 BC) as well as other examples. In the repeated lists of soldiers that Yoyote & Lopez (1969: 11) discussed (Qadesh P 88-89), the arrangement is a descending one: *sr*, *kḏn*, *wˤw*, and *qrˤw*. But there the final two are to be contrasted as we see once more that the footsoldier preceded a charioteer, the man of lesser importance. In Poem 199 we read the same arrangement but with *snni* replacing *qrˤw*. But Poem 265-266 provides the best arrangement in a descending order: *sr* – the army official or superior, the 'charioteer' *snni*, and then the footsoldier, the *wˤw*. This last case is of particular importance as it subsumes all high-ranking army men under the general rubric of *sr*, but nonetheless located the 'second man in the chariot' to a status higher than a mere infantryman.

In Poem 25 the same order in the dichotomy is repeated, and thereafter, perhaps including the disposition of the enemy (Kitchen, 1979: 11.1-4): "and their chiefs were with him there, each man with his infantry (*mšˤ*); and the chariotry (*nt-ḥtri*) were exceedingly numerous, without their equal".

Yet later in Poem 67 we read that the Hittite king sent his men (*rmṯ*) and horse teams (*ḥtrw*) to attack the Egyptians. Overtly, but little recognized, is this contrast to the Egyptian set-up, one that, however, was dependent upon the tactics of the Hittite monarch. Namely, that he depended upon his chariots to maul the second Egyptian division and then to hasten to the Egyptian camp. For this reason the Poem notes the men and the animals (teams of horses) and so ignores any division between infantry and chariotry. At this point the stress is upon the three men to a chariot set-up of the Hittites. Yet in the Bulletin (B) (B 100) the same order of the division is noted that we find right at the beginning of the Poem (P 25 and 28).

By the time we reach the important tactical error of the king the Poem indicates that Ramesses was 'alone' with his 'followers' when marching (P 56). Note once more that second key word which bothered Yoyotte & Lopez so much. Was Pharaoh's intimate bodyguard, shall we say his 'immortals', distinctly pinpointed, or is this word used merely to indicate the troops of the first division? The latter cannot hold as the account goes on to say that the division of Amun was following upon Ramesses. Yet close to the end of the narrative, Ramesses berates his army and maintains that only his team of horses plus Menna as well as his 'butlers' supported him (P 272-274). Were these men also his intimate protectors or *šmsw*?

The crucial point of this section of the account is that there were only three major witnesses to Ramesses' valor, in the following order: the king's chariot team of horses – both horses which are named – Menna, and the household butlers. The brief remarks indicate just how few are claimed to have known the great personal success of Pharaoh, according to the official account of course, and possibly also how only these three groups aided Ramesses. But the passage also proves that the 'great ʿtr of his majesty', when named, was the horse that one saw in the relief.

The ideal nature of the chariot warrior is perfectly evident from the account of the Poem. Granted that the orientation is solely royal, it is nevertheless the case that personal orientation of the elite hero of war is at the heart of the matter. Hence, the present author disagree with Assmann (1983) who placed, albeit quite reasonably, this narrative's presentation under the rubric of piety. True, that aspect was part of the presentation of Ramesses as was – and here Assmann did not fail to notice the direct of intent – the king's attack upon his officials who failed to recognize the Hittite king's strategy. But the entire composition centers around the warrior pharaoh to such a degree that his personal feelings are represented side-by-side with the topoi connected to charioteer warfare. Ramesses alone is prepared for battle. His protective coverings are listed and his 'great horse' (ḥtr ʿ3), or 'horse team' is likewise mentioned. After all, we are dealing with an idealized aspect of New Kingdom warfare. In the Bulletin as above, for example (B 6 with B 86) as well as in other 18th Dynasty military narratives – not to mention one special account of Ramesses that took place later in Asia – the Egyptian ruler will don his protective cover when he is about to depart from camp, independently of whether he is expecting immediate combat (Kitchen, 1979: 174.8-175.12; Sethe, 1907b). After he 'appeared' and was ready for combat Ramesses enters the fray in a 'gallop' (m ifd). Granted that all of this is commonplace, especially the emphasis upon the solitary role of the Egyptian monarch. The subsequent aspect is the discovery by Ramesses that he was surrounded by 2,500 enemy chariots, and that their leaders were the 'champions', if we use Gardiner's translation of pḥrrw (1960: 9, 19). Von der Way (1984: 301), however, preferred the simple literal translation of 'Läufer' whereas Kitchen included both (Kitchen, 1979: 31.10-15 and 1996: 5; O'Connor, 1990: 83; Schulman, 1964: 38-39). Lichtheim (1976: 64) interestingly preferred 'fast troops', which at least provides the reader with a feeling that reflects the velocity of these war vehicles; the word 'runners' is sometimes preferred.

Immediately thereafter, after Ramesses 'found' that he was alone and called upon Amun for help, he shoots with his right hand and captures with his left. His chariot enemies failed miserably in combat when they could neither shoot their arrows nor employ their javelins – note once more the expected physical role of fighting. Even in the second onslaught ordered by Muwatallis, the same occurred. We shall leave off the expected slaughter which Pharaoh accomplished and turn instead to his short dialogue with Menna, the qrʿw w. The king reacts, as he did earlier, to the threat by 'entering' into the enemy host just as he 'entered' into the Hittite chariot attack at home base (P 81, 221, and 280 are the same; see B 94 with Reliefs [R] 18 and 19). And Menna is required to 'stand firm' (smn tw), in the chariot of course, while his lord engages in combat with the foes.

Let me add some obvious parallels from the 18th Dynasty at this moment, but in a summary fashion as we have be able to signal the major components of the 'perfect chariot warrior' from the Qadesh inscriptions of Ramesses. Thutmose III, in his account of the Megiddo campaign, highlights the following parallel or identical themes. The king first is girdled with the required accouterments and then he is in his chariot. Amenhotep II records this is in a similar fashion, but his two main war accounts stress over and over that he 'went forth' 'on a (team of) horses' (Helck, 1955: 1304.10, 1305.1 and 17, 1307.4, 1308.3 – Memphis Stela; 1312.3, 1313.11 [yet restored]; and see 1314.17 for the armor as in 1311.6 – Karnak Stela). Yet it is from his Sphinx Stela that we derive much needed supplementary data concerning a charioteer's desired physical and mental attributes (Beylage, 2002: I 43-63, II 592-600). Horsemanship was required as well as drawing a bow. Specifically shooting while riding was remarked positively to Thutmose III on behalf of his son, Amenhotep II.

In the major account of Merenptah (1212-1201 BC) at Karnak, on the other hand, the narrator's orientation is somewhat different (Gnirs, 1996: 13; Heagren, 2010: 15-96, 72-74 in particular; Manassa, 2003: 104-107). In column 11 of that inscription the two divisions of the king's army are the archers and chariots; the importance of the archer sector of Merenptah's host is elsewhere indicated (columns 27 and 33). By column 30 the division into infantry and chariotry is resumed, and in the expected order, but with *mnf3it* employed for the first term (Edgerton & Wilson, 1936: 54, note 20d). In the lengthy Year 5 War Inscription the same division can be seen and also with *mnf3it*, likewise with the narrative accounts of year 8 and 11 – the old translation of 'militia' does not suffice (*Ibidem*). It is as if this other general term is used within the three literary accounts in a more restricted sense of footsoldiers. Note that, as well, the older word *snni* occurs at Medinet Habu for the more up-to-date *terminus technicus qrʿw* (Yoyotte & Lopez, 1969: 11). But perhaps the most important, and indeed unique passage that can be cited from Merenptah's lengthy account is highly important for our research (Manassa, 2003: 42-43, 91-92). It refers to Pharaoh's troops and not himself: "Now the chariot warriors (*snni*), who were upon his majesty's horse teams (*ḥtriw* = chariots of course), placed themselves behind him, saw that [...]" (column 38). Column 45, on the other hand, lists the prominent military officials before the standard duality of infantry-chariotry, as follows: *ṯsw-pḏwt, mnf3it, nt ḥtri*. This broken section supports the conclusions of Yoyotte & Lopez (1969: 6-7, 9), and the preference for *mnf3it* over *mšʿ* in this narrative can be reiterated once more.

MEDINET HABU DATA

How did the chariot men perform at Medinet Habu?

Year 5 Campaign

The *Iw.tw* Text and Scene – figure 1 (Heinz, 2001: 301 [pl. I.6] = Epigraphic Survey 1930: pls. 15-16; Kitchen, 1983: 12).

Top Left – security chiefs of the great span, chiefs of the *šmsw* who are "among the retinue of his majesty" (Gnirs, 1996: 55; Kitchen, 1983: 13).

These are the most intimate non-royal participants in the military who are in close proximity to the king. It is self-evident here that we have the solution to the Yoyotte-Lopez criticism of Schulman. Only the third group appear to be armed, this time with sickle-shaped swords and spears; they also hold shields. The other two, located to the front, have no war equipment to be seen. All of the men wear long cloaks. This is the system:

front row: two men, one of whom is a bugler
second row: three men; add the one in the front ?; all hold little 'control' whisks
third row: four men, as before
fourth row: six warriors

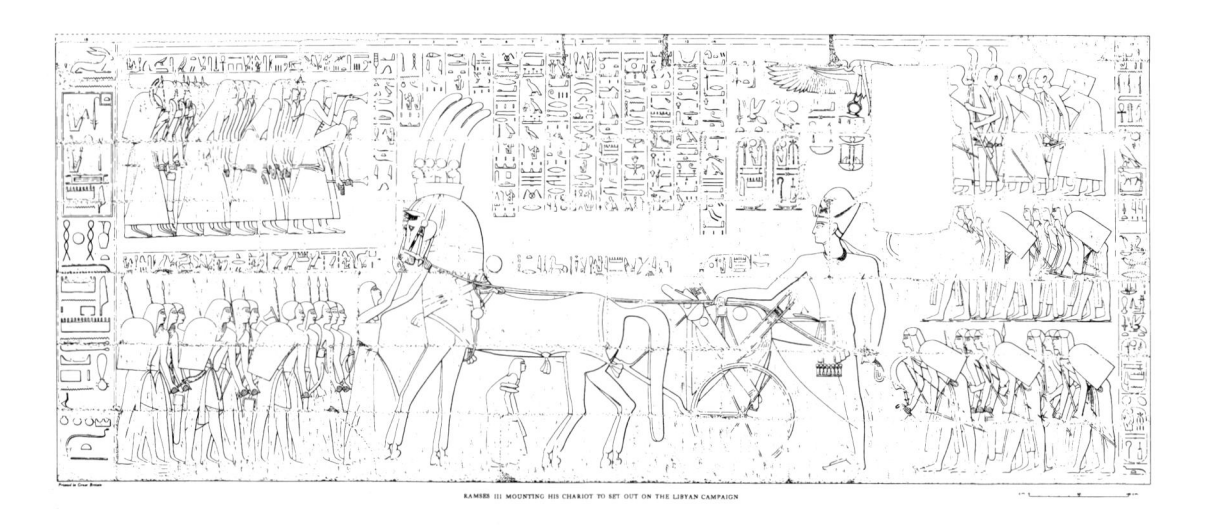

Figure 1. Disposition of soldiers. Ramesses III. Medinet Habu (MHI16). From: Heinz (2001: 301 [pl. I.6]).

Lower Left – *kḏn*, chief transport officials (*mškb*), *qrʿw* (Gnirs, 1996: 55; Kitchen, 1983: 13; Schulman, 1964: 120, note 206).

All the men possess sickle-shaped swords, leather (not metal) helmets, short kilts, and spears. Two quivers and one ax with the men can be seen. They are organized into rows having five, three, and then again three men, with the foremost the only group that has small protective caps. However, one of them seems to possess the large head protection seen in the two rear groups. The six rear men possess the quivers.

The thrust of the imagery is set into a front and rear system. In the former scene, which refers to the troops before Pharaoh, the charioteers can be seen, whereas to the rear of the king are the royal princes (bottom), archers (middle) and attendants (who are not going to war?) at the top. We cannot determine exactly the arrangement of the march, but we can establish that this scene refers to the more significant warriors or the sectors of the army that were the most important. The following depiction places the chariot division at a greater distance from the pharaoh than the footsoldiers. This may reflect the actual state of affairs, but it can be argued that the mustering of the vehicles and horses took more time and was located separate from the actual organization of the infantry. In the following scene the charioteers are placed behind the foreign contingents of footsoldiers.

March to the West

Figure 2 (Heinz, 2001: 301 [pl. I.7] = Epigraphic Survey, 1930: pl. 17).

The actual advance westward is given. The mustering is over. In the main scene the archer division is immediately in front of Ramesses (the men carry bows and there is an alternating pattern of sickle-shaped swords and battle axes). To the left and again in front of the king – temporally slightly later than the earlier depiction – are rows of five men apiece, each representing infantry. This must be a company of such warriors, all of whom have shields and weapons in their hands. Note once more the sickle-shaped swords alternating with the ax setup. They are in the very front, but followed by the leaders of the 'guard', *šmsw*, of the great span, and the chiefs of the transport officials (Gnirs, 1996: 55; Kitchen, 1983: 13.10; Schulman, 1964: 120, note 206). Hence, this sector, carved in the middle but behind the archers, reveals its close proximity to Pharaoh, notwithstanding the presence of the Amun standard being driven by one man in a chariot, all before Ramesses.

The charioteers, *kḏn* and *qrʿw*, are placed at the bottom of the composition following the non-Egyptian contingents of infantry (Gnirs, 1996: 30; Kitchen, 1983: 13.11-14). In this case, unlike in the Qadesh campaign, the chariots are located solely to the rear of the footsoldiers.

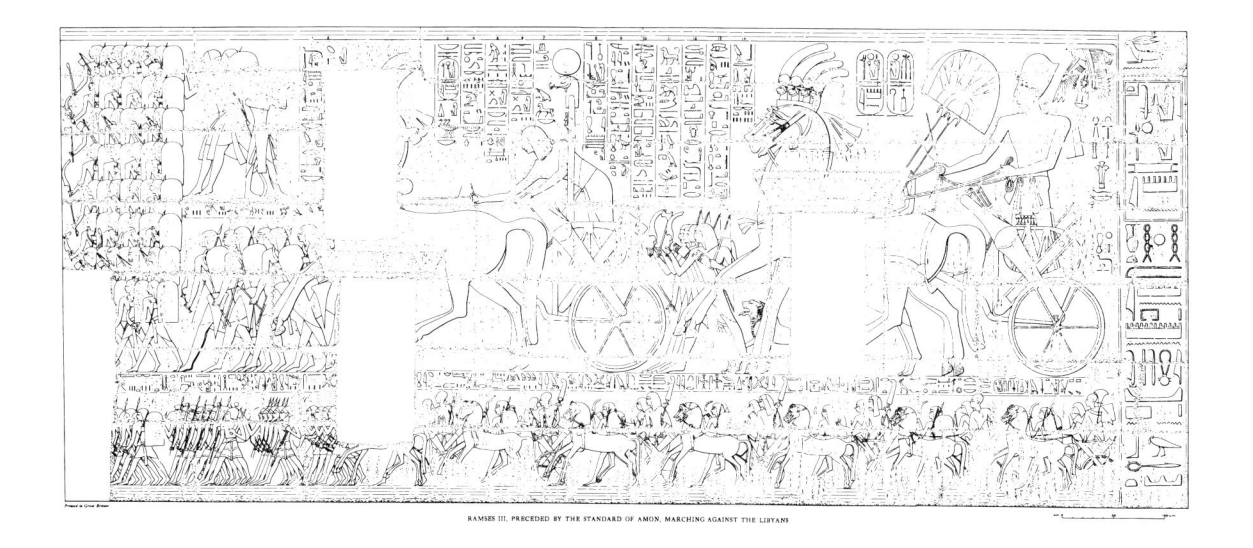

Figure 2. Setting out for war. Ramesses III. Medinet Habu (MH17). From: Heinz (2001: 301 [pl. I.7]).

Their order is as follows: Egyptian, Sherden, Asiatics and Nubians. One assumes that the most trustworthy and able men are foremost. The same may be seen in the depiction of Ramesses III hunting lions (Epigraphic Survey, 1930: pls. 35-36; Gaballa, 1976: 123; Heinz, 2001: pl. I.17; Kitchen, 1983: 31).

This bottom register covers the entire width of the panel. The list is: "[…] troop commanders of the chariotry, and the chiefs of the royal stables' ' (Gnirs, 1996, 30; Kitchen, 1983: 13.11-14). They are depicted to the rear of the foreign contingents or mercenaries. In addition to the two men in each chariot there is a third on their right side, brandishing a sickle-shaped sword, and holding a shield. It is assumed here that the specific title associated with these men is lost in the text. None of these soldiers belong to the archer component, and if the scene is taken to represent a reasonable set-up, then this infantry contingent marched right in front of the king's own chariot whereas the others, foreigners and fast moving vehicles, were further away. On the other hand, note the presence of four archers just in front of the king's chariot.

If one views the Thutmose IV text in conjunction with the Qadesh reliefs, then the chariot divisions, and not merely the higher-ups in the sector, were further away at the four sides of the infantrymen: right, left, front, and rear. Finally, Edgerton & Wilson (1936: 7) laid some stress upon the bugler in the uppermost register to the left. At this point in the proceeding he must have called the entire host to action.

Year 8 Campaign

Figure 3 (Spalinger, 2011: 193-197; Essche(-Merchez), 1989; 1994; O'Connor, 2000).

The archers play a secondary role in these proceedings. Edgerton & Wilson (1936: 37, but with 'many details omitted'; Heinz, 2001: 306 [pl. I.15] = Epigraphic Survey, 1930: pls. 30-31) maintained that the march against the enemy is virtually identical to that depicted for the first Libyan war. The visual nature adheres to the same template. Yet the foremost rows of footsoldiers are not archers but rather

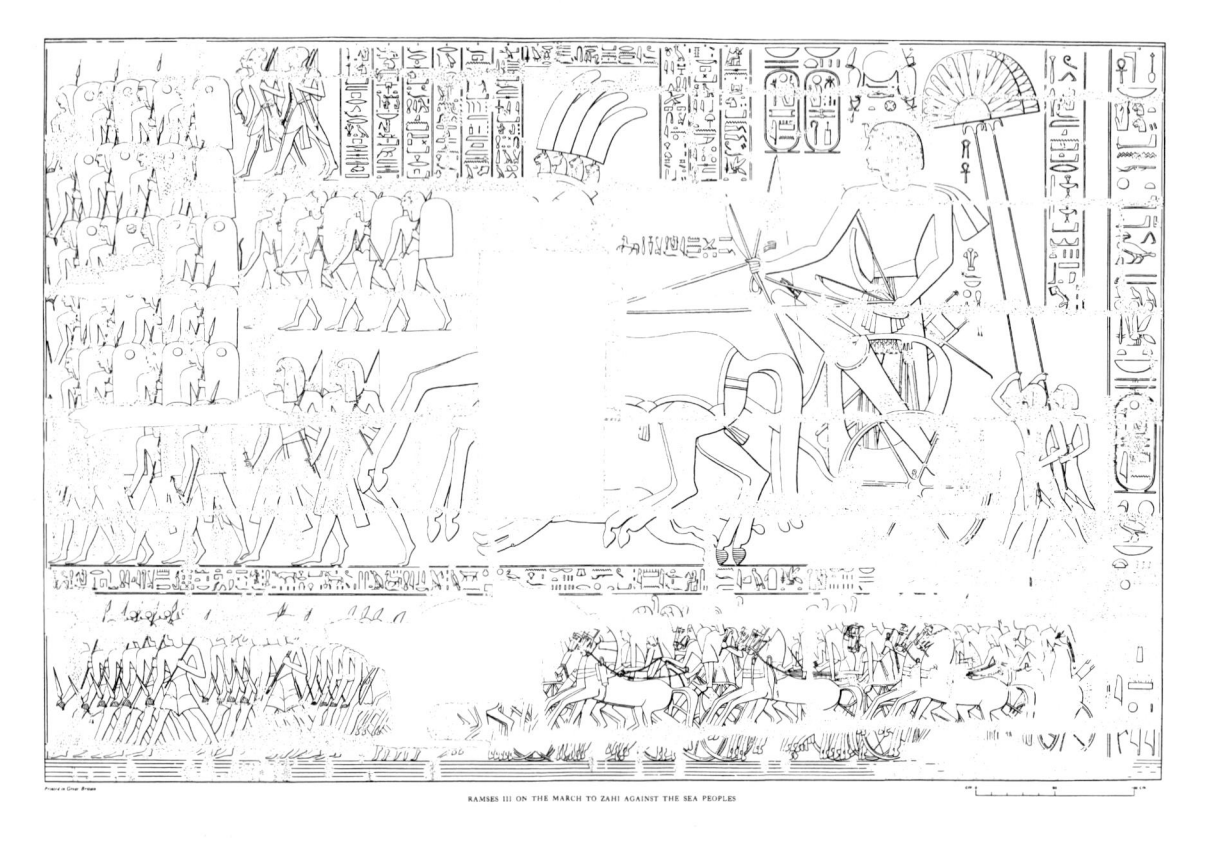

Figure 3. Immediate disposition to set out for war. Ramesses III. Medinet Habu (MHI31). From: Heinz (2001: 306 [pl. I.15]).

typical Egyptian infantrymen who carry spears, although here five men 'fit' into one row. Behind them are the more elite warriors and at least here we can argue for complete identity.

Below there is the lengthy 'frieze' of foreign contingents preceding chariot troops. But only Sherden, Asiatic, and Nubians may be found. Behind them come the elite charioteers and their supporters. Here, it was the rather different nature of the enemy and their location in Asia that present a completely different viewpoint than earlier. Unlike the two recent wars with the western invaders, Ramesses' tactics avoided emphasizing the archer divisions.

The first snapshot of victory, however, is not this one but the issuing of the war material to the king's army. Virtually everything relating to a soldier's need is included: sickle-shaped swords, spears, quivers, bows, helmets, and shields. Surely to be added are at least arrows if not also battle axes. Next is the king's speech to his high officials, the *ḥ3wtjw* (Kitchen, 1983: 27.15 – handing the weapons first to the 'leaders'; Gnirs, 1996: 14, 16; Schulman, 1964: 49; Yoyotte & Lopez, 1969: 10). In the middle of the depiction one caption refers to handing this equipment to the infantry and chariotry, but then specifies "the troops of Sherden, and Nubians" (Kitchen, 1983: 28.15-16). The order here is clear: Egyptians before foreigners and, as one of the earlier depiction reveals, the Egyptian infantry preceded the Sherden who, in turn, are carved in advance of the Nubians. A second phrase notes that the royal infantry and chariotry are just now received these weapons and war equipment (Kitchen, 1983: 29.2).

The process of the disbursement was as follows:

A) Official reception announced by a bugler. Pharaoh is outside and at a rostrum. He speaks to his officials (*srw*), his 'companions' (*smrw*), and the leaders (*ḥ3wtiw*) of his infantry and chariotry (Gnirs, 1996: 16 on the 'court' nature of the *srw* and *smrw*). They are ordered to secure the war material for the campaign;

B) The weapons, etc. are then distributed to the two divisions of the Egyptian army;

C) Two scribes insure that the proper number and type are given to the Egyptian troops as well as the foreigners (Sherden and Nubians here) while two officials receive and then give additional equipment to these two divisions of the army (Kitchen, 1983: 28.15-29.1): the men left of center who receive war equipment are mainly issued archery components);

D) The crown prince speaks to the *imiw mš⁽*, the important *ḥriw pdwt* and *tsw pdwt* (Yoyotte & Lopez, 1969: 7);

E) The officials (civilians again) and overseers of the *mni3it* (here this must refer to the army) speak to the crown prince who is, after all, the generalissimo of the army (Kitchen, 1983: 29.7-9);

F) Then all is ready for the march.

Why this scene was not included earlier is beyond the scope of this paper as it leads into the related but independent question of visual performance, space dispositions, and individual decisions on the part of the master designer. For the moment, it is sufficient to observe that the issuing of equipment only appears with respect to the northern campaign of the pharaoh. In the second half of the Year 8 battle accounts, either visual or written, this image does not occur. It is as if the topos of the king's march as well as the presentation of war material served both the land and seashore battles. After all, to the Egyptians, these two side of the Year 8 war were intimately linked.

Year 11 Campaign

Figure 4.

It is indicative of the independently minded chief designer of these war scenes at Medinet Habu that he did not parallel the depictions of the earlier Libyan war. The last relevant scene of use covers the final war of Ramesses in his eleventh regnal year (Heinz, 2001: 311 [pl. I.28] = Epigraphic Survey, 1932: 62-63; Kitchen, 1983: 49). Edgerton & Wilson (1936: 59) maintain that "It cannot be shown that this march has any necessary connection with a military campaign, and the accompanying inscriptions are quite general" and the original publications says that the king and his followers, military and civilian, are "on parade" (Epigraphic Survey, 1932: vii, caption to pl. 62). There are no chariots; likewise the 'runners' are missing. Instead we see

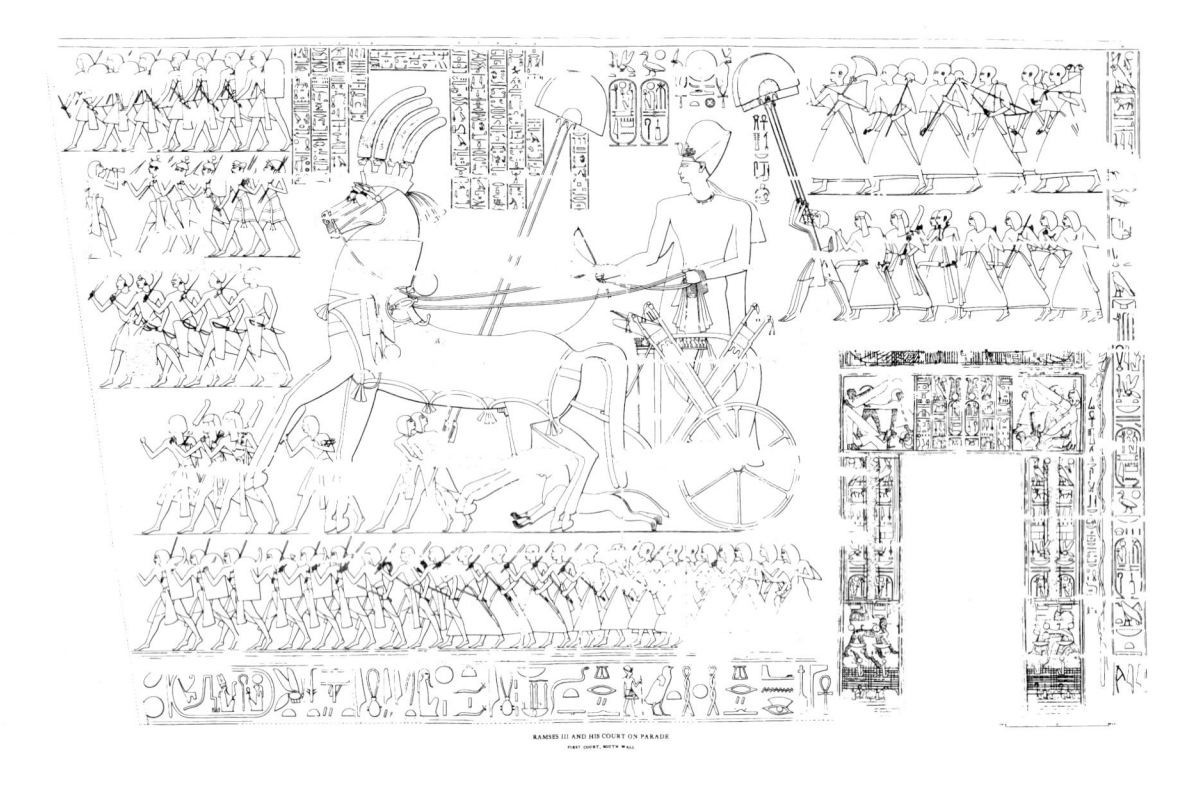

Figure 4. Another set-out to war. Ramesses III. Medinet Habu (MHII62). From: Heinz (2001: 311 [pl. I.28]).

footsoldiers. To the left of the marching king are four registers of these troops with a frieze of two types of officals (and guards ?) and military men:

A) Typical infantry are at the head, and the six carry shields and mainly have sickle-shaped swords as well (although one battle ax may be discerned);
B) Then come three men with control sticks (without shields);
C) Non-combatants but men of a very high rank. They also carry control sticks. It is presumed in the present paper that they include the *smrw* and *srw*, although this can be queried. The first group includes nine men; the heads are bare but wear long kilts;
D) The final group of non-combatants include six men with wigs; no object of social control is included in any of the hands of these officials.

This group of parading men may very well have marched at the king's side. Above and to the front of them are additional troops. This needs to be read from top to the bottom here, even if the highest register repeats much of the lowest. In both the Egyptian infantry can be recognized. Immediately below them is a bugler calling foreign troop into line. First are the Sea People Sherden (three men), followed in turn by two other foreigners who, by their garment and caps, are Sea Peoples as well (Darnell, 1991; Widmer, 1975: 71-75). The Sherden have horned helmets, Peleshet Tjeker, and Denyen have feather crests, and the Shekelesh wear caps. The identity of all the Sea Peoples is, however, troublesome (Widmer, 1975: 71-72 [c], 75). In fact, the garment worn by the last two men in the key scene is clearly represented on some Libyans at Medinet Habu (Epigraphic Survey 1930: pl. 18 – lower left; Gaballa, 1976: 157, note 222; Hölscher, 1937: 41-47; Widmer, 1975: 75). The register immediately below presents the Nubian contingents. Note the order once more: Egyptians, Sea Peoples, and Nubians. The first two of the latter group carry clubs and bows; the remaining three only bows. It is assumed here that the foremost southerners are in charge of their comrades in arms. Finally, at the upper right we can see other officials, who probably are the 'butlers'. Two of them are carrying vessels, one an ewer and washbasin combination. At least one of them with the bow could be a bodyguard if he is not just holding his master's bow. Note that in the second register from the top an army scribe is present.

The depiction seems not to represent a typical march to war, but rather that of a mustering, in preparation to setting forth for war. Spatial concerns might have limited the scenario, but with the bugler sounding his horn, is not all ready for the royal advance? Yet it is disconcerting that any general location of the footsoldiers remains unclear. One can assume that those infantry to the front of the monarch were located at his right side, but is this correct? Should one locate the more elite native soldiers there, such as, perhaps, those depicted at the bottom. Once more, the Egyptian pictorial evidence whilst useful is tantalizing, and it is best to stop speculation at this point and turn our attention to a final series of military reliefs from a different temple.

Abydos Reliefs of Ramesses II

Figure 5.

These depictions independently provide us with useful pictorial data (Heinz, 2001: 282 [pl. II.1]; Spalinger, 2003; 2011: 205-209, 166-168, 202-222; No Date). There, at least the protective nature of the chariotry is revealed as well as 'runners', whom have been seen before. The latter may be found, from the perspective of the viewer, inside the 'corralled' unit of footsoldiers. That is to say, the chariotry protect the infantry (see figure 6 for the marching of Ramesses II preliminary to Qadesh).

Looking carefully at the 'runners', one sees immediately that they are neither archers nor infantrymen carrying shields. In other words, they acted as a rightmost protective guard for the chariotry and possibly also for the infantry. At Medinet Habu an identical location for the infantry can be found on one side of the advancing chariots and their drivers (Heinz, 2001: 301 [pl. I.7]: year 5 campaign – lowest register).

The present source material does not allow us to conclude what the 'runners' were expected to do in battle. Schulman (1964: 39) argued that these men are "sometimes shown with a shield and a javelin", but he improperly referred to the Qadesh account of the Poem (P 85) wherein the Hittite side is discussed. In the Medinet Habu records it is once more that the Year 8 Sea Peoples' conflict provides the most information. In one passage these 'runners' are described almost as if the entire army was composed of them (Kitchen, 1983: 29.8), whereas a second mention is more significant (*Ibidem*: 40.11). The latter is the literary narrative of the same war, and owing to its importance, it is best to quote the entire passage (Kitchen 1983: 40.9-12; 2008: 34):

A) The infantry (*mnf3it*) of every picked man (see Kitchen 1983: 29.8 as well) of the Nile-Land – they were like lions roaring upon the mountain-crests;

B) The chariotry consisted of 'runners', of 'trained men', of all good/capable chariot warriors (*snniw*).

The literary nature of this narrative is self-evident here: note the two obsolete words *mnf3it* – which, from contact, has to indicate the footsoldiers, and *snni*.

But when the chariots move to battle, these 'runners' disappear. Indeed, the charioteers advance beyond their infantry comrades as well, if we assume that these Abydos reliefs tell the exact truth,

Figure 5. Orderly march close to Qadesh. Ramesses II. Abydos. From: Heinz (2001: 282 [pl.II.1], top).

Figure 6. Orderly march to Qadesh. Ramesses II. Luxor (L3). From: Heinz (2001: 289 [pl. IV.4]).

but they do not. In sum, the fragmentary scenes of Ramesses II at Abydos provide us with the 'second stage' of the Egyptian armies' advances, just as the Konosso Stela revealed a written account of the same situation of marching in war.

SUMMARY

The basic *modus operandi* for the use of the chariot sector within the Egyptian army before actual fighting took place and when the troops were marching to any destination can be delineated. For the sake of argument, let us assume that the pharaoh has decided to head the army in person, and the direction is northwards into Asia. Here, we face the obvious questions surrounding the final mustering of troops. No doubt it was not at Sile but rather first at Tell el-Daʿba/Avaris that the king set off on his war journey (Bietak, 2009a; 2009b, Forstner-Müller, 2011). In fact, Ramesses II ended up there when he returned from Qadesh (Kitchen, 1979: 100.1-5; the account of Papyrus (P.) Sallier III is important here). But in the two classical lengthy accounts of key northern campaigns, the Egyptian monarch is first cited at Sile, not at Avaris: Thutmose III advancing to Megiddo and Ramesses III likewise moving north to Qadesh (Sethe, 1907a: 647.12 – Thutmose III; Kitchen, 1979: 12.12-16 – Ramesses II's Poem 30). In the latter case, however, the earlier remarks of the narrative refer to the pharaoh's preparing his troops and setting north, all before he reached Sile (P. 25-29). That locality is the final stop in Egypt before entering Asia. Yet it cannot be left unsaid that Berlev (1997: 98-99) presented cogent reasons for locating the final mustering at Gaza, and interpreted a *crux passage* in Thutmose III's Annals very successfully (Redford, 1967: 60, note 27; 2003: 13-14; Sethe, 1907a: 648.10).

The march was prepared, in a logical fashion, with the major divisions separated, though the elite chariotry's first role, it seems, was to protect each company (or large grouping) of footsoldiers. 'Runners' were located on the lateral flanks, being set closer to the chariots than the infantry. Nonetheless, they provided an additional support to these partly vulnerable regular soldiers. The pharaoh, at the head of his troops, was protected by his personal guard as well as by effective and battle-trained troops who were superlative warriors. The chariots acted together as an effective protection on the army's left and right flanks, but the Abydos reliefs also indicate that they were also located in front of and at the rear of the corps of footsoldier companies. From Medinet Habu and Abydos we see some details concerning the physical location of the 'runners' can be seen, but their exact military service remains unclear. Ramesses II's Qadesh reliefs perfectly support this conclusion: see the arrival of the Naʿarn at the Egyptian camp as well as the attempt of the vizier to push forward the division of Ptah

(Heinz, 2001: 281 [pl. I.1 — Abu Simbel, arrival of vizier, messengers, and butler], 287 [pl. IV.1: L1], 288 [pl. IV.3: L1 — arrival of vizier], 289 [pl. IV.4: L1 — arrival of vizier with bareback messenger on horse behind him], and 291 [pl. V.1: R1]).

Medinet Habu also provides some representational detail concerned with the return of the Egyptian army, but not much. For the Year 5 campaign marching shield bearing footsoldiers who are Egyptian precede Sea Peoples' infantry (Heinz, 2001: 304 [pl. I.12] = Epigraphic Survey, 1930: pls. 24-25). Then come archers, higher Egyptian warriors (troop leaders?), and finally the elite in the army; all are on foot. The Seti I evidence once more is surprisingly uninformative on marches.

Because this study shall end 'on the road', a few words concerning the eventualities of attack can be given here. There is no evidence that what occurred in the army at the beginning of the 18th Dynasty was identical to what transpired during, for instance, the reign of Amenhotep III when the chariot division perhaps became too top heavy and in need of administrative reform (Gnirs, 1996: 21-23). Moreover, we cannot argue that the tactics of marching armies was the same under Thutmose III as it was under Ramesses II. How were the divisions arranged, for example? In columns, one supposes, but how many? The Thutmose IV example, provided at the beginning of this study, in fact refers to the marine disposition of the king's fleet in addition to his land-based troops, and the campaign was directed on the Nile upstream rather than a land-oriented war in Palestine or Syria. The Qadesh reliefs, on the other hand, reveal that the marching formation as evidenced in the Abydos depictions, also indicates the same basic march order of divisions far away from Egypt: chariots protect footsoldiers.

The multi-ethnic cohorts of footsoldiers present at Medinet Habu were not part and parcel of the mid-18th Dynasty's Egyptian army, Nubians excepted. Yet it is significant that these men *precede* the marching chariots. Whether or not this depiction is totally accurate is another matter. Although it has been remarked that the leading troops are Egyptians. The latter, apparently at all costs, were in control of the foreign troops.

The location of the chariots on the outside meant that they could veer off from the main body of troops without affecting the protection of Pharaoh. By this maneuver, the chariotry, or at least some of them, would be able to neutralize small bodies of enemy charioteers and infantry. In addition, they could perform their duties, some of which might have been mere reconnoitering, as quickly as possible. The heavier burdened infantry were therefore left 'inside', so to speak, of their protectors – note that the infantry carried shields. But when stopping for a day's rest, whether outside of a loyal city or in the field, it took time to separate the chariots from the horses and to line both up. The men, both footsoldiers and charioteers, would have rested more quickly. Of course, the faster moving cohort elite played no role in guard duty.

A final point needs to be addressed although it involves many unclear factors. Namely, the wear and tear on these vehicles. We are mainly dependent upon the pictorial evidence which, as has been stressed elsewhere, is open to multiple interpretations (Spalinger, 2011). Were the chariots themselves actually employed on the march over very long distances? Or do the war scenes just indicate the distribution of units? Surely the men received their weapons as well, but here the place for any direct advance into Asia was ultimately to be at Sile, as Papyrus [P] Lansing indicates (line 9.10), and not at Tell el-Da'ba (Epigraphic Survey 1930: pl. 29, the distribution of weapons, perhaps useful in this context; Heagren, 2010: 195-196).

If the chariots were deployed on the march, how long would they be able to travel before breaking wheels, axles, etc.? This depends upon the terrain as well as the distance traversed. As the chariots were designed in part for speed and maneuverability, would the majority have survived the trip through, for example, the hostile Sinai without breaking down several times? On the other hand, they had to be strong and capable of rapid maneuverability. Yet one may assume that the chariots were not necessarily assembled until a clear and less severe road system was at hand (see also Köpp-Junk, this volume). Finally, would it not make more sense to have deployed the divisions in the manner which Medinet Habu reveals, but only at the beginning and subsequently only on acceptable roads? In this context Berlev's (1997: 98-99) comments with regard to Gaza being the 'mustering center' of the

Egyptian army in the north makes perfect sense if only because at that point could the chariots travel with less difficulty than in the Sinai.

The situation of the Sinai was considerably different to the Egyptian army than northwards in Palestine and Syria. The Egyptian army could not travel as one unit between Sile/Tjaru and Gaza. This author believes that, following the 'Annals' of Thutmose III, the pharaoh with his protective body of soldiers was the last to depart from Sile. Then he met his already massed army in Gaza. Hence, the one-day stopover there by Thutmose III can be better explained (Spalinger & Oren, Forthcoming).

This issue needs further investigation. The Qadesh Poem with the reliefs at least indicate that divisions would be in formation, more or less, when on march but not near any possible expected battle site. This can be especially seen when the Hittite chariots 'sliced' through the Egyptian division of Re that was marching to the camp of the king (Kitchen, 1979: 26.12/16 [Poem – *šꜥf*; P 72], and 118.7/10 (Bulletin –ꜥq; B 79). But this may also be observed in the Thutmose IV example set in Egypt (subsequently, surely the chariots, horses, and troops were loaded into the royal ships). The pictorial evidence dealing with the Battle of Qadesh shows that, when traveling, the chariots of the Naʿarn protected the footsoldiers, in the front and the rear, as we have now come to expect. The division of Ptah, being somewhat relaxed when the vizier hastened to meet them, is shown marching in regular file with standard bearers and the division general in front of the chariots. In the present work it is presumed that the footsoldiers followed the elite troops. A clear picture can be drawn, on the other hand, with respect to the mustering, based on the pictorial evidence, as well as the actual march of the army, as described above. Across the Sinai, however, a different logistic movement northwards can be argued even if that situation remains sub judice.

CITED LITERATURE

Abd el-Razik, M. 1975. The Dedicatory and Building Texts of Ramesses II in Luxor Temple. Part II. – Journal of Egyptian Archaeology 61: 125-136.

Assmann, J. 1983. Krieg und Frieden im alten Ägypten. – Mannheimer Forum 83, 4: 175-231.

Berlev, O. 1992. Der Beamte. In: Donadoni, S. Ed. Der Mensch des Alten Ägypten. – New York/Paris, Campus Verlag/Éditions de la Maison des Sciences de l'Homme: 108-142.

Berlev. O. 1997. Review of Vandersleyen, C. 1995. L'Égypte et la vallée du Nil. Tome 2: De la fin de l'Ancien Empire à la fin de Nouvel Empire. – Orientalia 66: 98-99.

Beylage, P. 2002. Aufbau der königlichen Stelentexte vom Beginn der 18. Dynastie bis zur Amarnazeit. – Wiesbaden, Harrassowitz.

Bietak, M. 2009a. Perunefer: The principal New Kingdom Naval Base. – Egyptian Archaeology 34: 15-17.

Bietak, M. 2009b Perunefer: An Update. – Egyptian Archaeology 35: 16-17.

Boorn, Van den, G.P.F. 1998. The Duties of the Vizier: Civil Administration in the Early New Kingdom. – London/New York, Keagan Paul International.

Bryan, B. 1991. The Reign of Thutmose IV. – Baltimore, Johns Hopkins University Press.

Caminos, R. 1954. Late-Egyptian Miscellanies. – London, Oxford University Press.

Černý, J. 1947. Graffiti at the Wadi el-Allaki. – Journal of Egyptian Archaeology 33: 52-57.

Darnell, J. 1991. Supposed Depictions of Hittites in the Amarna Period. – Studien zur Altägyptischen Kultur 18: 113-140.

Dietrich, M. & O. Loretz. 1981. Die Inschrift der Statue des Königs Idrimi von Alala. – Ugarit Forschungen 13: 201-269.

Edgerton, W.F. & J. Wilson. 1936. Historical Records of Ramses III. – Chicago, University of Chicago.

Epigraphic Survey. 1930. Earlier Historical Records of Ramses III. – Chicago, Oriental Institute of the University of Chicago Press.

Epigraphic Survey. 1932. Later Historical Records of Ramses III. – Chicago, Oriental Institute of the University of Chicago Press.

Essche(-Merchez), Van, E. 1989. Quelques réflexions sur l'espace et le récit à Médinet Habou. – Annales de l'histoire de l'art et l'archéologie 11: 7-14.

Essche (-Merchez), van, E. 1994. Pour une lecture 'stratigraphique' des parois du temple de Ramsès III à Médinet Habou. – Revue d'Égyptologie 45: 87-116.

Faulkner, R.O. 1953. Egyptian Military Organisation. – Journal of Egyptian Archaeology 39: 32-47.

Fischer, H. 1973. Hands and Hearts (Berlin 1157). – Journal of Egyptian Archaeology 59: 224-226.

Fischer, H. 1977. More Ancient Egyptian Names of Dogs and Other Animals. – Metropolitan Museum Journal 12: 173-178.

Fischer-Elfert, H.-W. 1983. The Suffering of an Army Officer (Anastasi III 6,8-10 = LEM 27,11-15). – Göttinger Miszellen 63: 43-45.

Forstner-Müller. I. 2011. The Topography of New Kingdom Avaris and Pi-Ramesses. In: Collier, M. & S. Snape. Eds. Ramesside Studies in Honour of K.A. Kitchen. – Bolton, Rutherford Press: 23-50.

Gaballa, G.A. 1976. Narrative in Egyptian Art. – Mainz, Philipp von Zabern.

Gardiner, A. 1932. Late-Egyptian Stories. – Brussels, Fondation Égyptologique Reine Élisabeth.

Gardiner, A. 1937. Late-Egyptian Miscellanies. – Brussels, Fondation Égyptologique Reine Élisabeth.

Gardiner, A. 1947. Ancient Egyptian Onomastica I. – Oxford, Oxford University Press.

Gardiner, A. 1960. The Kadesh Inscriptions of Ramesses II. – Oxford, Oxford University Press.

Gnirs, A.M. 1996. Militär und Gesellschaft. Ein Beitrag zur Sozialgeschichte des Neuen Reiches. – Heidelberg, Orientverlag.

Greenstein, E.L. & D. Marcus. 1976. The Akkadian Inscription of Idrimi. – Journal of the Ancient Near Eastern Society of Columbia University: 59-96.

Habachi. L. 1957. Two Graffiti at Sehel from the Reign of Queen Hatshepsut. – Journal of Near Eastern Studies 16: 88-104.

Heagren, B.H. 2010. The Art of War in Pharaonic Egypt: An Analysis of the Tactical, Logistic, and Operational Capabilities of the Egyptian Army (Dynasties XVII-XX). – Auckland, University of Auckland (Unpublished Ph.D dissertation).

Heinz, S.C. 2001. Die Feldzugsdarstellungen des Neuen Reiches: Eine Bildanalyse. – Vienna, Akademie der Wissenschaften.

Helck, W. 1955. Urkunden der 18. Dynastie. Heft 17. – Berlin, Akademie Verlag.

Helck, W. 1957. Urkunden der 18. Dynastie. Heft 19. – Berlin, Akademie Verlag.

Helck, W. 1958. Urkunden der 18. Dynastie,. Heft 21. – Berlin, Akademie Verlag.

Hölscher, W. 1955. Libyer und Agypter: Beiträge zur Ethnologie und Geschichte libyscher Völkerschaften nach den altägyptischen Quellen. – Glückstadt/Hamburg/New York, J.J. Augustin.

Kitchen, K.A. 1979. Ramesside Inscriptions: Historical and Biographical II. – Oxford, Blackwell.

Kitchen, K.A. 1983. Ramesside Inscriptions: Historical and Biographical V. – Oxford, Blackwell.

Kitchen, K.A. 1996. Ramesside Inscriptions: Translated and Annotated. Translations II. – Oxford/Cambridge MA, Blackwell.

Kitchen, K.A. 1999. Ramesside Inscriptions: Translated and Annotated. Notes and Comments II. – Oxford/Malden, Blackwell.

Kitchen, K.A. 2008. Ramesside Inscriptions: Translated and Annotated. Translated V. – Malden, Oxford/Carlton, Blackwell.

Lichtheim, M. 1976. Ancient Egyptian Literature II. – Berkeley, University of California Press.

Liverani, M. 2004. Leaving by Chariot for the Desert. In: Liverani, M. Ed. Myth and Politics in Ancient Near Eastern Historiography. – Ithaca, Cornell University Press: 85-95.

Manassa, C. 2003. The Great Karnak Inscription of Merenptah: Grand Strategy in the 13th Century B.C. – New Haven, Yale University Press.

Manassa, C. 2007. Review of Patrik Lundh, Actor and Event: Military Activity in Ancient Egyptian Narrative Texts from Thutmose II to Merenptah. 2002. – Journal of Egyptian Archaeology 93: 305-308.

O'Connor, D. 1990. The Nature of Tjemhu (Libyan) Society in the Later New Kingdom. In: Leahy, A. Ed. Libya and Egypt. – London, Centre of Near And Middle Eastern Studies, SAOS & The Society for Libyan Studies: 29-113.

O'Connor, D. 2000. The Sea Peoples and the Egyptian Sources. In Oren, E. Ed. The Sea Peoples and their World: A Reassessment. – Philadelphia, University Museum, University of Pennsylvania: 85-102.

Oller, G. H. 1989. The Inscription of Idrimi: A Pseudo-Autobiography? In: Behrens, H., D. Loding & M. Roth, Eds. DUMU-E2-DUB-BA-A: Studies in Honor of Åke W. Sjörberg. – Philadelphia, University Museum: 411-417.

Redford D. 1967. History and Chronology of the Eighteenth Dynasty of Egypt. – Toronto, University of Toronto Press.

Redford, D. 2003. The Wars in Syria and Palestine of Thutmose III. – Leiden, Brill.

Schulman, A. 1964. Military Rank, Title and Organization in the Egyptian New Kingdom. – Berlin, Bruno Hessling.

Sethe, K. 1907a. Urkunden der 18. Dynastie: historisch-biographische Urkunden. 1907. – Leipzig, J.C. Hinrich.

Sethe, K. 1907b. Mißverstandnisse Inscriften. – Zeitschrift für Ägyptische Sprache 44: 35-41.

Spalinger, A. 2002. The Literary Transformation of an Ancient Egyptian Narrative: P. Sallier III and the Battle of Kadesh. – Wiesbaden, Harrassowitz.

Spalinger, A. 2003. The Chariot Frieze at Abydos. – Ägypten und Levante 13: 163-199.

Spalinger, A. 2006. The Paradise of Scribes and the Tartarus of Soldiers. In: Spalinger, A. Ed. Five Aspects of Egypt. – Göttingen, Seminar für Ägyptologie und Koptologie: 5-50

Spalinger, A. 2007. Transformation in Egyptian Folktales: The Royal Influence. – Revue d'Égyptologie 58: 7-51.

Spalinger, A. 2010. Ramesses II at Luxor: Mental Gymnastics. – Orientalia 79: 425-479.

Spalinger, A. 2011. Icons of Power: A Strategy of Reinterpretation. – Prague, Charles University in Prague, Faculty of Arts.

Spalinger, A. No Date. Mathematical Factors of the Battle of Kadesh. In: Spalinger, A. Ed. Time and the Egyptians: Feasts and Fights. – New Haven, Yale Egyptological Studies 10.

Way, Von der, T. 1984. Die Textüberlieferung Ramses' II. zur Qadeß-Schlacht. – Hildesheim, Hildesheimer Ägyptologische Beiträge.

Widmer, W. 1975. Zur Darstellungen der Seevölker am Großem Tempel von Medinet Habu. – Zeitschrift für Ägyptische Sprache 102: 67-77.

Yoyotte J. & R. Lopez. 1969. L'organisation de l'armée et les titulaires de soldats au nouvel empire Égyptien. – Bibliotheca Orientalis 26: 3-19.

CHARGING CHARIOTS:
PROGRESS REPORT ON THE TANO CHARIOT IN THE EGYPTIAN MUSEUM CAIRO

André J. Veldmeijer, Salima Ikram & Lucy Skinner

INTRODUCTION

During the 2008 season, the Ancient Egyptian Leatherwork Project (AELP) located a cache of leather objects in the Egyptian Museum, Cairo; figure 1). The cache consisted of several folders of red and green leather containing numerous large and small fragments, as well as objects made of thicker beige leather, decorated in green.[1] All had single JE and SR numbers (JE 88962; SR 14530). This acquisition was recorded on *Dossier du Service* 32-2/101, as being purchased from Georges Tano, the noted Cairene dealer, in 1932; no other information was available for these pieces. Well over 300 fragments have been recorded from these folders.

This find is of particular importance, uniquely preserving the leather components of an ancient chariot. Leather is rarely preserved archaeologically, and when it is, even in the dry conditions of Egypt, it tends to be in small pieces, rather than on this grand scale. As a result, the Tano material allows us to study chariots from a more holistic basis, this find filling in the gaps of earlier research. Examinations show that this leather was actually used, as there are many signs of wear such as abrasions where it has rubbed on the chariot framework. Thus, this object does not only aid in explaining the construction of a chariot, but also its life history.

The present contribution will discuss the progress of the Egyptian Museum Chariot Project (EMCP), including the conservation and some preliminary results on the study of the manufacturing technology.

THE TANO CHARIOT

Methodology

The leather fragments, called, for convenience, the 'Tano Chariot' after the dealer, consists of both large and small pieces (Veldmeijer & Ikram, 2012). The group (figure 1) include parts of the bow-case, the main portion of the casing (consisting of a double layer of leather: one side green and the other red) and side filling (one layer of red leather) as well as the straps and ties to connect the chariot together and to the horses (including neck and girth straps). Clearly all the portions of the chariot are present. Some of the leather pieces are highly decorated with leather appliqué work, while others are more plain. The leather falls into two main groups, based on colour and robustness: red and green fine leather and beige and green robust leather (figure 1).

In order to make sense of the many pieces of leather and to identify them with chariot parts the first step was to create an inventory of the items. Each piece was numbered – in the case of pieces which are under one centimetre, several were grouped together if they were of the same colour and might have come from the same piece. Then a verbal description was made (unless the fragment was too fragile and needed prior conservation treatment), the piece was photographed, and then drawn. Subsequently, the fragments were conserved (see below for details), re-housed and placed in a new cabinet which was put into magazine Room 19

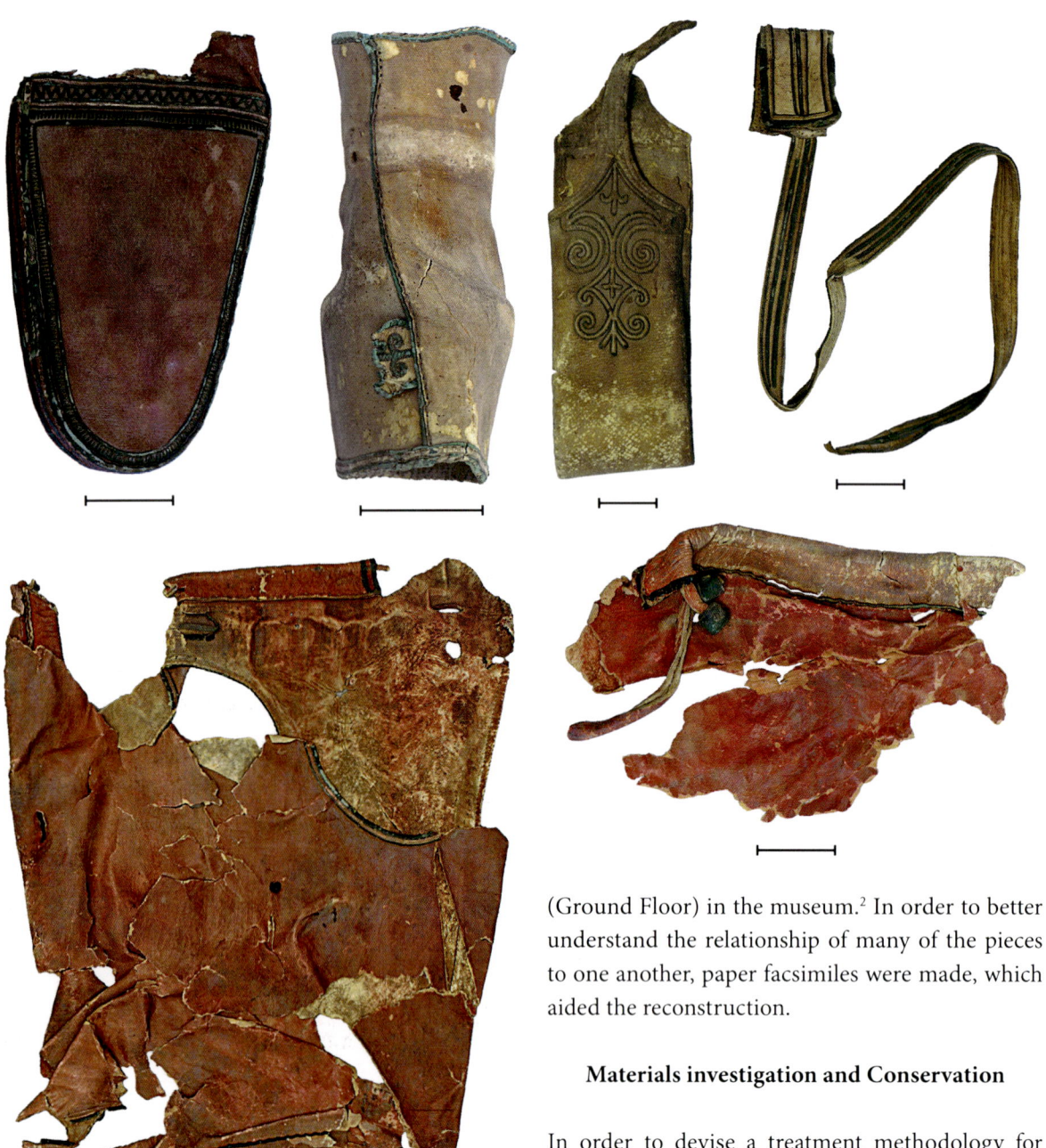

Figure 1. Examples of the so-called Tano Chariot (before conservation). From left to right and top to bottom: bottom of bow-case; nave hoop; neckstrap; rein and two pieces of red casing. Scale bars are 50 mm. Photographs by A.J. Veldmeijer. Courtesy of the Ministry of State for Antiquities/Egyptian Museum Authorities.

(Ground Floor) in the museum.[2] In order to better understand the relationship of many of the pieces to one another, paper facsimiles were made, which aided the reconstruction.

Materials investigation and Conservation

In order to devise a treatment methodology for the Tano Chariot, a good understanding of leather chemistry and the possible processing methods was vital. It was also necessary to identify other factors that may have influenced the leather's condition – such as the original archaeological milieu and the storage environment in the Egyptian museum.

From the onset it was decided that the larger fragments, which were difficult to handle, in bad condition and highly deformed, would be prioritized for treatment as these were impossible to study, draw and photograph in their deteriorated state. Many of the smaller fragments could at least be carefully studied and photographed without the need for prior conservation treatment. When

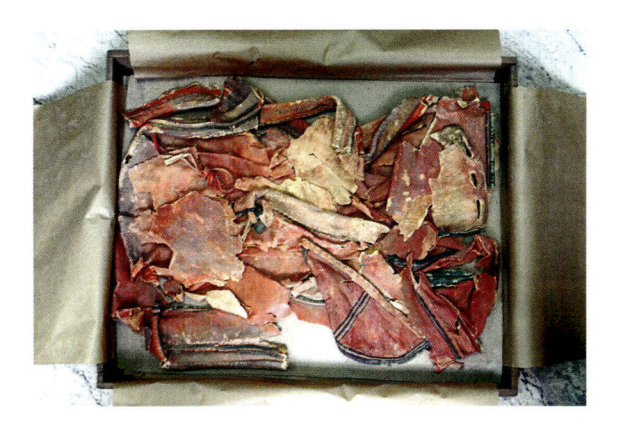

Figure 2. Two of the brown paper and cardboard folders in which the Tano Chariot was stored originally. Photographs by A.J. Veldmeijer. Courtesy of the Ministry of State for Antiquities/Egyptian Museum Authorities.

Figure 3. Archival cardboard boxes were specially made for proper storage. Photograph by A.J. Veldmeijer.

the team first examined the chariot leather in the museum, the fragments were wrapped in brown paper and cardboard folders (figure 2) and stacked on top of each other inside a series of shallow wooden boxes. This method of storage was untenable as the pH of the paper is acidic which could accelerate the rate of leather decay. Also, the leather was overcrowded and compression of the stacked fragments added to its distortion, intensifying folds and cracks. Thus, archival quality corrugated cardboard was imported. This was used to construct shallow chemically stable trays, fastened together in the corners using locally purchased polyethylene cable tie fasteners in lieu of glue or tape which tends to fail in the dry heat of Egypt (figure 3). The trays' raised sides offer protection and support for the leather, without crushing it when the fragments are placed in a single layer. The trays were lined with acid free tissue paper and stored in a map cabinet (figure 4) that protects the leather from dust, vermin and also buffers the local climate from rapid fluctuations in relative humidity.

Once the leather had been repackaged, some portions were moved to the objects conservation lab in the Egyptian Museum, Cairo to carry out preliminary tests determining the condition of the leather, to examine it for identification of possible curing or tanning techniques and to devise an appropriate treatment methodology.

Condition

We can safely assume that the chariot leather had originated from a place with a regular and extremely stable environment in terms of temperature and a low relative humidity with little fluctuation (see also below). If not, the condition of the leather would have been much worse, potentially causing the collagen to turn to gelatin – as was the case with much of the leather from the tomb of Tutankhamun where many leather objects had degenerated into little more than a resinous mass due to high level of humidity possibly caused by the last-minute plastering of the walls before closing the tomb (Veldmeijer, 2010b: 35). Carter (1927: 26, 104) noted that the last thing to be done in terms of tomb preparation was the painting of the tomb. Building upon this, it has been suggested by Mitchell that the paint still might have been damp when the tomb was sealed, and this was the source of the mould on the tomb's walls. He says (http://www.seas.harvard.edu/news/2011/06/tut-tut-microbial-growth-pharaohs-tomb-suggests-burial-was-rush-job): "We're guessing that the painted wall was not dry when the tomb was sealed". It should be noted that though the paint might indeed have still been damp at the time of sealing the tomb, it was not necessarily the source of the mould. It is more likely that the humidity is from water seepage, as posited by Scezepanowska & Cavaliere (2005: 42-47).

Considering the Tano Chariot is of great antiquity the appearance of much of the chariot leather, both on the grain surface and the flesh surface, is good. But appearances can be deceiving and in fact, there has been intense chemical degradation of the collagen fibres. The first sign of this is an accumulation of powdered leather at the bottom of the old paper folders and on the fingers when the flesh surface is touched. There has been loss of fibre strength and breakage of the collagen network that usually gives leather its strength. Since this has been damaged, the leather is frail and can easily break or split when handled.

Fats and oils can, with time, induce oxidation by producing high-energy self-perpetuating radicals that catalyse the oxidation of proteins (Florian, 2006: 38-41). Pollution may have expedited oxidation after the leather left its find-spot and arrived in the Egyptian Museum. In the case of the chariot leather then, at least while it was still in a sealed stable environment, oxidation would have occurred very slowly. Subsequently its accumulative effect has been subtle yet substantial, changing the outward appearance of the leather very little, but on a molecular level dramatically.

Other indications that the leather is highly deteriorated are the dark and glossy spots or splashes located on a few of the leather fragments (figure 5). These look like the effect of water, which has caused gelatinisation of the collagen – effectively turning it to hide glue. During the pH tests, a drop of water was added to tiny samples of the leather. These leather fibres dissolved almost instantly in water. This is a reaction that does not normally happen to leather in good condition (Larsen *et al.*, 2012: 61). Thus, there are clear indications that, for conservation, water-based adhesives and consolidants should be avoided, and humidity levels must

Figure 4. A map cabinet was obtained to store the cardboard boxes. Photograph by A.J. Veldmeijer. Courtesy of the Ministry of State for Antiquities/Egyptian Museum Authorities.

Figure 5. Dark and glossy spots or splashes located on a few of the leather fragments indicating gelatinisation of the collagen – effectively turning it to hide glue – caused by water. Photograph by L. Skinner. Courtesy of the Ministry of State for Antiquities/Egyptian Museum Authorities.

be maintained below 70% relative humidity to ensure that condensation and water droplets do not form on the leather surface.

Treatment

The EMCP team had the shared desire to unfold the leather and return distorted pieces (as close as possible) to their original shape, but there was a huge challenge to find a way to achieve this without using humidification, a technique sometimes used by conservators for softening and reshaping organic materials such as textiles, basketry and leather (Kite *et al*, 2006:125).

An alternative method considered was to place the leather in an alcohol-saturated environment to make it more pliable. This has been used effectively by conservators for reshaping fragile basketry (Personal Communication, Nancy Oddegard). However, when trials were carried out on a small fragment of the chariot leather, even after a few sessions inside a solvent tent, the leather did not respond favourably and it became much stiffer and darker in colour. Presumably the alcohol had a desiccating effect on the leather, removing remaining free water or lubrication around the desiccated fibres (Bowden & Brimblecombe, 2002: 63). Thus this technique was abandoned.

Despite reservations about the effect of water on the chariot leather, it was decided after carrying out some controlled tests, using slightly elevated humidity (while vigilantly monitoring to avoid the formation of condensation) at room temperature (25° C) could be used successfully for softening and reshaping fragments. The Egyptian Museum's conservation lab kindly granted access to use a large humidity chamber.[3] By very gradually increasing the relative humidity (RH) to about 65 +/- 5% and holding it there for an extended period, it was possible, slowly and gently over the space of a few days, to very gradually, lift folds and flatten creases in some of the leather fragments. The increase in humidity was particularly useful for 'setting' the leather into its new shape by applying gentle weight in strategic areas and allowing the RH to drop back to ambient conditions. In this way much of the most decorated and distorted fragments have been unfurled. However, for the hardest creases nothing was effective for softening the leather and so these have been left as they were. Investigations into a more effective technique are ongoing.

After testing, it was discovered that the beige coloured leather is especially sensitive to water and the large thick girth strap and nave hoops were found completely unresponsive to humidification. The reason why this leather feels and reacts differently than the red/green leather is unclear for now but it suggests that the initial curing/processing method could have been different.

Another important mission was to find a suitable consolidant to strengthen the leather and secure the powdery flesh surface. A few consolidants were tested on tiny samples and most caused unfavourable darkening to the leather. Cellugel, a commercially available mixture of Klucel G (hydroxypropyl cellulose) dissolved in the solvent isopropanol, did not darken the leather and dealt very effectively with the powdering surfaces. It also strengthened the leather structure substantially. Unfortunately Klucel G is not a particularly flexible polymer and causes some stiffening. This means that any reshaping of the leather has to take place before consolidation and the Cellugel can be applied only after deformations have been removed.

For rejoining and supporting splits and cracked areas, consolidation alone was not enough and edges could not be rejoined without some additional support. Japanese tissue backing tabs, torn to shape and adhered with Klucel G dissolved in ethanol were used (figure 6). The tabs can be easily removed without damaging or leaving traces on the leather. Finely

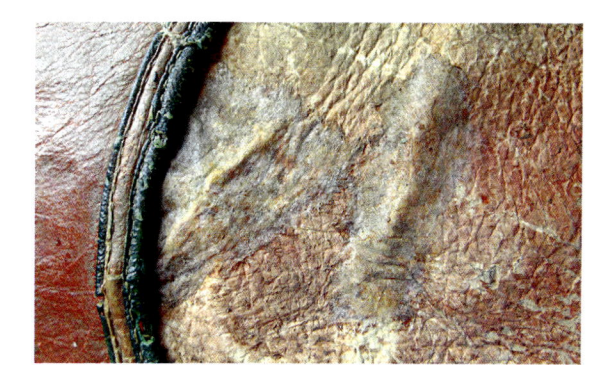

Figure 6. Repairs to the leather executed using tinted Japanese tissue strips. Photograph by L. Skinner. Courtesy of the Ministry of State for Antiquities/ Egyptian Museum Authorities.

torn tissue was turned into a sticky pulp with the same adhesive and inserted into small voids and areas where cracks required additional support. The tissue used was a handmade mulberry paper that has been dyed a light beige colour to blend somewhat to the leather, but that still remains recognisable as an intervention. Where the repairs were applied to the verso of the leather, no further attempt was made to conceal them. However, where the tissue continued to be visible on the front, for example where tissue pulp was used as a fill, water-colour paint pigments mixed with Klucel G were used to tone in the repairs so that they were not too visually obtrusive.

Information on the Leather and its Preparation

Skin Type

The grain surfaces (the top surface) of the green and the red leather fragments are smooth, uniform in appearance and the sheets are fine and thin (between one and two millimeters); the flesh surface (the inner surface of the corium) is soft and spongy. The even thickness and texture suggests that the skin was expertly processed from high quality hides. Most of the red and green leather was evidently flexible and stretchy when it was first manufactured, suitable for tying over a wooden chariot frame. Only the bow-case is stiff, but this is due to the use of several layers, as well as other constructional features. It is possible that a different processing method, *i.e.* avoiding the treatment to make the leather stretchy and supple, may have been used where the stiffness of the leather was an important factor for the function (see also below concerning the skin processing).

Micro-photographs of the follicle pattern (figure 7) show wave-like rows, with larger holes (where guard hairs originally grew) next to a few smaller follicle holes left by the underfur. This follicle pattern is typical for goat or sheepskin (Haines, 1985). Sheepskin has a tendency to split or delaminate between the grain surface and the flesh layer because of a high concentration of fat cells and globular proteins in this zone, creating a loose, open and weak network of collagen fibres (Reed, 1972: 42). Although it does have other condition problems, the chariot leather is not delaminating and there is no obvious differentiation between the grain and the flesh layers. Thus, the red and green leather is probably made from goat and not sheepskin. However, the skin of a wild animal (which generally produce more consistently high quality skins than domesticated animals), such as an antelope species might have been used to fabricate such high status items (*Ibidem*: 37). In order to recognize alternate skin types it would be necessary to have access to a wide collection of leather reference samples.

The beige coloured leather that forms, among others, the neck and girth straps and the nave hoops, is generally thicker than the red and green coloured fragments (figure 8). The leather of the nave hoops measures up to three millimeters in cross-section.

Figure 7. Micro-photograph of the red leather grain surface. Photograph by L. Skinner. Courtesy of the Ministry of State for Antiquities/Egyptian Museum Authorities.

Figure 8. Micro-photograph of the beige leather grain surface. Photograph by L. Skinner. Courtesy of the Ministry of State for Antiquities/Egyptian Museum Authorities.

It is also much stiffer and more brittle, and the flesh surface is much more compact and less fibrous. Its follicle pattern has holes that are regular in size and evenly-spaced out over the surface, consistent with bovine (cattle) skin (Haines, 1985). Typically bovine leather is more robust, with a tougher handle than goatskin, but is less easily stretched or manipulated into soft and decorative edgings (Reed, 1972: 38). Using the more robust and less stretchy bovine hide to construct the straps and other more load bearing pieces of the chariot and harness makes good technological sense.

LEATHER PREPARATION

Skin Processing

Skin processing is shown on the walls of, among others, the tomb of Rekhmire (Theban Tomb [TT] 100) in Sheikh abd el-Qurna (figure 9). In one part of the scene the skins are being scraped to remove flesh, globular proteins and fats, to de-hair the skin and, also as part of the 'beaming' or 'staking' process to loosen the fibres, make the leather flexible and more readily able to absorb oils, fat and colorants (Thomson, 2006a: 69). Other parts of the scene shows an animal hide, hair still attached, being dipped into a large vessel, possibly containing sesame oil (Schwarz, 2000: 58), but this is debated and no analyses have been carried out to date (about oil from the tomb of Tutankhamun, see Carter, 1927: 176-178).

The historic methods of converting putrescible scraped and prepared skin to durable 'leather' include oil curing, smoke tanning, alum tawing and vegetable tanning (Van Driel-Murray, 2000: 302-306; Schwarz, 2000: 25-64; Thomson, 2006b: 2). There has not been a great deal of reliable scientific research carried out to learn about ancient Egyptian leather tanning techniques and thus far the EMCP team has not had an opportunity to use research methods to elucidate this information.

The colour of the chariot leather, beneath the green and red surface stain, is light beige, which matches the tone we might expect from vegetable tanned or oil cured skin. Alum tawing usually produces a white leather, easy to dye or stain, which is soft and supple, but being only a pseudo-tan makes it sensitive to water: if alum is washed out, the 'leather' reverts into untreated skin and will start to rot.[4] The presence of alum (potassium aluminium sulphate) can be identified via spot testing for aluminium or elemental analysis using X-ray fluorescence spectroscopy (Thomson, 2006c: 59). It is possible that oxidation of the fats or oils used as lubricants would cause alum tawed skin to darken with age (Personal Communication, Abdelazak Elnaggar).

Spot tests have been carried out for aluminium using ammonium hydroxide and sodium alizarin sulphonate (Odegaard *et al.*, 2000: 34). Interestingly, the results show that there is aluminium present in the green leather and red leather but not in the beige leather. It is a possibility, therefore, that the red and green leather is alum tawed, while the beige leather is prepared using another method. Alternatively, the alum may have been used for something else in the manufacturing process, such as a mordant to aid in the application of the green and red surface stain, a common use of alum from the later New Kingdom onwards (Van Driel-Murray, 2000: 304). If this were the case, if elemental analysis were carried out on the grain and flesh surface of the leather, one might expect a higher concentration

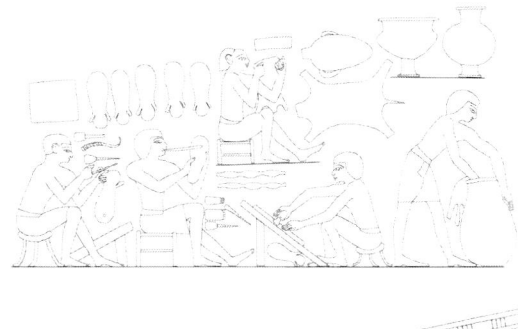

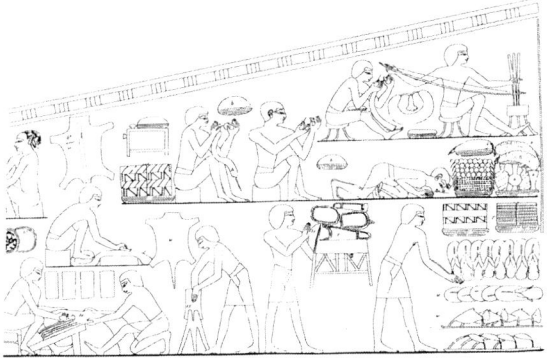

Figure 9. A leatherworking scene from tomb of Rekhmire. From: Davies (1943: pl. LII, LIV).

of aluminium, potassium and sulphur on the grain surface than the flesh surface, since the colour was applied only to one side of the skin. Alum tawing might also be distinguished from a mordant were we able to detect the presence of egg or of flour, but to find out this would require analysis of the leather using Gas Chromatography–Mass Spectrometry (GC-MS) or High-Performance Liquid Chromatography (HPLC), which both are costly and inaccessible in Egypt at the time of writing.

The existence of vegetable tanned leather in Egypt from the Pharaonic era is uncertain. Some scholars believe that vegetable tanning was not introduced to Egypt until the Greco-Roman period (Van Driel-Murray, 2000:305), and that the identification of vegetable tanned leather and the existence of a leather tannery at Gebelein dating to the Predynastic period (*Ibidem*: 305-306) are incorrect. Rather, these finds date to the Greek occupation of the site in the late 1st Millenium BC. It should be noted that the chemical spot tests used to detect vegetable tannins can give unreliable results when the leather is contaminated with soil minerals or coloured with vegetable dyes (*Ibidem*: 315).[5] Nevertheless, spot tests for vegetable tanning have been carried out on tiny samples of the red/green coloured chariot leather using the ferric chloride test (Thomson, 2006c: 59). Vegetable tannins are indicated by the development of a dark blue/black stain. In all cases the results were negative, allowing us to tentatively rule out vegetable tanning.

Oil curing involves the use of unsaturated fatty acids such as brain or fish liver oil. The curing effect of oil tanning on the skin is due to an aldehydic reaction and oxidation of the fats (Covington, 2006: 30). If the chariot leather had been oil cured, this may be discovered if the fats or oils could be identified analytically, also using GC-MS or HPLC. However, all kinds of leather preparation involve the application of oils – for softening and lubricating the skin – and so it may be difficult to discern one from another.

Colour

The chariot leather is coloured red, green or beige. At first sight the colours appear fresh and new. However, they are not as vibrant as they must have been when first applied. In some areas edging strips or the top layer of leather in stacked sheets have become detached, revealing the original vivid colours, with some lighter areas as a result of its original use (figure 10).

The green colour forms a homogenous surface layer with a slight sheen, which has penetrated a short distance into the grain surface (figure 11A). The red stain by contrast, is a thinner layer although no less glossy or intense in colour (figure 11B). The green is stiffer, more 'scale-like' and has flaked off

Figure 10. Vivid colours are visible beneath the decoration. Photograph by A.J. Veldmeijer. Courtesy of the Ministry of State for Antiquities/Egyptian Museum Authorities.

Figure 11. Micro-photograph of green (A) and red (B) leather grain surface showing flaking. Photographs by L. Skinner. Courtesy of the Ministry of State for Antiquities/Egyptian Museum Authorities.

more readily than the red. There are strong similarities between the Tano Chariot and pieces excavated at Amarna (Veldmeijer, 2010a; figure 12).

It is quite apparent, that the pigment was applied to the green and red leather exclusively as a topcoat on the grain surface rather than as a dip-dye that would have resulted in uniform colouration throughout the leather, on the recto and the verso. The correct terminology for describing this superficial application method is 'staining'. To attain such an even tone the stain must have been applied liberally as a liquid and rubbed or smeared over the surface of the leather using a rag or something similar. A faint hint of green and red colouration evident on the verso of many of the fragments is likely due to the liquid stain soaking through the leather when it was first applied, drawing pigment grains through to the flesh surface.

Neither the pigments nor the binding media have yet been definitively identified. Red textiles from this period have been analysed and found typically to be dyed using red ochre (Vorgelsang-Eastwood, 2000: 278) or madder (Chenciner, 2000: 34), an organic colorant derived from plant roots (Eastaugh *et al.*, 2012: 50). It was apparently introduced to Egypt during the 18th Dynasty and produces an intense red dye, if bound to a mordant such as alum (Chenciner, 2000: 229).

At the Metropolitan Art Gallery in New York, Surface Enhanced Raman Scattering (SERS) has successfully identified madder lake as a surface colorant on a possible Middle Kingdom leather object, tentatively identified as quiver, from the collection. This proves that madder lake pigments were being manufactured seven centuries earlier than previously thought (Leona, 2009: 14759).

The green leather has a very deep rich colour, similar to malachite (copper carbonate) or Egyptian green (copper-wollastonite). Copper test-strip papers were used to detect whether copper was present on the green leather, with positive results. Copper based colorants can take many forms: malachite, organic salts of copper including copper formates, and copper acetates (also known as verdigris – of which there are many variants), copper resinates and copper proteinates (which are verdigris-protein complexes), and copper oleates and stearates (which are oils or waxes that have reacted with cupric salts, Scott, 2002: 270-298). The green and the red colourants will be investigated further in the future.

FIRST RESULTS: CHARIOT MANUFACTURING TECHNOLOGY

Forms and Cutting

It is possible that some sort of pattern might have formed the basis for cutting out the basic forms for the different parts of the body of the chariot, although it is possible that measured drawings on the leather, executed without a pattern, were used. Presumably the harness would have been cut based on measurements, as it is today. The tools used for the cutting were probably made from copper-bronze alloys, as seen in the tomb of Rekhmire (figure 9; see also Schwarz, 2000: 81-100), although flint could also have been used, as it was commonly used throughout ancient Egyptian history for butchery and animal processing, along with other activities (*e.g.* Ikram, 1995: 63-72).

Stitching

Two types of material were used in stitching the chariot leather (as opposed to the harnessings)[6]: flax zS_2 thread (see Veldmeijer, 2005 for terminology on cordage) was mainly used for adding decoration and, occasionally, in places that were not subject to large force/stress. However, the elements that needed to be reinforced as they were

Figure 12. Flaking green surface coating of chariot leather fragments from Amarna. Photograph by A.J. Veldmeijer. Courtesy of Ägyptisches Museum und Papyrussammlung, Berlin.

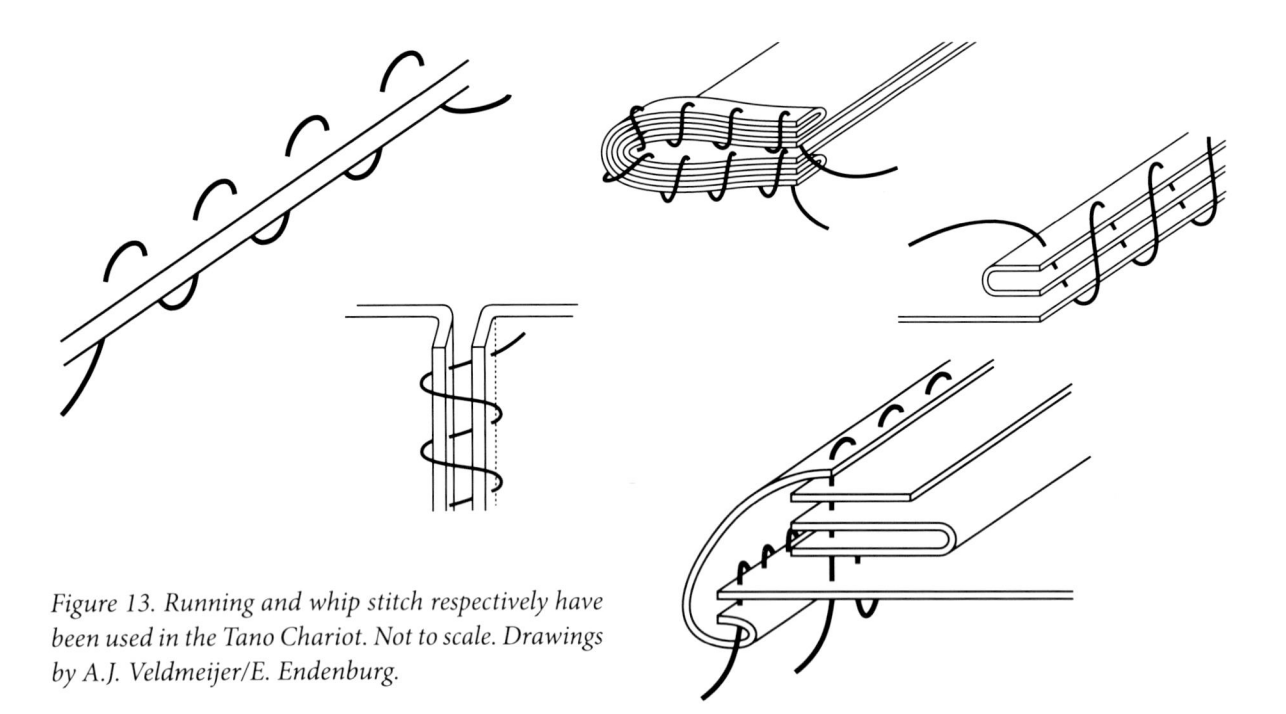

Figure 13. Running and whip stitch respectively have been used in the Tano Chariot. Not to scale. Drawings by A.J. Veldmeijer/E. Endenburg.

subject to increased stress were secured with sinew thread (also zS_2).

A variety of stitches were identified (figure 13). The simpler running stitch was predominantly used in applying the decoration, a technique also seen in other leatherwork whereas in edge bindings whip stitching was used, often in combination with running stitches. Whip stitches were also used to secure larger pieces of leather together, sometimes in a double row. Several tubes were extended by overlapping, one inside the other, and securing with whip stitch. Some of the harnessing elements were secured at the overlap with whip stitch, but at the edge with running stitching. The ends of some straps are rolled up and the edges secured with whip stitch butt seam or with the edges folded inside. It is interesting to note the absence of more decorative stitching, such as the slit-pull technique seen in the leather from, supposedly, the tomb of Amenhotep III (AJV Personal Observation) and non-chariot, contemporary leatherwork. The absence of sailor stitch, however, can be explained by the fact that this is mainly used to repair cracks, as seen in a leather Stubbed-Toe Ankle Shoes (Veldmeijer, 2013).

Edge Bindings

A wide variety of edge bindings were registered (figure 14). The simplest one is an edge to which a folded piece of green leather is applied and se-

Figure 14. Some examples of edge bindings in the Tano Chariot. Not to scale. Drawings by A.J. Veldmeijer/E. Endenburg.

cured with whip stitch, the fold facing away from the edge. These are found at the edges of the tube; as tubes contain drawstrings, they were probably used in tying the leather to the chariot frame or forming connections of some sort. In one case, the folded strip of leather was secured with running stitches, but given the fact that this is the only example, it might point to a repair, possibly carried out by a non-professional, or someone who was not involved with making the original. If this had been part of the original, it might reflect a different leatherworker, in which case more examples might have been expected.

Some of the tube-ends have a triple-strip-decoration, alternating red and green that are secured with whip stitching but without stair-step overlapping, in which the strip at the edge is secured over the edge with whip stitching. Other edge bindings, combined with appliqué, consist of several strips of leather that overlap in stair-step fashion (and some of which are folded lengthwise to create relief). The set is finally secured at the edge with a strip that is sewn with whip stitching at the reverse after which it is pulled over it and further secured at the obverse with running stitches. This type of edge binding is also seen in the beige/green leather, *viz.* the nave hoop, but the number of layers of overlapping strips of leather is fewer, and restricted to beige and green. A type of edge binding only seen in the nave hoops consists of a lengthwise folded strip of green leather that is secured with whip stitch to the edge of the *fleur-de-lys* decoration (see below) rather than on top of the edge of the leather proper. This technique is often seen in footwear that is dated to later times and is, until now, unique in Pharaonic leatherwork.

Seams and Other Constructional Features

Passepoils are small strips of leather that are sandwiched between two larger pieces. They reinforce the seam and make a stronger bind. Passepoils are identified in the Tano Chariot, consisting of a lengthwise folded strip that is secured with the other two pieces by means of running stitch. It is the earliest record of passepoil to date.

The edges of tubes are connected to the side fill as well as the main casing (figure 15). They are secured with running stitch. The edges at the obverse are covered with a triple-strip decoration, but there are exceptions: pieces of the main casing are without (note that the tube is secured to a double layer of leather, as the main casing consists of two layers). Several tubes have been secured to the main piece of leather by including a passepoil, usually without the triple-strip decoration.

The straps that make up part of the rein system clearly shows its purpose: they are made of thicker, stronger leather, folded lengthwise two or three times, and secured with several rows (up to five) of running stitch (figure 16). The number of rows might be related to the use of flax thread: possibly, fewer rows might have been necessary if sewn with sinew.

Decoration

Aside from colouring the leather, the decoration in the Tano Chariot consists only of appliqué work. Strips of leather, alternating red and green applied in stair-step overlapping fashion, predominate. The folding of some of these strips, together with the final strip at the edge being pulled over itself, creates relief. In some cases, the bow-case being the most obvious example, strips were made to bulge to give the same effect of relief. Relief was also obtained by stuffing, which will be discussed below. Alternative to these appliqué are triple strip decoration, again alternating green and red, but not overlapping: these are secured with the edges against each other (butt seam). In contrast to the former, which are secured by means of running stitch, these are secured with whip stitches, also to the base layer (figure 17). In the bow-case, a rare glimpse in the decisions of the leatherworker can be seen as seemingly two individual strips were made out of one wider strip by cutting it lengthwise, but not entirely: the cut drops short before the end. The two parts that were thus obtained were spread out as to flank the individually inserted centre strip of a different colour. Also the nave hoops show strip-appliqué, but as mentioned, these are less elaborate.

More elaborate motifs adorn the bow-case: rows of icicles and zigzag. The harnessing shows mainly

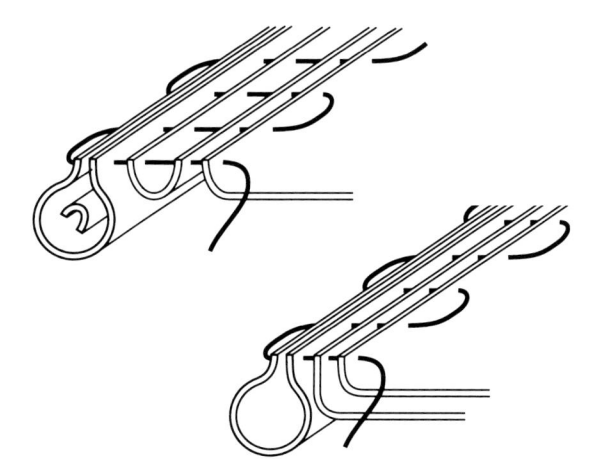

Figure 15. Two varieties of attachment of the tube to the body leather: with and without a passepoil. Not to scale. Drawings by A.J. Veldmeijer/E. Endenburg.

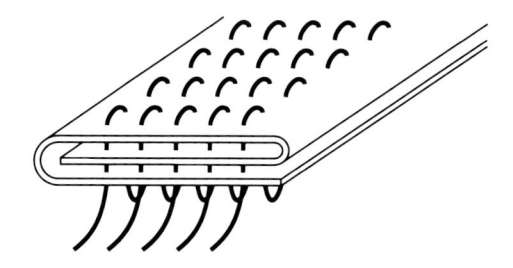

Figure 16. Example of the stitching of some of the reins. Not to scale. Drawings by A.J. Veldmeijer/E. Endenburg.

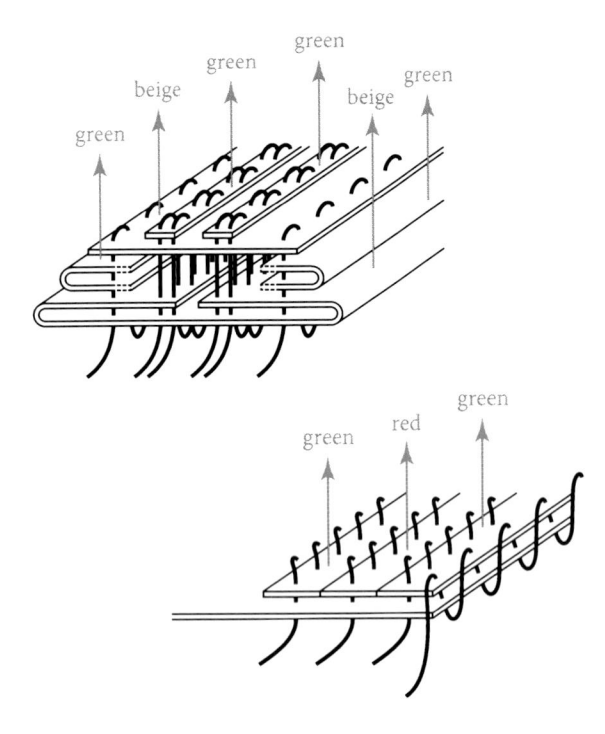

Figure 17. Two ways of applying decorative strips of leather. Not to scale. Drawings by A.J. Veldmeijer/ E. Endenburg.

floral appliqué, and the nave hoops sport *fleur-de-lys* designs. The decoration at the ends of the harnessing consists of a green folded strip that is filled with beige. Note that the strip of green under the central beige fill usually is much wider than the green visible at the obverse. As stitches are made slightly away from the edge, due to which the edge protrudes slightly from the underlying layer. The beige centre is stuffed, probably with vegetable material, to create relief, a technique also recognised in some of the Amarna chariot leather (Veldmeijer, 2010a: 23-24). This relief makes the design more visible, and is aesthetically pleasing.

USE OF LEATHER IN CHARIOTS[7]

The choice of using leather for chariots rather than dressed thin wood, as seen in two chariots from Tutankhamun (Littauer & Crouwel's A4 and 5) and the one from Thutmose IV (CG 46097) seems obvious: "As compared with leather, a lighter and more resilient material, the relatively large wooden surfaces [Littauer & Crouwel's] A1, A2 [the State Chariots], the chariot of Yuya and Tuiu, and in particular that of Thutmose IV, would have tended to reduce the flexibility of the body and its ability to withstand strain. The material bespeaks a limited use, and this is confirmed by the elaborate decoration of these chariots" (Littauer & Crouwel, 1985: 74). Clearly, the choice is dependant on the function of the chariot. Leather would be a poor choice for a state chariot as it is a flexible material, unsuitable for decorating by insetting with glass, semi-precious stones, or coating with metal foil and gilding. A rigid, solid base, such as wood coated in gesso would be more suitable for this purpose and the decoration less likely to fall off while the chariot was ridden.

But could there have been other reasons? Or alternatives? Clearly, the above-mentioned physical problems are the main reason for not using wood for certain types of chariots. Alternatives are fairly non-existent. Textile or cartonnage, although possible as a chariot casing, would be impractical in the extreme; basketry chariots might be possible, albeit not for warfare, and there is no evidence for such constructions from Egypt although examples of basketry bodies of carts are known from Rome (Blanc *et al.*, 2006: 45). Thus, leather chariots that weigh less than wooden ones, and can therefore move faster and are more manoeuvrable, would be more appropriate for hunting and even warfare than those made of solid wood. Granted, wood would protect the person in the chariot more than leather, but thick leather might repel arrows and entangle spears as well. Experiments show the resilient character of leather.[8] The floor of chariots was typically made of leather or rawhide strips that were woven together (see also Crouwel, this volume), making it flexible and shock resistant; this required a strong sense of balance of the part of the passengers, but would also cushion them from jarring movements (see Sandor, this volume).

Rawhide and sinew were also used in chariot production (the latter particularly in chariots with leather casing and their accoutrements). Rawhide is very effective in chariot construction as it binds things tightly and securely as it shrinks upon wetting: such properties was valuable wherever different portions of the frame and the body needed to be tightly joined, such as the overlap of the two parts of the floor frame, the joints in naves, spokes, and felloes, or as tyre around the entire wheel. When rawhide was used in the construction of a chariot there was no fear of nails jolting loose at inopportune moments. This material was particularly ideal in Egypt where there was little chance of the rawhide becoming damp and thus coming loose. Rawhide was also used on wheels for a smoother ride, but also protected the wooden wheel from damage.

The choice of using leather, stretched over the wooden frame, with a rawhide floor and lashings helped to create the perfect chariot that has never been surpassed in lightness, swiftness, strength and riding qualities. It is yet to be seen if one can establish whether the finer details of using leather, rawhide, or sinew were inventions of the Egyptians or adaptations of established chariot technology introduced from the Near East.

DISCUSSION

As the Tano Chariot is the only virtually intact leather chariot body from ancient Egypt, it is key in our understanding of the modes of construction, and provides a comparison in manufacturing techniques with the fragments from other chariots. However, there are also questions that are specific to the Tano Chariot that need to be addressed.

First among these is why is the leatherwork of the chariot found separated from its frame? Although there is no clear answer, one can speculate based upon the evidence. The Tano Chariot shows considerable evidence for wear: areas along the upper railing are discoloured, and the upper surfaces are rubbed off, probably due to repeated gripping on to the railing. Moreover, several areas show secondary slits cut into the leather (evidenced by the lack of enhancement of their edges, which is unlike other, original, slits and openings), suggesting that these were cut into the leather to adjust it during use. Furthermore, the leather is faded in many places, as well as abraded, indicating that it was exposed to the elements and saw some action. Clearly it was not made specifically as a funerary offering. Perhaps the drawstrings along the edges of the casing provide a clue: these might have been used to secure the casing to the frame of the chariot. Possibly, instead of giving an entire chariot, the old leatherwork was placed in a tomb – a part symbolic of the whole. Or, this might have been a spare leather cover, perhaps the second class version which was buried with the deceased. As mentioned above, the condition of the leather clearly indicates that it was never in contact with or buried directly into soil or sand and must have originated from a tomb or a similar context with a stable environment that would have ensured the preservation of organic materials with some degree of suppleness preserved. Leather finds from urban contexts such as Amarna, although still relatively good compared to leather finds from many sites elsewhere in the world, are usually very fragmented, brittle and overall in poorer condition. Furthermore, ancient workshops are unlikely to have been the target of antiquities' thieves.

The second question is to whom might the chariot have belonged? The less elaborate, and possibly standardized decoration with only the bow-case showing any elaborate designs, seems to suggest that it was a non-royal chariot as pictorial evidence shows far more elaborate decoration on royal chariots than on those made for the elite (Sabbahy & Ikram, In Preparation). Of course, it is possible that this was a simple, every-day chariot used for private hunts by royalty, but there is no strong evidence to support this theory. Thus, for the moment, the Tano Chariot is thought to have belonged to a member of the elite who was buried in a rock-cut tomb in the dry heat of Upper Egypt.

The third and final question is, what is the date of the Tano Chariot? Based on historical and pictorial evidence, it is clear that it cannot date to earlier than the 18th Dynasty. If it belongs to an elite individual, it is more likely to date from the latter part of the reign of Thutmose III onward, when chariots are more commonly featured in tombs' decoration (Sabbahy & Ikram, In Preparation). Future study still needs to be carried out on the decorative features and construction methods to see if these provide more clues to the date of the Tano Chariot.

The work on the Tano Chariot is by no means complete and the analyses of the data has just begun. In collaboration with our Egyptian colleagues, the team needs to carry out scientific analysis to identify preparation techniques and colorants; conservation treatment will be continued and further research is necessary in order to better understand this unique find.

NOTES

1. The material is under the curatorship of Ibrahim el-Gawad, to whom we are grateful, as we are to the directors of the Egyptian Museum (Dr. Wafaa el-Seddik, Dr. Tarek el-Awady, Dr. Lotfi Abdel Hamid, Dr. Sayed Amer & Mr. Mohammed Ali). We thank the Ministry of State for Antiquities (MSA) for their kind permission for working with this important material. The work was made possible due to a grant of ARCE's Antiquities Endowment Fund (backed by USAID).
2. See also www.leatherandshoes.nl, where details of the Project are posted, including a blog.
3. We are grateful to Dr. Hoda and the conservation team at the Egyptian Museum Cairo for their help and support during the course of this project.
4. The same problems arise with oil-cured skins.
5. More on the problems of this field test, see Veldmeijer (2011 and references therein).
6. See Veldmeijer (2010a: 19-24) for a useful overview of stitching in ancient Egypt.
7. This section is adapted from a contribution by AJV & SI to the 'Why Leather' conference at UCL Institute of Archaeology in London (8 September 2011).
8. See for example the discussion on http://www.myarmoury.com/talk/viewtopic.php?t=24741 instigated by the information given by Renfrew & Bahn (1996: 312-313). More on related topics in Cheshire (In Press).

CITED LITERATURE

Blanc, N., F. Gury, D. Mordant & M. Pichonnet. 2006. Weide statt Plastik. – Abenteuer Archäologie 2: 42-45.

Bowden, D. & P. Brimblecombe. 2002. The Thermal Response of Parchment and Leather to Relative Humidity Changes. In: Larsen, R. Ed. Microanalysis of Parchment. – London, Archetype.

Carter, H. 1927. The Tomb of Tut.ankh.amen II. – London, Cassel & Co.

Chenciner, R. 2000. Madder Red: A History of Luxury and Trade. – Richmond, Curzon

Cheshire, E.J. In Press. Cuir Bouilli Armour. In: Harris, S. & A.J. Veldmeijer. Eds. Proceedings of the 'Why Leather' Conference of the Archaeological Leather Group.

Covington, A.D. 2006. The Chemistry of Tanning Materials. In: Kite, M. & R. Thomson. Eds. 2006. Conservation of Leather and Related Materials. – London, Routledge.

Davies, N.D.G. 1943. The Tomb of Rekhmire at Thebes. Volume I, II. – New York, The Metropolitan Museum of Art.

Driel-Murray, van, C. 2000. Leatherwork and Skin Products. In: Nicholson, P.T. & I. Shaw. Eds. 2000. Ancient Egyptian Materials and Technology. – Cambridge, Cambridge University Press: 299-319.

Eastaugh, N., V. Walsh, T. Chaplin & R. Siddall. 2012. Pigment Compendium: A Dictionary of Historical Pigments. – London, Routledge.

Florian, M.-L.E. 2006. The Mechanisms of Deterioration in Leather. In: Kite, M. & R. Thomson. Eds. Conservation of Leather and Related Materials. – London, Routledge.

Haines, B. 1985. Identification of Leather. In: Fogle. S. Ed. Recent Advances in Leather Conservation. Proceedings of a Refresher Course, June 1984. – Washington, The Foundation of the American Institute for Conservation: 12-16.

Ikram, S. 1995. Choice Cuts: Meat Production in Ancient Egypt. – Leuven, Peeters.

Kite, M., R. Thomson & A. Angus. 2006. Materials and Techniques: Past and Present. In: Kite, M. & R. Thomson. Eds. Conservation of Leather and Related Materials. – London, Routledge.

Larsen, R., D. Vestergaard, S. Poulsen, K. Mulen Axelsson & S.N. Frank. 2012. Transformation of Collagen into Gelatin in Historical Leather and Parchment Caused by Natural Deterioration and Moist Treatment. ICOM-CC, Leather and Related Materials Working Group. Interim meeting, August 29-31. – Offenbach am Main, ICOM-CC.

Leona, M. 2009. Microanalysis of Organic Pigments and Glazes in Polychrome Works of Art by Surface-Enhanced Resonance Raman Scattering. – Proceedings of the National Academy of Sciences 106, 35: 14757-14762.

Odegaard, N., S. Carroll & W.S. Zimmt. 2000. Material Characterization Tests for Objects of Art and Archaeology. – London, Archetype.

Reed, R.,1972. Ancient Skins, Parchments and Leathers. – London/New York, Seminar Press Ltd.

Renfrew, C. & P. Bahn. 1996. Archaeology: Theories, Methods, and Practice. – London, Thames & Hudson.

Sabbahy, L. & S. Ikram. In Preparation. Images in Motion: Chariots in Egyptian Art. In: Veldmeijer, A.J. & S. Ikram. Eds. [An Ancient Egyptian Chariot]. – Leiden, Sidestone Press.

Schwarz, S. 2000. Altägyptisches Lederhandswerk. – Frankfurt am Main etc., Peter Lang

Scott, D.A. 2002. Copper and Bronze in Art: Corrosion, Colorants, and Conservation. – Los Angeles, Getty Publications.

Scezepanowska, H. & A.R. Cavaliere. 2005. Tutankhamen's Tomb. A Closer Look at Biodeterioration, Preliminary Report. In: Rauch, A., S. Miklin-Kniefacz & A. Harmsse. Eds. Schimmel – Gefahr fur Mensh und Kultur durch Microorganismen; Fungi, A threat for People and Cultural Heritage through Micro-Organisms. – Stuttgart, Thesis Verband der Restauratoren: 42-47.

Thomson, 2006a. The Manufacture of Leather. In: Kite, M. & R. Thomson. Eds. Conservation of Leather and Related Materials. – London, Routledge.

Thomson, 2006b. The Nature and Properties of Leather. In: Kite, M. & R. Thomson. Eds. Conservation of Leather and Related Materials. – London, Routledge.

Thomson, 2006c. Testing Leathers and Related Materials. In: Kite, M. & R. Thomson. Eds. Conservation of Leather and Related Materials. – London, Routledge.

Veldmeijer, A.J. 2005. Archaeologically Attested Cordage. Terminology on the Basis of the Material from Ptolemaic Roman Berenike (Egyptian Red Sea coast). – Eras 7 (online journal Monash University).

Veldmeijer, A. J. 2010a. Amarna's Leatherwork. Part I: Preliminary Analysis and Catalogue. – Norg, DrukWare (unrevised republished by Sidestone Press in 2011).

Veldmeijer, A. J. 2010b. Tutankhamun's Footwear: Studies of Ancient Egyptian Footwear. – Norg, DrukWare (unrevised republished by Sidestone Press in 2011)

Veldmeijer, A.J. 2011. Sandals, Shoes and Other Leatherwork from the Coptic Monastery Deir el-Bachit. Analysis and Catalogue. – Leiden, Sidestone Press.

Veldmeijer, A.J. 2013. Studies of Ancient Egyptian Footwear. Technological Aspects. Part XVII. Leather Stubbed-Toe Ankle Shoes. – Jaarberichten Ex Oriente Lux: [not yet known].

Veldmeijer, A.J. & S. Ikram. 2012. With contributions by L. Skinner. Preliminary Report of the Egyptian Museum Chariot Project (EMCP). – Bulletin of the American Research Center in Egypt: 7-11.

Vorgelsang-Eastwood, G. 2000. Textiles. In: Nicholson, P.T. & I. Shaw. Ancient Egyptian Materials and Technology. – Cambridge, Cambridge University Press.